"WHAT SHALL WE NAME THE BABY?"

BIBLICAL
ABSALOM (Hebrew—"Father of Peace")
DASIA (Hebrew—"The Law of the Lord")

AFRICAN
EPATIMI (Ibo—"Man of Patience")
HADIYA (Swahili—"A Gift from God")

EUROPEAN
KEENAN (Irish—"Little Ancient One")
BONITA (Spanish—"Good, Pretty")

AFRICAN-AMERICAN
LeBRON (Detroit attorney **LeBron Simmons** was
a dedicated advocate
for the poor and underprivileged)
JARENA (**Jarena Lee** was a black woman evangelist and
author in the nineteenth century)

PROUD HERITAGE

11,001 NAMES FOR YOUR AFRICAN-AMERICAN BABY

ELZA DINWIDDIE-BOYD

AVON BOOKS  NEW YORK

PROUD HERITAGE: 11,001 NAMES FOR YOUR AFRICAN-AMERICAN BABY is an original publication of Avon Books. This work has never before appeared in book form.

AVON BOOKS
A division of
The Hearst Corporation
1350 Avenue of the Americas
New York, New York 10019

Copyright © 1994 by Elza Dinwiddie-Boyd
Cover photo by Steven Jones
Published by arrangement with the author
Library of Congress Catalog Card Number: 93-90638
ISBN: 0-380-77340-6

First Avon Books Printing: March 1994

AVON TRADEMARK REG. U.S. PAT. OFF. AND IN OTHER COUNTRIES, MARCA REGISTRADA, HECHO EN U.S.A.

Printed in the U.S.A.

RA   10   9   8   7   6   5   4   3   2   1

In Loving Memory of Those Who Named and Nurtured Me
Dave Dinwiddie and Artemisia Elizabeth Baker Dinwiddie

Acknowledgments

When I consider acknowledging individuals who contributed to the making of this book, the list becomes extensive. Prudence will not allow me to name each person who supplied names of friends and family, insight into African-American naming practices, or just good old moral support, but all should know that many heartfelt thank-yous vibrate in their direction.

Compiling this book has been most labor-intensive; in fact, to label it backbreaking is only slightly engaging in hyperbole, so it seems appropriate to thank first my family for endowing me with the stamina and foundation to sustain the pace. Thank you:

Frederick Odell Dinwiddie, for assuming the role of family patriarch;

Thelma Etoria Avant Dinwiddie, for expecting this work of me;

Lorene Oretha Pollard, for being an example of determination and willpower;

William Scott Pollard, for being a model of faithfulness to duty;

Lily Jean Russell, for her Christian insight and encouragement;

Alvin Russell, for his example of dedicated hard work;

Katherine Brown, for her warmth, generosity, and cheerful willingness to offer a very talented helping hand;

Juanita Lorene Marshall, for her unfailing dedication to family.

A very special word of appreciation is extended to

Katherine Johanna Herberta "Kathy" Boyd for her research. Thank you, Kathy, for so carefully, thoroughly, and efficiently searching thousands of pages of newspaper and magazine copy for all those choice examples of creativity.

Janis Ahmed deserves a medal for her efficiency in reviewing, transferring, organizing, categorizing, and copying names.

The kind and thoughtful assistance offered by Mary E. Belden of Charleston Heights, S.C., deserves special recognition. Upon hearing from her jazz musician son Bob about the project, this retired librarian organized a collection effort that netted thousands of names. It is people like you, Mrs. Belden, who give humanity a good name. A special note of gratitude goes to those individuals who responded to the alert sounded by Mrs. Belden: Kathi Carr, North Charleston High School librarian; Kay Passailaigue; William "Billy" Wooten; Lonnie Hamilton; and Theodore Collier, retired principal of Bonds Wilson High School.

The insight and assistance of librarian Sharon M. Howard, curator of Research and Reference at the Schomburg Research Center for Black Culture, helped get the work on track from the start.

Thank you, my teacher friends from around the nation, for lists of created names: Sandra McKinney, Linda Odumade, Aljenae Wilson, and Maria Zubritiski.

Asante sana to my African colleagues who contributed names and information about African naming: Rosina Ampah, Daniel Awdowiya, Dame Babou, Pat Endromeda, David Mbouri, and Vickie Earabah Ward. A special word of thanks goes out to Ogonna Chuks-orji for breaking the ground with his *Names from Africa: Their Origins, Meaning, and Pronunciation* (Johnson Publishing Co., 1972).

I am so grateful to Ambassador Robert Van Lierop, Esq., for his enthusiastic and active support of this project. Bob, mere words cannot convey just how much it meant to me to have you take time out from your high-powered schedule to find and give me so many of the names listed in the created sections. Thank you to Michael Rashiid Adderley for compiling my first list of contemporary names from among his school chums.

And for my sisters of the collective I must acknowledge my indebtedness to Adrienne Ingrum, for her recommendation; my agent Marie Brown, for her continuing support of me and her dedication to black writers; Tonya Bolden, for her daily support, empathetic ear, and helpful hints on all the little details no one else cares to hear; Mildred Greene, for being there; and Safiyyah "Laverne" Marks for collecting all those pretty names.

And to my friends at Avon Books, thank you: Lisa Wager for putting my name forth; Gwen Montgomery and Tom Colgan for your enthusiasm, your support, and especially your gracious attitudes.

A very special acknowledgment is extended to my life partner, my cothinker, my husband, Herb Boyd, whose patience, good sense, and keen intellect shepherded me through, and without whom I cannot imagine my life.

And when it is all said and done, it is ultimately by the grace of God that I have done this work, and I thank my Savior for His blessings.

Contents

It is through our names that we first place ourselves in the world.

RALPH ELLISON, c. 1969

To The Parents

Choosing your baby's name is one of the most important things you will do. It is your child's name that will first set him or her apart from all others, that identifies little Monique or Darren as a unique individual. It can represent your hopes for him; it can intimate your feelings about her. As in the case of my goddaughter Ola, who is named for her paternal great-grandmother, it may connect your child to your family's history. Your baby's name is one of the first words he or she will learn. And, yes, you are indeed wise to want to make just the right choice. After all, it is the baby who will have to wear the name you assign. This baby names book has been written just for you. It is rooted and grounded in black culture and designed to suit the needs and the tastes of black parents.

Proud Heritage: 11,001 Names for Your African-American Baby allows the African-American parent to take a close look at the pool of names we use. It will also give you insight into our naming practices and heritage, and will tell you and your child something about the important people who have answered to a particular name.

If you want a name to inspire and motivate your child, you will find it here. If you want a name that sounds pretty, you will find it here. If you want a name that provides an exceptional role model, you will find it here. If you are determined to name the baby after a historical figure, you will find it here. And if you want an unusual name, you have thousands to choose from, as the newly invented names proliferate and show no sign of abating.

Perhaps you have already selected a name and want to know its meaning. Or you are trying to decide among several choices and want to know more about each of them.

It could be that you want to go truly Afro-centric and give the baby a name from the continent of Africa. Maybe you want to give your child a traditional American name such as Paul or Marie and worry about how that will play among the new creations. Or you think you have invented a new name and want to see just how creative and imaginative you've been. On the other hand, you may wish to give your child a name that has been in your family for several generations. If so, you can use this book to check the spelling variations, meaning, language of origin, and historical figures attached to it.

The book's organization is user-friendly. It is divided into two parts by gender, and the names are listed alphabetically. Each part contains several sections. In the first section you will find European-based or traditional American names, such as Katherine and Herbert. In the second section are names from Africa, such as Kofi and Efua. In both the traditional European-based American and the African sections, you will find language origins, meaning, significance, and sometimes a brief history of the name. The third and final section contains a lengthy list of the very chic, trendy, and au courant, newly created names such as Shalonda and Deryx. Throughout there are comments on interesting people.

Since this is not a scholarly work, the emphasis is not on the etymology of a name, but on its relationship to African-American culture, history, and naming practices. It is compiled for black parents who want to place their newborn's name squarely in the African-American tradition. But there are secondary usages too. It can assist those who are seeking to change their names to better reflect their self-concepts. Readers can refer to *Proud Heritage* to learn more about black naming preferences. And, finally, this book is for any reader who wants to know more about African-American names and some of the people who bore them.

African-American names and naming practices are intriguing facets of our sociocultural heritage. The process and the results provide a fascinating glimpse at the complexity of the black experience in America. As you turn the pages of this book, you will find more than a name for baby. You will find, culture, history, trends, and a people's innate propensity to distinguish themselves.

PROUD HERITAGE

11,001 NAMES FOR YOUR
AFRICAN-AMERICAN BABY

Introduction

*For in the dim beginnings, before I ever thought con-
sciously of writing, there was my own name, and
there was, doubtless, a certain magic in it. From the
start I was uncomfortable with it, and in my earliest
years it caused me much puzzlement. Neither could I
understand what a poet was, nor why exactly my father had chosen to name me after one.*

—RALPH WALDO ELLISON
"Hidden Name and Complex Fate"

When I was asked to compile a book of names for
African-American babies, I wondered just how one would
distinguish the names of black people from those of other
Americans. I knew that our African names had been left
behind and captive Africans had been forced to use the
names of those who enslaved them. But now I realize that
African-American names are the names that we have used:
those from other cultures and those we have created. We
have taken names such as John and Harriet, names that we
were first forced to carry, and forever imprinted them on
the pages of history. I also wondered how to find the
names and, when I figured out my research method,
whether there were enough names available to justify a
substantial book. Well, now I chuckle when I am asked
how one defines and researches the names used by black
Americans. With my attention focused on our names as
something more than personal handles, they suddenly appeared around every corner, in the literature at the turn of
every page, on the children, and on the lips of the adults.

The work of college professor, sociologist, and
forklorist Dr. Newbell N. Puckett has been central to the
compilation of *Proud Heritage. Black Names in America,*

1

published by G. K. Hall Publishers in 1975 and edited by
Murray Heller, is based on Puckett's research into "the
genesis, use and metamorphosis of the names of black
Americans." Puckett's untimely death precluded the com-
pletion of his work. Heller, with the full cooperation of
Puckett's widow, edited and brought to publication a portion of Puckett's pioneering efforts.

Puckett searched records of all sorts, including birth
registries, school and college rolls, armed service rosters,
and census data to trace the naming practices of blacks.
Keenly aware of the importance of a name and its impact
on the individual, Puckett dug deeply into various archives
and collected approximately 500,000 names: 340,000
names used by blacks. His collection consists of names
used by blacks in America from 1619 to the mid-1940s.

The Harvest

The names from Puckett's collection included here are se-
lectively taken from lists of names of free blacks in both
the North and the South. This selection process is designed
solely to follow the practice of accentuating the positive. I
opted for names that the individual wearing the name possibly had some say in selecting. A name's image is also
considered. Pejoratives like Sambo—which probably is a
distortion of the African Samba and an example of our
heritage turned against us—and sound patterns that have
been the butt of jokes have been deliberately omitted.

Using European-American names as his standard,
Puckett identified a long list comprising tens of thousands
of black names that he labeled unusual. Today we might
call these names created or invented. Puckett's lists of unusual names make a strong and early case for black American creativity in naming our children. They are, indeed,
evidence of African-Americans taking our right to name
ourselves—a right lost on the shores of enslavement—
back into our own hands. The sheer volume of the list of
unusual names documented by Puckett is staggering, and
appears to account for more than one-third of the entire
collection.

I have culled the various lists in *Black Names in America* to identify interesting examples: names that demonstrate flair, unusual sound combinations, spelling variations, and trends. You will find them among the traditional American names. These names that are apparently a result of black inventiveness are not listed in the newly created section, as Puckett makes no claim that they are inventions of recent coinage. Additionally, they are also located in the European-based traditional American section to place them in terms of time period. As Puckett distinguished his unusual names as those not found among the basic stock of traditional American names, it therefore seemed appropriate that these names used by our foreparents should actually be placed in the traditional American category. Nevertheless, it is my strong hunch that the greater portion of them are evidence of African-American inventiveness set firmly in our early American history.

Names in this volume not taken from Puckett's collection were appropriated from a number of sources: school rolls, church rolls, newspapers, magazines, sports rosters, almanacs, history books, and encyclopedias.

The resourceful word-of-mouth proved to be most bountiful. People who heard about the book were quick to offer names of family and friends. At every mention, I was met with a fascination so powerful, so astounding that it was overwhelming. As the word spread, names—especially the created ones—were coming faster than I and my assistant could record and process them. And they still come. Invariably, individuals responded with excitement and sometimes exhilaration over the recent explosion of created names. Along with my informants, I discovered the beauty in them.

Affirming the Right to Name Ourselves

The right to name ourselves has been a major issue for black Americans. As a group we have at various points in our history rejected and accepted the labels colored, Negro, black, Afro-American, and African-American. As we have struggled for a respectable identity, our personal names and our group name have been paramount. In the pages that follow, you will watch the evolution of African-American naming from 1619 into the 1990s. At no other point in our history have we demonstrated a more zealous passion about our personal names than we do today with the electrifying surge of newly created names and spelling variations.

The giving of a personal name is a highly emotional bestowal. For African-Americans it is an even more profound and transcendent ceremony. Our right to name ourselves has often represented our freedom, our reclamation of self, our need for distinction in an often oppressive culture; our need to proclaim, "I am somebody!"

In keeping with that syncretistic tendency of black Americans, newly created names reflect a blending of Africa and Europe that often results in something unique and distinctive.

Our Naming History

Lerone Bennett in *Before the Mayflower* and Ivan Van Sertima in *They Came Before Columbus* document an African presence in what is now the Americas centuries before the arrival of Christopher Columbus. Also historical records indicate that African explorers accompanied such European conquistadors as Balboa, Cortez, and Ponce de Leon to the New World. Despite this early presence of free Africans, the unhappy fact is that the vast majority of our ancestors didn't come as explorers but as captives, forced into bondage, with their African names, like their languages, shorn and replaced by European designations.

Our African foreparents were given the names of the period. In these early days of American history, the basic naming practices came from the British Isles. Wave upon wave of immigration has broadened that tradition to include Western Europe. Nevertheless, Anglicized names continue to dominate the basic stock of American first names. The history of these names is ancient and can be traced through the Norman Conquest of England to Latin and Greek. They are also influenced by the Germanic, the

Celtic, and Old English or Anglo-Saxon languages; the Nordic influence brought by the Danish presence in ninth century England, the Norman-French period, the Middle English period, and the modern period, which starts with the tremendous growth in the English language that began with the sixteenth century.

Like so much of our history, naming ourselves has not been accomplished without heartache and struggle. Just as the American experience has dictated the naming and re-naming of ourselves as a group, it has soundly impacted upon the evolution of our preferences and practices in per-sonal names. From George Washington Carver to Jawanza Kunjufu, our history is replete with those who have very deliberately chosen personal names to reflect their aspira-tions and self-concept.

Following the Civil War, we emerged with European names. But even then we varied the spelling and the pro-nunciation. Of course, in some cases these variations were the result of spelling and pronunciation errors, but in many other cases variations are our own ethnic statement.

America is the blend of the New World and the Old. At the very essence of the African-American being is the blending of Africa and Europe. In dance, music, speech, and dress, we too have forged the old and the new. In our names we have sought affirmation and distinction that has been denied. Removed forcibly from our lingustic context, we have sought to use personal names to affirm our hu-manity, to reclaim a lost identity.

The Power in a Name

It is probably a stretch to imply that a name can make or break you, but it is important for parents to consider the potential of a positive name.

Not long ago, one of my students described a memora-ble experience. Having just completed an all-day Church World Services seminar that celebrated women, Janis said that a most profound moment occurred when the Asian-American women talked about the inspirational impact of their names. It seems that each of these women had been given a name with a very positive meaning, and each woman had sought to live up to her name. Moved to tears by one woman's description of the continuing source of inspiration derived from the beautiful name her father had given her, Janis realized just how important a personal name is. A further example of a name's power was noted in the epigram by Ralph Ellison.

Far more than their meanings, the power that drives the names in this volume comes from those individuals of remarkable achievement who are called by them. Following the principle that ideal naming enhances, even stimulates, positive growth, the names of famous and not-so-famous role models are included. Some of them, like Martin, Malcolm, Maya, and Sojourner, are larger-than-life icons whose stories depict overcoming horrendous obstacles to heralded accomplishment. The power of these names is derived from those everyday people like you and me—friends, relatives, and casual acquaintances, good citizens, hardworking, God-fearing individuals—who valiantly face and conquer the vicissitudes of a day. They are our aunties and uncles. (In West Africa, these are respectable titles younger generations use to refer to an older person of great esteem.)

I urge you to consider carefully the selection of the name your child will carry. It is a good idea to try the name out on others before your son or daughter is born to see what kind of response it gets. If you get several unfavorable reactions, you might be wise to reconsider. Repeat the name aloud, as a whisper, as a shout, and see how it feels to you. Will you be comfortable calling it across a crowded playground? Will it inspire an unfavorable nickname that can take hold and stick? If yours is not a home birth, take this book to the hospital with you to facilitate any change of heart you might have after looking at the baby.

If the name you select for your child has been used by a family member and/or a high achiever, encourage the child to study the habits of this role model, to learn more about that person's life. Do not hesitate to let your child know where his or her name comes from, and why you selected it. Again, accentuate the positive.

The Bounty

Many types of names from which to choose are listed here. There are names from Europe, Africa, Asia, and the Americas. There are occupational names; flower names; place names; jewel names; tree names; biblical names; animal names; names of months and days; and names from history, mythology, literature, and religion. And, finally, there are those names that we create, the ones that sound and look good to us.

In all cultures, parents want to give the newborn a name that will enhance the child's progress through life, and in that regard black parents are no different.

This is a baby names book filled with names used by black people. Our names entitle our existence. A name may tell of the place one comes from; or it may tell of one's occupation, clan, or family; or it may define a spirit or a characteristic. But no matter what type of name we choose, our identity and our individuality are often derived from it.

Names from Africa

A proverb among the Yoruba of Nigeria cautions parents to "consider the state of your life before you name a child." Throughout the continent one finds that names are often intended in a very literal sense to clarify circumstance, family and clan connections, character attributes, or character flaws.

Africans tend to value highly family and family history, thus African naming is a family affair. Universally, African naming ceremonies and rituals contain three major components:

- They are a spiritual package reconnecting the living with their ancestors. A newborn baby may be named for a family trait. This practice reconnects the clan with its past. For example, if a family has been known over the generations for producing brave warriors, the child's name might reflect this attribute.
- They are a social commentary on who you are and what the family is all about. A God-fearing, God-loving family among the Yoruba of Nigeria may use the name Olutoyin, which translates as God is enough to praise, or Olulaanu, which means God has mercy.
- They reflect the hopes and aspirations of the family. Africans are expressing a universal human response when the names they give their offspring reflect their desires for them.

However, naming in Africa doesn't necessarily stop at birth. As social commentary, your name can be changed to describe your current circumstance or what you have be-

come. And on this score our cousins across the great sea
make no bones about it; if you have grown to become a
negative your new name will say so. A very literal description of what the child has become is found in
Bamwoze, a boy's name in Uganda, which means the child
who is spoiled, or in Walugyo, a Uganda boy's name,
which means he doesn't like to give, but he likes to be
given. A girl may be called Katebulanya, meaning trouble-
maker. A boy or girl who has become a liar will be re-
named Kalimbira. A very literal circumstantial name is
Najjawambi, a Ugandan girl's name, which means the
mother died after the birth, or the unisex Mulekwa, which
means one who has no father.

Communication specialist and college teacher W.
Adewale Legunleko says that among the Yoruba of south-
western Nigeria and their kinfolk in Togo and the Republic
of Benin, a baby's name is taken from the family's
Oriki—a recapitulation of ancestral deeds, worth, and
place in history. To the casual student of this cultural wa-
tershed, the Oriki seems nothing more than a praisesong.
Legunleko warns us not to take this pedestrian view of the
Oriki, as it is the central key in the name ceremony of the
Yoruba child. Tradition holds that every child has a natural
Oriki by virtue and circumstances of birth and family history. The Oriki extolls the grandeur of royalty, the deeds of
the accomplished; it accentuates their honor and celebrates
their achievements as a reminder for the next generation to
emulate.

The example below is taken from the hours-long Oriki
of Legunleko's mother, 80-year-old Aduke Ibidun Bakare
of Lagos, Nigeria. This excerpt gives a brief history of her
father's ancestors.

Ibidun ani
Omo Nmere Ogudu
Omo Ara Isheri
Omo oloko
Iwaju oloko nsowo
Eyin oloko nso odigba ileke
Omo kaf'owo wa kaf'aje wa

Ka f'ogedegede owo wa oko de Isheri . . .

Sweet and lovely one
Child of Nmere Ogudu [the sturdy one]
Begotten of the great and candid warrior
Child of Isheriland [their famous homestead]
Child of the great seafarer
The bow of his boat is laden with great wealth
The stern laden with priceless beads
Child of the great pilot
Who paddles with bare hands
Paddles with oars
Guided his boat without a paddle all the way to Isheri . . .

The Arabic Influence

Since the invasions of the seventh century, Arabic has greatly influenced African languages. The Hausa and Swahili names listed in this section have a great resemblance to Arabic. Although not as apparent, Wolof is also influenced by Arabic.

In some cases the same name will have different meanings among different ethnic groups. Where the language of origin is not known, the country or region is noted.

Language, Country and Region

Language	Country	Region
Abaluhya	Uganda	East
Akan	Ghana	West
Arabic (most prominent)		
Ateso	Uganda	Uganda
Bachopi	South Africa	Southern
Benin	Nigeria	West
Ewe	Ghana	West
Fante	Ghana	West
Ga	Ghana	West
Hausa	Nigeria	West
Ibo	Nigeria	West
Kikuyu	Kenya	East
Lomwe	Malawi	Southern
Luganda	Uganda	East
Luo	Uganda, Kenya	East
Mudama	Uganda	East
Mugwere	Uganda	East
Mukiga	Uganda	East
Muneyankole	Uganda	East
Musamia	Uganda	East
Musoga	Uganda	East
Ndali	Tanzania	East
Ndebele	Zimbabwe	Southern
Ngoni	Malawi	Southern
Nguni	South Africa	Southern
Nwera	Kenya	East
Nyakyusa	Tanzania	East
Pulaar	Senegal	West

Language	Country	Region
Rwanda	Rwanda	East
Shekiri	Nigeria	West
Shona	Zimbabwe	Southern
Swahili	Tanzania, Kenya, Uganda	East
Tiv	Nigeria	West
Tswana	Botswana	Southern
Twi	Ghana	West
Wolof	Cote D'Ivoire, Gambia, Senegal	West
Xhosa	South Africa	Southern
Yao	Malawi	Southern
Yoruba	Nigeria	West
Zaramo	Tanzania	East
Zulu	South Africa	Southern

Newly Created Names:
A Black American Legacy

Traditionally black names have been no different from white names in the U.S.—that is, with the exception of those several hundred thousand unusual names documented by Dr. Puckett. But since 1980 Americans have experienced a veritable explosion of newly created names and spelling exaggerations and variations. This originality in naming children has touched nearly every class, race, and region, but experts agree that it is largely and profoundly the legacy of African-Americans.

The current quest for originality and individuality in names can be traced directly back to the apex of black consciousness in the politically charged 1960s and 1970s. We were exhorted by the militants among us to get rid of "ole massa's" name and return to our African roots. Grown men and women rushed in to change their names from Donald Gene to Sekou, from Gerald to Kwame, from Patricia to Noni, and from Effie Jean to Efua. Newborn babies were called Malik and Monifa, Kenya and Kenyatta, Sundiata and Nzinga, as we proudly celebrated and asserted our African past. In many instances our new names represented only cosmetic changes. For others, they spelled a genuine metamorphosis, a transformation of character seeking higher standards and lofty ideals.

The trend toward placing an ethnic stamp on our names is now in full bloom. According to Leonard Ashley, an English professor at Brooklyn College in New York, "Blacks are refusing to take white people's names. They are saying we are different. We are going to have our own Christmas holiday, we are going to have our own names."

When parents are asked why they chose a name such as

Sheshandra, Donesha, or Daquan, they most often respond that it sounds pretty. Some of the most popular phonemes used in the creation craze are Da, De, La, Le, Sha, and Ja.

At the turn of the century, according to Ashley, the ten most popular names in each gender category sufficed for half of all boys and girls. But today the top ten accounts for an estimated 25 percent of all American names. The other 75 percent are largely names rarely seen in this country until recent years.

According to Jerrilyn McGregory, a professor of African-American studies and English at the University of Georgia, "Basically the majority of African-Americans are now naming outside the tradition. It's a statement of cultural identity. Some people predicted it to be a fad, but it seems to be going beyond one generation." And if Puckett is to be believed, it started centuries ago.

Names
for Boys

Traditional American

Names for Boys

Every person comes into this world seeking his name. This is the centrality of life. By one's name is not meant the name upon a birth certificate, nor the name by which one's parents call him. Rather, what is the name by which God knows you?

—Herman Watts, "What Is Your Name?"
Philpot, ed., *Best Black Sermons*, 1973

Can you sense a man's hurt at not knowing the name he's called by, or to what his name calls him?

—Aime Cesaire
Tragedy of King Christophe, 1963

Note: You'll also notice some created names as you read through the European based names. These are names that have become more common and widely enough used to be included here.

Aaron *Biblical/Hebrew:* Enlightened, lofty. Aaron, the brother of Moses, was the first high priest of the Jews. Aaron Douglas was the best known painter during the Harlem Renaissance.

Abel *Biblical/Hebrew:* Breath, the second son of Adam and Eve.

Abraham *Biblical/Hebrew:* Father of a mighty nation, blessed by God. In the early 1800s, many free blacks used this name.

Abram *Biblical/Hebrew:* The exalted father; Abraham's name before God changed it. Abram Harris was a writer during the Harlem Renaissance.

Absalom *Biblical/Hebrew:* Father of peace. This third son of King David was renowned for his handsome appearance. Absalom was a common given name among free blacks in the 18th and 19th centuries. It is rare today. Absalom Jones and Richard Allen founded the African Methodist Episcopal Church in 1746.

Acie An African-American original. University of Iowa's Acie Earl was a top defensive player in the Big Ten collegiate conference in 1993.

Adam *Biblical/Hebrew:* Mortal, man of the red earth; the first human created by God. Reverend Adam Clayton Powell Jr. represented Harlem in the U.S. Congress for over 20 years. He was loved and respected by black Americans all over the nation because of his dedication

20

to freedom and justice and his outspoken representation of blacks. For many years he was the only black on Capitol Hill.

Addison *English:* Son of Adam. Addison Gayle, the noted black literary critic and writer, wrote *The Black Aesthetic.*

Adger This unusual name, quite likely an African-American creation, seems to have first appeared in the 20th century. Its origins and meaning are unknown. Photographer Adger Cowans is a colleague and former protege of the legendary Gordon Parks.

Adolph *German:* Noble wolf. Wolf in the definition of a German or English name always refers to courage or the courageous. Because of its association with Nazism and Adolf Hitler, this name is rarely used. Adolfo is a Spanish form. Adolphus is a Latin form, and Adolphe is a French form. Adolph Caesar, a well-known stage and screen actor, came to prominence in 1984 with an Oscar nomination as Best Supporting Actor for his outstanding portrayal of Sgt. Walters in *A Soldier's Story.* Adolpho Birch Jr. was the long-time chaplain for Howard University.

Adonis *Greek:* A handsome lord. In Greek mythology, Adonis was a most beautiful lad. Adonis Jordan was a member of the starting five for the Kansas University 1992–93 basketball team.

Adrian *Latin:* Black or dark one from the Adriatic Sea. Also Adrien. In its earlier form, Hadrian, the name was borne by a Roman emperor and six popes. Adrian Dantley is a former Detroit Pistons basketball star.

Ainsworth *English:* A place name meaning from Ann's estate.

Alain This French form of Alan (see below) is growing in popularity. Writer and educator Alain Locke's influential work on the Harlem Renaissance makes him one of our important scholars and historians.

Alan *Irish:* Handsome, cheerful, harmonious one. Alan

Young, CEO of Alan Young Buick-GMC Truck, Inc. led the dealership he founded in 1979 to a record-setting $34 million in sales in 1991.

Albert *English:* Noble and brilliant. Albert W. Johnson Sr. is the founder and CEO of Al Johnson Cadillac-Avanti-Saab, Inc., the nation's 17th largest black-owned automobile dealership. Albert Hughes and his twin, Allen, directors of the popular film *Menance II Society,* at the tender age of 21 were veteran video directors.

Alden *English:* Wise, friendly; a surname sometimes used as a given name. Alden J. McDonald Jr. is the chief executive of Liberty Bank and Trust Co., the nation's 20th largest black-owned bank.

Aldrich *German:* Wise ruler. In 1981, Aldrich Allen, a former Grambling Tiger, was drafted by the Atlanta Falcons, but did not play. The football team for Grambling, a historic black college, is well-known for its superb play, having sent numerous players to the pros, and for the outstanding coaching of Eddie Robinson Jr. African-Americans travel from all over the country to see the Grambling Tigers play.

Alex A dimunitive for Alexander (see below). Also Alec. Alex Haley, author of *Roots,* received worldwide acclaim for tracing his family history back to Africa.

Alexander *Greek:* Defender and helper of humankind. Made popular by Alexander the Great. Clergymen Alexander Crummell, a descendant of West African royalty, was born in 1819 in New York to free parents.

Alfred *English:* Supernaturally wise, elf counselor. The mythical elves were esteemed by the ancients as supernatural beings who influenced and advised mortals wisely. Alfred N. Thompson is the CEO of Consolidated Beverage Corp., one of the top 100 black-owned and operated industrial/service companies.

Allen An alternate spelling for Alan (see above). A popular first name among free blacks in the 19th century. Its popularity has continued until today.

Allison *English:* Son of the highborn. Also Alison. More common as a girl's name. Allison Davis, renowned psychologist and educator, was one of the first to point out the inadequacies of intelligence tests for measuring the educational potential of children from low-income families.

Alonzo The English form of Alphonso (see below). Alonzo Mourning, a basketball star for Georgetown, was a top NBA draft choice in 1992. In 1993 he distinguished himself as a rookie with the Charlotte Hornets. Alonzo Babers won the 400-meter Gold Medal in the 1984 Olympics.

Aloysius *Latin:* The very wise; a form of Louis (see below) or Luigi. An unusual name appearing among free blacks in the nineteenth century. Rarely used in the 20th century.

Alphonso *German:* Noble, ready for battle. Also Alphonzo. A favorite of black American families for many generations. In Spanish, the variation Alonso is frequently used by royalty.

Alrutheus This unusual name is probably of African-American coinage. Alrutheus Ambush Taylor, a well-known historian and educator who died in 1955, dedicated his entire career to black colleges.

Alston *English:* One from Al's town. Also Allston. Alston Burleigh was a musician and actor during the Harlem Renaissance.

Alton *English:* A place name meaning old town. Alton Maddox is an activist lawyer in New York City.

Al-Tarik Al-Tarik Mack is a high school student in Newark, N.J.

Alvesta An African-American original. Alvesta Stewart Evans was the father of Doris Saunders, who in 1949 established the library for *Ebony* magazine.

Alvin *English:* Noble friend. Alvin Ailey founded the Alvin Ailey American Dance Theatre and won international fame as both dancer and choreographer. Alvin F. Poussaint, associate professor of psychiatry at Harvard

Medical School, was a consultant on "The Cosby Show." Until the recent explosion of newly created names, Alvin and its many variations have been a clear favorite among African-American parents. The use of Ailwyn, Alvan, Alven, Alwyn, Alvyn, Aylwin, Elvin, Elwyn, and Elwin can probably be safely attributed to our penchant for the unusual in naming our children.

Alvis *Scandinavian:* All-knowing.

Ambrose *Greek:* Immortal, divine.

Americus Americus Vespucius is the Latin name of Amerigo Vespucci, the Italian navigator after whom America is name. In Italian, Amerigo means home ruler.

Amos *Biblical/Hebrew:* Burdened, troubled. Very popular at the turn of the century, Amos fell on hard times after black activists in the 1960s condemned the popular radio and TV comedy "Amos and Andy" as perpetuating racist stereotypes.

Anderson *English:* Son of Andrew (see below). By the turn of the century, Anderson became a common given name. Anderson Hunt played guard on the 1990 NCAA championship University of Nevada at Las Vegas basketball team and now plays professional ball in Europe. Anderson Thompson is a noted scholar and teacher.

Andre The Spanish form of Andrew (see below). This name is rapidly gaining popularity. Andre Ware won the prestigious Heisman Trophy in 1990 and is a quarterback for the Detroit Lions. Andre Watts is an internationally famous concert pianist.

Andrew *Biblical/Greek:* Manly; one of the 12 apostles. This is an often used first name. Andrew Jack was a free black patriot who fought in the American Revolution. Andrew Young, a faithful lieutenant of Martin Luther King, became the first black ambassador to the UN. Andrew "Rube" Foster was the founding father of U.S. baseball's Negro Leagues.

Anfernee An African-American original. Anfernee

Hardaway was named one of Dick Vitale's Colossal Collegians during the 1992–93 basketball season.

Angelo *Greek:* Messenger, angel. Popular among free blacks in the 17th century. Angelo Herndon was a political activist in the 1930s.

Anson *German:* Son of the divine. Anson E. Rhodes of Detroit's Renaissance High School was one of *Ebony* 's 1993 Top High School Seniors.

Anthony *Latin:* Worthy of great praise, beyond price, valuable. A popular name among black Americans for centuries. Anthony Bettis was a free black patriot who fought in the American Revolution. Anthony Mason is a power forward for the New York Knicks. Anthony Peeler is a guard for the L.A. Lakers. Avant-garde alto saxophonist and composer Anthony Braxton has a long association with the Art Ensemble of Chicago.

Antoine French for Anthony (see above). Very popular in recent years. Antoine Carr is a power forward with the San Antonio Spurs.

Anton This German form of Anthony (see above) is growing in popularity.

Archibald *German:* The truly bold, sacred prince, or genuine.

Archie Originally the English pet name for Archibald (see above), it is now an independent name. Archie Shepp is a versatile musician and university professor. Light-heavyweight champion of the world Archie Moore continued boxing into his 50s.

Ardell *Latin:* Eager, industrious.

Aris *Greek:* A prefix for words like aristocratic. The origins and meaning of this unusual name are obscure. Physician Aris T. Allen was elected to chair the Maryland Republican Committee in 1977.

Armon *Hebrew:* Castle. Armon Gilliam, a power forward for the New Jersey Nets, plays a finesse game.

Armond *Italian:* Warrior. Armond White is a film critic for the New York-based *City Sun,* a weekly newspaper.

Armstead Armstead is listed among free black first names since the 18th century. Its origins and meaning are unknown.

Arna The origins of this name are unclear. It may be a variation of Arnan, a Hebrew name meaning quick and joyful, or it could have come from the German Arno, meaning wolf, or Arne, meaning eagle. More than likely, Arna is an African-American invention. The prolific writer Arna Wendell Bontemps has contributed innumerable plays, poems, short stories, novels, and other writings to African-American literature. With Langston Hughes, he edited *The Poetry of The Negro 1746–1949* and *The Book of Negro Folklore.*

Arnall *German:* Strong as an eagle, gracious. Also Arnell.

Arnett *French:* Little eagle. Arnett Cobb was a robust tenor saxophonist of the Texas school of honkers and shouters.

Arnold *German:* Strength of an eagle. Arnold Rampersad is a historian and biographer of Langston Hughes.

Arsenio *Greek/Spanish:* The virile or masculine one. Arsenio Hall is the host of the enormously popular "Arsenio Hall Show," which outstripped Johnny Carson's "Tonight Show" in the ratings.

Arthur *English:* Noble, brave as a bear. Arthur Ashe, the famous tennis player, was the first black to win the U.S. Open. Following this victory in 1968, Ashe went on to claim many titles, including the prestigious Wimbledon. Living up to his name, Ashe bravely confronted an HIV infection acquired through a blood transfusion during open heart surgery and continued his many community endeavors. In 1992, *Sports Illustrated* named him Athlete of the Year. Arthur Mitchell was the first black Democrat elected to Congress.

Arvarh The origins of this rare name are not known. Educator and historian Arvarh E. Strickland became a professor of history at the University of Missouri in 1969.

Arvin *German:* A friend of the people. Also Arvine. When Arvine Bradford opened his office in Pocomoke City, Md., in 1950, he became the first black physician to practice medicine in that city.

Asa *Biblical/Hebrew:* Healer, physician. An unusual name sometimes used by freed African-Americans, especially during the latter half of the 19th century. Asa Spaulding was president of North Carolina Mutual Life Insurance Co. When he was appointed to the board of directors of W. T. Grant Co., Spaulding became the first African-American to serve on the board of a major nonminority corporation. Asa Hilliard is a leading proponent of Afro-centric thought.

Ashford *English:* A place name meaning dweller at the ash tree ford. This surname is also used as a given name.

Ashley *English:* A place name meaning from the ash tree meadow. Originally a surname, then a male given name, Ashley is now quite popular among white parents as a girl's name. Its popularity as a girl's name is growing among black parents.

Ashton *English:* A place name meaning from the ash tree farm.

Aubrey *French:* Blond ruler, elf ruler, spirit ruler. The name Aubrey came to England with the Norman Conquest. Originally a man's name, it is now often used by white families for girls.

Audie A nickname for Audley (see below) sometimes used as an independent name. Also Auddie.

Audley *English:* Old friend.

Augie A short form of Augustine (see below). Augie Conduah, Crenshaw High School class of 1993, Los Angeles, is one of *Ebony*'s Top High School Seniors.

August German and English form of Augustus (see below). Playwright August Wilson won the Pulitzer Prize in

1987 for *Fences* and again in 1990 for *The Piano Lesson*.

Augustine   A variation of Augustus (see below).

Augustus   *Latin:* Exalted one. Augustus Caesar was the first emperor of Rome. Augustus "Gus" Savage was a congressman from Illinois.

Aurven   This name probably represents an African-American spelling of Ervin or Irving (see below). In 1937, physician Aurven Colston DeBerry became the senior attending oral surgeon at St. Agnes Hospital in Raleigh, N.C.

Autrey   This surname is sometimes employed by black parents as a given name. Autrey Lane Howell, a former Grambling Tiger, was drafted in 1963 by the New York Giants.

Avery   *English:* Elf ruler; a form of Alfred (see above) and Aubrey (see above). Avery Brooks, a stage and TV actor, is best known for his portrayal of the mysterious Hawk in the TV series "Spencer for Hire" and "A Man Called Hawk."

Avon   *English:* A river in central England. The use of Avon as a given name appears to be restricted to African-American parents. Avon Long was a singer and dancer at the famous Cotton Club in the 1930s.

Bailey   *English/French:* Public official, person in charge.

Barclay: *English:* A place name meaning dweller at the birch tree meadow.

Barnet *English:* Of honorable birth.

Barry *Irish:* Great spearman or marksman. Barry Harris is a highly respected jazz pianist. Barry Sanders is a running back for the Detroit Lions.

Bartholomew *Biblical/Hebrew:* Farmer's son; one of the 12 apostles. Also Bart, Bartel, Barth, and Bartlett. Bartholomew Robinson played tight end with the 1991–92 Gambling Tigers.

Barton *English:* A place name meaning barley was grown here.

Basie The surname of William "Count" Basie. Young Basie Allen was given the Count's last name in celebration of his grandfather's love for the great bandleader's music.

Basil *Greek:* Of royalty. Basil is a popular name among Caribbean-American parents. Basil Raymond Darling graduated in 1993 from the College of New Rochelle, School of New Resources.

Bayard *English:* Reddish-brown haired, powerful. Bayard Rustin was a chief organizer of the 1963 March on Washington.

Baz The origins of this name are unknown. Also Bass. Baz Reeves was a deputy U.S. marshal in the Indian Territory for 32 years. He traveled all over Texas and Oklahoma making arrests.

Ben Diminutive for Benjamin (see below), sometimes used as a given name. Also Benny. As senior vice-president and A&R general manager of the Black Music Division of Warner Brothers Records, Benny Medina is the coproducer of NBC TV's "The Fresh Prince of Bel-Air."

Benedict *Latin:* Blessed. This name is rarely used, perhaps because it is best known for Benedict Arnold, the American Revolutionary general who became a traitor.

Benito A diminutive for Benedict (see above). The use of this name fell off dramatically after WWII and its association with the infamous Benito Mussolini. Benito

Sylvain, a Haitian diplomat, was an organizer of the Pan-African Congress of 1900.

Benjamin *Biblical/Hebrew:* Fortunate. Reverend Benjamin Hooks was executive director of the NAACP from 1977 to 1993. Benjamin Banneker, inventor, astronomer, mathematician, and gazetter, served on the commission that surveyed and designed Washington, D.C. Benjamin Chavis became executive director of the NAACP in April 1993.

Benji A diminutive for Benjamin (see above) rarely used as an independent name. At the beginning of the 1991 season, Benji Roland left Tampa Bay to join the Atlanta Falcons football team.

Bennett *Latin:* Blessed.

Bernard *German:* Brave as a bear. Bernard King is a star forward for the New Jersey Nets. Bernard Bell is the author of *The Afro-American Novel and Its Traditions.*

Berry A botanical name often used for both boys and girls. The legendary Berry Gordy, founder of Motown Records, launched the careers of Smokey Robinson, Diana Ross, Marvin Gaye, and Michael Jackson, to name but a few.

Bert *English:* Shining brightly. Bert Johnson is the publisher of *Excel* magazine. Bert Collins is the CEO of North Carolina Mutual Life Insurance Co., founded in 1898—the nation's largest black-owned insurance company. Bert Andrews was famous for his photographs of black performers on Broadway.

Bertram *German/English:* Bright raven, he shall be famous.

Bertrand *German:* Bright shield. Bertrand A. Hall was a leading agriculturalist and civic leader in Guilford County, N.C., until his retirement in 1973. Bertrand Jennings is a dentist in Chicago.

Bill A diminutive for William (see below), Bill is often used by African-Americans as an independent name. Bill "Bojangles" Robinson began his legendary dancing career at age 8 and is considered the dean of the tap dancers.

Bishop *Greek:* An overseer. A popular name among free blacks of the 19th century, it's out of fashion today.

Blaine *Irish:* Thin. Detroiter Blaine Denning starred in high school basketball and later played with the Harlem Globetrotters.

Blair *Irish:* Child of the fields; surname now used as a first name for boys. Recently it has been used for girls as well. Actor Blair Underwood plays the Harvard-educated lawyer Jonathan Rollins on "L. A. Law."

Blake *English:* Of dark skin.

Bloise A surname infrequently used as a given name.

Bonaparte This surname of Napoleon was sometimes used by free blacks in the 19th and early 20th centuries.

Booker *English:* An occupational name for one who copies books. The great educator Booker T. Washington rose from humble origins to found Tuskegee Institute. Booker Little was a promising jazz trumpeter before his death in 1961 at age 23.

Borel The origins of this name are uncertain; it is apparently an African-American invention. Borel C. Dauphin is the CEO of Williams Progressive Life & Accident Insurance Co., the nation's 13th largest black-owned insurer.

Boris *Russian:* Warrior.

Boston *English:* A place name meaning a town near the thicket. Boston Ballard was a free black patriot who served in the American Revolution.

Boycereid This unusual name is found among contemporary men. Boycereid Sloan lives in South Carolina.

Boyd *Scottish:* Blond, fair-haired; a surname infrequently used as a given name. Saxophonist and violinist Boyd Atkins composed "Heebie Jeebies," which was made famous by Louis Armstrong.

Brad *English:* 7'1" Brad Daugherty covers the center lane for the Cleveland Cavaliers as if he is broad.

Bradford *English:* A place name meaning broad river crossing.

Bradley *Scottish:* Broad clearing in the woods. *English:* A place name meaning wide meadow.

Bran *Irish:* Raven. The dove, the raven, and the phoenix are symbols of continued life or rebirth.

Brand *English:* Fiery. Also Brandy.

Brandon *English:* A place name meaning from the beacon hill. The popularity of Brandon has mushroomed.

Branford This variation of Bradford (see above) may have originated in the Marsalis family. Branford Marsalis, the hot young tenor saxophonist, joined Jay Leno on "The Tonight Show," replacing Doc Severinsen as the show's bandleader. Branford, the brother of Wynton, composed the show's new theme song.

Brant *English:* Fiery.

Brent *English:* A place name meaning from the steep hill. Brent Wade is the author of *Company Man,* the first novel written about the black experience in corporate America. Brent is quite a fashionable name among today's black parents.

Brenton This variation of Brent (see above) appears to be a contemporary African-American invention. Also Brentton. Brentton Birmingham is a rising young star on the Manhattan College 1992–93 basketball team.

Brian *Irish:* The strong. Also Bryan. This name has been very popular for several generations now. Brian Shaw is a guard for the Miami Heat. Brian Roche Russell, husband and father, lives in Oklahoma City.

Brimmer The origins of this unusual name are not clear. In 1991, Brimmer Brown Jr. was a tight end for the famous Grambling State University's Tigers football team.

Bristol *English:* Rich, noble, powerful.

Britus This invention reflects a variation of Brutus (see below). Britus Twitty was a Detroit entrepreneur and salesman.

Broadus An unusual name of obscure origins. Broadus Eugene Sawyer is a well-known accountant, economist, and college professor.

Brock *English:* A badger. Brock Peters is a movie actor.

Brook *English:* A stream, dweller at the brook. Also Brooke. Brook Benton was a famous rhythm and blues singer. Since the fame of movie actress Brooke Shields, the name is probably more associated with girls.

Bross The origins of this unusual name are unclear. Bross Townsend is a well-known jazz pianist who has toured the world accompanying famous singers such as Dakota Staton.

Bruce This is the Scottish form of the old French name Brieux, a place name meaning dweller in the thicket or woods. In 1989, J. Bruce Llewellyn led the investment group that paid Time, Inc. $420 million for Lenfest Communications, the largest cable TV corporation owned by African-Americans.

Brutus *Latin:* Brutus was one of the assassins of Julius Caesar. The name fell into disfavor around the turn of the century.

Bryant *Irish:* Strong, virtuous. Bryant Gumble is a popular TV host.

Buck *English:* A male deer. American: A dashing figure. Buck was frequently used during the late 19th century. Buck Williams is a power foward for the Portland Trailblazers.

Bud A diminutive for Buddy. The career of Bud Powell, the most important pianist in the development of the bebop style of jazz, was greatly hampered after he sustained a head injury during a racial incident.

Buford *French:* A shallow stream where the oxen cross. Also Bufford.

Burford *English:* Dweller at the castle ford.

Burnell *Irish:* Brown skin. Burnell K. Moliere is the CEO of A Minority Entity, Inc., one of the top 100 black-owned industrial/service companies.

Byford *English:* From the river crossing.

Byrd *English:* Birdlike.

Byron *English:* A place name meaning barn for cows. This surname was first used as a given name in tribute to the poet Lord Byron. NBA star Byron Houston is a small forward for the Golden State Warriors. Byron Scott is an NBA guard.

Cade *Irish:* Spirit of battle. Reverend Cade Jones lives in New York City.

Caesar *Latin:* Emperor. This title was used by Roman emperors from Augustus to Hadrian, most notably by Julius Caesar. Birth by operation is called caesarean because Julius Caesar was born that way. Caesar Power was a free black patriot who served in the Revolutionary War.

Calbert *English:* An occupational name meaning calf herdsman. Calbert Cheaney, a senior with Indiana University's 1992–93 basketball team, is considered one of the top players in his class.

Caldwell *English:* Cool, clear spring. NBA star Caldwell Jones is one of three brothers who played in the pro ranks.

Caleb *Biblical/Hebrew:* A dog. The connotation is a positive one signifying both a bold stance and faithful affection. Caleb was one of the 12 men sent by Moses to spy on Canaan. It was very popular in the 18th and 19th centuries.

Calvert A form of Calbert (see above.)

Calvin *Latin:* Bald one. A very popular name among black American parents for several centuries now. Calvin B. Grigsby is CEO of Grigsby Brandford & Co., the leading black-owned investment bank. Calvin Lockhart is the handsome actor of *Cotton Comes to Harlem* fame.

Canada A country in North America. Canada Lee (born Lionel Cornelius Canegata) was a stage and film actor of the 1930s and 1940s.

Cardell An unusual name of African-American origins. Cardell Jones is the head coach at Alcorn State University, football rivals of the Grambling Tigers.

Carey *Welsh:* Dweller at the castle. Also Cary.

Carl A German form of Charles (see below), which means countryman or husbandman. Its popularity has recently begun to fade. Carl T. Rowan, the prizewinning journalist, was the first black to sit on the National Security Council. Carl Martin, a Howard University graduate, is a member of the explosive singing group Shai.

Carlisle *English:* A place name meaning one from the fortified tower or walled city.

Carlos The Spanish form of Charles (see below) or Carl (see above). African-Americans have had Spanish given names since their arrival on this continent with the Spanish explorers.

Carlton American version of the English Carleton, meaning from the farm of Carl. Carlton L. Guthrie is the CEO of Trumark, Inc., one of the top 100 black industrial/service companies.

Carrington *English:* A surname sometimes used as a given name. Carrington Lewis Davis, a distinguished educator with degrees from both Harvard and Columbia, headed the Department of Foreign Languages and the Classics at Morgan State College in Baltimore.

Carroll   *Irish:* Champion.

Carson   *Scottish:* Son of Charles.

Carter   *English:* A cart driver. Carter G. Woodson, the famous historian, dedicated his life to the study of black history. Among his important works is *The Negro in Our History.*

Carvel   *English:* From the estate in the marshes. Carvell is a French variation. Carvel E. Simmons is an aerospace engineer who founded Simmons Enterprises, one of the top 100 black industrial/service companies.

Carver   *English:* He who carves wood.

Cassius   *Latin:* Vain. Cassius Clay, the legendary heavyweight champion of the world, later changed his name to Muhammad Ali. Throughout his boxing career, Ali's bold predictions of winning, his frequent "ain't I pretty" quip, and his outspoken bravado certainly lived up to the meaning of Cassius.

Cato   *Latin:* All-knowing. Cato Robinson was one of several free black patriots with the same first name who fought in the American Revolution. This name was very popular in the 17th and 18th centuries.

Caudilla   An unusual name said to be of Spanish origin, sometimes used by black parents around the turn of the century. Caudilla Leander Baker, a well-known federal employee in Rochester, N.Y., was often cited and highly respected for his civic activities and distinguished public service.

Cazzie   This unusual name is probably an African-American invention. The University of Michigan star Cazzie Russell was a triple threat on the basketball court, playing with equal skill the positions of forward, center, and guard.

Cecil   *Latin:* Blind one. Not often used by white families, but common among African-American given names, especially in the 20th century. Cecil B. Willis is the chief executive of Peninsula Pontiac-Oldsmobile, the sixth largest black-owned automobile dealership in the country. Cecil Banks is a Detroit public school teacher.

Cedric *English:* War chief. The name, probably invented by Sir Walter Scott for use in his literary landmarks *Ivanhoe* and *Little Lord Fauntleroy,* has recently been growing in popularity. Cedric Ceballos, at 6'7", is a small forward for the Phoenix Suns.

Chance *English:* Good fortune. Rarely used by black parents.

Chancellor *French:* Keeper of records; a surname infrequently used as a given name. Historian and college professor Chancellor Williams is the author of *The Destruction of Black Civilization.*

Chandler *English:* Candlemaker, he provides light. In the fall of 1917, Chandler Owen and A. Philip Randolph cofounded and coedited *The Messenger,* a radical black magazine.

Channing *English:* Knowing. Channing H. Tobias, minister and educator, won the Spingarn Medal in 1948 for contributions as a spokesman for civil liberties.

Charles *German:* Strong, manly. The name Charles has been enormously popular among African-Americans for several generations. Although its use may have peaked during the first half of the 20th century, it remains a frequent choice. Charles H. Houston, as dean of Howard University Law School, was Thurgood Marshall's teacher. Physician Charles Drew's research in blood plasma lead to the founding of the first blood bank. Charles Dutton is an actor.

Charlie A form of Charles (see above). Charlie Parker, a brilliant alto saxophonist/composer, was one of the most influential figures of the modern jazz movement.

Chauncey *English:* Chief secretary, record keeper; a contraction of Chancellor (see above). Also Chance, Chaunce. In 1987, running back Chauncey Allen amassed a team record 1,866 yards for the Grambling Tigers.

Chester *Latin:* Fortress, camp. English: A place name meaning dweller in a fortified town. Chester Himes, a famous black writer, is the author of *The Lonely Crusade* and *Cotton Comes to Harlem.*

Chico *Spanish:* Boy, lad.

Chilton *English:* A place name meaning farm near the well, or town by the river. Chilton Eugene Baker lived in Dallas.

Chris This diminutive of Christopher (see below) is sometimes used as an independent name. Chris Webber, the center of the University of Michigan 1992–93 basketball team, was named one of Dick Vitale's Colossal Collegians.

Christian *Greek:* Christlike. Rare in black families.

Christopher *Greek:* One who carries Christ in his heart. This name was particularly popular among African-American parents during the 1960s and 1970s. Christopher Edley Jr. is the first black deputy director of the Office of Management and Budget. Christopher Williams is a musical heartthrob and member of the group Shai. He is a balladeer blessed with good looks, just like his musical predecessor, Billy Eckstine. Christopher Martin Dinwiddie is a member of the class of 1993, Howard University.

Chuck A popular nickname for Charles (see above). Also Chucky, Chuckie.

Cirus An alternate spelling for Cyrus (see below).

Clarence *Latin:* Illustrious. Clarence Mitchell, a reporter for the *Baltimore African American,* joined the NAACP as labor secretary in the 1940s. Named director of the Washington Bureau, he became the nation's top civil rights lobbyist. His numerous successful efforts include the passage of the Civil Rights Act of 1964.

Clark *English:* A clergyman, a learned man. French: A scholar. Clark Terry, jazz trumpeter and flugelhorn player, performed with Count Basie and Duke Ellington and appeared regularly on Johnny Carson's "Tonight Show."

Claude *Latin:* Lame one; a form of Claudius. The connotation is positive, indicating that a handicap may spark greater achievement. By the turn of the century, Claude appears as a common given name. Journalist Claude Barnett became widely recognized as an authority on African art. Born in the hill country of Jamaica, poet Claude McKay, a key figure in the Harlem Renaissance, was published by the time he was 21.

Clay *German:* To stick together.

Clayborne *German/French:* A place name meaning a boundary marked by clovers, or a brook near a clay bed. Also Claiborn, Claiborne, Clayburn, Claybourne. Clayborne Carson is a prolific scholar and college professor.

Clayton *English:* A place name meaning one from a town near the clay bed. Clayton "Pegleg" Bates lost his leg in a car accident at age 12. Although he had a pegleg, he was considered the number one dancer in the country during the Harlem Renaissance. Clayton Riley is a writer and radio personality.

Cleary *Irish:* Scholar.

Cleavon *English:* Of the cliff. Cleavon Little was a comedian and movie actor.

Clement *Latin:* Merciful one, gentle, kind. Also Clemons, Clemmons.

Clemente The Spanish form of Clement (see above). Running back Clemente Gordon in 1989 compiled a record 3,093 yards for the Grambling Tigers.

Cleo A diminutive for Cleophus (see below) that is sometimes used as an independent name. Cleo Fields, a lawmaker from Louisiana, was the youngest person elected to the 103rd Congress.

Cleon *Latin:* Renowned father.

Cleophus *English:* One who comes to give a speech.

Cleophus "Cleo" Miller, Jr. was a well-known pro football player. Cleophus Roseboro is a dedicated teacher and counselor in Detroit.

Cleveland *English:* A place name meaning land near the steep bank; the name of a city in Ohio.

Cliff *English:* A steep bank. Cliff Waldron accumulated a grade point average of 96.5 at the East New York High School of Transit Technology. An honor roll student for four straight years, he was valedictorian of the class of 1993.

Clifford *English:* A place name, one who dwells at the ford near the lake. Clifford Alexander graduated cum laude from Harvard University. President Jimmy Carter appointed him the first black Secretary of the Army.

Clifton *English:* One from the cliff estate or town. In the early 20th century, Clifton appears as a common given name and remains popular today. Before his appointment to President Clinton's Cabinet, Clifton R. Wharton Jr. was the chairman and CEO of TIAA-CREF, the world's biggest pension fund and third largest insurance company. In that position he was one of the 40 most powerful black executives in the country.

Clint *English:* A town on a hill.

Clinton *English:* A dweller in a town on the hill. Clinton Edwards is a New York City photographer.

Clobert This name likely represents an African-American invention based on an alteration of Colbert (see below). Clobert Bernard Broussard became a vice chairman of the St. Louis Mayor's Council on Human Relations in 1944. He had been active in trying to secure recreational facilities for the city's African-American citizens.

Clovis *German:* Great fighter. In 1967, Clovis C. Campbell became the first African-American elected to the Arizona Senate.

Cloyce *Latin:* A nail; a form of Clavus.

Clyde *Welsh:* From a warm and sheltered place. Clyde

Drexler, the superstar guard for the Portland Trailblazers, was a member of the 1992 Olympic Dream Team.

Clydell   A form of Clyde (see above).

Colbert   *English:* Famous man of the sea.

Colby   *English:* The dark-haired one.

Coleman   *English:* Dove. On Nov. 6, 1973, Coleman Young, a brilliant union organizer, was elected mayor of Detroit. He was the first black mayor of the nation's fifth largest city.

Colin   *Irish:* Young and manly. Gen. Colin Powell of Operation Desert Storm fame was the first black national security adviser and the first black chairman of the Joint Chiefs of Staff, the highest military position in the U.S.

Columbus   This surname of Christopher Columbus is listed by Puckett as an unusual name found among African-Americans during the late 19th and 20th centuries.

Comer   The origins of this unusual name are not evident. It may have come from the Arabic Coman (ko MAHN) meaning noble one. Or it may have come from the Ghanaian Ewe name, Commie (KO mee), which means born on Saturday. Comer has been used over generations by African-Americans. In 1990, Comer Cottrell, as president of Pro-Line Corp. paid $1.5 million for the Bishop College campus.

Commodore   *American:* A naval officer. This unusual name was occasionally used by African-American parents around the turn of the century.

Congo   This name, believed to have African origins, was used by freed blacks in the 16th and 17th centuries. Congo Zado was a free black patriot who fought in the Revolutionary War.

Conrad   *English:* Giver of courageous advice. Conrad Hipkins is the CEO of Automated Sciences Group, Inc. An information services and technology company, it is the 37th largest black industrial company in the country.

Conroy   *Irish:* Wise adviser.

Constantine   *Latin:* Constant, steadfast. Physician Constantine Clinton Barnett helped to establish a mental hospital for blacks in West Virginia in 1926.

Conway   *Welsh:* A surname sometimes used as a given name.

Conwell   This name is apparently an African-American invention. In 1902, in Wilmington, Del., physician Conwell Banton, became the superintendent of Edgewood Sanitarium, a hospital for tuberculosis patients.

Cooper   *English:* An occupational name meaning one who makes and repairs barrels.

Cordell   *French:* One who makes ropes.

Corder   This unusual name of unknown origins may be an African-American creation. Corder Ward was a defensive tackle for the 1991 Grambling Tigers.

Corey   *English:* Dweller at the hill hollow. Also Cory, Corie. Corey Williams is a guard for the NBA champion Chicago Bulls. Corie Blount was a member of the University of Cincinnati basketball team that surprised sportscasters and writers by reaching the Elite Eight in the 1993 NCAA tournament.

Corlis   *English:* Benevolent. Also Corliss. Freshman Corliss Williamson of the 1992–93 Arkansas University basketball team is one of the top five players in his class.

Cornelius   *Latin:* Like a horn, the cornel-cherry tree. This name was popular among African-American parents through the first half of the 20th century, but its use has declined somewhat in recent decades. Cornelious Thornton, vice-president and senior research analyst for Goldman, Sachs & Co., has been on *Institutional Investor* magazine's list of Wall Street's most outstanding brokerage analysts for 14 straight years, ranking first for the last 7.

Cornell   A form of Cornelius (see above). Also Cornall,

Cornel. Cornel West, writer, theologian, and philosopher, is a professor of black studies and theology.

Cottrell Apparently an African-American invention, this name is used infrequently. Cottrell Laurence Dellums was a vice-president of the Brotherhood of Sleeping Car Porters and a key figure in the union's development.

Council *Latin:* A group of people.

Count *French:* Companion. Also Countee. Count Basie was a world-renowned bandleader. Countee Cullen, a poet during the Harlem Renaissance, combined poetic sensitivity with an alert racial consciousness. His most famous poem, "Heritage," describes his love of Africa.

Courtney *English:* Court dweller. This name was fairly popular among black Americans right into the 20th century. Among contemporary white families, it is now more often used as a girl's name. Courtney N. Blackman is a member of the *Black Enterprise* board of economists convened yearly in the magazine's New York headquarters to evaluate the economic development of black America. Actor Courtney Vance starred in *Fences*.

Craig *Scottish:* One who dwells at the crag or rock. This surname migrated to given name status mid-century. Its popularity has steadily increased among both black and white families. Craig Polite is a clinical psychologist and coauthor of *Children of the Dream*.

Craigory This unusual name is probably an African-American creation. Craigory Sam played center with the 1991 Grambling Tigers football team.

Crawford *English:* From the crow ford.

Crispus *Latin:* Curly-haired one. Crispus Attucks was the first to fall during the Boston Massacre.

Cuba *Spanish:* A small island off the coast of Florida first colonized by the Spanish. Cuba appears on Puckett's list of unusual names as early as the 17th century. Its use as a given name is rare but remains into the 20th century. Drummer and innovator Cuba Austin was a full-time member of McKinney's Cotton Pickers, a popular jazz band of the 1920s. Cuba Gooding is the young star of *Boyz N the Hood.*

Cudjoe   This unusual name for freed blacks is believed to have African origins, but its meaning is unknown.

Cuff   This early African-American name is believed to have African origins. It was the first name of several black patriots who fought in the American Revolution.

Cuffee   An unusual name that is believed to have African origins, but unfortunately its meaning was left on those shores.

Cullen   *Irish:* Handsome.

Curt   This diminutive for Curtis (see below) is infrequently used as an independent name. Throughout the 1960s, Curt Flood was a brilliant center fielder for the St. Louis Cardinals. Curt Stewart is a filmmaker and instructor at Rutgers University, Livingston campus.

Curtis   *French:* Courteous, court-bred. Curtis has been a popular African-American name for several generations. Curtis Fuller is a well-known jazz trombonist. At 6′3″, Curtis Blair of the Houston Rockets is short by NBA standards. Curtis J. Crawford, vice-president of AT&T's Microelectronics Division, is one of the top 40 black executives in the country.

Cyril   *Greek:* Lordly. Journalist Cyril Briggs was an editor of the *Amsterdam News* and founder of the African Blood Brotherhood.

Cyrus   *Persian:* Sun, throne. This name was very popular among free blacks during the 17th, 18th, and 19th centuries, but fell out of fashion in the late 20th century. The famous Persian emperor Cyrus allowed the Jews to rebuild Jerusalem. Cyrus Vassall was a free black patriot who fought in the American Revolution.

D'Army D'Army Bailey works at the National Civil Rights Museum in Memphis.

Dale *German:* A place name meaning one who dwells in the dale. Dale Davis is the nearly 7'-tall center for the Indiana Pacers.

Dalton *English:* A place name meaning from the valley town.

Damien *Greek:* A tamer of men.

Damon *Latin:* A demon spirit. However, the Damon of ancient Syracuse who offered his life for his friend Pythias has caused the name also to mean loyal friendship. Damon Bailey is a loyal guard for the Indiana Hoosiers 1992–93 basketball team. Jurist Damon Keith won the NAACP Spingrarn Award in 1974 for steadfast defense of constitutional principles and distinguished public service.

Dan Short for Daniel (see below). Journalist Dan Burley was an editor of the *Chicago Defender,* New York *Amsterdam News, Ebony,* and *Jet.* He became famous for his *Chicago Defender* column, "Everybody Goes When the Wagon Comes."

Dana *English:* A place name meaning from Denmark. Originally a masculine name, it is now very popular among white parents as a girl's name. Dana Barros is a guard for the Seattle SuperSonics.

Danan Wide receiver Danan Hughes was a 1993 draft pick by the Kansas City Chiefs.

Daniel *Biblical/Hebrew:* God is my judge. Also Danny. Daniel has remained popular over several centuries. Physician Daniel H. Williams founded the first interracial hospital in Chicago in 1881. In August 1975, Gen. Daniel James became the first black four-star general in the U.S. Army.

Darby *English:* A place name meaning a home by the water or a park with deer. It is sometimes used for girls. African-American parents have used the name sparingly.

Darence One source calls this name American and says that its blending of Darrell and Clarence means shining, gentle, open. However, it is remarkably similar to the current generation of new creations that are flowing out of the African-American naming experience.

Darius *Greek:* Wealthy one. *Persian:* A king. A well-used name until recently.

Darnell *English:* A place name meaning the hidden spot. Also Darnall.

Darnley Darnley Osborn is an administrator at the College of New Rochelle, School of New Resources, in New York.

Darren *Irish:* Little great one. Also Daryn. This surname was first used as a given name in America.

Darryl *French:* Little dear, beloved one. Also Darrel, Darrell. The spelling Darryl is enormously popular. Darryl Strawberry is a well-known outfielder for his hometown Los Angeles Dodgers. Darrell Walker is a reserve guard for the Chicago Bulls.

Darwin *English:* Dear friend. Also Derwin. Darwin Davis is an executive with Equitable Life Insurance Co. Derwin Webb is a college basketball star.

Dave A loving form of David (see below). Dave Bing, the former Detroit Pistons basketball star, is the founder and CEO of the Bing Group, the nation's 10th largest black-owned industrial company. Pianist Dave Burrell was introduced to jazz by his mother at an early age.

Davey A pet form of David (see below). Also Davy, Davi.

David *Biblical/Hebrew:* Beloved. King David was blessed of God. Since the 17th century, David has been enormously popular among black parents and is still a favorite name. David Humphreys was captain of the Second Company of the Fourth Regiment, a company of free black patriots who fought valiantly in the American Revolution. David Johnson at 6'7" is a small forward for the Portland Trailblazers. David Robinson was a top draft choice for the San Antonio Spurs. David N. Dinkins became the first black mayor of New York City. David Simily is an elementary school student.

Davin *Scandinavian:* Bright, intelligent. Davin Harris was a guard on the 1992–93 University of Illinois basketball team.

Dawson *English:* A surname of earlier centuries that became a given name in the 20th century.

Dean *English:* A place name meaning valley; an occupational name meaning church official. This surname migrated to first-name status in the 20th century.

Defield An unusual name of unknown origins, but quite likely an African-American creation. Defield T. Holmes is a prominent educator and scientist who has devoted his life's work to instruction in black colleges.

Dehart This unusual name resonates with African-American originality. Dehart Hubbard held the national championship in broad jumping from 1922 to 1927. He earned a Gold Medal at the 1924 Olympics in Paris, making him the first African-American to win an Olympic Medal.

Deinaba Newly created. Deinaba George is a student at City College of New York.

Dekovas Newly created. Dekovas Johnson belongs to the Little Rock Missionary Baptist Church in Detroit.

Delano This obscure family name possibly means either nighttime or nut tree in French. It gained wide recognition as the middle name of President Franklin Delano Roosevelt. Many black parents admired this president and his wife, Eleanor, as most sympathetic to the needs of black Americans, thus its occasional use.

Delbert   *English:* Noble and brilliant. Delbert W. Mullens is the chief executive of the 35th largest black company in the nation, Wesley Industries, Inc.

Dell   *French:* From Del, which means of the. Dell Curry is a guard for the Charlotte Hornets.

Delmar   *Latin:* Of the sea. Also Delmer.

Delmont   *English/French:* Of the sea. Also Delman, Delmon. Delmont O. Dapremont Jr. is the chief executive of Coastal Ford, Inc., one of the top 100 black-owned automobile dealerships.

Delroy   *French:* The king.

Delvin   *Greek:* A dolphin.

Delwyn   *English:* Proud friend.

Demarre   An African-American original. Demarre Lavelle, age 16, is a talented flutist.

Demetrius   *Greek:* Belonging to Demeter, Greek fertility goddess. This unusual name has sometimes been used by black parents. It may not be favored because Demetrius, a silversmith of Ephesus, led disturbances against St. Paul.

Demond   An African-American creation. Actor Demond Wilson played Lamont on the popular 1970s TV sitcom "Sanford and Son."

Denton   *English:* Dweller in the valley town.

Dennis   *Greek:* From Dionysus, the god of wine and revelry. Also Denis. Dennis Rodman, who at 6'8" is a small forward, led the NBA in rebounds. Dennis Haysbert played Paul Cater in *Love Field*.

Denzel   *English:* A place in Cornwall; first a surname, then a given name. Also Denzil, Denzell, Denzyl. Academy Award–winning actor Denzel Washington starred as Malcolm X in director Spike Lee's film.

Derby A form of Darby (see above). This name was very popular among free black parents during the 17th and 18th centuries. Two free black patriots with this first name served in the same regiment during the American Revolution.

Derek *German:* The people's ruler. In a field of giants, Derek Harper at a mere 6′4″ is a point guard for the Dallas Mavericks.

Dermot *Greek:* Free from envy.

Deron *English:* Dweller near a small rocky hill. Also DeRon. DeRon Hayes was a forward for the 1992–93 Penn State Nittany Lions.

Derrick This form of Derek (see above) is by far the most favored among black parents. In the last decade its use has soared. Derrick Bell, civil rights activist and former Harvard law professor, wrote the popular *Faces at the Bottom of the Well.*

Derwin *English:* Beloved friend.

Desmond *English:* Gracious protector. Desmond Howard, a wide receiver for the University of Michigan Wolverines football team, won the Heisman Trophy in 1991.

Devaughn An unusual name that appeared in the early 20th century and is thought to be an African-American invention.

Devin *Irish:* Poet, savant. Devin Rowe is a designer.

DeWayne An African-American invention. Physician DeWayne France Davis in 1923 became the assistant health commissioner for the city of Charleston, W. Va.

Dewey *Welsh:* Beloved one. Dewey Redman is a gifted and beloved jazz saxophonist.

Dexter *Latin:* Dextrous one, skillful. Dexter Gordon, a famous jazz musician and actor, was equally adept on the stage or on the tenor sax.

Dick This pet name for Richard (see below) has often been used by black parents as a given name. Dick

Gregory, activist, writer, and comedian, developed the formula for the popular Bahamian diet.

Diego   A Spanish form of James (see below), meaning the supplanter. Many free blacks in early American history carried Spanish names.

Dino   *Italian:* Dino is a short form of names such as Bernandino. A small number of black parents have used this name over several generations now.

Dion   *Greek:* From Dionysus, the mythological god of wine. Also Deion. Two-sport phenom Deion Sanders enjoys both a football and a baseball career.

Dixon   *English:* Dick's son; a surname infrequently used as a given name.

Dock   An unusual name employed infrequently by black parents in the late 18th century. Contemporary use appears confined to a nickname status.

Dominic   *Latin:* Belonging to God. Also Dominick.

Dominique   The French form of Dominic (see above). Dominique Wilkins is the Atlanta Hawks superstar.

Don   It is not unusual for this pet name of Donald (see below) to be used by African-American parents as a boy's first name. Pitcher Don Newcombe had a distinguished career with the Brooklyn Dodgers.

Donald   *Irish:* Brown stranger. Donald Bogle is one of the country's leading experts on blacks in film and popular American culture.

Dondre   An African-American original. In 1992, when Dondre Green was a senior at St. Frederick High School in Louisiana and a member of the school's golf team, his white teammates forfeited a championship game rather than play at a country club that barred Dondre.

Donnell   *Irish:* A surname now used as a given name.

Donnie   A pet form of Donald sometimes used as an independent name. Donnie Hathaway was a popular R&B singer.

Donovan   *Irish:* Dark warrior.

Dorian *Greek:* Gift. Also Dorion, Dorien, Dorean. Dorian S. Boyland is the chief executive of Greshan Dodge, Inc., the 70th largest black-owned automobile dealership in the country.

Douglas *Scottish:* Black water. Originally a girl's name, by the 19th century it was used almost exclusively for boys. Douglas Holloway, a senior vice-president of USA Network, chairs the National Association of Minorities in Cable.

Doyle *Irish:* Dark stranger. B. Doyle Mitchell Sr. is the chief executive of Industrial Bank of Washington, the nation's fourth largest black-owned bank.

Drake *Greek:* Dragon.

Drew *Welsh:* Wise one; diminutive for Andrew (see above). Also Dru, Drue. Former football pro Drew Pearson is the CEO of a sports manufacturing company in Texas.

Dudley *English:* A place name meaning from the people's meadow. Dudley Randall is the founder of Broadside Press, a Detroit-based small press most famous for publishing the poetry of Gwendolyn Brooks and Don L. Lee (Haki Madhubuti).

Duffy *Scottish:* From Duff, meaning dark face.

Duke *French:* A leader. Edward Kennedy "Duke" Ellington was a famous bandleader who rose to the top of the music world. He wrote over 2,000 songs and led his band before packed houses in every major country in the world.

Duncan *Scottish:* Brown warrior.

Dupree Apparently a surname used infrequently by black parents as a first name. Dupree Daniel Davis became an assistant state's attorney in Illinois before World War I.

Durant *Latin:* The enduring one.

Dutch *German:* The German.

Dwayne *Irish:* Little dark one. Also Duane. Duane

Ferrell is a swing man for the Atlanta Hawks basketball team. Dwayne Stephens, a member of the Michigan State Spartans, has accumulated impressive statistics for the 1992–93 basketball season.

Dwight *Dutch:* White or blond one. In 1974, Dwight Scales, with 60 points, was the scoring leader for the Grambling Tigers football team. Dwight "Doc" Gooden is a superstar pitcher with the New York Mets.

Earl *English:* A chief or nobleman. *Irish:* A solemn pledge. Also Earle. Earl G. Graves is the founder of the popular *Black Enterprise* magazine. A leading exponent of black entrepreneurship, he has done much to advance black businesses. Hall-of-Famer Earl "The Pearl" Monroe was a top draft choice when he joined the Baltimore Bullets. He was named Rookie of the Year for the 1967–68 NBA season.

Early *English:* The earl's shelter. Also Earlie. Historian Earlie Endris Thorpe taught at several black colleges before his 1962 appointment to the faculty of North Carolina Central University.

Earvin *Irish:* Handsome. *English:* Sea friend. An alternate spelling for Irvin (see below) or Irving, this name is now highly recognizable due to the prominence of Earvin "Magic" Johnson, whom some believe to be the greatest professional basketball player of all time. Johnson was a leading player on the 1992 Olympic Dream Team, and is the proud owner of five NBA championship rings won during his years with the L.A. Lakers. Although his questionable sexual practices have resulted in his becoming HIV-infected, Magic has continued to flash his bright smile, charm his public, and display himself as a fierce competitor. He has vowed to beat the virus.

Eason An unusual name whose origins and meaning are obscure. It may be a purely African-American invention or it could be a form of Easton (see below).

Easton *English:* One from East town.

Eaton *English:* A place name meaning from the riverside estate, one from the riverside village.

Eaves This unusual name, sometimes employed by black Americans predominantly in the 19th century, may have come from the Welsh Evan (see below). However, its origins are unclear; it first appears in the 19th century according to Puckett's *Black Names in America*.

Ebenezer *Biblical/Hebrew:* Rock of help. Ebenezer Don Carlos Bassett is reputedly the first black man appointed to the diplomatic service. He became the U.S. minister to Haiti in 1869.

Eddie This diminutive for Edward (see below) is sometimes employed as an independent name. It has also been used for girls: Eddie Mae. Actor Eddie Anderson became famous for his lifetime role as Rochester, Jack Benny's valet. The indefatigable Eddie Robinson has built an incomparable record for over 50 years as football coach of the Grambling Tigers. It is said that he has done more for football than any other person. Eddie Murphy is a contemporary film star and comedian.

Edgar *English:* Wealthy spearman. This royal Anglo-Saxon name survived the Norman Conquest. In 1913, Edgar Sampson Ballou established a dental practice in Montclair, N.J.

Edison *English:* Edward's son. Edison R. Lara Sr. is the chief executive of Westside Distributors, one of the top 100 black-owned companies.

Edmond *English:* Wealthy, fortunate, and happy protector. This spelling of Edmund was very popular in the
19th century and is still used in the 20th. The variation
Edmondson is also used as a first name, though rarely.

Edolphus This African-American variation of Adolphus
is rare. Edolphus "Ed" Towns represents the 11th District in New York in the U.S. Congress.

Edric *English:* Child of power and good fortune.

Edward *English:* Wealthy defender. The sustained popularity of Edward began in the 19th century and continues
for both black and white parents. Edward Bradley, the
noted TV news journalist, captured America's attention
with his riveting on-the-scene coverage of the Vietnam
war. In 1981, he became a coeditor and correspondent
on the perennially popular "60 Minutes." Edward
Gardner is the CEO of Soft Sheen Products, Inc., a manufacturer of black hair-care products.

Edwin *English:* Rich in friendship, prosperous friend.
Also Edwyn. Since its revival in the 19th century, this
name is frequently used by black and white parents.
Edwin D. Biagas is the founder and CEO of Biagas
Pontiac-Buick, Inc., one of the top 100 black-owned au-
tomobile dealerships.

Egbert *English:* Bright sword. Rarely used by black parents.

Egypt This African country that traces its roots back into
antiquity is considered the cradle of civilization. According to Puckett, it is an unusual name sometimes
used by free blacks in the 19th and early 20th centuries.

Elam *Biblical/Hebrew:* A place name meaning the high-
lands. Infrequently used as a first name.

Elbert *English:* Noble and bright; a form of Albert (see
above).

Elden *English:* A place name meaning from Ella's
mound. Also Eldon. Elden Campbell is a center and forward for the L.A. Lakers.

Elder *English:* Older, wiser.

Eldridge *German:* Mature counselor. English: Fearful, terrible. Eldridge Cleaver, the former Black Panther and black power advocate, is the author of *Soul on Ice,* his autobiography. Following many years of expatriation in Algeria, he returned to the U.S., professing a Christian conversion experience.

Eldzier This rare name is probably of African-American coinage. Eldzier Cortor is a well-known artist in the Chicago area.

Electa This name appears on a list Puckett calls unusual black names in the North. Its origins are unclear.

Elgin *English:* White, noble. Elgin Baylor, the former L.A. Lakers star, in one game against the New York Knicks scored 71 points, a total second only to Wilt Chamberlain's 100 points for a single game.

Eli *Hebrew:* The highest. Also Ely, Elie. Eli Fontaine is a versatile percussionist.

Elias The Greek form of Elijah (see below), and the New Testament spelling of the great prophet's name.

Elijah *Biblical/Hebrew:* The Lord is my God; an Old Testament prophet. Like many other biblical names, Elijah has been popular among black parents since the 17th century. Elijah Fisher exemplifies the great black preachers of the 19th and early 20th centuries. He led the Olive Baptist Church in Chicago from 1902 until his death in 1915. Elijah "Zeke" Jackson, an electrical engineer, is the chief executive of Navcom Systems, Inc., one of the nation's top 100 black-owned companies. Elijah Tillery is a middleweight boxer. Elijah Muhammad was founder of the Nation of Islam.

Elisha *Biblical/Hebrew:* The Lord is my salvation; the prophet who succeeded Elijah. Elisha P. Murchison was an editor and clergyman.

Ellic The origins of this unusual name are unclear; it may be a variation of Alec. Also Ellick, Elick. Although appearing frequently in 19th century, there are few contemporary examples of its use.

Elliott   *French:* Jehovah is my God. Also Eliot, Elliot. The spelling Elliott has been most popular among blacks. Anthropologist Elliott Skinner became chairman of Columbia University's Department of Anthropology in 1969.

Ellis   An English form of Elijah. Pianist Ellis Marsalis is the father of Wynton and Branford.

Ellison   *English:* The son of Ellis.

Ellsworth   *English:* From the estate of a noble one. Also Elsworth. Ellsworth Davis is the night photo editor for the *Washington Post.*

Elmer   *English:* Noble, famous. At the age of 15 Elmer Snowden was playing the banjo and guitar with the legendary pianist and composer Eubie Blake.

Elmo   *Greek:* Friendly, lovable. Infrequently used by black parents.

Elmore   *English:* Dweller at the elm tree moor. The 7′, 290-pound Elmore Spencer is a center for the L.A. Clippers.

Elonza   Apparently an African-American variation of Alonzo (see above), this name appeares in the early 20th century.

Elrick   A contemporary American invention probably akin to Elroy (see below).

Elrod   *Hebrew:* God is the ruler; a variation of Elrad.

Elroy   *Latin:* The king.

Elston   *English:* From the estate of the noble one. New York Yankee Elston Howard in 1963 became the first black player from the American League to win the Most Valuable Player award.

Elton   *English:* From the old estate. Elton Carter was a starting forward for the 1992–93 Penn State Nittany Lions basketball team.

Elvern   *English:* Spring.

Elvert A variation of Elbert (see above.)

Elvin *English:* Elf friend; a variant form of Alvin (see above). Elvin Jones gained prominence as a drummer in the John Coltrane quartet. Elvin Hayes was the first black to play with the University of Houston's basketball team. Elvin Philips lives in Muskogee, Okla.

Elvis *Scandinavian:* All wise. Football player Elvis Patterson was a standout secondary player for the New York Giants.

Elvoid This unusual name first appears in the 19th century and is quite probably an African-American invention.

Elvy Although its origins are unclear, it may be a pet name for Elvin (see above).

Elzey This unusual name was infrequently used in the 19th century. It is apparently an African-American invention.

Emery *German:* Industrious ruler.

Emile *French:* To emulate, to be industrious. Emile Barnes emulated his great blues teachers to sustain his career as a clarinetist from 1919 to 1951.

Emlen With his historic induction in 1967, Emlen Tunnel became the first black player to enter football's Hall of Fame.

Emmanuel *Biblical/Hebrew:* God is with us. Also Immanuel. Isaiah in his prophecy of the coming of Jesus Christ called Him Emmanuel. This frequently used biblical name has remained popular well into the 20th century.

Emmerson This surname that is related to Emery (see above) is sometimes used as a first name.

Emmett *Hebrew:* Truth. *English:* Diligent. Also Emmitt. Emmitt J. McHenry is the CEO of Network Solutions, Inc., the 17th largest black-owned service company. Emmett Walker Jr. is the president of an international transportation service.

Emory A spelling variation of Emery (see above).

Endris The origins of this unusual name are not clear. It appears to have roots in African-American invention.

Ennis *Irish:* Only. choice. Ennis Cosby is the son of Bill and Camille Cosby.

Enoch *Biblical/Hebrew:* Dedicated.

Enrique *Spanish:* One who rules his household; a form of Henry (see below).

Ephraim *Biblical/Hebrew:* Fruitful; one of the two sons of Joseph. Also Efraim, Efrem.

Erasmus *Greek:* To love. This name was frequently used by black parents in the 18th and 19th centuries. Today it is used rarely, if at all.

Eric *Scandinavian:* Honorable ruler. Also Erich, Erik. Eric is becoming increasingly popular as a boy's name. Eric Floyd is a guard with the Houston Rockets basketball team. At age 7, Eric Yergan set up a Kool-Aid stand on a Long Island street corner. Today, the 38-year-old senior vice-president at Paine Webber Group, Inc., sells treasury bills to foreign governments and is ranked among the top ten executives in his division.

Erlie An unusual African-American name cited by Puckett.

Ernest *English:* Earnest one. Also Earnest. Journalist Ernest Reese is a sportswriter for the *Atlanta Constitution*. Ernest E. Just was a scientist, a Howard University professor, and a leading zoologist who made contributions in the field of experimental embryology.

Ernie A diminutive for Ernest (see above). Ernie Ladd was a defensive tackle with the San Diego Chargers when they were a championship team. Ernie Banks had an outstanding career as one of the first black players with the Chicago Cubs baseball team.

Errol *Latin:* To wander. *German:* Earl or nobleman. Internationally famous pianist Errol Garner learned to read music very late in his career; he played by ear.

Erskine *Scottish:* Ascending or high cliff. The migration of Erskine from a last name to a first name occurred in the 20th century. Trumpeter and bandleader Erskine Hawkins began playing the drums when he was only 7 years old; he learned the trombone before taking up the trumpet at age 13.

Erwin *Scottish:* Beautiful. Also Ervin, Irvin.

Esau In the Bible, Esau is the son of Isaac and the twin brother of Jacob. This name is listed among Puckett's common given names. It is now largely out of fashion.

Essex *English:* From the East.

Estee *Italian:* From the East. Also Estes, Este.

Ethan *Hebrew:* Firm, strong.

Etheridge An obscure surname rarely used as a given name. Esteemed poet Etheridge Knight was published by Dudley Randall's Broadside Press of Detroit.

Eubie A nickname for Hubert (see below). James Hubert Blake, called Eubie for most of his life, is known to millions around the world for his many musical contributions as composer and pianist. He died at the ripe old age of 97.

Eudell Apparently an African-American invention of the 19th century. Also Eudelle. It was popular in the South during the early 20th century but is now obsolete.

Eugene *Greek:* Wellborn. Eugenio is a Spanish variation. Eugene has been frequently used by black parents for several generations; Eugenio is sometimes used. Eugene Flood Jr., who holds a doctorate in finance, is a trader in Morgan Stanley & Co.'s mortgage-backed securities area.

Eulis *Greek:* Sweet-speaking. Also Eulice, Euliss.

Evan *Welsh:* Jehovah has shown favor; a variant of John.

Evander A form of Evan (see above). Boxer Evander Holyfield is respected by sportscasters and writers for having been a dignified heavyweight champion of the world. They often referred to him as a gentleman.

Evans As a first name, this surname means son of Evan.

Everett *German:* One who is strong. Everett Barksdale, a staff musician for CBS Radio during the 1940s, came to prominence as a guitarist when he joined the Art Tatum trio.

Evers This surname of slain civil rights activist Medgar Evers is now used as a given name. Evers Burns is called a frontcourt flash by Dick Vitale for his collegiate performance on the University of Maryland's 1992–93 basketball team.

Everson This unusual name may be an African-American original. Everson Walls, a former Grambling Tiger, played pro football with the Dallas Cowboys and New York Giants until 1991.

E'Vinski This name resounds with the tones of an African-American invention. E'Vinski Davis played center for the 1991–92 Grambling Tigers football team.

Ewart *English:* Herder of the ewe. Also Ewert. Trade unionist Ewart Guinier was the first chairman of Harvard University's Department of Afro-American Studies. His daughter, Lani, is an acclaimed instructor at the University of Pennsylvania Law School.

Eyton Eyton Aderson was a 1993 champion in the New York Public School Athletic League's annual competition.

Ezekial *Biblical/Hebrew:* God will strengthen. Also Ezekiel. Ezekiel Tupham was a free black patriot of the American Revolution.

Ezell Probably a form of Ezekial (see above) and an African-American invention. Also Ezil. Ezil Bibbs was the eighth choice in the 1974 professional football draft. This former Grambling Tiger went pro with the New York Giants.

Ezra *Biblical/Hebrew:* Salvation. Born in 1852, educator Ezra Eziekel began teaching in North Carolina in a log schoolhouse that he built. He is considered the founder of Fayetteville State University.

Ezzard A form of Ezra. Ezzard Charles held the boxing heavyweight championship from 1949 to 1951.

Fabrice *Latin:* One who works with his hands.

Fairfax *English:* Blond.

Farrell *Irish:* Champion.

Farris *English:* Strong. *Irish:* The chosen one. Also Faris, Ferris.

Fayard This name is apparently an African-American blend. Fayard Nicholas is the younger half of the famous Nicholas Brothers dance team.

Felder The origins of Felder are uncertain; however, it was sometimes used by black Americans in the 19th and early 20th centuries.

Felipe *Spanish:* One who is fond of horses; a form of Phillip (see below). Rare in black families.

Felix *Latin:* Happy. Felix came into vogue around the turn of the century.

Felton *English:* A place name meaning settlement on the field, or the town in the garden.

Fenton *English:* Settlement on the marsh. Fenton Johnson was born in Chicago in 1888. The legendary James Weldon Johnson called him one of the "first revolutionary Negro poets."

Fenwick An English surname sometimes used by free blacks as a given name in the 19th century.

Ferdinand *German:* Bold voyager.

Fernando The Spanish form of Ferdinand (see above).

Field *English:* An occupational name for one who works in the field. Rare.

Fielding A form of Field (see above.)

Filbert *English:* Very brilliant.

Filmore *English:* Very famous.

Finis The origins of this unusual name are not clear. Although it is a rare name, Finis has appeared among black men and women as a first name. Finis Henderson III is a dynamic nightclub entertainer.

Finley *Irish:* Brave soldier. Also Findley.

Finney *German:* From Finland. Also Finn. Finney was occasionally used by blacks in the 19th century.

Fisher An unusual first name employed by free blacks in the 19th century.

Flanders Flanders, a location in England, is an unusual name used by freed blacks in the 19th century. Rare in the 20th century.

Fleming *English:* Man from the lowlands.

Flemister The origins of this unusual name may rest in Flanders, but its meaning is not known and its use is rare.

Fletcher *English:* Arrow maker. Fletcher Henderson, pianist, bandleader, and arranger, held a degree in chemistry and mathematics from Atlanta University. Henderson, who led the most important of the pioneering big bands, had a special gift for discovering new talent. Louis Armstrong is among his many stellar discoveries.

Flint *English:* A brook. The name of a city in Michigan.

Floyd *Welsh:* Gray-haired. Floyd was rapidly gaining in popularity among black parents at the turn of the century. Floyd Patterson, heavyweight champion of the world, was noted for his quiet, gentlemanly manner. Floyd Thacker is CEO of the Thacker Organization, one of the nation's top 100 black companies.

Fontaine *French:* A source of water.

Ford *English:* A road.

Foreman This unusual first name infrequently used by black parents in the late 19th and early 20th centuries means one who is in charge.

Forrest *Latin:* Outdoors. *English:* A woodsman. Also Forest. Actor Forrest Whitaker won critical acclaim for his portrayal of Charlie Parker in *Bird,* a biopic produced by Clint Eastwood. Forest J. Farmer, as president of Acustar, Inc., a subsidary of Chrysler Corp., is one of the 40 most powerful black executives in the nation.

Fortune *Latin:* Strong, fortunate. The use of this name in the 18th, 19th, and 20th centuries may very well express the hope of black parents for their sons.

Francesco This Spanish form of Frances (see above) was quite popular among free blacks in the 16th and 17th centuries. Also Francisco.

Francis *Latin:* Freeman. This name has been popular among free black parents since the 17th century. Its popularity may be declining in the later half of the 20th century. In 1934, Francis Atkins became president of Winston-Salem State Teachers College, a historic all-black college.

Frank Frank, a pet form of Francis (see above), has been a common given name since the 1800s. Author Frank Yerby wrote his best-selling novel *The Foxes of Harrow* while working 12 hours a day in a Long Island war plant during World War II. His romantic historical novels have sold over 20 million copies. Frank Robinson was the first baseball player ever to win the Most Valuable Player award in both the American and the National Leagues.

Franklin *English:* Freeholder. Franklin became especially popular among black parents during the presidency of Franklin Delano Roosevelt, who was considered sensitive to the needs of black Americans. Franklin Brasfield opened a successful dental practice in Pittsburgh in 1926. Franklin D. Greene is the chief executive of Republic Ford, Inc., the nation's 32nd largest black-owned automobile dealership. Franklin Pryor is the young son of actor and comedian Richard Pryor.

Frantz The French form of Francis (see above).

Fraser *French:* One who makes charcoal.

Fred This pet form of Frederick (see below) has been common since the 1800s, but during the last decade or so its popularity has begun to wane. Tenor saxophonist Fred Anderson Jr. was a founding member of the Association for the Advancement of Creative Musicians in Chicago. Fred Hampton was a Black Panther who did much for the youth of Chicago.

Freddie A pet name for Frederick (see below). Freddie Poe is the owner of a fast-growing automobile dealership in Michigan.

Frederick *German:* Peaceful ruler. Also Fredrick. Popular since the 17th century, Frederick's use has fallen off in recent decades. Frederick Douglass rose from slavery to power and prominence. His autobiography did much to assist the abolitionist movement. He was the first black U.S. marshal; first black recorder of deeds; bank president; and eloquent orator and journalist. Douglass used all his talents to fight slavery—the "evil institution." His memory is enshrined in Rochester, N.Y. Frederick Rawlings Baker was a school teacher who served the families of eastern Texas until his death in the early 20th century. At age 37, Frederick Terrell is a senior banker for First Boston. On any given transaction, 20 to 30 people report directly to him.

Freeman *English:* One born free. The reason for this name's popularity among free blacks and freedmen during the pre–Civil War era is obvious.

Fritz *German:* A form of Frederick (see above).

Fulbert *German:* Brilliant.

Fuller *English:* An occupational name meaning one who shrinks cloth. Fuller Gordy is the father of Berry Gordy, the founder of Motown and the Motown sound. Fuller Gordy was well-known in Detroit for his commitment to family and his entrepreneurial spirit.

Fulton *English:* From a field near the town. Fulton Bradley was a popular radio commentator in Detroit during the 1960s.

Furman *Latin:* From the wilds. Also Ferman.

Gabe A diminutive for Gabriel (see below). An unusual name found among free blacks in the 19th century.

Gabriel *Biblical/Hebrew:* God is my strength. A common given name among free blacks in the 19th century. The name became prominent after the enslaved Gabriel Prosser planned a revolt to involve 32,000 slaves in about 1800.

Gail A diminutive for Gaylord (see below), but more often used for girls. Also Gale, Gayle. Gayle Sayers, the former professional football star, is now CEO of Crest Computer Supply, one of the nation's top 100 black-owned companies.

Gaines *English:* To increase in wealth.

Gaius *Latin:* To rejoice. Gaius Bolin was the first black graduate of Williams College.

Galen   *Greek:* Calm, healer. Galen was a second-century Greek physician whose research provided a basis for medical practices for 1,500 years.

Galloway   *Scottish:* Man from the land of the stranger.

Galt   *Norse:* High ground. A rarely used first name.

Gamaliel   The meaning and origin of this unusual name are not known. It appears among free blacks in the 17th century. Gamaliel Terry was a free black patriot who fought in the American Revolution.

Gardelle   *German:* A guard or watchman. Also Gardell.

Gardner   *English/French:* Keeper of the garden. The internationally respected Reverend Gardner C. Taylor is known to his fellow clergymen as the prince of preachers or as a preacher's preacher.

Gareth   *Welsh:* Gentle.

Garfield   *English:* A surname meaning field of spears. Quite a stylish name choice by African-American and West Indian parents in the early 20th century. Former NBA star Garfield Heard, in the middle of the 1993 season, became the first black head coach of the Dallas Mavericks.

Garland   *French:* A prize, a wreath of flowers. Also Garlin. Playwright Garland Anderson was the first black to have a full-length production on Broadway.

Garnet   *English/French:* Keeper of the grains. Also Garnett. Garnett Mims was a rhythm and blues singer.

Garrett   *English:* A good spear thrower. Although sparingly used by black parents, this form of Gerald (see below) has been more often employed by white parents.

Garrick   *English:* An oak spear.

Garth   *German:* Garden. Garth Fagan is a leading choreographer.

Gary   *German:* A spear. The name is steadily growing in popularity. Gary Grant is a point guard for the L.A. Clippers.

Gaston   *French:* Man from Gascony.

Gavil An unusual name of unknown origins, found on Puckett's list. Perhaps it is an African-American variation of Gavin (see below).

Gavin *Welsh:* White hawk. The name is gaining in popularity.

Gaylor Found on Puckett's list of unusual names.

Gaylord *English:* Cheerful, jolly.

Gayraud Gayraud is surely an African-American invention. Gayraud S. Wilmore is an ordained Presbyterian minister. This former dean of the New York Theological Seminary is best known as coauthor of *Black Theology: A Documentary History, 1966–1979.*

Gene A short form of Eugene (see above). Gene Baker and Ernie Banks were the first black baseball players with the Chicago Cubs.

Geoffrey *English:* The peaceful one.

George *Greek:* A farmer, one who tills the soil. In use as early as the 17th century by free blacks, George remains a favored name. The free black patriot George Jackson fought in the American Revolution. Botanist, chemist, and educator George Washington Carver's extensive research into soil building and plant disease revolutionized the economy of the South. Ex-heavyweight champion George Foreman has made a remarkable comeback.

Gerald *German:* Rules by the spear. Enormously popular over several generations. Gerald Wilkins, a former New York Knick, is now with the Cleveland Cavaliers. Gerald Gladney is an editor who lives and works in New York.

Gerard *German:* Brave spearman. Also Gerrard, Gerrod.

Geronimo *Spanish:* Sacred. This name is best known for the last great Native American Apache warrior chief. It has been rarely used by black parents.

Gevin Found on Puckett's index of unusual names.

Gibson *German:* A surname that comes from Gilbert (see below). It was quite popular among both black and white parents as a given name during the latter half of the 19th century and the first half of the 20th.

Gideon *Biblical/Hebrew:* One who cuts down; a judge of Israel who won great battles through faith in God. An unusual name used by free blacks in the 19th century, it is obsolete in the 20th century.

Gilbert *German:* Bright lad. A common given name among free blacks in the 19th and early 20th centuries that is somewhat less popular today.

Giles *Greek:* A shield that protects. Sparingly used by black parents.

Gillance This African-American variation of Giles (see above) is noted among contemporary adult males.

Gillian A form of Giles (see above). This name was used by free black parents through the 19th century. However, it is rarely used today.

Gilmore *Scottish:* Servant of the Virgin Mary.

Gino *Italian:* Gino is a short form of names such as Giovanni.

Gladstone *Scottish:* From the town near the clearing in the woods.

Glascow *English:* A surname. Also Glasco. Sometimes employed by black parents of the 18th and 19th centuries, it is out of fashion today.

Glendon *Scottish:* From the shady valley.

Glenn *Irish:* From the secluded wooded valley. Also Glen, Glyn, Glynn.

Glover *English:* Glove or paw. Popular in early 20th century.

Glydon This name appears on Puckett's list of unusual black names in the 19th century. It is apparently an African-American blend or variation.

Godfrey *English:* Of God's peace. Godfrey appears on Puckett's "In the Beginning: 1619–1799" list as a name frequently used by free blacks. Comedian, actor, and civil rights advocate Godfrey Cambridge won critical acclaim as an actor on Broadway, in television, and on film.

Goffee This name may have African origins and is apparently an African-American invention. In use as early as the 17th century, it is rare today, if used at all.

Golden An unusual name first used in the late 19th century, rarely used in the 20th. Also Goldie. Goldie Sellers went to the Denver Broncos from the Grambling Tigers as a top draft choice in 1966.

Goodman *English:* The good man.

Goodwin *English:* Good, faithful friend.

Gordon *English:* From the marshes. It began to gain popularity among black parents in the early 1930s. Gordon Parks is an internationally esteemed photographer, writer, film director, and music composer.

Gowan *Scottish:* Wellborn; a variation of Owen (see below). This name has been infrequently used by black parents.

Grady *Irish:* A man of rank. Grady Tate is a popular jazz drummer.

Grafton Although this name sounds British, its origins are unclear. There is the remote possibility that it is an African-American invention. Grafton Tyler Brown, born in 1841, was the first noteworthy black artist to work in California. His drawings and paintings of landscapes in the West were collected and exhibited by the Oakland Museum.

Graham *English:* One from a farm home.

Granger *French:* Farmer.

Grant *French:* Great, tall. Grant S. Shockley, a distinguished clergyman and educator, became president of the International Theological Center in Atlanta in 1975. Grant Hill, a star player with the 1992–93 Duke Blue Devils, is one of Dick Vitale's Colossal Collegians.

Grantley *English:* A place name meaning one from Grant's meadow.

Granville *French:* The big town. Granville T. Woods invented the third rail and the automatic air brake system now used in subways, both of which help to reduce accidents.

Gray *English:* To shine.

Grayson *English:* The son of an earl.

Green A common given name among southern free blacks in the 19th century, this name remained popular into the 20th century, but appears to have fallen out of use.

Greenage Used by free blacks as early as the 17th century. There is no record of its use today.

Greg This short form of Gregory (see below) is often used by black parents as an independent name. Greg Calhoun is CEO of Calhoun Enterprises, a company founded in 1984 that has grown into one of the top 30 largest black-owned businesses.

Gregory *Greek:* Vigilant watchman. An immensely popular name over several generations. Gregory T. Baranco is CEO of the third largest black-owned automobile dealership in the nation.

Griffin *English:* Strong and powerful. Also Griffith.

Guion Just where this unusual name originated is not known. Lt. Col. Guion S. Bluford Jr., as one of a crew of five on the eighth flight of the space shuttle, became the first black American to travel in space.

Gunter *German:* War. Also Gunther.

Gus This short form of Gustave remained a common given name until the early 20th century.

Gustavo *Spanish:* Often used by free blacks in the 17th and 18th centuries.

Guy *Latin:* Lively. Guy Watson was a free black patriot who fought in the American Revolution. Linebacker Guy Prather played pro ball with the Green Bay Packers from 1981 to 1985.

Gylan An unusual name of uncertain origins. Gylan Kain was a member of the popular Last Poets.

Hadley *English:* Child from the heather meadow.

Hale *English:* Hero in good health.

Hall *English:* Dweller at the hall or manor house.

Hallam *English:* Dweller at the slope.

Hamilton *English:* Beautiful mountain. Hamilton Glover is the chief executive of the Advance Federal Savings & Loan Association, one of the top financial companies owned by blacks. Hamilton Holmes and Charlayne Hunter-Gault were the first black Americans to integrate the University of Georgia.

Hamlet *German:* Little home. This name of a famous Shakespearean character was infrequently used in the 17th through 19th centuries. Its use in the 20th century seems to have disappeared altogether. Hamlet Earl was a free black patriot who fought in the American Revolution.

Hamlin *English:* A variation of Henry (see below).

Hammond *English:* A home; a form of Hamlet (see above). This surname sometimes serves as an unusual given name.

Hampton *English:* Town or village. Hampton, a surname, is occasionally used as a given name. Hampton University is a top black college. Lionel Hampton, himself an institution, is a well-known example of its use as a surname. Hampton Hawes was a respected jazz pianist.

Hanes A surname that is related to the German Hans, which is a form of John (see below). Hanes Walker Jr. is a highly respected political scientist.

Hank This nickname for Henry (see below) is sometimes used as an independent name. Hank Aaron surpassed Babe Ruth's all-time record to become the home run king.

Hanley *English:* Meadow.

Hannibal *English:* A steep hill. Hannibal, a general from Carthage, an ancient city-state in North Africa crossed the Alps with a contingent of elephants and invaded Italy. The use of the name has endured. Hannibal Allen, a free black patriot, served in the American Revolution. Hannibal Peterson is a well-known jazz trumpeter.

Harcourt *French:* A fortified dwelling. Nickname Harry (see below).

Hardy *German:* Strong. Also Harding. Harding Bennett Young served as dean and professor of business administration at Atlanta University and as professor of business management at Georgia State University.

Harford *English:* From the hare ford.

Hark An unusual name of obscure origins.

Harley *English:* The meadow of the hares.

Harold *English:* Army commander. Harold Miner is a member of the Miami Heat basketball team. Harold W. Lundy became the fourth president of Grambling State University in 1991.

Haron This distinctive name, apparently an African-American invention, appears in Puckett's index of unusual names.

Harper *English:* One who plays the harp. Harper LeBell is a member of the Atlanta Falcons football team.

Harrell The Scandinavian form of Harold (see above).

Harris *English:* Son of Harry (see below). Also Harrison.

Harry This nickname for Henry (see below) or diminutive for Harold (see above) and Harcourt (see above) is often employed as an independent name, and has maintained popularity. Harry Williams was a free black patriot of the American Revolutionary War. Harry W. Brooks is the CEO of Advanced Consumer Marketing, one of the top 100 black-owned businesses of the 1990s. Radical thinker and theorist Harry Haywood was a major figure in political circles in the 1930s. Sociologist Harry Edwards pioneered the movement for racial equality in sports management.

Hart *English:* Stag. This name appears on Puckett's list of unusual black given names.

Hartford *English:* From the stag ford. Hartford Smith Jr. is a widely respected professor of social work at Wayne State University in Detroit. His groundbreaking work in nontraditional education set the stage for the university's alternative degree College of Life Long Learning.

Hartley *English:* From the stag wood. Rare.

Harvey *French:* Strong and ardent. Harvey Grant is a forward with the Washington Bullets.

Harwood *English:* Dweller in the hare wood.

Haskell *Hebrew:* Intellectual. Also Haskel.

Hawthorne *English:* One from the field of hawthorns.

Hayes *English:* From the hedged place.

Hayward *English:* A surname meaning bailiff. Used as a given name since the 19th century. Hayward R. Gipson Jr., vice-president and general manager for Corning's Vitro International, is one of the 40 most powerful black executives employed by a nonminority corporation.

Haywood *English:* Dweller near the hayfield. Multireedist Haywood Henry recorded with Ella Fitzgerald.

Heath *English:* From the large open field.

Hector   *Greek:* Steadfast. Hector Williams, a free black patriot, fought in the American Revolution.

Heman   The origins of this name are obscure and its use is rare. It is found among free blacks in the 17th century. Heman Rogers was a free black patriot who fought in the American Revolution.

Henderson   *English:* Son of Henry (see below). Used regularly, though not frequently, by black families.

Henley   *English:* Dweller in the high meadow. Also Hendley.

Henry   *German:* Ruler of the home. A common given name since the 19th century. Henry Harvey is a popular two-name combination. In 1836 Henry Blair obtained the first patent issued to an African-American.

Herbert   *English:* Bright, excellent ruler. This name endures in popularity among black families. Herbert Douglas "Herb" Boyd is an award-winning journalist and scholar of African-American history.

Hercules   *Greek:* Glorious. In Greek mythology, Hercules, the son of Zeus, was renowned for his great strength. This name is rarely used in the 20th century.

Herman   *German:* Soldier. Herman J. Russell is the CEO of H. J. Russell & Co., the fourth largest black-owned industrial company in the nation.

Herschel   *Hebrew:* Deer. Also Hershel. Football star Herschel Walker is a running back.

Hersey   The exact origins of this name are not clear, but it appears to be an African-American creation. Hersey Hawkins plays professional basketball with the Philadelphia 76ers.

Hezekiah   *Biblical/Hebrew:* God is my strength. The use of this very popular name of previous centuries has fallen off during the latter half of the 20th century.

Hilliard   *Greek:* Cheerful. Also Hillard.

Hilly   A nickname for Hilliard (see above). Hilly Saunders is an uncompromising activist in New York City.

Hilton *English:* A town on the hill. In 1969, Hilton Crawford was a defensive back for both the San Francisco 49ers and the Buffalo Bills.

Hiram *Biblical/Hebrew:* Of noble birth. This once well-used name rarely occurs in the latter half of the 20th century. Hiram R. Revels, the first black U.S. senator elected in Mississippi, served from 1869 to 1871.

Hobart *Danish:* Bart's hill. Also Hobert.

Hobson *English:* Son of Robert (see below).

Hollis *English:* Dweller near the holly bushes. In 1983, Hollis Brent led the Grambling Tigers in the total number of yards gained.

Holman *German:* Island in the river.

Holmes *German:* Son of Holman (see above).

Holt *English:* Dweller in a wooded area.

Homer *Greek:* A pledge or security. This name of the ancient Greek poet credited with writing the *Iliad* and the *Odyssey* is rarely used. Homer Tutt was a playwright during the Harlem Renaissance.

Horace *Greek:* To see, to behold. Horace Silver is a well-known jazz pianist. Power forward Horace Grant is a superstar member of the championship Chicago Bulls. Social scientist Horace Cayton coauthored *Black Metropolis* with St. Clair Drake.

Hosea *Biblical/Hebrew:* Salvation. Activist Hosea Williams worked closely with Martin Luther King.

Houston *Scottish:* A surname meaning from Hugh's town; the name of a city in Texas. Houston Baker is a noted author, literary critic, and college professor. Houston Markham is a football coach for Alabama State University. Houston Person is a famed saxophonist.

Howard *English:* Noble watchman. This surname of one of the great houses of British nobility has maintained enduring popularity in black families since the 19th century. Howard Lee is a popular two-name combination. Howard Thurman, preacher, philosopher, and mystic, developed the nonviolent love ethic that influenced Martin Luther King Jr.

Howell *Welsh:* Eminent, remarkable.

Howie A nickname for Howard (see above).

Hoyt An unusual name sometimes used by black parents. Hoyt Fuller was a leading black intellectual and journalist.

Hubert *German:* Bright, shining mind. Hubert Davis shocked sportswriters by performing well above expectations during his rookie year with the New York Knicks.

Huddie An African-American derivation of Hudd, a pet form of Richard (see below) now obsolete. Blues singer Huddie "Leadbelly" Ledbetter made a major contribution to the revival of folk music in America.

Hugh *English:* Intelligent. Hugh Mulzac was a steamship captain in the ill-fated Black Star Shipping Line organized by Marcus Garvey. South African–born Hugh Masekela is loved around the world for his trumpet playing.

Hughlyn A variation of Hugh (see above), quite possibly the name was originally a blend of both parents' names. Or perhaps it is a variant spelling of Hulan (see below). Hughlyn F. Pierce was a vice-president of Chase Manhattan Bank until he became president of the black-owned Freedom Now Bank.

Hulan An unusual name of uncertain origins. In 1953 Hulan Jack was the first black politician to be elected as borough president of Manhattan.

Humphrey *German:* Strength. *English:* Peace. Also Humfrey, Humphery, Humphry. Rare.

Hunter *English:* One who hunts.

Huntley *English:* From the hunter's meadow.

Huxley *English:* A field of ash trees.

Hyde *English:* A measure of land.

Hyder *English:* One who prepares hides for tanning.

Hyland *English:* One who lives in the high lands. Also Hylan.

Hyman *Hebrew:* Life.

Ian *Scottish:* God is gracious. Ian Hart of the Bronx, N.Y. was valedictorian of his class at Alfred E. Smith High School in 1993.

Ichabod *Biblical/Hebrew:* The glory is gone. This commonly used given name in early American history has fallen out of favor in the 20th century among both black and white parents. Ichabod Northrup was a free black patriot who fought in the American Revolution.

Ignatius *Latin:* Fiery one. An unusual name infrequently used.

Ike This diminutive for Isaac (see below) is well-known as the nickname of President Dwight Eisenhower. Guitarist Ike Turner gained wide acclaim performing with his wife, Tina.

Immanuel A form of Emmanuel (see above).

Inge *Scandinavian:* Protection. The use of Inge by black parents has occurred, but rarely.

Ingram *Scandinavian:* Raven of peace. Seen more as a surname, Ingram is sometimes used as a given name.

Inman An unusual name of unclear origins. Inman Jackson joined the Harlem Globetrotters in 1929 and introduced the clowning they are now known for. Until that time their play had been orthodox. Inman Russell lives in Taft, Okla.

Innis *Scottish/Irish:* From the island. Also Ennis.

Ira *Hebrew:* Watchful one. In December 1990, Ira D. Hall was named treasurer of IBM US. His job of keeping the company liquid to the tune of more than $1 billion per day makes him one of *Black Enterprise* magazine's 40 most powerful African-American executives.

Iran *Persian:* An Islamic state in Southwestern Asia. Iran Barkley was International Boxing Federation super middleweight champion until his defeat in 1993.

Irvin *Irish:* Handsome. Also Earvin, Irving, Irvine, Ervin. Irvin Church was named by Dick Vitale as a backcourt ace during the 1992–93 collegiate basketball season.

Irwin *English:* Boar friend.

Isaac *Biblical/Hebrew:* Laughter; the beloved son born to Abraham when he was 100 years old. The name Isaac has remained popular since the 17th century. At least two of the free black patriots who fought in the American Revolution had this given name. Since the 1960s, its use by black parents has fallen off. Isaac Hayes was a popular singer of soul music in the 1960s and 1970s. Isaac Lang Jr. is the CEO of Black River Manufacturing, Inc., an auto parts maker.

Isadore *Greek:* Gift of Isis, the Egyptian goddess of the moon. Also Isidor, Isidore, and Isador, Izzy. In 1964, Isadore Haynes, a former Grambling Tiger, joined the Kansas City Chiefs as a running back.

Isaiah *Biblical/Hebrew:* Salvation of God; an Old Testament prophet. Also Isiah. Enormously popular in late 19th and early 20th century, the name is rarely used now. The Detroit Piston superstar Isiah Thomas, a point guard, is well-known for his bright smile and his close relationship with his mother.

Isham *English:* From the iron one's estate. The name

Isham appeared in southern cities during the latter half of the 19th century. Its use in the 20th century is rare at best.

Ishmael *Biblical/Hebrew:* The Lord will hear. This name has gained literary prominence for its use in the first line of Herman Melville's *Moby Dick:* "Call me Ishmael." Ishmael Reed is a noted author, essayist, and anthologist.

Ishtar *Babylonian*: Meaning unknown. Noted among contemporary boys.

Israel *Biblical/Hebrew:* The name given Jacob by the Lord. Rarely used.

Ivan *Russian:* God is gracious, a form of John (see below). Actor Ivan Harold Browning of the Harlem Renaissance played in the first openly romantic scene between blacks onstage. Actor Ivan Dixon is best known for his movie performance in *Nothing But a Man* and his TV role in "Hogan's Heroes."

Ivano Ivano appears to be an African-American version of Ivan (see above). Ivano Newbill was a guard with the Georgia Tech Yellow Jackets in the 1992–93 basketball season.

Ives *English:* Little archer. Rarely used.

Ivory Origins and meaning unclear. Ivory Joe Hunter was a popular rhythm and blues singer during the 1950s.

Izera This unusual name, which appears on Puckett's list, is quite likely an African-American creation.

Jabez *Hebrew:* Born in pain.

Jack This pet name for John (see below) is sometimes used as an independent name. Jack Arbus was a free black patriot of the American Revolution. Jack Johnson was the first black heavyweight champion of the world.

Jackie This nickname for Jack (see above) was originally used as an independent name for boys, but recently it has become associated with girls as a pet name for Jacqueline. Jackie Robinson was the first black to play professional baseball in the major leagues.

Jackson This surname means son of Jack (see above). Its use as a given name was immensely popular in the late 18th and early 19th centuries, but is less so today.

Jacob *Biblical/Hebrew:* One who holds back. Jacob, a son of Abraham, is considered the father of Israel. His name was changed to Israel by the Lord, and the 12 tribes of Israel were descended from his 12 sons. Like many other biblical names, Jacob has experienced sustained use in black families over several centuries.

Jacques *French:* A form of Jacob (see above). Jacques has been consistently but infrequently used over the centuries.

Jade This name for a precious stone found in Asia and Africa appears on Puckett's list of unusual names in southern cities. Nowadays, it is more often used for girls.

Jaime *Spanish:* (pronounced HI mee) or Scottish (pronounced JAY mee) pet name for James (see below).

Jake A diminutive for Jacob (see above). Jake is sometimes used as an independent name, but less frequently in recent years.

Jalil Jalil represents a spelling variation of the Arabic Jaleel, which refers to majesty.

James The English form of Jacob (see above). James has experienced undiminished and enormous popularity since the 17th century. It is one of the most often used given names for boys in black families, and many remarkable black men have answered to James. James Armistead was a spy for the Continental Army during the American Revolution. James Baldwin was a noted novelist, essayist, and playwright from Harlem, who died in France. James Weldon Johnson, one of black America's most versatile men of letters, wrote the poem "Lift Ev'ry Voice and Sing." James Brown is considered the king of soul. James Turner is an author and leading black scholar who chairs the Black Studies Department at Cornell University. James H. Cone is a Charles A. Briggs Distinguished Professor of systematic theology at Union Theological Seminary.

Jamieson *English:* Son of James (see above). Also Jameson.

Jan *Dutch/Slavic:* A form of John (see below). Jan Matzeliger invented the shoe lasting machine, which revolutionized the shoe industry.

Jarek *Slavic:* January.

Jarmon *German:* German. Also Jerman.

Jaron *Hebrew:* To sing, to cry out. Jaron Jackson of Harlem is a promising middleweight boxer.

Jarrell This variation of Gerald (see above) is quite probably an African-American creation.

Jarrett *English:* Brave with a spear.

Jarrod *Hebrew:* To descend. Also Jared. The use of this name is growing. Jarrod Bunch brought new blood to the 1992 New York Giants football team. Jarrod Ellis played offensive guard with the 1991 Grambling Tigers.

Jarvis   *English:* A conqueror. Jarvis Tyner is a long-time political activist and brother of pianist McCoy.

Jason   *Hebrew:* The Lord is my salvation.

Jasper   *Greek:* A semiprecious gemstone. *Persian:* He who holds the secret or the treasure. Also Jaspar. Jasper Brown Jr. is listed in the 1950 edition of *Who's Who in Colored America* as an influential social worker in Philadelphia who dedicated his life's work to boys.

Javan   *Biblical/Hebrew:* A son of Japeth, Noah's son, born to him after the flood. Also Javin, Javon. Although rare, Javon is now being heard more often.

Jay   *Latin:* Jay bird. Jay Humphries is a guard for the Utah Jazz.

Jean   The French form of John (see below).

Jedidiah   *Hebrew:* Beloved of the Lord. Also Jedediah.

Jeff   A short form of Jeffrey (see below) or Geoffrey (see above), sometimes used as an independent name. Jeff Sanders is a power forward for the Atlanta Hawks.

Jefferson   A surname meaning the son of Jeffrey (see below) or Geoffrey (see above), occasionally used as an independent name. The self-educated Jefferson Long was the only African-American from Georgia to serve in the U.S. Congress in the 19th century.

Jeffrey   *English:* God's peace. Also Jeffery. Jeffery Shamberger is the CEO of the nation's 98th largest automobile dealership.

Jenkin   *Flemish:* Little John (see below).

Jenner   An English variation of John (see below).

Jennings   *English:* A descendant of John (see below).

Jerald   A modern spelling of Gerald (see above). Also Jerrald.

Jeremiah   *Biblical/Hebrew:* God will uplift; a major

prophet of the Old Testament. A common given name since the 18th century. Only in very recent generations has this biblical name's popularity fallen off slightly.

Jeremy A pet form of Jeremiah (see above) infrequently used by black parents as an independent name.

Jermaine An African-American variation of Jarmon (see above). Jermaine Jackson, an older brother of Michael, was a member of the popular Jackson Five.

Jerome *Greek:* A sacred or holy name. One of the finest small forwards in the NBA, Jerome Kersey, plays for the Portland Trailblazers.

Jerrell This name resonates with the sounds of contemporary African-American linguistic invention.

Jerrick This unusual name seems to be an African-American creation.

Jerrold A spelling variation for Gerald (see above).

Jerry A diminutive for Jerome (see above) or Jeremiah (see above) that is sometimes used as an independent name. Jerry Butler was a famous crooner of the 1950s and 1960s. His smooth rendition of tender ballads is often heard on oldies radio shows.

Jess A nickname for Jesse (see below).

Jesse *Biblical/Hebrew:* The Lord exists; the father of King David. The popularity of this biblical name dates back to the 16th century. Jesse Owens, the formidable athlete who succeeded at the 1936 Olympics in the face of Nazism, and Reverend Jesse Jackson are two of the most famous examples. Reverend Jackson's son, Jesse Jackson Jr., received a law degree from the University of Illinois at Urbana-Champaign College of Law, class of 1993. His father delivered the convocation address. Jesse H. Turner Jr. is the CEO of Tri-State Bank of Memphis, the nation's 18th largest black-owned bank.

Jethro *Hebrew:* Preeminence. Infrequently used.

Jim This pet name for James (see above) is sometimes

used as an independent name. Jim Brown is a former professional football player and a movie star.

Jimel Notorious Los Angeles gang member Jimel Barnes attended the historic Kansas City peace talks between street gang members from cities around the country.

Jimmie This spelling of a diminutive for James (see above) is another indication of our desire to distinguish names, as it has been mainly used by black American families, unlike Jimmy, which is mainly used by white American families.

Joachim *Hebrew:* God will judge.

Joe This diminutive for Joseph (see below) is sometimes used as an independent name. Joe Black was a pitcher for the Brooklyn Dodgers. The indomitable Joe Louis became the pride of black America when he won the heavyweight championship in 1937.

Joel *Biblical/Hebrew:* Jehovah is the Lord; an Old Testament prophet.

Johann A form of John (see below). Also Johannes, Johan, Jochanan. Rare.

John *Biblical/Hebrew:* God is graceful, God is merciful; a contraction of Jochanan, Johanan. John was one of the 12 apostles, who wrote one of the four Gospels of the New Testament. The popularity of John as a given name for boys has been preeminent among black parents. It is surely one of the all-time most popular names, and many distinguished African-American men have been called John. Ten men named John are listed in one company of free black patriots who fought valiantly in the American Revolution. John Hicks is a well-known jazz pianist. John Coltrane revolutionized jazz on the tenor saxophone. John A. Williams is a highly respected author and college professor. The formidable John Johnson is the founder of *Ebony* magazine, the patriarch of a family business empire, and one of America's richest men. John Hope Franklin is an outstanding historian. John Oliver Killens was a dedicated writer.

Johnnie A pet form of John (see above). Also Johnny, Johnie, Johney, Jonny, Johney. Johnny Newman is a small forward for the Charlotte Hornets.

Johnson *English:* A surname meaning son of John (see above), sometimes used as an independent name. Also Johnston.

Jon A variation of John (see above). Trumpeter Jon Faddis leads and directs the Carnegie Hall Jazz Band.

Jonah *Biblical/Hebrew:* A dove; an Old Testament prophet. Jonah Jones was an important jazz trumpeter.

Jonas The Greek form of Jonah (see above).

Jonathan *Biblical/Hebrew:* God has given; the son of King Saul. Also Johnathan, JoNathan. Although rare, the name has sometimes been used by black parents. Jonathan Henderson Brooks, a minister and poet, won several writing awards. As president of CBS Television Stations, a $500 million division of the CBS Broadcasting Group, Johnathan A. Rodgers is the highest-ranking black in his field and one of the 40 most powerful black executives in the land.

Jonel A name that is probably of African-American origins. Jonel Leonard Brown is listed in the 1950 *Who's Who in Colored America* as a dedicated educator who served as assistant state director of education of Negroes in Texas. This occurred before the *Brown v. Board of Education* Supreme Court decision outlawed school segregation.

Jordan *Biblical/Hebrew:* To descend. Occurring consistently among new generations, Jordan has been steadily growing in popularity since the 19th century. Jordan A. Frazier is the CEO of Midfield Dodge, Inc., one of the top 100 black-owned automobile dealerships. Jordan Segue attends St. Paul's Elementary School in Grosse Point, Mich.

Jory Jory Luster is the CEO of Luster Products Co.

Joseph *Biblical/Hebrew:* God will add the increase. A common given name. Like, John, Jesse, and David, Joseph has been frequently used over many generations. Joseph Jarmon is a highly respected avant-garde jazz musician. Joseph Lowry is executive director of Southern Christian Leadership Conference, the organization founded by Martin Luther King Jr. Joseph S. Colson Jr., as a vice-president of AT&T, is one of the 40 top black executives in the country. Actor Joseph Phillips appeared on NBC-TV's "The Cosby Show."

Josh A short form of Joshua (see below). Josh Gibson, the Babe Ruth of Negro baseball, was prevented by racial discrimination from receiving the national fame he deserved. Josh White was an internationally recognized folksinger.

Joshua *Biblical/Hebrew:* The Lord is my salvation. Joshua Jones was a poet and novelist of the Harlem Renaissance. Joshua I. Smith is the CEO of The Maxima Corp., the 18th largest black-owned industrial company in the nation.

Josiah *Biblical/Hebrew:* Fire of the Lord. Very popular in the 18th and 19th centuries among free blacks. Reverend Josiah S. Caldwell was an outstanding bishop of the African Methodist Episcopal church at the turn of the century. Josiah Henson is reputed to have been the model for Harriet Beecher Stowe's character Uncle Tom.

Josias The Greek form of Josiah (see above).

Joubert *English:* Praise or brilliance of God. Rare.

Juan Spanish form of John (see above). In fairly frequent use for many generations.

Juba This name may well have African origins. Its use is concentrated in the 17th and 18th centuries.

Juber This name may have African origins. Its use is apparently confined to earlier centuries. Juber Holland was a free black patriot of the American Revolutionary War.

Judd A form of Jordan (see above). Sometimes used in earlier centuries, but rare today.

Jude *Biblical/Hebrew:* Praise. Rare.

Judea *Biblical/Hebrew:* A land where God's people resided. Rare.

Judson *Hebrew:* Judah's son. Rare.

Jules The French form of Julius (see below). As the use of Julius decreases among black parents, the popularity of Jules is on the rise. Jules Bledsoe pursued a successful career as a concert baritone in the U.S. and Europe during the Harlem Renaissance. When photographer Jules Allen is not working in his bustling Harlem studio, he is roaming the urban landscape and countryside capturing black life and contemporary history in pictures.

Julian *Greek:* Soft-haired, light-bearded. First appears in use by black parents in the 20th century. Julian "Cannonball" Adderley is considered one of the foremost jazz alto saxophonists. Civil rights activist Julian Bond was the first black elected to the Georgia State Legislature.

Julio The Spanish form of Julian (see above). Rare.

Julius *Latin:* Youthful. Best known as Julius Caesar. Basketball Hall of Famer Julius "Dr. J" Erving played with the Philadelphia 76ers for many years.

Junius The Latin form of junior. Junius "Buck" Buchanan, a Grambling Tiger, was the first round draft choice of the Kansas City Chiefs in 1963.

Jupiter *Latin:* The supreme Roman deity; the fifth planet of the solar system. In 1771 poet Jupiter Hammon became the first black American to have his work published.

Jurard An African-American variation of Jarrod (see above).

Justin *Latin:* Justice. Also Justus. Guard Justus Thigpen was a key player for the 1992–93 Iowa State Cyclones basketball team.

Several of the names on this list are enjoying a burst of popularity. It is interesting that some of them have meanings that refer to individuals of darker hues.

Kacey *Irish:* Brave.

Kade An alternate spelling for Cade (see above).

Kadeem An African-American original. Actor Kadeem Hardison starred in the sitcom "A Different World."

Kai (kye) *Welsh:* Keeper of the keys. An unusual name used in America almost exclusively by black parents. In 1992, Kai Burrell, a sophomore, was a talented lineman for the Grambling Tigers.

Kaiser *German:* Emperor. Rare.

Kal A diminutive for Kalton and Kalvin (see below). Kal Daniels is a left fielder for the Chicago Cubs.

Kalton *Greek:* Beautiful.

Kalvin An alternate spelling for Calvin (see above).

Kanavis An African-American original. Kanavis McGhee brought new blood to the New York Giants when he was drafted in the second round in 1993.

Kane *Welsh:* Beautiful. *Irish:* Warrior's son. This name first appears on the list Puckett entitles "In the Beginning, 1619–1799."

Kaream An obviously African-American variation of the

Arabic Kareem popularized by basketball legend Kareem Abdul Jabbar. Also Kareen.

Karl An alternate spelling of Carl (see above). Karl Malone is the Utah Jazz basketball superstar who lent his superior talents to the 1992 Olympics Dream Team. Karl Lancaster of Cheyney College led his conference in rebounding during the 1992–93 academic year.

Keane *English:* Of keen wit or keen eye.

Kecalf (kelf) Kecalf, the son of soul diva Aretha Franklin, is an aspiring rap artist.

Kedem *Hebrew:* From the East.

Kedrick *Irish:* A gift of splendor.

Keeley *Irish:* Handsome. Also Kealy, Keely.

Keenan *Irish:* Little ancient one. Keenan Ivory Wayans is the creator and executive producer of the popular TV show "In Living Color."

Keith *Irish:* From the battle place. Welsh: From the forest. Over the last several decades, the use of Keith has grown steadily and rapidly. It is fast becoming a popular first name for boys. Keith A. Hasty is chief executive of Best Foam Fabricators, Inc., one of the nation's top 100 black businesses.

Kekey An unusual name of uncertain origins. Also Kiki.

Kelby *Scandinavian:* Place by the spring.

Kelly *Irish:* Lively, aggressive. Recently this name is most often used for girls. Kelly Miller was a noted sociologist and college professor. Kelly Wyatt is a world-class classical pianist and composer.

Kelsey *English:* One who dwells at ship island. Used for boys by black parents, for girls by white parents.

Kelton *English:* Dweller in the town where ships are built.

Kelvin *Irish:* From the narrow river. Also Kelvan, Kelven. During the annual Black and Gold game, Kelvin Reddix made seven tackles for the Grambling Tigers.

Kemper   *English:* A variation of Kemp, which means fighter, warrior. Violinist Kemper Harreld was one of the founders of the National Association of Negro Musicians in 1919.

Ken   A diminutive for any one of the boys' names beginning with the letters Ken. This nickname is rarely used as an independent name.

Kendall   *English:* From the valley of the river Kent. Also Kendal, Kendell. Kendall Gill is a guard for the Charlotte Hornets.

Kendrick   *English:* Royal ruler. Kendrick Warren, the 6'8″ junior who played for the Virginia Commonwealth Metros 1992–93 basketball team, is considered a brawler on the inside, where he averaged 19 points per game.

Kennard   *English:* Brave, strong.

Kenneth   *Irish:* Handsome. Kenneth has held enduring popularity since the early 19th century. The research of Kenneth B. Clark, the noted sociologist, was instrumental in helping Thurgood Marshall persuade the Supreme Court to overturn school segregation.

Kenny   A diminutive for Kenneth (see above) that is today rapidly growing in popularity as an independent first name. New Jersey Net guard Kenny Anderson is a future great in the NBA.

Kenrick   *English:* Royal or bold ruler.

Kent   *Irish:* Royal chieftain; a county in England.

Kenton   A form of Kent (see above).

Kentrell   *English:* Royal power.

Kenway   *English:* Royal or bold warrior.

Keon   *Irish:* A form of John (see above).

Kermit   *Irish:* Free man. Kermit Alexander was an exciting running back in college and the pros.

Kern   *Irish:* Little dark one.

Kerry   *Irish:* Son of the dark one. Kerry Brown earned a starting position during his freshman year with the 1992–93 Grambling Tigers.

Kerwin *Irish:* Little black one.

Ketter This unusual name appeared on Puckett's list early in our history.

Kevin *Irish:* Handsome. Since the 1960s, the use of this name has soared. Kevin Powell is a young writer whose star is rising. Kevin Gamble is a small forward for the Boston Celtics.

Khary A spelling variation of the Swahili Khari.

Khephra An unusual name of uncertain origins. Khephra Burns writes a quarterly column on African-American culture for *Essence.*

Kier Kier Gist is a member of Naughty by Nature. The group made a splash on the hip-hop scene with its debut album. The members, Treach (Anthony Cross), Vinnie (Vincent Brown), and Kier all live in East Orange, N.J.

Kimball *Irish:* Bold kin. Rarely used.

King *English:* Ruler. Use of King as a given name was quite common in earlier centuries among free blacks.

Kirby *English:* Dweller in a cottage by the water. Kirby Puckett is an All-Star outfielder with the Minnesota Twins.

Kirk *Scottish:* Church. Kirk Lightsey is a widely acclaimed jazz pianist.

Kirkland *Scottish:* A church's land.

Kit A nickname for Christopher. Also Kitt. When used as an independent name, the spelling Kitt has been the more frequent choice of black parents.

Knoll *English:* A round, smooth hill.

Knolton An African-American variation of Knoll noted among contemporary males.

Kolby *Polish:* The dark-haired boy; a short form of Jacob.

Kurt *German:* Brave and wise.

Kyle *Irish:* Chief.

La Quarius Newly created. This name is noted among elementary school students in Detroit.

Labert This name is another demonstration of the African-American fondness for blending La with a wide variety of endings that often make the new name a unique creation.

LaBron Also LeBron. Although used for several generations by black parents, these names smack of that African-American penchant for creating new sounds in naming their children. LeBron Simmons, a noteworthy attorney in Detroit during the 1950s and 1960s, was a staunch advocate for the poor and underprivileged.

Lacey *Latin:* From Latius's estate. Also Lacy. Rare.

Lad *English:* Manservant, young man. Also Ladd. Although Lad is listed in Puckett's free black names, 1800–60, there is apparently little or no use of it as a given name in the 20th century.

Lafayette Marquis de Lafayette, a French nobleman, joined Gen. Washington's army in 1777. His fame spread throughout the country, and his surname was often taken as a first name by free black and white parents. Rare in the 20th century.

Lamar *French:* Of the sea. Also Lemar. First used by black parents in the late 19th century, Lamar remains in frequent use today. Lamar McGriggs played for the New York Giants football team.

Lamb   This unusual name, which refers to a young, gentle sheep, is found in Puckett's list of free black names, 1700–1800.

Lambert   *German:* His country's brightness, the brightness of the land.

Lambold   This unusual name of uncertain origins appears in Puckett's list of free black names, 1700–1800.

Lamont   *Irish:* A man of the land. Also Lamond. Lamont Dozier was a leading member of the Holland-Dozier-Holland songwriting team of Motown fame.

Lance   A French diminutive for Lancelot. In the tales of King Arthur, Sir Lancelot was the most famous of the Knights of the Round Table. Lance Blanks comes off the bench for the Detroit Pistons. Lance Alexander is a member of the singing group Lo-Key.

Lander   *English:* An open grassy area, a lawn. Also Landor, Landan.

Landon   *English:* Landowner. Rare.

Lane   *English:* A narrow path or roadway between hedges.

Langston   *English:* A long narrow town, a tall man's town. Poet Langston Hughes is one of the most prolific and respected black writers of all time. Langston University, a historically black college, is located in a historically all-black town in Oklahoma of the same name.

Lany   A pet name for names beginning with Lan. Also Lannie. Infrequently used by black parents as a given name.

Lark   This name of a bird is infrequently used by black parents as a given name for boys and by white parents for girls.

Larnell   Apparently a recent African-American creation, only a few generations old. Also Larney.

Larrimore   *French:* Armorer. Rare.

Larron *French:* A thief. Its meaning might hinder its use.

Larry This diminutive for Lawrence (see below) is often used as an independent name. Larry L. Hovell is CEO of Bay City Chrysler Plymouth, Inc., one of the top 100 black-owned automobile dealerships. The former UNLV college star Larry Johnson is now the superstar of the Charlotte Hornets pro basketball team.

Lars A Scandinavian form of Lawrence (see below). Lars Kate is a basketball player with the University of Georgia.

Larvall *English:* Dweller near the well in the lowlands. Also Larvell.

LaSalle *French:* The hall. NBA stalwart LaSalle Thompson is an Indiana Pacer.

Latham *English:* A district, a division.

Lathrop *English:* Villager.

Laval An African-American original. Laval Perry is the CEO of All American Ford, Inc., the nation's 71st largest black-owned automobile dealership.

Lavar An African-American original. Also Levar, Le Var, LaVar. Popularized in the late 1970s when actor Le Var Burton played Kunte Kinte in the TV miniseries of Alex Haley's *Roots*.

Lavon An African-American original.

Lawanza Newly created. Lawanza Spears was a cum laude graduate of the class of 1993, Howard University.

Lawrence *Latin/English:* From the place of the laurel trees. Also Laurence. Lawrence is by far the more often used spelling of the name by all American parents. It became popular among black parents in the late 19th century. Laurence Edward "Larry" Doby joined the Cleveland Indians baseball club in 1946 and became the first black player in the American League. Lawrence Hall had a brief career with the Harlem Globetrotters. Lawrence Moten of the Syracuse Orangemen basketball team was the 1991–92 NBA Rookie of the Year. The fearsome linebacker Lawrence Taylor has had a distinguished career with the New York Giants.

Lawson *English:* Son of Lawrence (see above); aristocratic surname now used as a given name.

Lawton *English:* Settlement on a hill. Rare.

Lazarus *Biblical/Greek:* God has helped. In the New Testament, Jesus raised Lazarus from the dead. Lazarus Sims came off the bench for the Syracuse Orangemen in their 1992–93 season.

Leander *Greek:* Lion man, brave one.

Leandro *Spanish:* Man fierce as a lion. Also Leandre.

Ledell An African-American creation.

Ledyard The origins of this name are unclear. It is apparently a surname used as a given name.

Lee *English:* From the pasture meadow. Popular since late 19th century. Lee Elder, a well-traveled pro golfer, finished second to the great Jack Nicklaus in 1968 while playing in the American Golf Classic. In 1974 he became the first African-American eligible for the Masters golf tournament.

Leggett *French:* An envoy.

LeGrand Also Legrant. The use of these first names appears to be confined to African-Americans. Perhaps they are originals.

Leigh An alternate spelling for Lee (see above). During the Harlem Renaissance, actor Leigh Whipper received accolades for his role in a play based on John Steinbeck's *Of Mice and Men.*

Leighton *Hebrew:* Belonging to God. Also Layton, Leyton.

Leland *English:* A pasture. Also Leeland.

Lemmy A nickname for Lemuel (see below) rarely used as a given name.

Lemon An unusual given name that appears on Puckett's early list.

Lemuel *Biblical/Hebrew:* Belonging to God. Rare. Lemuel Peterkin is a veteran New York City photographer.

Len A pet name for Leonard (see below) or Lennard (see below) rarely used as a given name. Also Lenn, Lynn. In 1967 Lynn Swann of the Pittsburgh Steelers won the Most Valuable Player award for his outstanding performance in the Super Bowl.

Lennard A variation of Leonard (see below). Also Lennart.

Lennox *Irish:* The land of many elm trees.

Lenny A short form of Leonard (see below) or of names beginning with Len. Lenny Moore was a superb running back with a good pair of hands.

Lent This unusual given name was found among free blacks and is listed by Puckett, "In the Beginning, 1619–1799." Lent Munson was a free black patriot of the American Revolution.

Lenus Although it appears a few times in the 17th century among free blacks, the origins of this unusual name are obscure.

Lenvil *French:* Dweller is the tenant house near the town.

Lenwood *English:* Dweller in the tenant house in the woods.

Leo *Greek:* Lion. Leo Watson was an innovative vocalist and scat singer during the 1930s and 1940s.

Leon *Greek:* Lion. In February 1978, Leon Spinks defeated Muhammad Ali to become heavyweight champion of the world; in September 1978, Ali regained his title. Leon Eastmond is CEO of Al Eastmond and Sons, one of the top 100 black-owned industrial companies.

Leonard *German:* Strong as a lion. Leonard Goines is a highly regarded musicologist.

Leopold *German/English:* A bold free man. Rare.

Lerone The origins of this name are not clear; it may

come from the French Lerond, which means the round. Also Leron. Lerone Bennett Jr. is executive editor of *Ebony* magazine and author of the widely read *Before the Mayflower.*

Leroy *French:* The king. The chief executive of Ozanne Construction Co., Inc., the 88th largest black-owned company, is Leroy Ozanne. The formidable slugger Joe DiMaggio called LeRoy Robert "Satchel" Paige, who began his professional baseball career in the Negro Leagues, the best pitcher he ever faced.

Leslie *English:* Dweller at the small dell. Also Lesley. This boy's name gained popularity around the turn of century and has maintained it until today. But recently it is more frequently used for girls. Lesley Vandahoss Baker lives in Dallas. His middle name is said to be after the first name of a famous black Methodist bishop of the late 19th century. Lesley Dwight Dinwiddie lives in Tulsa, Okla.

Lester *English:* From Leicester. Lester Young, a famous jazz tenor saxophonist of the swing era, is loved by jazz enthusiasts for his sensitive interpretation of ballads.

Levander *French:* A man from the East.

Leverett *French:* Baby rabbit.

Levert This name may be an African-American variation of similar names from the French.

Levi *Biblical/Hebrew:* Joined, united. Also Levy. In the Bible, Levi was Jacob's third son; his mother was Leah. Levi's descendants were the Levites or priests who served in the Temple of God. Levi Wartkins was the founding president of Owens College, now Lemoyne-Owen College.

Lew A diminutive for Lewis (see below). Lew Alcindor was Kareem Abdul Jabbar's name before he changed it.

Lewis *English/German:* Renowned fighter. Lewis Martin was a free black patriot who fought in the American Revolutionary War. An associate of Thomas Edison's,

Lewis H. Latimer supervised the installation of the first electric lighting of the streets of New York City.

Lex *Latin:* Law. Rare.

Lexius This unusual name of obscure origins appears among free blacks in the 18th century.

Liberty This given name is on Puckett's list of free black names, 1700–1800.

Lige This unusual name may have African origins.

Limas An unusual name appearing on Puckett's list of free black names, 1700–1800.

Lincoln *English:* From the colony by the pool.

Lindell *English:* One who dwells near the linden tree dell.

Lindon *English:* Dweller by the hill with lime trees. Also Lyndon.

Lindsay *English:* Linden tree island. Also Lindsey. Although black parents have typically used Lindsay as a boy's name, white parents recently have begun to use it as a girl's name. Lindsey Hairston was a high school All-American basketball player from Michigan in the 1960s.

Linford *English:* Dweller near the linden tree ford. Also Linfred.

Link *English:* An enclosure. Rare.

Linton A form of Lindon (see above).

Linus *Greek:* Flax-colored hair.

Lionel *Latin:* Young lion. Also Lyonel. Lionel Hampton is an internationally famous vibraphonist and bandleader. Lionel Richie is a well-known pop star.

Llewellyn *Welsh:* Ruler who is like a lion. J. Bruce Llewellyn is CEO of Garden State Cable TV.

Lloyd *Welsh:* Gray-haired. In 1959, Lloyd Richards became the first African-American to direct a Broadway play. Lloyd Price was a popular rhythm and blues singer in the 1950s.

Logan *Scottish:* Low meadow.

London A city in England, rarely used as a given name, but it appears on Puckett's list of unusual black names.

Lonear This unusual name appears to be an African-American creation. Lonear Heard is the CEO of James T. Heard Management Corp., one of the top 100 black-owned companies.

Lonnie A diminutive for Alonzo (see above) sometimes used as an independent name. Lonnie Peek is a political consultant and businessman in Detroit. Baseball player Lonnie Smith appeared in several World Series.

Lonnon This unusual given name was found among free blacks in the 18th century.

Lonzie A nickname for Alonzo (see above) rarely used as a given name.

Lord A few black parents have used this name, which connotates authority and power, perhaps to emphasize their value to the parents or to endow the children with a sense of power.

Lorenzo The Italian form of Lawrence (see above). Also Lorenza. Lorenzo Pace is an established artist in New York City.

Lot *Biblical/Hebrew:* To cover; the Nephew of Abraham. Rare.

Lou A diminutive for Louis (see below) sometimes used as an independent name. Actor Lou Gossett Jr. won an Oscar in 1983 for his portrayal of Foley, the tough Marine drill sergeant, in *An Officer and a Gentleman.*

Loudos This unusual name is found in Puckett's free black names, 1700–1800.

Lougo This unusual name is found in Puckett's free black names, 1700–1800.

Louis *English:* (pronounced LOO iss). *French* (pronounced loo wee): Great fighter. While serving in the Army Medical Corps during WWI, physician Louis T. Wright discovered the technique for giving a smallpox injection. Louis Armstrong was loved around the world for his mastery of the trumpet and his distinct singing voice.

Love   This unusual given name is found from time to time in 19th- and early 20th-century records.

Lovell   *French:* Young wolf.

Lowell   *English:* Beloved.

Lucas   A form of Luke (see below).

Lucien   *Latin:* Light, a child born at dawn. Also Lucian.

Lucius   *Latin:* He brings light and knowledge. Lucius "Lucky" Millender was an outstanding jazz bandleader of the 1930s and 1940s. Lucius Jackson was a forward for the 1992–93 Syracuse University Orangemen basketball team. Lucius Harris was a 1992–93 backcourt ace for the Long Beach State basketball team.

Lucky   A nickname for Lucius (see above).

Lud   An unusual name of obscure origins, rarely used in the 20th century.

Luke   *Greek:* The giver of light; the author of the Gospel of Luke and the Book of Acts in the New Testament. First baseman Luke Easter was a powerful hitter for the Cleveland Indians in the 1950s.

Luther   *German:* Famous warrior. Luther Wright is an emerging superstar on the Seton Hall Pirates 1992–93 basketball team. Popular singer Luther Vandross performed at the Lincoln Memorial celebration held in honor of the 1993 presidential inauguration.

Lutrell   This name sounds like an African-American original.

Luzerne   *French:* Glowworm.

Lydell   *English:* From the wide dell.

Lyle   *French:* One from the isle. Lyle Atkinson is a well-known jazz acoustic bassist.

Lyman   *English:* Man of the meadows.

Lymore   An unusual given name of obscure origins.

Lyndall *English:* From the lime tree dell.

Lyron *Hebrew:* The lyrical one.

Lysander *Greek:* He liberates.

Three of the most exciting, dynamic and influential leaders of the 20th century have names that begin with M: Marcus, Martin, and Malcolm.

Mac *Scottish/Irish:* A surname prefix meaning son of. Also Mc.

MacArthur *Irish:* Son of Arthur (see above). Also McArthur. Artist McArthur Binion is well-known for his unique approach and technique.

Macclennon The origins of this name are unclear; perhaps it is an African-American variation of Maclean, or it may be a case of using the mother's family name as a given name. Also McClennon. Born in Waco, Texas, McClennon Phillip Harvey was the managing editor of the *Waco Messenger* and a member of the advisory board of Paul Quinn College.

Macdonald *Scottish:* Son of Donald (see above); a powerful Scottish clan. Also McDonald. Given the widespread awareness of the fast-food chain McDonalds, it is quite unlikely that contemporary parents will select this as a given name.

Macdougal *Scottish/Irish:* Son of the dark stranger. Also McDougal.

Maceo (ma SA oo)   *Spanish:* From Matthew's estate. Harlem Renaissance musician Maceo Pinkard is the composer of "Sweet Georgia Brown." Maceo Rojas lives in Teaneck, N.J.

Mack   A pet form of Mac (see above) rarely used as a given name.

Mackenzie   *Irish/Scottish:* Son of the wise ruler, son of Kenzie the fair, favored one. Also McKenzie.

Mackinley   *Irish/Scottish:* Son of the learned or skilled one. Also McKinley. As a child in Mississippi, McKinley Morganfield played in a muddy creek so often that his grandfather started to call him Muddy. His friends added Waters. Muddy Waters was the legendary blues singer, guitarist, and composer who developed the Chicago blues or urban blues sounds.

Maclean   *English:* Son of Leander (see above). Also McClean.

Madison   *English:* Son of a mighty warrior.

Magnus   *Latin:* The great one. Journalist, editor, and publisher Magnus L. Robinson worked as a reporter on a Baltimore newspaper, the *Bee.* In 1886, he founded the *National Leader.*

Major   *Latin:* Greater; a military rank and a surname occasionally used as a given name. Major R. Owens is a Democratic congressman from New York. From 1898 to 1900, Major Taylor was the world's fastest bicycle rider.

Malachi   *Biblical/Hebrew:* Messenger of God; the prophet who wrote the final book of the Old Testament. Like other biblical names, it has been well used by black parents. Bassist Malachi Favors is a founding member of the Art Ensemble of Chicago.

Malcolm   *Scottish:* A disciple of St. Columba. Also Malcom. It is a favorite name of Scottish royalty. Malcolm X is surely our most famous Malcolm, and for many he is our royalty. Like Martin Luther King Jr., he loved his people, sought their freedom from oppression, and lost his life in the struggle.

Mallory *German:* Army counselor.

Malvern *Welsh:* Bare hill.

Mamon The origins of this unusual name are not clear. Mamon Powers Sr. is the CEO of one of the top 100 black-owned industrial companies.

Manfred *German:* Man of peace. Rare.

Manley *English:* Dweller at the hero's meadow.

Manning *English:* Son of the hero. College professor Manning Marable is one of our most prolific writers and gifted thinkers. He is a leading black intellectual.

Manny *English:* nickname for Emanuel (see above), Manfred (see above), Manning (see above), or Manley (see above), used as early as the 17th century by free blacks. Also Mannie. Mannie L. Jackson is a senior vice-president for Honeywell Industries and one of the nation's top 40 black executives employed by a nonminority company.

Mansfield *English:* Dweller in the field by the small river.

Manu *Hindu:* A mythical creator of humankind. Manu Dawson is a highly respected natural foods counselor in the New York area.

Manuel *Spanish:* God is with us; a form of Emanuel (see above).

Manus *Irish:* Great king. This name was found occasionally among free blacks of the 17th and 18th centuries.

Manville *French:* He comes from the great estate.

Marcel The French form of Marcellus (see below).

Marcellus *Latin:* Little warlike one; its root is the Roman god of war, Mars. Banker Marcellus Anderson is a well-known business executive.

Marcus *Latin:* Little hammer, warlike one. This original form of Mark (see below) is also derived from Mars, the Roman god of war. Marcus Belgrave is a well-known jazz trumpeter and composer. Marcus Garvey's fierce post-WWI leadership certainly reflects the meaning of this name. His dynamic oratory excited and galvanized African-Americans and blacks in Latin America and the West Indies to organize around self-help, race pride, and Pan-African ideals.

Mario An Italian form of Mark (see below). Mario Van Peebles is an actor and director.

Marion This French masculine form of Mary has come to be almost exclusively used for girls. Cellist Marion Cumbo became widely recognized at the annual convention of the National Association of Negro Musicians during the 1920s. In 1970, he founded Trian Presentations, an organization dedicated to promoting black concert artists and composers. Marion Brown is a musician, painter, writer, and teacher.

Mark *Latin:* From Mars, the Roman god of war. The use of Mark as a boys' name is growing in popularity among black parents. Mark wrote the second Gospel of the New Testament. Mark Jackson, the professional basketball star, has played with the New York Knicks and the L.A. Clippers. Mark Aguirre was a recent addition to the Detroit Pistons when they defeated the L.A. Lakers and Magic Johnson for the 1989 NBA championship. Hip-hopper Mark Winston Griffith is the founder of Central Brooklyn Credit Union in the Bedford-Stuyvesant section of Brooklyn.

Marland *English:* From the land of the lake.

Marley *English:* One who lives near the lake meadow.

Marlon *French:* Blackbird. Also Marlin. At 6'9", Marlon Maxey is a power forward for the Minnesota Timberwolves NBA team. Trumpeter Marlon Jordan is making a name for himself in jazz circles. Marlon Wayans is a member of the famous Wayans family.

Marlow *English:* From the hill by the lake.

Marquis (mar KEE) *French:* A nobleman whose title ranks below a duke and above an earl. Also Marques. Marques Haynes played with the Harlem Globetrotters from 1946 to 1952. He was billed as the world's greatest dribbler.

Mars *Latin:* The god of war. This name is best known for its use in Spike Lee's *She's Gotta Have it*.

Marshall *English:* Military cavalry officer or caretaker of horses. In America, a marshal is an officer of the law.

Martice An Atlanta native, Martice Moore spent his senior year as a guard/forward at Georgia Tech. He was rated among the top transfer students in the NCAA.

Martin *English:* Warrior. The beloved Martin Luther King Jr. stood up for what he believed and gave his life for freedom's cause.

Martinez The Spanish form of Martin (see above); a surname occasionally used by black parents as a given name.

Marty A nickname for Martin (see above) sometimes used as an independent name. Marty Conlon is a center for the Sacramento Kings.

Marvin *English:* Well-known friend. Appears around turn of century as a common given name.

Mason *French:* A worker in stone.

Mathis A form of Matthew (see below).

Matthew *Biblical/Hebrew:* Gift of god; the apostle Matthew wrote the first book of the New Testament. On April 6, 1909, half-frozen Matthew A. Henson literally stood on top of the world when he reached the North Pole 45 minutes before Admiral Peary. Matthew Augustine is the CEO of Edtrex Industries, one of the top 100 black-owned companies.

Maurice *Latin:* The dark-skinned one. Maurice Hunter, a handsome, dark, muscular Zulu who was born in South Africa, came to America with his parents in 1910. As a model he posed for illustrations in most of the popular white magazines of the period as well as for the most successful artists, such as Norman Rockwell. Maurice F. Jones, as the president of Xerox's Office Document Systems Division, is one of the nation's top 40 black exec-utives employed by nonminority companies.

Maury A nickname for Maurice (see above) sometimes used as an independent name. Also Morrie, Maurie. In 1959 the brilliant fielding of Los Angeles Dodger Maury Wills helped the team win the World Series.

Maxwell *English:* From Mack's well.

Mayfield *English:* From the warrior's field.

Mayhew The French form of Matthew (see above).

Maynard *French:* Powerful. In 1973, attorney Maynard Jackson was elected the first black mayor of a major southeastern city: Atlanta.

Mayo An English variation of Matthew (see above).

McCarroll *Irish:* Son of Carroll (see above).

McCleary *Irish:* Son of Cleary (see above). McCleary Stinnett, a dancer who was also called a jack-of-all trades, is considered one of the Harlem Renaissance's most remarkable personalities.

McCoy A Scottish surname used from time to time as a given name. McCoy Tyner has won international ac-claim as a jazz pianist.

Mead *English:* From the meadow. Also Meade. Meade Lux Lewis was a remarkable pianist who helped popu-larize the boogie-woogie style.

Medgar The meaning and origins of this name are ob-scure. It may be an invention or a family name. Civil rights leader and lawyer Medgar Wiley Evers was a leader in the civil rights movement until he was assas-sinated at the entrance of his home in Jackson, Miss., in 1963.

Mel A diminutive for names such as Melvin (see below) and Melton (see below), it is rarely used as an indepen-dent name. Mel Farr, the former star of the Detroit Lions football team, is the CEO of the nation's fifth largest black-owned automobile dealership.

Meldrick *English:* Powerful. Like the meaning of his

name, Meldrick Taylor is a potent boxer and former welterweight champ.

Melton An unusual name of obscure origins, sometimes used by black parents. It may be related to Mertin (see below).

Melvin *Irish:* Chief. Melvin Booker of the University of Missouri's basketball team is considered a backcourt ace. Melvin "Mel" Tapley, a reporter with the *Amsterdam News* for over 40 years, has been the New York paper's arts and entertainment editor for the past decade.

Mercer *English:* Merchant or storekeeper. Bandleader and trumpeter Mercer Ellington—Duke's son—is carrying on his father's illustrious tradition.

Merle *French:* Blackbird. In 1963, Merle M. McCurdy became the U.S. attorney for the Northern District of Ohio.

Merrill *French:* Little famous one.

Merritt *English:* Worthy.

Mertin *English:* From the town by the sea. Also Merton.

Mervyn *Welsh:* Sea hill. Also Mervin.

Meshach *Biblical/Hebrew:* Mesach was one of the three Hebrew men of the Old Testament who survived the fiery furnace. The spelling Meshack is found among free blacks of the 18th and 19th centuries. TV star Meshach Taylor led a star-studded gala heralding the black family at the 1993 Indiana Black Expo.

Meyer *Hebrew:* The bearer of light.

Mial This name is found on Puckett's list of unusual names. Its origin and meaning are unknown.

Micah *Biblical/Hebrew:* Like unto the Lord; an Old Testament prophet.

Mical (me KAL) A variation of Michael (see below).

Michael *Biblical/Hebrew:* He who is like God. In use since the 18th century, but experiencing a stupendous upsurge in popularity among black parents since the

1950s, Michael easily rivals and perhaps now overtakes John, James, Joseph, and David as a boy's name. Among white parents, Michael has been one of the top 50 names for most of this century. Superstars Michael Jordan and Michael Jackson are surely the most famous of African-American Michaels. Michael Rashiid Adderley is a high school student in Brooklyn and Michael Danny Dinwiddie is a playwright in Los Angeles.

Mick A rarely used nickname for Michael (see above).

Mickey A pet name for Michael (see above) that is now sometimes used as an independent name. Mickey Leland, a U.S. representative from Texas, was the chairman of the Congressional Black Caucus and the House Select Committee on Hunger until his untimely death.

Midian The origins of this unusual name are not known. Midian O. Bousefield was a well-known physician in Chicago from 1914 until 1948.

Mifflin The meaning and origins of this unusual name are unclear. Born a free man in Philadelphia in 1823, Mifflin Wister Gibbs traveled to San Francisco in 1849. In 1855, he founded *Mirror of the Times,* California's first black newspaper.

Miguel (mi GEL) The Spanish form of Michael (see above) sometimes used by black parents.

Mike A popular diminutive for Michael (see above).

Milan (mee LAHN) *Latin:* A soldier.

Milburn *English:* From the mill stream.

Miles *English:* Merciful. Also Myles. Shown among Puckett's common given names as early as 1800. Our most famous Miles is Mr. Davis, one of the greatest jazz trumpeters.

Milford *English:* A place name meaning from the ford near the mill. Rare.

Milfred This name may be an African-American invention derived from Milford (see above).

Miller *English:* An occupational name meaning one who grinds grain.

Milo A variation of Miles (see above).

Milt A popular diminutive for Milton (see below). Milt Jackson is a world-famous jazz vibraphonist. Milt Campbell was only 18 years old when he finished second in the 1952 Olympics decathlon competition in Helsinki.

Milton *English:* Dwells in the town near the mill. Appears on Puckett's list "In the Beginning, 1619–1799". Milton Brown is a star forward for the 1992–93 Oklahoma State Cowboys' basketball team.

Mingo An unusual name of unknown origins. Mingo Freeman was a free black patriot of the American Revolutionary War. Rare.

Mitch A diminutive for Mitchell (see below) rarely used as an independent name. Mitch Richmond is an off guard for the Sacramento Kings.

Mitchell *English:* A form of Michael (see above). Mitchell Butler of UCLA's 1992–93 basketball team is a deft ballhandler with great leaping ability.

Moddie An unusual name that appears to be an invention. Scientist Moddie Daniel Taylor served on the University of Chicago's Manhattan Project during WWII.

Mole An unusual name found on Puckett's list "In The Beginning, 1619–1799."

Monk An unusual name found on Puckett's list "In the Beginning, 1619–1799."

Monkieta Monkieta Juan Lucas graduated magna cum laude from Howard University in 1993.

Monroe *Irish:* Dweller at the river's mouth. In 1888, physician Monroe Alpheus Majors became the first African-American to pass the medical examination given by the State Board of California. Monroe Work was an outstanding scholar and researcher during the first decades of this century. Monroe Sharp is a small farmer in Hopkinsville, Ill. *

Montgomery *French:* From the wealthy one's hill castle.

Monti A nickname for Montgomery (see above) occasionally used as an independent name. Monti M. Long is the CEO of one of the top 100 black-owned automobile dealerships.

Mookie An unusual African-American nickname that has gained status as a given name. Its origins are not clear, but its similarity to Mookinga (see below) is striking. Mookie Wilson is a well-known former professional baseball player. Mookie Blaylock is a professional basketball player.

Mookinga This unusual name is listed on Puckett's very early list and apparently has African origins.

Moore *French:* A dark handsome man; from the moors.

Mordecai *Biblical/Hebrew:* Warrior, warlike, derived from the Babylonian mythical Marduk, god of war. Mordecai, cousin of Queen Esther, saved the Jewish people in Persia from extermination. Educator Mordecai Wyatt Walker in 1922 delivered the Harvard commencement address on postwar racism.

Morefield The origins of this name are not clear.

Morgan *Welsh:* He dwells by the white sea.

Morland *English:* Dark-skinned one from the land of the Moors, or from the wildlands. Also Moreland.

Morlon An African-American variation of Morland (see above). Also Morlan. Morlan Wiley is a reserve point guard with the Atlanta Hawks.

Morrell *English:* Dark-complexioned one.

Morris *Latin:* Dark-skinned.

Morrison *English:* Son of Maurice (see above).

Moses *Biblical/Hebrew:* Taken out of the water. Moses obeyed God and led the children of Israel out of Egypt. Moses Gunn is an actor.

Mozell This name is uniquely African-American. Noted sociologist Mozell Hill taught at Langston University in Oklahoma. He finished his career as a college professor at New York University.

Murphy *Irish:* Sea warrior.

Murray *Irish:* Warrior who dwells by the sea.

Myron *Greek:* Fragrant, sweet oil. Myron Bush was the first African-American elected to the City Council in Cincinnati.

Naaman *Biblical/Hebrew:* Honorable, good, pleasant, beautiful. Naaman the leper, the captain of the army of the king of Syria, visited the prophet Elisha and was healed by the Lord. Rare.

Namon The origins of this unusual name are not clear.

Nance *English:* The masculine form of Nancy. Also a surname.

Napoleon *Greek:* Lion from the woodland. *French:* Man from Naples. The exact origins and meaning of this name are in dispute, but those listed here are the most accepted. The name was made famous by Napoleon Bonaparte. In America it is almost exclusively used by black families, although it is falling out of vogue.

Nassau The use of this unusual given name appears from 1877 to 1937.

Nat Diminutives for Nathan (see below) or Nathaniel

(see below). Also Nate. They appear on Puckett's list "In the Beginning, 1619–1799" as given names used by free blacks. Nat "King" Cole was a giant in the entertainment field who rose from a $5-a-night jazz pianist to a $25,000-a-week entertainer. He was the first black host on network TV. His remarkable program ran for nine months without sponsors because advertisers were afraid of negative reactions from Southern customers. He was the father of Natalie Cole.

Nathan *Biblical/Hebrew:* He gave; the prophet who brought the Lord's reprimanding message to King David. Found on Puckett's list of most common names among free blacks in the South from 1800 to 1860, its frequent use has continued until today. Scholar Nathan Huggins was a well-known historian and Harvard University professor of African-American studies. Nathan Hare and his wife, Julia, are well-known sociologists. Nathan Sams, who taught flying at Tuskegee Institute, became the first black to manage an airfield when he took over Hatbox field in Muskogee, Okla. in 1948.

Nathaniel *Biblical/Hebrew:* A gift of God. Listed in Puckett's "Most Common Free Black Names in the South, 1800–1860." The use of Nathaniel by black parents has held steady for well over 100 years. Nathaniel "Nate" Singleton was a star wingback for the 1991–92 Grambling Tigers. Nathaniel "Sweetwater" Clifton was the first black in the NBA. Nathaniel R. Goldston III is the CEO of The Gourmet Co., the nation's 30th largest black-owned service company. Many distinguished African-American men answer to Nathaniel.

Naulbert A rare name that may well be an African-American original, found on Puckett's list of unusual names.

Navora Navora Bacon was a key linebacker on the Grambling Tigers 1992–93 football team.

Nayland *English:* Dweller at the island. Rare.

Nead This unusual name of obscure origins is first noted in 1800–60. It is perhaps an alternate spelling of Ned (see below).

Neal *Irish:* Chief, champion. Also Neil.

Ned This diminutive for Edward (see above) or Edmond (see above) implies wealth. It has been used as an independent name for several centuries now. Ned Fields and Ned Freeman were free black patriots who fought in the American Revolution.

Needham An unusual name that may well be an African-American linguistic invention. Needham Roberts, a volunteer from Harlem, fought in WWI in the 15th New York Infantry, better known as the Hell Fighters. Along with Henry Johnson, he was awarded the Croix de Guerre for bravery in WWI by the French government.

Neeley A variation of Neal (see above). Also Neely. Neely Fuller Jr. is a sociologist and Pan-African theorist.

Nehemiah *Biblical/Hebrew:* God comforts. This is an Old Testament prophet's name that was quite popular among the Puritans, but has been used in this century almost exclusively by black families. Nehemiah Pitts is a music promoter and cultural maven.

Nelson *Irish:* Son of Neal (see above). A common given name used by black parents by the turn of the century.

Nemroy An unusual name of obscure origins.

Neptune *Latin:* Roman god of the sea. Found among free blacks in 17th century. Rare today.

Nero *Latin:* Strong, stern. This name is best known for the demented emperor who fiddled while Rome burned.

Nesbit *English:* Dweller at the bend in the road. Rare.

Nestor *Greek:* Wise elder. Rare.

Nevalon Nevalon Mitchell Jr. is deputy chaplain at Fort Sill, Okla.

Newbold *English:* Dweller from the town by the tree or from the new building. More common as a surname.

Newell *French:* A form of Noel (see below) most often

used as a surname but sometimes used as a given name. Also English place name. "From the manor."

Newman *English:* A new man; a surname sometimes used as a first name.

Newport This name of a city in Rhode Island is found among free blacks from 1800 to 1860.

Newton *English:* Dweller from the new estate or new town.

Nicholas *Greek:* The victorious one. Also Nichols, Nickolas, Nickolaus.

Nick Nickname for Nicholas (see above) rarely used as an independent name. Also Nicky, Nickey.

Nigel *Irish:* Champion. Sometimes used by African-American parents of West Indian descent who come from former British colonies such as Barbados. Nigel Hodges is a guard on the Alabama-Birmingham Blazers 1992–93 basketball team.

Niles Son of Neal (see above). Also Nyles.

Nimrod *Biblical/Hebrew:* Rebel. Found in the 19th century. If in use today, rare.

Nisom This name found on Puckett's list of unusual names sounds like an African-American creation.

Noah *Biblical/Hebrew:* Rest, peace, long-lived. Noah Watson Moore Jr. was elected a Methodist bishop in 1960. Noah Brown Jr. is a noted community activist and teacher in Detroit.

Noble *Latin:* An aristocrat. Noble Sissle was a lyricist, actor, and bandleader who gave Lena Horne her first job on the road.

Noel *French:* Christmas. The use of this name for boys remains consistent but not widespread.

Nolan *Irish:* Renowned, famous. Also Noland, Nolen. Nolan Richardson is the first black head coach of the Arkansas Razorbacks.

Norbert *German:* Shining one from the North. In 1846,

Norbert Rilleux revolutionized the sugar-refining process when he invented a vacuum pan evaporator.

Norman *English/French:* Man of the North. Gained popularity after WWI, but recently its use has fallen off. Norman Leroy McGhee is a prominent lawyer in the Cleveland area.

Norris *Scottish:* One from the North.

Northcliff *English:* Dweller at the north cliff. Rare.

Northrop *English:* From the north farm. Rare.

Norton *English:* Dweller in the north town. Occasionally used by black parents.

Norval *English:* From the north valley.

Norvell *English:* From the north estate. Also Norvill.

Norwell *English:* Dweller at the northern well.

Norwood *English:* From the woods in the north.

Nunnelly Cited among unusual names, 1800–60, on Puckett's list.

Oakley *English:* From the field of oak trees. Also Oakleigh.

Obadiah *Hebrew:* Servant of God. Also Obediah. Appears on Puckett's list of free black names, 1800–60. The use of this given name for boys remained a common practice, particularly among southern blacks, well into the 20th century.

Obert   *German:* Brilliant, wealthy.

Obie   This diminutive for Obadiah (see above), which first appears on Puckett's 1877–1937 list, is remarkably similar to the Nigerian Ibo Obi. Singer Obie Benson was one of the original Four Tops.

Octave   A variation of Octavius (see below). From 1866 to 1877, Octave Rey was a police captain in New Orleans. He was famous for his prodigious memory; he knew the name of every person in the city. When he died in 1902, the white city fathers gave him a public funeral, a most extraordinary event for an African-American in the South in those days.

Octavius   *Latin:* The eighth-born child.

Oddia   An unusual name of uncertain origins, 1877–1937. Also Oddias, Oddis.

Odell   *Scandinavian:* Wealthy one.

Odie   A diminutive for Odell (see above). Also Odey. Odie C. Donald, as president of Bell South Mobility, a cellular company, is one of the nation's top 40 black executives affiliated with a nonminority corporation.

Oliver   *Scandinavian:* Kind, affectionate. *French:* From the olive tree grove. This name has been in frequent use since the turn of the century. Oliver Miller is a forward and center for the Phoenix Suns.

Olivier   The French form of Oliver (see above). Olivier Stephenson is a New York City journalist.

Ollie   This diminutive for Oliver (see above) is sometimes used as an independent name. Reverend Ollie Wells is a well-known pastor in the Harlem community. His ministry pays special attention to the needs of children.

Olphin   This unusual name is found on Puckett's list of free black names, 1800–60.

Onando   This unusual name noted in the 1800s may be an African-American variation of Orlando (see below), or of the Spanish Ordando.

Orange This rare use of the name of a fruit as a given name appears in Puckett's index of unusual names.

Ordaway An African-American variation of Ordway (see below).

Ordell In all probability this name is an African-American variation of Odell (see above).

Ordway *English:* Warrior with a spear.

Orenthal Orenthal James "O.J." Simpson, now the star of Hertz Rent a Car commercials, was a winner of the prestigious Heisman Trophy while in college. As a professional football player with the Buffalo Bills, O.J. bettered Jim Brown's single season rushing record.

Orford *English:* From the cattle ford.

Orion *Greek:* Son of fire and light. The Orion constellation contains three of the brightest stars in the heavens. Rare.

Orlando The Spanish and Italian form of Roland (see below). Orlando Woolridge is a star power forward for the Detroit Pistons.

Orlee Orlee Smith was the father of the famous journalist and civil rights activist Daisy Bates.

Ormond *Irish:* Red. *English:* Man of the sea. *Scandinavian:* Serpent, symbol of immortality. Also Ormonde, Orman, Ormand.

Ornell An African-American variation of Arnall (see above).

Ornette *Hebrew:* Light, cedar tree. Saxophonist and composer Ornette Coleman is world-famous for his unorthodox and abstract treatment of jazz.

Orrin *Hebrew:* Pine tree. *Irish:* Pale-skinned. Also Orin, Orren, Oren, Oran. Orrin Cromwell Evans was an outstanding journalist who became city editor for the *Philadelphia Tribune.* Saxist Oran Coltrane is the son of the immortal jazz artist John Coltrane.

Orscinio An African-American variation. Orscinio Brown is a high school basketball player of some distinction. He scored 19 points in the New York Public School Athletic League Tournament in 1993.

Orson   *English:* Son of the spearman. *French:* Little bear.

Orton   *English:* Dweller in the town by the shore.

Orvall   *English:* Strong as a spear. Also Orval.

Orville   *French:* From the golden estate or town.

Orvin   *English:* Courageous friend.

Orzell   This unusual name pulsates with the sounds of an African-American linguistic blend. Orzell Billingsley Jr. was a noted civil rights lawyer in Birmingham, Ala. He led the move to incorporate black municipalities.

Osborn   *German:* Divinely strong. Also Osborne. Osborn Perry Anderson, a free black who was a printer by trade, was one of five blacks in the small band of followers of abolitionist John Brown, who tried to capture the U.S. arsenal at Harpers Ferry, Va. Anderson went on to fight on the side of the Union in the Civil War.

Oscar   *Scottish:* Warrior. Oscar Robertson was the NBA Most Valuable Player in 1964. He is now CEO of one of the nation's top 100 black-owned companies. Producer and director Oscar Micheaux pioneered black filmmaking.

Osceola   Osceola was a leader of the Native American Seminole people. The name is found on Puckett's list of unusual names.

Osiah   This name appears to be a spelling variation of Isaiah (see above). Osiah Johnson was a coach for the Grambling Tigers in the mid-1930s.

Osman   *English:* Protected of God.

Osmond   *Scandinavian:* God's friend. Also Osmin, Osmund, Oswin. Rare.

Ossie   A diminutive for names beginning with Os, sometimes used as a given name. Actor Ossie Davis is perhaps our most prominent bearer of this name.

Oswald   *German:* Of divine power. Given its negative association with the assassination of President Kennedy, this name has fallen into disfavor.

Otey An unusual name that is probably an African-American creation. Otey Matthew Scruggs is a historian and educator.

Otha From the German Otto (see below), which means prosperous. Also Otho. This name fell into disfavor around the turn of the century because of the aggressive German armies assembled by Otto von Bismarck.

Othello The male lead in a Shakespearean play of the same name. Also Othela. Othela Harrington, a freshman center for the 1992–93 Georgetown Hoyas, is one of the five best players in his class.

Otis *Greek:* Of keen hearing. Also Ottis. This name has been in regular use by black parents for over 100 years. Otis Redding was well-loved for his progressive renditions of popular blues tunes. Otis Thorpe is a power forward for the Houston Rockets. Otis B. Young became the first black pilot to fly the 747 jumbo jet when in 1970 he flew the Pan Am World Airways inaugural nonstop flight between London and Los Angeles. Running back Ottis Anderson of the New York Giants won the MVP award for his spectacular performance in the 1991 Super Bowl.

Otto *German:* Prosperous.

Overn From Puckett's index of unusual names.

Overton *English:* From the upper town.

Owen *Welsh:* Wellborn. Owen Dodson was the author of many poems and plays.

Oxey This diminutive for Oxford (see below) is found as a given name on Puckett's 1800–60 list.

Oxford *English:* Where the ox cross the stream.

Ozell This name is apparently an African-American creation. Ozell Bonds is an educator and entrepreneur.

Ozzie A diminutive for Oswald (see above) that is sometimes used as a given name. Shortstop Ozzie Smith of the St. Louis Cardinals is a perennial All-Star.

Pace   This rare use of a word meaning rate of movement as a given name occurs in the 1700s. There is some evidence of its use by black parents as a boy's name in the 20th century. Rare.

Paddy   *Irish:* This nickname for Patrick (see below) is rarely used as a given name. However, it showed up in *Black Names in America.*

Palmer   *Latin:* Palm bearer, one who makes a pilgrimage carrying a palm.

Paraway   The origins and meaning of this unusual name are unknown.

Paris   *French:* The capital city of France. Also Parris. In Greek mythology, Paris was the prince of Troy whose love for Helen led to the Trojan Wars. Paris was first noted among blacks in 1877. This name remains a favorite boy's name among black parents. In white families it is used infrequently, and then only for girls.

Park   *English:* Dweller in the park or enclosed woodland. Also Parke.

Parker   *English:* One who keeps the park, forest ranger; a surname that is sometimes employed as a given name. Rare.

Parlan   *Scottish:* A farmer, son of the earth.

Parlett An African-American original. Parlett Longworth Moore dedicated his entire career as a high school principal and college professor to the education of African-Americans.

Parma The origins of this unusual name are unknown. It appears on Puckett's list of 1800–60.

Parnell *French:* Little Peter (see below). Also, Parnal, Parrnell, Pernel, Pernell. This name has been frequently chosen by black parents over several generations.

Parren This unusual name is quite likely an African-American linguistic blend. Representative Parren Mitchell was the first black congressman elected from Maryland's Seventh District.

Parry *Welsh:* Son of Harry (see above).

Parson *English:* A minister who heads a parish.

Paschal *Hebrew:* Born at Passover or Easter. Also Pascal.

Patrick *Latin:* Noble one. First noted in the 1800s, Patrick enjoys popularity today. Patrick Ewing is the superstar center for the New York Knicks basketball team. Patrick L. Beauchamp is the CEO of Beauchamp Distributing Co., one of the top 100 black-owned companies.

Patterson Surname rarely used as a given name.

Paul *Latin:* Little. Paul the apostle of Jesus Christ wrote 14 of the books of the New Testament. This enormously popular name first appears among free blacks in the 1700s. The oustanding architect Paul R. Williams is internationally distinguished for designing some of California's most beautiful mansions. Concert singer Paul Robeson was the first black actor to play Othello on the American stage. A genuine Renaissance man, he spoke all the modern European languages, read in 20 others including Chinese, acted in films, held a law degree, and was a star athlete. He was also a champion of human rights. Poet Paul Laurence Dunbar was the first black writer to achieve national recognition.

Pawley This nickname for Paul (see above) is infrequently used as a given name.

Paxton *German:* An itinerant trader who carries packs of goods. *Latin:* Town of peace.

Payne *Latin:* One from the country. Also Paine.

Payton *English:* Dweller at the fighter's estate. Also Peyton.

Pearce *French:* Rock, stone; an early form of Peter (see below). Also Pierce.

Pedro *Spanish/Portuguese/Greek:* Rock, character as strong as a rock; a form of Peter (see below). Pedro Alonzo Nino was the navigator on the *Niña,* one of Columbus's three ships.

Pelham *English:* From Peola's residence; the surname of a distinguished English family. *Latin:* From the pellis (the skin of a fur-bearing animal), thus a dweller in a town with a tannery. Pelham C. Williams is the CEO of Williams-Russell and Johnson, Inc., one of the top 100 black-owned businesses.

Pelton *English:* From an estate by a pool.

Penrod *German:* Famous commander.

Percival *French:* Stalwart one. Also Perceval. Sir Percival was a knight of King Arthur's Round Table who sought the Holy Grail. Some historians consider him the legendary Black Knight, and of African descent.

Percy A diminutive for Percival (see above) also used as an independent name. It first appears on Puckett's 1887–1937 list. Neglected by white parents, its use among black parents has sustained. The well-known businessman and politician Percy Sutton is considered a pillar of the Harlem community.

Perrin *French:* Little Peter (see below). Also Perren, Perryn. Used infrequently by black parents.

Perry *English:* Wanderer. Following a distinguished career as editor, state legislator, lawyer, and judge, Perry

B. Jackson became judge emeritus of the Cuyahoga County Common Pleas Court in Cleveland.

Pervis *Latin:* Through the way. Also Purvis. In the 1986 NCAA Division I Championship game, Purvis Ellison was the most outstanding player.

Pete A diminutive for Peter (see below), infrequently used as a given name.

Peter *Greek:* Rock, stone. Peter was the disciple Jesus was referring to when He said, "Upon this rock I shall build my church." As a first-century preacher, Peter spread the Gospel far and wide. Peter has been immensely popular as a boy's name for several centuries. Seven men with the given name Peter were among the Second Company of the Fourth Regiment who fought in the American Revolution.

Pettus An unusual name of unknown origins found on Puckett's list. One source says it is a variation of Peter (see above). Also Pettis.

Pharoah The title of the rulers of ancient Egypt. Also Pharaoh. This name first appears on Puckett's 1800–60 list. Its use is very rare. Pharoah Saunders is a jazz saxophonist who often performed with John Coltrane.

Phil A nickname for Phillip (see below) rarely used as a given name.

Philander *Greek:* Fond of men. Rare.

Philandus This name appears to be an African-American variation of Philander (see above). It first appears on Puckett's list of unusual names, 1877–1937.

Philbert *German:* Illustriously brilliant. Also Filbert. Philbert X, the brother of Malcolm X, is a Muslim minister in Michigan.

Philemon *Greek:* Affectionate.

Phillip *Greek:* A lover of horses. Phillip was one of the twelve apostles of Christ. The name first appears on Puckett's 1700–1800 list, and it retains a regular use. Phillip G. Price is the CEO of Red Bluff Ford-Mercury,

Inc., one of the top 100 black-owned automobile dealer-ships.

Philo *Greek:* Loving. Philo Freeman and Philo Phillips were free black patriots who fought in the American Revolution. Philo is rare today.

Phineas The meaning of this name is disputed. One source says it comes from the Egyptian and means dark-skinned, while others claim it means a mouth of brass. Some say its origins are Hebrew, and it means oracle. Its use is extremely rare. Phineas Strong was a free black patriot who fought in the American Revolution. Phinease Newborn was a popular jazz pianist.

Pierre A French form of Peter (see above). Rare. During the 1870s, Pierre Cazenave, an undertaker in New Orleans, developed a method of embalming so perfect that it was compared to the secret formulas of the ancient Egyptians; he never revealed his secret. Pierre Sutton replaced his father, Percy, as the CEO of Inner City Broadcasting Corp., the 45th largest black-owned company in the country.

Plato *Greek:* Broad-shouldered. Plato, the great Greek philosopher, was a student of Socrates. Its use as a given name is extremely rare. Plato Alderson, a free black patriot, served the cause of democracy fighting in the American Revolution.

Pluria Pluria Marshall heads the National Black Media Coalition in Washington, D.C.

Polidore An extraordinarily unusual name of unknown origins, but pol comes from the Greek and means a crown. Also Polydore. The names were found on Puckett's 1800–64 list. There is no evidence of the use of this name today.

Pomp A diminutive for Pompey (see below.) Three black patriots who served in the American Revolution answered to this first name.

Pompey *Latin:* A tendril, young shoot. Pompey first appears on Puckett's 1800–60 list of most common given names in the South. Its use today is rare.

Porter *Latin:* The gatekeeper; a surname is sometimes used as a given name. Porter Grainger was an actor and writer during the Harlem Renaissance. Porter Troupe is the son of writer Quincy Troupe.

Powell *Welsh:* Son of Howell (see above). This name is most often seen as a surname.

Prentice *English:* A learner, apprentice. Also Prentiss.

Prescott *English:* One from the priest's dwelling. Infrequently used.

Preston *English:* From the priest's settlement. In 1961, Preston Powell of the Grambling Tigers was the Seventh-round draft choice of the Cleveland Browns football team.

Prezell An African-American original. Prezell Robinson is a sociologist and educator.

Price *English:* Value. Most often seen as a surname, but infrequently as a given name.

Primus The origins of this unusual name are not known. Primus Rhodes was a free black patriot who fought in the American Revolutionary War. Primus Lew was a musician in the colonial army prior to the revolution.

Prince This name that indicates royalty has been enormously popular among black Americans for centuries. Nine free black patriots who served in the American Revolution had this first name. In the latter half of the 20th century, its popularity as a boy's name has begun to diminish. Historian Prince Edward Wilson is a well-known educator. Singer/entertainer Prince is a superstar.

Produs *English:* To be proud.

Psrial This most unusual invention was found in the 1920 census records.

Purnal *English:* From the pear tree grove.

Purvus *French:* To provide food.

Putnam *Latin:* A gardener.

Q

Qadeer   This represents an African-American spelling of the Arabic Quaadir, which means powerful, mighty, capable. Also Quadeer.

Quade   *Irish:* A variation of McQuade, a surname.

Quash   Noted in Puckett's list "In the Beginning: 1619–1799."

Quennel   *French:* Dweller at the little oak tree.

Quentin   *Latin:* Fifth child. Also Quintin, Quinton.

Quillan   *Irish:* Little cub. Also Quillon. Rare.

Quinby   *Scandinavian:* Dweller at the woman's estate. Most often used by West Indian parents.

Quince   A variation of Quincy (see below).

Quincy   *French:* From the fifth son's estate. Poet and college professor Quincy Troupe is the coauthor of Miles Davis's autobiography. Quincy Jones is an award-winning composer and arranger.

Quinland   The origins of this name are not known. Quinland Gordon, an Episcopal priest, was named dean of the Absalom Jones Theological Center in Atlanta.

Quinn   *Irish:* Wise. Former Boston Celtic Quinn Buckner is the head coach of the Dallas Mavericks.

Quintos   Documented on Puckett's 1800–64 list.

Radcliff *English:* From the red cliff. Also Radcliffe.

Radford *English:* From the red ford.

Rafael (rah fah EL) *Hebrew:* God has healed. Also Raphael. The choice of this name by black parents is in a recent surge. Rafael Addison is a short forward for the New Jersey Nets.

Rafe A short form of Rafael (see above), noted on Puckett's 1919–37 list.

Rafer An African-American variation of Rafael (see above). In 1960, Rafer Johnson won an Olympic Gold Medal for his performance in the decathlon competition.

Ragis An unusual name noted on Puckett's 1800–60 list.

Rainey Perhaps a variation on the German Rainer, which means counsel. It appears on Puckett's 1937 list.

Raleigh *English:* Dweller at the meadow of the roe deer. Also Rawley.

Ralph *English:* Wolf counsel. While its popularity among white parents trailed off early in the 20th century, its use has remained steady among black parents. Reverend Ralph Abernathy was one of Martin Luther King's closest advisers. He replaced him as the president of the Southern Christian Leadership Conference. Ralph J. Bunche was the first black to receive the Nobel Peace Prize. Until his death, Ralph Cooper was the producer of the Apollo's famed amateur night.

Ralston   *English:* From Ralph's estate.

Ramon   *Spanish:* Mighty protector; a form of Raymond (see below).

Ramsey   *English:* Dweller on the ram's island.

Ramson   *Latin:* To redeem.

Rance   *French:* A type of marble.

Rand   A diminutive for Randall (see below) infrequently used as a given name.

Randall   A form of Randolph (see below). Also Randal, Randell. As executive director of TransAfrica, Randall Robinson is a leader in the anti-apartheid movement. Randall Cunningham is quarterback for the Philadelphia Eagles.

Randolph   *English:* Wolf shield. Wolf refers to courage or the courageous.

Randy   A nickname for Randolph (see above) occasionally used as a given name. Randy White is a forward for the Dallas Mavericks.

Ransford   *English:* From the raven's ford.

Raoul   A French form of Ralph (see above). Rare.

Ravell   The origins of this name may lie in African-American linguistic inventions.

Raven   *English:* A large bird from the crow family. Rare.

Rawley   This form of Raleigh (see above) appears in Puckett's 1700–1800 list.

Rawlins   *French:* Son of wolf counsel; a surname derived from Roland (see below) sometimes used as an independent name.

Ray   *French:* An honored title. *English:* A diminutive for names beginning with Ray. In 1951, boxing great Sugar Ray Robinson defeated Jake LaMotta to win the middleweight championship of the world.

Rayburn   *English:* From the roe deer brook. Also Reyburn, Raybourne.

Rayford   *English:* The ford over the stream. Also Raford.

Raymond *German:* Mighty or wise protector. Also Raymund. Raymond has enjoyed a good deal of popularity until quite recently. Philadelphia lawyer Raymond Pace Alexander established a fine reputation for his civil and criminal trial practice.

Rean Rean Graves was editor of the *Baltimore Afro-American* at the peak of the Harlem Renaissance.

Reavo The origins of this unusual name are not known. Reavo Braxton says his mother heard the name in *Aloma of the South Seas,* a 1941 Paramount film.

Reece *Welsh:* Ardent, fiery. Also Reese, Reis.

Reed *English:* The red-haired one. Also Read, Reid.

Reeve *English:* Steward.

Reggie A nickname for Reginald (see below) infrequently employed as an independent name. Reggie Miller is an off guard for the Indiana Pacers.

Reginald *English/German:* Judicious, wise counselor, mighty and powerful ruler. Reginald Lewis, who died in 1993, initiated the largest leveraged buyout ever accomplished by a black man and become a billionaire. Reginald Durham was valedictorian of his Automotive High School graduating class of 1993. Reginald "Reggie" Jackson is a member of baseball's Hall of Fame.

Remington *English:* Dweller at the estate of the raven family.

Remy A diminutive for Remington (see above) infrequently used as a given name.

Renaldo The Scottish form of Reginald (see above).

Rene *French:* To rise again, to be reborn. Found principally among African-Americans from the French-speaking Caribbean. Rene John-Sandy is the founder and publisher of *Class* magazine.

Renfred *English:* Mighty peacemaker.

Renil Noted in 1937.

Renny *Irish:* Little, but mighty and powerful. Renny Freeman is a social activist and counselor in Detroit.

Renzo A diminutive for Lorenzo (see above) rarely used as a given name.

Reuben *Hebrew:* Behold, a son. Also Ruben. The use of this name by free blacks first appears on Puckett's 1700–1800 list. Its use has held steady ever since.

Rex *Latin:* King. Rare. Actor Rex Ingram portrayed a number of significant roles during his long Hollywood career, including De Lawd in *Green Pastures.*

Rexford *English:* The king's ford.

Reynard *French/German:* Mighty, brave fox. Also Rennard.

Reynolds A form of Reginald (see above).

Rias An African-American variation of the Welsh Rhys, which means ardent or fiery. It appears on Puckett's 1937 list.

Rice Noted by Puckett.

Rich A diminutive for Richmond (see below) or Richard (see below).

Richard *German/English/French:* Powerful king. For centuries, this name has been an enormously popular choice. Four men named Richard were among the free black patriots who fought in the American Revolution. Very recently, because of the quest for unique, extraordinary names, the use of Richard has fallen off slightly. The esteemed novelist Richard Wright is one of our most famous Richards. He is the author of *Black Boy* and *Native Son,* required reading in many schools. Richard Greene was the first black chancellor of New York City Public Schools. Richard Allen was a founder of the African American Episcopal Church. Comedian and actor Richard Pryor is world-renowned for his comedic genius.

Richie A diminutive for names beginning with Rich. Richie Havens is an activist and sought-after folksinger.

Richman *English:* A powerful man.

Richmond *German:* Powerful protector. Richmond Barthe was a prominent sculptor.

Ricky A nickname for Richard (see above) that is occasionally used as a given name. Also Rickey. In 1990, Rickey Henderson was the American League's Most Valuable Player. In 1991, he broke Lou Brock's record for career stolen bases.

Riddick An African-American original. In 1991, Riddick Bowe defeated Evander Holyfield to become heavyweight champion of the world.

Riddock *Irish:* From the smooth road.

Riley *Irish:* Courageous.

Riordan *Irish:* The king's poet.

Rivington *English:* Dweller in the town near the brook.

Roarke *Irish:* Famous king.

Robert *English:* Bright with fame. Robert first appears on Puckett's 1700–1800 list. It has remained eminently popular until the recent craze for the unusual. Author Robert L. Allen is senior editor of the *Black Scholar.* Robert Smalls was a pilot on the armed Confederate steamer the *Planter.* He took the boat and fled into the Union lines. At over 38 years of age, Robert Parrish of the Boston Celtics is currently the oldest starter in the NBA.

Robin This form of Robert (see above) is now more often used for girls. Robin Harper is a gifted painter.

Roby A short form of Robert (see above), noted among free black names, 1800–64.

Rock *English:* Dweller from the rock. Also Roc. Rare.

Rocquieth Rocquieth Jackson is an artist who works in oils.

Rodman *German:* Famous man. *English:* One who clears the land. Rare.

Rodney *German/English:* From the famous one's island. Rodney Monroe is an off guard for the Atlanta Hawks. Rodney Rogers, a power forward for the Wake Forest

Demon Deacons 1991–92 team, is one of Dick Vitale's Colossal Collegians.

Roger *German:* Famous spearman. Also Rodger. Roger Craig has been a dependable running back in the NFL for several years. Roger Wilkins is an author and political consultant.

Rohan Newly created. Rohan Williamson is a member of the Little Rock Missionary Baptist Church in Detroit.

Roland *German:* From the famous estate. Also Rowland. Concert singer Roland Hayes, a former member of the fabled Fisk Jubilee Singers, sang in concert halls around the world and was the first black to sing before racially mixed audiences in the South.

Rollie A diminutive for Roland (see above) sometimes used as an independent name. Also Rolly.

Rollin A form of Roland (see above).

Roman *Latin:* Man from Rome. Roman is first noticed as a free black given name on Puckett's 1800–60 list. It has experienced good use since. Roman Jones-Bey is a masseur.

Romare (ro MARE) The exact origins of this name are not known, but it appears to come from the French. The paintings and collages of Romare Bearden are treasured around the globe.

Romeo *Italian:* Pilgrim to Rome; best known as the hero of Shakespeare's Romeo and Juliet. Rare.

Rommel This last name of a famous WWII German general is noted by Puckett, 1877–1937. Also Rummel, Rummeal.

Romolo *Italian:* A Roman. Rare.

Ron A diminutive for Ronald (see below) infrequently used as a first name. Ron Anderson is a swing man for the Philadelphia 76ers.

Ronald *German:* Mighty, powerful; a contraction of Reginald (see above). For the better part of the 20th century, Ronald has been well-used by black parents. As a vice-president of First Boston, Ronald T. Gault is one of the nation's 25 "hottest blacks on Wall Street."

Roosevelt *Dutch:* From the field of roses. First appearing on Puckett's 1919–37 list, Roosevelt has been often used by black parents. Roosevelt "Rosey" Grier was voted All-Pro twice while with the New York Giants. Grier was a bodyguard for Robert F. Kennedy at the time of his assassination.

Rory *Scottish:* The red one. Rare. Guard Rory Sparrow was an NBA standout for many years.

Roscoe *Scandinavian:* From the deer woods. Roscoe Brown Jr. is a highly esteemed educator and past president of Bronx Community College in New York.

Ross *Scottish:* Dweller on the peninsula.

Rouse Noted on Puckett's 1877–1937 list.

Rowell *English:* Dweller at the deer spring.

Roy *French:* King. *Irish:* Red. Roy Wilkins, a former newspaperman, became the executive director of the NAACP.

Royal *Latin:* King.

Royce *French/English:* The king's son.

Royd *Scandinavian:* Dweller at the clearing in the forest.

Rozelle Collected by Puckett.

Ruddie *German:* Red.

Rudelle This name rings with the sound of an African-American creation. It first appears on Puckett's 1937 list.

Rudolph *German:* Famous wolf. Also Rodolph.

Rudy A nickname for Rudolph (see above). Rudy Richardson is a clarinetist with a number of top bands.

Ruford *English:* Dweller at the red ford.

Rufus *Latin:* Red-haired. Rufus Callehorn was a free black patriot who fought in the American Revolution. Harlem Renaissance entertainer and actor Rufus

Greenlee toured Russia while still in his teens. Rufus
Thomas is a soul singer.

Rulus   An unusual given name documented by Puckett,
1919–37. It may be a variation of Rufus (see above).

Rupert   A variation of Robert (see above). Educator
Rupert J. Picott served as president of the American
Teachers Association.

Russell   *French:* Red-skinned. Russell Robinson Debow,
III, associate judge of Cook County, Illinois, was an ad-
ministrative assistant to Mayor Richard T. Daley.

Rusty   *French:* Red-haired. Rare.

Rutley   *English:* From the red meadow.

Ryan   *Irish:* Kingly. Ryan Thompson is a promising baseball player for the New York Mets.

Ryas   Noted on Puckett's index of unusual names.

Rylan   *English:* Dweller at the rye farm. Also Ryland.

Ryle   *English:* From the rye hill.

Saba   This name may have African origins. It appears on
Puckett's 1800–64 list.

Sabra   This unusual name appears on Puckett's 1800–64
list.

St. Clair   *French:* A place name in honor of the Saint Clair.
The Anglicized Sinclair is derived from this name. Bibli-
cally, "saint" refers to anyone who accepts Jesus Christ
as his or her personal savior. Thus, all Christians are

saints. St. Clair Drake was an eminent anthropologist. St. Clair Bourne is a talented documentary filmmaker.

Salisbury *English:* From the stronghold.

Salvador *Spanish:* Savior. Also Salvatore, Salvadore.

Sam Diminutive for names such as Samuel (see below), Samson (see below), and Sampton (see below). Also Sammy, Sammie. Sammy Davis Jr., the consummate entertainer, was universally loved for his showmanship. Sam Johnson is the CEO of S&J Enterprises, the fourth largest black-owned automobile dealership in the nation.

Sampson A variation of Samson (see below.) Sampson Cuff was a free black patriot in the American Revolution.

Sampton From Puckett's index of unusual names, 1877–1937.

Samson *Biblical/Hebrew:* Sun. Samson was a warrior and Hebrew judge who lost his strength when Delilah cut his hair. Samson Hazzard was a free black patriot who fought in the American Revolution.

Samuel *Biblical/Hebrew:* His name is of God; a prophet of the Old Testament for whom two books are named. Samuel has been a popular name among African-Americans for several centuries. In 1821, Samuel E. Cornish organized the first black Presbyterian church in New York City. In 1827, with John B. Russwurm, Cornish founded the first black newspaper in the U.S. Samuel Metters is CEO of Metters Industries, Inc., one of the top 100 black industrial companies.

Sanborn *English:* Dweller near the sandy brook.

Sancho *Spanish:* Saint. Rare.

Sanco Noted, 1800–64.

Sandor *Slavic:* He who helps others. Also Sander.

Sandy This diminutive for Alexander (see above) is found as an independent name among free blacks in the nineteenth century. Today, largely taken as a diminutive for Sandra, it is generally used for girls. Sandy Burns was an entertainer who performed widely in vaudeville. But in order for this African-American to get work, he had to appear in blackface.

Sanford *English:* Dweller near the sandy ford. Sanford Wright is a teacher and social scientist.

Sango Just where this unusual name originated is not clear. It may have roots in Africa. It appears among free blacks in the 19th century.

Sanks This unusual name appears on Puckett's 1877–1937 list.

Santana *Spanish:* Saint. Santana Datsun is on the Tampa Bay NFL team.

Santo *Spanish/Italian:* Sacred. This unusual name appears among free blacks of the 18th century.

Sargent *Latin:* A military man. Also Seargent. This name is found among free blacks of the late 19th century. Artist Sargent Johnson celebrated in his work what he described as the "natural beauty of the Afro-American."

Saul *Biblical/Hebrew:* Asked by God; the first king of Israel. This was Paul's name before his conversion to Christianity. Rare.

Schisms An unusual name found among free blacks in the 19th century.

Scipio *Latin:* Scipio was the Roman general who defeated Hannibal in the Second Punic War. Scipio Brown and Scipio Dalton were free black patriots who fought in the American Revolution.

Scott *English:* Dwells in Scotland. Composer Scott Joplin is considered the king of ragtime. Scott Williams is a forward and center for the championship Chicago Bulls.

Scotty Nickname for Scott (see above). Also Scottie. Scottie Pippen is a superstar small forward with the Chicago Bulls and was a member of the 1992 Olympics Dream Team.

Seabert *English:* Glorious, bright hero. Also Sebert.

Seafus Quite likely an African-American original, it first appears on Puckett's 1937 list.

Sean *Irish:* God is good; a variation of John (see above). Also Shawn, Shon, Shaun. Following actor Sean Connery's enormously popular portrayal of Agent 007 in the movies, the use of this name among black parents surged and became widespread. Sean Green is an off guard for the Indiana Pacers. Shawn Burras was quarterback for the 1991–92 Grambling Tigers. Actor Shaun Baker aspires to match his idol, Sammy Davis Jr.

Sear An unusual name found among free blacks in the 18th century. Sear Kimball was a free black patriot of the American Revolution.

Searle *German:* Armed. Also Serle.

Seaton *English:* From the town by the sea. Also Seton.

Sebastian *Greek:* August, revered. Rare.

Sebion Noted in 1877.

Sebold *English:* Bold victory.

Sebron The origins of this unusual name are not known.

Sedale An African-American original. Sedale Threatt, a power guard, is a member of the L.A. Lakers basketball team that nearly upset the favored Phoenix Suns led by Charles Barkley. Sedale's mother says she gave him the name because it sounded pretty.

Sedgewick *English:* Victorious town.

Seeley *English:* Happy, blessed.

Seifred *German:* Peace. Also Seigfred.

Selby *English:* From the manor house.

Seldon *English:* Dweller in the willow tree valley.

Selvin This variation of Selwyn (see below) appears among free black names in the late 19th century. Also Selvyn. Selvyn Michael is vice-president and comptroller of the nation's largest black-owned newspaper, the New York *Amsterdam News.*

Selwyn *English:* Good friend. Selwyn Cudjoe is an accomplished teacher and scholar.

Semaj This name was coined when the parents spelled James backwards. Semaj Wilson is from Detroit.

Semmie This unusual name was noted on Puckett's 1899–1937 list. Also Simmie.

Seneca *Native American/Iroquois:* Standing rock. Seneca Turner, a law school graduate, is a college administrator and poet in New York City.

Sennett *French:* Elderly, wise one. Also Sennet.

Sennie This nickname for Sennett (see above) is found among free black names in 1877.

Sereno *Latin:* Calm, peaceful one.

Serge *Latin:* The attendant. Rare.

Serico The meaning and origins of this unusual name are not known. It appears among free blacks in the 17th century. Serico Collens was a free black patriot who fought in the American Revolution.

Seth *Biblical/Hebrew:* The appointed; the third son of Adam and Eve. Rare. Seth Joyner plays for the Philadelphia Eagles.

Sethard This unusual name is probably of African-American coinage, derived from Seth (see above). As a professor of sociology at the University of California at Santa Barbara, Sethard Fisher wrote numerous articles and scholarly papers on black life in America.

Sewell *German:* Victorious at sea. Also Sewald, Sewall.

Sexton *English:* Church official.

Sextus *Latin:* Sixth son.

Seymour *German:* Victorious at sea.

Shadrack *Biblical:* Meaning unknown; one of three men thrown into the fiery furnace. They maintained their faith in the Lord and survived unharmed.

Sha-keith Sha-keith Mills is a championship sprinter at New York City's McClancy, a Catholic high school.

Shandue Shandue McNeill is a point guard at Archbishop Molloy High School in Queens, N.Y.

Shane This variation of Sean (see above) means the Lord is gracious. Also Shaine, Shayn, Shayne. Shane Oubree was a defensive back for the 1992–93 Grambling Tigers. Shane Mack is an outfielder for the Minnesota Twins.

Shank An unusual name of obscure origins that appears on Puckett's lists.

Shannon *Irish:* Wise. Appearing among male names, 1877–1937, Shannon is used today almost exclusively for girls in white families.

Shaquille An African-American variation on the Arabic. At center, Shaquille O'Neal is the Orlando Magic's superstar. He is affectionately called Shaq by his fans.

Sharp Just where this unusual name originated is not clear. Its use is extremely rare. Sharp Rogers was a free black patriot of the American Revolution. Sharpe James is the mayor of Newark, N.J.

Shaw *English:* From the shady grove.

Shedrich Meaning unknown. This unusual name appears among African-Americans around the turn of the century.

Shedrick This name appears to be of African-American origins. Appearing around World War I, perhaps it is a variation of Cedric. Also Shedric. Shedrick Covert is a student at the College of New Rochelle, School of New Resources.

Sheffield *English:* Dweller near the crooked field.

Shelby *English:* From the estate by the ledge. Shelby Steele is a college professor and author with a neoconservative outlook.

Sheldon *English:* From the protected valley with steep sides. Also Shelden, Sheldin.

Shelley *English:* Dweller at the ledge-meadow.

Shelton   *English:* From the settlement near the high plateau. Shelton "Spike" Lee is our most celebrated filmmaker.

Shep   A nickname for Shepherd (see below). Also Shepp.

Shepherd   *English:* An occupational name for one who tends sheep. Rare.

Sherard   *English:* Brave. This name for boys is growing in popularity.

Sheridan   *Irish:* Wild man. Rare.

Sherley   *English:* A bright clearing. Appearing in the 1800s, this once masculine name is now exclusively used for girls. The common spelling is Shirley.

Sherman   *English:* One who shears the sheep. Sherman W. Smith Jr. became a judge of the Superior Court in Los Angeles in the early 1950s.

Sherwin   *English:* Good friend.

Sherwood   *English:* From the shining forest. Sherwood Forest in England was the home of Robin Hood, who is said to have robbed from the rich to give to the poor.

Shiloh   *Hebrew:* The one to whom it belongs. Rarely used in the 20th century.

Shim   Found among free black males in the early 19th century, this name is probably an African-American spelling of the biblical Shem, which means renown. Shem was one of the three sons of Noah.

Shubael   This name has a decidedly African-American ring. Shubael Johnson was a free black patriot who fought in the American Revolution.

Shubel   This unusual name is found on Puckett's 1800–64 list.

Sias   A name of unknown origins found among free blacks in the early 19th century.

Sibby   This diminutive for Sibley (see below) is found among free black males in the 19th century.

Sibley   *Latin:* Prophetic.

Sid   A nickname for Sidney (see below)

Siddell *English:* From the wide valley.

Sidney *French:* From St. Denis. Also Sydney. This name has been widely used and remains so. In 1964, actor Sidney Poitier became the first African-American to win an Academy Award as Best Actor for his role in *Lilies of the Field.* Displaying a precocious musical talent as a child, Sidney Bechet achieved international fame as a clarinetist and soprano saxophonist. Sydney L. Small is the CEO of American Urban Radio Networks, one of the top 100 black-owned companies.

Sigh Collected on Puckett's 1800–64 list.

Silas A form of Sylvanus (see below). Also Sylas. Silas was a companion of Paul the apostle.

Silax An unusual name of unknown origins.

Simeon *Hebrew:* God heard him. Simeon Golar is an influential jurist in the New York City area.

Simon *Hebrew:* Heard by God. Simon Peter was one of the twelve apostles. This name is found among free blacks in the 17th century. Simon Estes is among the foremost opera singers.

Sims Son of Simon (see below). Also Simms. E. Simms Campbell was an illustrator and cartoonist whose work appeared in such magazines as *Esquire* during and following the Harlem Renaissance. For forty years he was one of the country's most successful cartoonists and illustrators.

Sinclair *Latin:* Illustrious. *French:* From St. Clair.

Sindey This unusual name appears on Puckett's list entitled "In the Beginning, 1619–1799."

Sindred This unusual name is of obscure origins. It appears among free black males in the 18th century.

Sipeo This variation of Scipio (see above) is found among free blacks in the 17th century. Also Sipio.

Siva *Hindi:* Destroyer.

Skeet *English:* The swift one.

Skerry *Scandinavian:* From the rocky island.

Skip *Scandinavian:* Ship's owner. Also Skippy, Skipper.

Slade *English:* Dweller in the valley. Also Slayde.

Sloan *Irish:* Warrior. Also Sloane. Recently, among white families, this name is more often used for girls.

Smith *English:* A worker with a hammer (blacksmith, goldsmith, silversmith); a surname that is sometimes used as a given name.

Socrates *Greek:* The name of the great Greek philosopher. A rare occurrence of this as a given name among black men is recorded in 1919.

Solomon *Biblical/Greek:* This son of David and Bathsheba wrote the Book of Proverbs, Ecclesiastes, and the Song of Solomon.

Sonnie A very popular nickname meaning son or boy that has often been used as a given name. Also Sonny. Sonny Liston was a heavyweight champion of the world until he was defeated by Muhammad Ali. Sonnie Sowtice was a free black patriot who fought in the American Revolution. Sonny Rollins is a well-known jazz saxophonist.

Spalding *English:* From the split meadow.

Spencer *English:* Provider. Also Spence, Spenser. Spencer Williams was a profilic songwriter and arranger.

Spike A popular nickname. Spike Lee is the leading black filmmaker of the day.

Spud A popular nickname for boys for several generations. Spud Webb is a guard for the Sacramento Kings.

Squire *English:* An aide to a knight. Rare.

Stacey *Latin:* Stable, prosperous. Stacey Augmon had a notable career as a college player with UNLV, and his star is rising as a small forward on the Atlanta Hawks basketball team.

Stafford *English:* From the stony road.

Stan A diminutive for Stanley (see below) sometimes used as an independent name.

Stanley *English:* From the stony meadow. First appearing on Puckett's 1937 list, it has been a popular name among black parents for several generations. Acoustic bassist Stanley Clarke reached large audiences playing pop jazz on an electric bass.

Stanton *English:* From the settlement on the stony ground.

Stedman *English:* Farmstead owner, dweller at the farmstead. Also Steadman, Steadmann. Public relations executive Stedman Graham asked Oprah Winfrey to be his wife on October 10, 1992.

Stephen *Greek:* A crown, garland. Stephen was the first Christian martyr. This name continues to be quite popular. Stephen Junius Wright received his Ph.D from New York University in 1943. He was president of Fisk University from 1957 to 1966. Stephen Yelity is the CEO of Accurate Information Systems, Inc., one of the top 100 black-owned service companies.

Sterling *English:* Genuine, of excellent quality. A member of Phi Beta Kappa, Sterling Allan Brown has been called the dean of African-American poets.

Steve A diminutive for Stephen (see above) that is frequently used as a given name. Also Stevie. Musical genius Stevie Wonder enjoys international acclaim for his composing and singing. Born blind as Steveland Judkins in Saginaw, Mich., in 1950, he had his first million-seller at the tender age of 13.

Steven An alternate spelling of Stephen (see above).

Stewart *English:* An administrator.

Stillman *English:* Quiet.

Stinson *English:* Son of Stone.

Stokely The meaning of this English name is uncertain; it may be an occupational name. Student activist and civil rights leader Stokely Carmichael was a leading advocate of black power, a term which he helped popularize.

Stonewall An unusual name noted on Puckett's 1899–1937 list.

Stoney A nickname based on the word stone. Stoney Brooks was for many years a chief aide to Andrew Young.

Stuart An alternate spelling for Stewart (see above).

Suffield *English:* From the south field.

Sullivan *Irish:* Dark eyes.

Sumner *Latin:* Church official. *French:* One who calls people to court.

Sunna The origins of this unusual name are not known.

Sunny A name from nature that is used for both boys and girls.

Sussex An unusual name that appears among free blacks in the 17th century.

Sutton *English:* From the south estate.

Swain *German:* Youth.

Swan This name of a beautiful bird is noted on Puckett's 1800–64 list.

Sweeney *Irish:* Little hero.

Sylvanus *Latin:* Forest dweller. Also Silvanus. This name is found among free black males in the 17th century.

Sylvester *Latin:* From the wooded area. Also Silvester. Sylvester Stewart (Sly Stone) was a soul artist with a huge following in the 1960s and 1970s.

Tab *German:* Shining, brilliant. This name was found among free blacks of the 18th century.

Tabor *Hungarian:* From the fortified camp.

Tack This unusual name is noted in 1899. There is no evidence of its use today.

Tad *Welsh:* Father; an English nickname for Thaddeus. Also Tadd. Pianist Tadd Dameron was considered one of the top composers and arrangers in the 1940s.

Taft *English:* Dweller from the river estate. Taft, Okla. is historically an all-black town. Taft Jordan was a fine singer and trumpeter.

Taggart *Irish:* Son of the prelate.

Tait *Scandinavian:* Cheerful. Also Taite.

Talbot *English:* Bloodhound. *German:* Valley bright. Also Talbert, Tolbert.

Taliaferro The middle name of Booker T. Washington.

Tally A nickname for Talbot (see above). Rare.

Talmadge *English:* From the lake between the towns. Talmadge James is a devoted teacher in Detroit.

Tanton *English:* From the quiet river town.

Tarleton *English:* Thor's town.

Tarrant *Welsh:* Thunder. Also Taran.

Tashambe This unusual name is apparently an African-American variation of the African Tshombe.

Tate   *English:* Cheerful. *Native American:* A great talker. Tate George is a guard for the New Jersey Nets.

Taylor   *English:* An occupational name for a tailor. Taylor Emmanuel Gordon was a popular singer and writer during the Harlem Renaissance. Taylor Segue is a promising young attorney in Detroit.

Teague   *Scottish:* Poet.

Tearle   *English:* Stern one. Also Thearl.

Teasdale   *English:* From the settlement by the river Tees.

Ted   A diminutive for Theodore (see below) and Edward (see above). Also Teddy, Teddie. Ted is occasionally used as an independent name. Bandleader Teddie Hill was a mainstay in Harlem during the 1930s.

Tedmond   *English:* National protector. Also Tedman, Tedmund.

Telford   *French:* Ironworker. *Latin:* A shallow stream.

Tepio   An unusual name of unknown origins found among free blacks in the 17th century.

Terence   *Latin:* Smooth, polished one, tender. Also Terance, Terrence. During the 1991–92 school year, high school basketball star Terrence Rencher won the distinction of "Mr. Basketball" in New York State.

Terrill   *English:* Thunder ruler; from Thor, the mythical Old Norse god of thunder. Also Terrel, Terrell, Tirrell, Tyrell, Tyrelle, Tyrrell. This name is enjoying a burst of popularity among black parents, particularly the spelling Terrell. Terrell Brandon is an off guard with the Cleveland Cavaliers. Terrell Binion is a tax accountant and business consultant in Michigan.

Terris   *English:* Son of Terrill or Terence. Also Terriss.

Terry   A diminutive for Terence (see above). Within the last two decades, the use of Terry as an independent name is widespread among black parents. Terry Dehere of the 1992–93 Seton Hall Pirates basketball team, a senior, was distinguished as one of the top five players in the country in his class. Terry Porter is a star member of the Portland Trailblazers.

Terryal A variation of Terry (see above).

Tevin An African-American variation. Tevin Campbell, a native of Texas, soared onto the music scene in 1990 via the Quincy Jones album "Back on the Block."

Thad A diminutive for Thaddeus (see below).

Thaddeus *Greek:* Gift of God, stouthearted, courageous. *Latin:* He who praises. Also Thadeus. Thaddeus Lot is an innovative educator in Houston. Thaddeus Drayton was an actor during the Harlem Renaissance.

Thadford *English:* From Thaddeus's ford.

Thales An unusual name found among free blacks of the 18th century. Perhaps the name is derived from Thalia, the muse of comedy in Greek mythology.

Tharon *Greek:* Hunter, untamed. Also Theran, Therron, Theron, Theon.

Thatcher *English:* An occupational name referring to one who builds and repairs roofs, roofer. Also Thaxter.

Thayer *German:* From the nation's army.

Theo A diminutive for Theobald (see below) or Theodore (see below).

Theobald *German:* The boldest one. Also Theobold.

Theodore *Greek:* Gift of God. Also Theodor. A common given name among free blacks of the 18th century. Theodore Cable was the first black athlete to win an intercollegiate weight championship. In 1912, he threw the hammer 162′4½″.

Theophilus *Greek:* Beloved of God. Also Theophillus. In the New Testament, Theophilus is the person to whom Luke's Gospel is written. Theophillus Lewis was a drama critic during the Harlem Renaissance.

Theotis Pharmacist Theotis James Holmes is listed among *Ebony*'s 1993 most eligible bachelors.

Thirman An unusual variation of Thurman (see below).

Thirman Milner is an executive for the Food Marketing Institute, the lobbying arm of the nation's food retailers.

Thomas   *Greek:* A twin. This name of one of the twelve apostles appears among free blacks in the 17th century, and has experienced enduring popularity since, until the recent explosion of unusual and newly coined names. Four free black patriots of the American Revolution answered to Thomas. Thomas A. Farrington is CEO of one of the nation's top 100 black-owned companies, Input Output Computer Services, Inc. Thomas Bradley was elected mayor of Los Angeles in 1973.

Thompson   *English:* Son of Tom (see below); a surname infrequently used as a given name. Also Tomson, Thomson.

Thorley   *English:* From the thorn meadow.

Thornton   *English:* Dweller at the thorny estate.

Thorpe   *English:* From the farmhouse.

Thurgood   *English:* Thor is good. Before his appointment as the first black justice on the U.S. Supreme Court, Thurgood Marshall successfully argued many cases before the highest court in the land. His most famous case was *Brown v. Board of Education,* which struck down the nation's school segregation laws.

Thurlow   *English:* From Thor's hill.

Thurman   *English:* Protected by Thor, the Norse god of war and thunder. Also Thormond, Thurmon, Thurmond, Thurmund. The Thurman spelling of this name is perhaps the most popular among black Americans. Thurman Thomas is a key ingredient in the Buffalo Bills running game.

Thurston   *Scandinavian:* Thor's stone. Also Thurstan.

Tibe   An unusual name of unknown origins found among free blacks in the 18th century.

Tilden   *English:* Dweller in the fertile valley.

Tilford   *English:* From the fertile ford.

Tilton   *English:* From the good one's estate.

Tim   Diminutive for Timothy (see below). Also Timmy, Timmie. Occasionally Tim is used as an independent name. Comedian Tim Moore is best known as the Kingfish in the television version of "Amos and Andy." Tim Perry is a forward for the Philadelphia 76ers.

Timothy   *Greek:* He who honors God. Reverend Timothy Mitchell is the pastor of Ebenezer Baptist Church in Flushing, N.Y.

Tingo   The origins and meaning of this unusual name are not known. It is found among free blacks in the 18th century.

Tinsley   *English:* From the fortified meadow.

Tip   A nickname for Thomas.

Titus   Many sources connect the name to Greek mythology and the titans, who were great, powerful giants. Others claim that the meaning of the name is unknown. Titus was a missionary to whom Paul addressed a letter that is now a part of the New Testament. Black parents have used the name for several generations. Since the 1950s, however, its use has tailed off.

Tobias   *Hebrew:* The Lord is good. Tobias appears as a common given name among free blacks in the 18th century.

Toby   A diminutive for Tobias (see above). Also Tobey. Toby appears among free black names in the 17th century.

Todd   *Scottish:* Clever, wily. Also Tod. Todd Burroughs is an emerging journalist.

Toland   *English:* From the taxed land.

Tom   This diminutive for Thomas (see above) has been popular among African-American parents as an independent name since the 17th century. Tom Lemonier was a composer during the Harlem Renaissance. Tom Hammonds is a forward with the Charlotte Hornets.

Tommy   A nickname for Thomas. Also Tommie, Tomie. After winning the 200-meter Gold Medal in the 1968

Olympics in Mexico, Tommie Smith, on the ceremony pedestal, raised his fist in defiance, expressing his support for black power.

Tone   Singer Tone Loc scored several top-selling singles before making his big screen debut in *Posse*.

Tony   In the last quarter of this century, this diminutive for Anthony (see above) has become a common given name. Also Toney. A review of the basketball teams in all the major college conferences, such as the Big Ten and the Big East, reveals at least one African-American player per team with the name Tony. Tony Bennett is a power guard for the Charlotte Hornets.

Tooler   An unusual name of unknown origins that may well be an occupational name. It appears among free blacks during the 17th century.

Torbert *English:* From the bright hill.

Torin *Irish:* Chief.

Torrance *Irish:* From the knolls or little hills. Also Torrence.

Tory   A nickname for Torrance (see above). Also Torrey, Torin.

Toussaint   The name of the great Haitian revolutionary, Toussaint L'Ouverture, whose tactics drained Napoleon's army. In 1923, Toussaint Tourgee Tildon, a psychiatrist, was one of the first African-American physicians on the staff of the Veterans Hospital in Tuskegee, Ala.

Tower   The origin of this name is unknown. It appears among free blacks in the 18th century.

Townly *English:* Dweller in the town meadow. Also Townley, Townlee. This name first appears among free blacks in the 17th century.

Townsend *English:* Dweller at the town's end.

Tracy *Greek:* The harvester. *English:* Courageous. Also Tracey. Since the 1960s, Tracy has become quite a fashionable name among black parents. Tracy Maitland, a

Merrill Lynch vice-president, is a top producer in convertible bond sales worldwide.

Travis *English:* Dweller at the crossroads. Also Travers, Travus. This name has gained in popularity over the last two decades. Travis Knight was a freshman member of the University of Connecticut Huskies 1992–93 basketball team. Travis Mays is a guard with the Atlanta Hawks.

Trayton The origin of this name is unknown.

Tredway *English:* Mighty warrior.

Tremain *Irish:* Dweller in the stony town. Also Tremayne, Tramaine, Tremaine. This name is experiencing a recent burst of popularity. Tremaine Hawkins is a noted gospel singer.

Trent *Latin:* The rapid stream. *English:* A river in England. Also Trenton. Trent Tucker is an off guard for the NBA champion Chicago Bulls.

Trevin *Welsh:* From the fair town.

Trevor *Irish:* Prudent, discreet, wise. *Welsh:* From the large estate.

Trey *English:* Third-born. The use of this given name among black parents is a recent trend. Its use probably has to do with its attractive sound and its unusualness. Trey Ellis is a young avant-garde writer.

Troy *Irish:* Soldier. *French:* From the place of curly-haired people. Also Troyes, Troi. Troy was the Greek city where the Trojan Wars were fought.

True A diminutive of Truesdale (see below). The use of this unusual name by black parents probably has little to do with any relationship to Truesdale and more to do with the desire to give children unusual and distinctive names that demonstrate their importance to us, or our hopes for their lives in an all too often hostile environment. The use of True as a given name has diminished considerably in the latter half of the 20th century.

Truesdale *English:* Dweller at the beloved ones' estate.

Truett   *English:* True.

Truman   *English:* A faithful or loyal man.

Tucker   *English:* He tucks or pleats the cloth; an occupational name most often seen as a surname, but occasionally as a first name.

Tudeus   Perhaps this unusual name represents an African-American variation of Tydeus, who in Greek mythology is the father of Diomedes and one of the heroes who helped recover the throne of Thebes.

Tui   An unusual name of obscure origins found among free blacks in the 18th century. There is no evidence of its use today.

Tunis   *Arabic:* The capital of Tunisia. An unusual given name found among 18th-century free blacks.

Tupac   An African-American original. Tupac Shakur had a starring role in the movie *Juice.*

Turner   *Latin:* He works with a lathe. *English:* Woodworker. This surname is infrequently used as a given name.

Ty   A diminutive of Tyler (see below).

Tyger   Tyger Williams wrote *Menace to Society.*

Tylan   An African-American original. Tylan Boyd attends Bishop Gallagher High School in Harper Woods, Mich.

Tyler   *English:* A house builder who makes tiles, bricks, and roofs.

Tymon   A variation of Timothy (see above).

Tyoka   An African-American original. Tyoka Jackson is a defensive lineman at Penn State.

Tyrone   *Greek:* Sovereign. *Irish:* From Owen's estate. Also Tyron, Tyronne. Tyrone, which appears to be the preferred spelling among black parents, has been well-used since WWII. But like other once enormously popular names, it is fast losing ground to the contemporary practice of name invention. Currently, several professional and college basketball players answer to this first name, including Tyrone Hill, a power forward for the Golden State Warriors.

Tyson   *English:* Son of the Teuton or German.

Udell   *English:* From the yew tree valley. Also Udel, Eudel.

Uland   *German:* From the noble land.

Ulfred   *English:* Wolf peace.

Uliss   A variation of Ulysses (see below). Also Ulice.

Ulmer   *English:* Wolf famous.

Ulric   *German:* Ruler of all. Also Ullric, Ulrich, Ulrick. Rare.

Ulysses   *Latin:* Wrathful; Ulysses is the Latin form of the Greek name Odysseus, and Ulysses was the hero of Homer's epic tale *The Odyssey.* Also Ulises. Ulysses appears on Puckett's list of most common given names, 1877–1937. The name has fallen out of favor in contemporary times. Journalist Ulysses Poston was one of the active leaders in Marcus Garvey's Universal Negro Improvement Association.

Unis   Documented among free black names, 1800–60.

Upshaw   *English:* Dweller in the upper woods.

Upton   *English:* Dweller in the upper town.

Upwood   *English:* From the upper forest.

Urban   *Latin:* A city.

Uri *Hebrew:* My light. Also Urie.

Uriah *Hebrew:* The Lord is my light. Appears among Puckett's most common given names, 1877–1937.

Uriel *Hebrew:* Angel of light.

Ursel *Latin:* Strong as a bear.

Urshell This name appears to be a variation of Ursel (see above).

Uthaw This unusual name is quite probably an African-American invention. Uthaw Mitchell is a respected businessman.

Valantine *Latin:* Strong. This variation of Valentine (see below) is found on Puckett's 1619–1799 list.

Valentine *Latin:* Strong. Also Valentin. Found among free black names of the 19th century, it was a common name among first-century Christians. The famous Christian martyr of this name is associated with a pagan festival for lovers, thus the celebration of St. Valentine's Day.

Vallis *French:* Welshman.

Van *Dutch:* From, of. A nickname for many Dutch surnames that begin with Van. Van is also a diminutive for Vance (see below). It is infrequently employed as an independent name.

Vance *English:* Grain thresher, dweller near the marshland.

Vandell An African-American original. Vandell Cobb's photographs can be seen in *Ebony*.

Vander While it may have origins in the Dutch Van (see above), this unusual name rings with the sounds of an African-American linguistic blend.

Varick *German:* Protecting ruler.

Vassar This name of a former all-women's college in Poughkeepsie, N.Y., appears on Puckett's 1877–1937 list.

Vaughn *Welsh:* Small one. Also Vaughan.

Vedery Found in 1899.

Vedie *Latin:* To see.

Vemer Found among free blacks in the 19th century.

Venchael This unusual name is obviously an African-American linguistic blend. Reverend L. Venchael Booth, pastor of the Zion Baptist Church in Cincinnati, called the meeting that led to the split of the National Baptist Convention and the formation of the Progressive National Baptist Convention.

Veo Found in Puckett's index of unusual names, 1877–1937.

Verdell *French:* Flourishing, green.

Verge *French:* Owns a quarter acre.

Verine An uncommon name of obscure origins found among black male names in the late 19th century.

Vern *Latin:* Youthful, springlike. Also Verne. Vern Fleming is a power guard for the Indiana Pacers.

Vernal *Latin:* Belonging to spring.

Vernell An African-American variation of Verdell (see above). Vernell Johnson is a gospel saxophonist.

Vernie A pet form of Vernon (see below).

Vernon *Latin:* Born in the spring. *French:* Little alder grove. It appears on Puckett's 1937 list. Vernon E. Jordan, former executive director of the National Urban League, headed President Clinton's transition team.

Verril　*German:* Masculine. Also Verel, Verrill, Verrall, Verrol, Veryl.

Vertner　The origins of this unusual name are not known. Architect Vertner W. Tandy designed St. Phillip's Episcopal Church in Harlem and Madame C. J. Walker's elaborate Villa LeWaro at Irvington-on-Hudson, N.Y.

Ves　Noted in the early 20th century.

Vic　A nickname for Victor (see below). Also Vick.

Victor　*Latin:* Victorious, conqueror.

Vince　This diminutive for Vincent (see below) first appears on Puckett's 1899 list.

Vincent　*Latin:* Conquering one. Theologian Vincent Harding is the author of *There Is a River: The Black Struggle for Freedom in America.*

Vinnie　A nickname for Vincent (see above) rarely used as a given name. Also Vinnie. Vinnie "Microwave" Johnson was a key member of the Detroit Pistons 1989 and 1990 championship teams.

Vinton　*English:* From the wine town. Vinton Randolph Anderson, a clergyman, was appointed to the President's Commission on Equal Employment Opportunities in 1963.

Virge　This diminutive for Virgil (see below) is found on Puckett's 1899 list.

Virgil　*Latin:* Rod or staff bearer; in ancient Rome, a staff designated an official. Also Vergil. Virgil is best known for the Roman poet Virgil. The name appears among free blacks of the 19th century. Once quite popular, it is now out of fashion. Virgil Hill is a light heavyweight champ from North Dakota.

Virgis　Noted in the 19th century. Virgis W. Colbert, vice-president of plant operations for Miller Brewing Co., is one of the nation's top 40 black executives employed by a nonminority corporation.

Visker　A rare name that appears to be an invention, found in Puckett's 1919 list.

Vohn This uncommon name is found on Puckett's 1877–1937 list.

Wadaran This rare name appears to be an African-American linguistic blend. Wadaran L. Kennedy was an outstanding agriculturalist who served the newly created system of Negro land-grant colleges for more than three decades.

Waddie An uncommon name, noted in 1877.

Wade *English:* From the river crossing. Wade Hampton McCree Jr., an outstanding jurist in the Detroit area, was appointed solicitor general by President Jimmy Carter.

Wadell This name is probably an African-American linguistic blend.

Wadsworth *English:* From Wade's estate; principally a surname infrequently employed as a given name.

Waggoner This rare name is found among free blacks of the 19th century.

Wagner *German:* He builds wagons.

Wakefield *English:* From the wet field.

Wakely *English:* From the damp meadow. Also Wakeley.

Walbert *English:* Well-fortified.

Walcott *English:* Dweller from the cottage behind the wall. Also Walcot, Wallcot, Wallcott, Wolcott, Wolcot.

Walden *English:* From the wooded valley. *German:* Ruler. Also Waldon, Walten.

Waldo *German:* Mighty.

Waley First noted among free blacks of the 19th century. While it does not occur often, Waley does appear in the 20th century.

Walford *English:* From the Welshman's crossing.

Walfred *German:* Peaceful ruler.

Walker *English:* Cloth walker. In medieval England, workers walked on wool to clean it. Principally a surname, Walker is found on Puckett's 1930s given name list.

Wallace *English:* Man from Wales. Also Wallis, Wallice. Wallace Warith Deen Muhammad assumed the leadership of the Nation of Islam—now the American Muslim Mission—from his father, Elijah Muhammad, upon his death in 1975. Wallace O. Stephens is CEO of Stephens Engineering Co., one of the nation's top 100 black companies.

Waller *English:* Wall builder. *German:* Ruler.

Wally A diminutive for Wallace (see above).

Walmond *German:* Protecting ruler.

Walt A diminutive for Walter (see below). Walt Williams is a swing man for the Sacramento Kings.

Walter *German:* Powerful warrior. Much like a powerful warrior, Walter White as executive secretary of the NAACP from 1931 to 1955 was in the forefront of the civil rights struggle.

Walton *English:* Dweller in the walled or fortified town.

Ward *German:* Protector.

Wardell *English:* From the watchman's hill. Before his death under mysterious circumstances in 1955, Wardell Gray was a deeply admired and emulated tenor sax virtuoso.

Ware *English:* Prudent, aware.

Warfield *English:* From the field by the dam.

Waring A variation of Warren (see below). Writer and poet Waring Cuney was an art and music columnist for *The Crisis* during the Harlem Renaissance.

Warner *German:* Warrior. As dean of music, Warner Lawson directed the Howard University choir for a quarter of a century.

Warren *German:* Protector. Percussionist Warren Smith is a member of Max Roach's group M'Boom. Warren Moon is a quarterback with the Houston Oilers.

Warrick *English:* Stronghold. *German:* Defending ruler. Also Warwick.

Warton *English:* From the estate by the dam.

Wash A diminutive for Washington (see below).

Washington *English:* From the astute one's estate. Although Washington is a surname, it is noted among given names in *Black Names in America.*

Watkins *English:* Son of Walter (see above).

Watson *English:* Son of Walter (see above).

Wave An uncommon name appearing on Puckett's 1919 list.

Waverly *English:* From the trembling aspen meadow.

Wayland *English:* From the estate by the highway. Also Waylon, Waylan.

Wayman A variation of Wyman (see below). Wayman Tisdale is a power forward for the Sacramento Kings. Wayman F. Smith III is one of the top 40 black executives as vice-president of corporate affairs for the Anheuser-Busch Co., Inc.

Wayne *English:* Wagon builder. Wayne Embry Sr. is CEO of an auto parts manufacturing company, one of the nation's top 100 black-owned companies. Wayne Shorter is an innovative composer and tenor saxophonist.

Weaver *English:* Clothmaker.

Webb *English:* Weaver. Also Weber, Webber.

Webster   *English:* Weaver. It is said that occupational names in old England ending in ter designated the feminine form. If that is so, then Webster referred to female jobs. When these jobs were taken over by men, the names were also adopted. Webster appears among free black given names in the 17th century.

Weddell   *English:* Dweller at the advancer's hill.

Welby   *English:* From the farm by the spring. Also Wellby, Welbey.

Welcome   *English:* Invited guest. Rare.

Weldon   *English:* Dweller near the spring by the hill. Saxophonist Weldon Irvine was a member of the Jazz Crusaders.

Welford   *English:* From the spring by the road. Also Wellford.

Wellesley   A form of Wesley (see below). Rare.

Wellington   *English:* From the prosperous one's estate.

Wells   *English:* Dweller by the springs.

Wendell   *German:* Wanderer. Also Wendall, Wendel, Wyndell. Wendell Barron is CEO of one of the nation's top 100 automobile dealerships. Reverend Wendell Anthony is the president of the Detroit chapter of the NAACP.

Wentworth   *English:* From the pale one's estate.

Werner   *German:* Defending warrior.

Wes   A diminutive for Wesley (see below).

Wesley   *English:* From the west meadow. The handsome actor Wesley Snipes is in his heyday.

West   This diminutive for Weston (see below) appears as a given name on Puckett's 1930s list.

Weston   *English:* Dweller at the west-facing farm.

Wheeler   *English:* One who makes wheels. Rare.

Whippy   An uncommon name appearing among free blacks in the 17th century. Its origins and meaning are not known.

Whitby *English:* From the white farm.

Whitcomb *English:* From the white hollow.

Whitfield *English:* From the small white field. Forced to leave the University of South Carolina in 1876, Whitfield McKinlay became a personal friend of President Theodore Roosevelt, who appointed him to the Housing Commission. His assignment was to investigate housing facilities among the poor of Washington, D.C.

Whitford *English:* From the white or clear ford.

Whitney *English:* From the white-haired one's island. Author, lecturer, and newspaper columnist Whitney M. Young was executive director of the National Urban League. Whitney Houston's magnificent display of this name has completed its crossover onto the girls' roster.

Whittaker *English:* Dweller at the white field.

Wilbert *German:* Bright and persevering.

Wilbur *English:* From the secure fortress. Also Wilber, Willbur. Appears on Puckett's 1919 list.

Wilfred *German:* Determined peacemaker. Also Wilfrid. Jamaican-born Wilfred Adolphus Domingo was an active political writer during the Harlem Renaissance.

Wilfredo The Italian form of Wilfred (see above).

Will A diminutive for names beginning with Will. It appears among free blacks in the 17th century. Composer, conductor, and violinist Will Marion Cook was internationally known by the turn of the century. Will Henry Bennett Vodery arranged the scores for more than 50 Broadway musical comedies.

Willard *English/German:* Bold, resolute. Author Willard Motley wrote the novel *Knock on Any Door.*

William *German:* Resolute protector. Since William the Conqueror's conquest of England, his name has remained in widespread use. It appears among free blacks in America in the 17th century. William rivals James, John, Paul, Charles, and Thomas in consistent and frequent use over centuries. Comedian William "Bill"

Cosby is perhaps our most recognizable William. William Wells Brown was the first American black to publish a novel and a play. Illinois Congressman William L. Dawson was the first African-American to chair a major House of Representatives committee. Self-educated, William Stanley Braithwaite became a nationally known anthologist during the Harlem Renaissance and professor of creative literature at Atlanta University. William G. Mays is CEO of the nation's 13th largest black-owned industrial company. Historian, philosopher, scholar, sociologist, and founder of the NAACP, William Edward Burghardt "W.E.B." DuBois is the author of *The Souls of Black Folk.* With over 50 books to his credit, and as a formidable advocate of civil and human rights, DuBois is considered one of the foremost influential figures in black history. There seems to be an endless list of accomplished and distinguished African-American men who have and do answer to William.

Willie   A diminutive for William frequently employed as an independent name. Also Willy. Appearing on Puckett's 1877–1937 list. Willie Burton is a small forward for the Miami Heat. Willie Anderson is an off guard for the San Antonio Spurs. Willie Mays is one of the greatest professional baseball players of all time.

Willis   *English:* Son of Will. Willis Richardson is said to be the first serious black writer to have a play produced on Broadway. Willis Reed was an All-Star center for the 1970 and 1973 NBA Championship New York Knicks.

Willoughby   *Dutch:* A house near the willow trees. Rare.

Wilmer   *German:* Beloved, famous, and resolute. Also Wilmar. Wilmer Ames was the founding editor of *Emerge* magazine.

Wilmot   *German:* Of a resolute spirit.

Wilson   *English:* The son of William (see above). It appears among free blacks of the 17th century, but this surname is rare today as a given name. Wilson Pickett is a dynamic soul singer.

Wilt A diminutive for Wilton (see below). Wilt Chamberlain, standing 7′ tall, was the greatest offensive player in the history of the NBA.

Wilton *English:* Dweller on the farm with the spring.

Wilver An African-American variation of Wilbur (see above).

Winfield *English:* From the friend's field. Rare.

Winfred An African-American variation of Wilfred (see above). Economist Winfred Octavius Bryson Jr. is an educator and banker.

Wingate *English:* Divine protection. Rare.

Winslow *English:* From the friendly hill.

Winston *English:* From the friendly estate.

Winthrop *English:* Dweller in the friendly village.

Winton *English:* Dweller at the friend's estate. Also Wynton. Wynton Marsalis is an internationally famous jazz and classical trumpeter and composer.

Wittum An African-American creation appearing in the 18th century.

Wolcott *English:* From the brave man's cottage or wolf cottage. In ancient European languages such as Teutonic and Anglo-Saxon, wolf refers to courage.

Wood *English:* From the forest. Appears on Puckett's 1930s list.

Woodrow *English:* Dweller at the hedge by the forest. Appears in the 1930s.

Woody This diminutive for Woodrow (see above) appears on an earlier list (Puckett's 1919 list) than the name for which it is a short version. Also Woodie. Woody Strode is a veteran actor. Woodie King Jr. is a director and producer.

Worley *English:* Dweller at the uncultivated land.

Worrell *English:* Dweller at the true man's estate.

Worth A diminutive for Worthy (see below) in rare usage.

Worthy   *English:* From the manor. Rare.

Wright   *English:* A carpenter.

Wyatt   *French:* Little warrior. Also Wyatte, Wiatt. Reverend Wyatt Tee Walker was an executive assistant to Martin Luther King and is pastor of Canaan Baptist Church in Harlem.

Wycliffe   *English:* From the white cliffs. Also Wycliff. Wycliffe Gordon is a young trombonist from New Orleans who has performed with the Marsalises.

Wylie   *English:* Charming, clever, beguiling. Also Wiley. Wiley Woodward is a writer.

Wyman   *English:* Warrior.

Wymer   *English:* Famous warrior.

Wynn   *English:* Friend. Also Wynne, Winn. Rare.

Xanthus   *Greek:* Golden-haired.

Xavier   *Spanish:* Bright, splendid. Xavier Nicholas is a blues historian and poet. Xavier McDaniel is a power forward for the Boston Celtics.

Xerxes   *Persian:* Royal prince.

Xylon   *Greek:* Dweller in the forest.

Yaff Appearing in the 1800s.

Yale *English:* From the corner of land. Rare.

Yaphet *Hebrew:* Comedy. Actor Yaphet Kotto has appeared in numerous films.

Yardley *English:* From the enclosed meadow.

Yates *English:* Dweller at the gate.

Yenix A very rare name appearing on Puckett's 1800–60 list.

Yochanan *Hebrew:* The Lord is gracious.

Yohanan A form of Yochanan.

Yon An unusual name appearing among free blacks in the 19th century.

York *English:* Dweller near the sacred Yew tree. York Champlin was a free black patriot who fought in the American Revolution.

Yves *French:* Little archer.

Z

Black Names in America contained a large number of apparent inventions beginning with Z. Most of these names are documented by Puckett in the records of the 1800s.

Zacchaeus *Biblical/Hebrew:* Clean.

Zach Diminutive for Zachariah (see below). Also Zack.

Zachariah *Biblical/Hebrew:* Jehovah has remembered. Also Zaccharias, Zacarisa, Zechariah. Appears on Puckett's list "In the Beginning, 1619–1799" list.

Zackenas This odd name appears among free black names in the 19th century.

Zackery An English variation of Zachariah (see above).

Zacko Noted in the 1800s.

Zadoc *Hebrew:* Just, righteous one. Also Zodoc, Zodok. Found among free black names of the 19th century.

Zadork A very odd name of obscure origins, noted in the 1800s.

Zale *Greek:* Power of the sea.

Zane A variation of John (see above). Also Zayne, Zain.

Zango The origins of this unusual name are not known. It is found on Puckett's list of 1800–60.

Zanza A rare name of unknown origins found on Puckett's 1800–60 list.

Zeb Diminutive for Zebedee (see below) and Zebadiah

(see below) found on Puckett's 1877–1937 list. Also Zebe.

Zebadiah *Hebrew:* Gift of God.

Zebedee An African-American variation of Zebadiah (see above). Found on Puckett's 1877–1937 list.

Zebiah A variant spelling of Zebadiah (see above) found on Puckett's 1800–60 list.

Zebron A name that sounds and looks like an African-American linguistic blend, appearing on Puckett's 1877–1937 list.

Zebulun *Hebrew:* To give honor to. Also Zebulen, Zebulon. Found among free blacks of the 19th century, but very rare in the 20th century.

Zed A diminutive for first names beginning with Zed.

Zeddock Found on Puckett's 1800–60 list.

Zedekiah *Hebrew:* The Lord is just. Also Zedekhian, Zedekias.

Zedick Found on Puckett's 1800–60 list.

Zekia Found on Puckett's 1800–60 list.

Zemiliano Noted in 1800–60.

Zemmie This rare name is found on Puckett's 1899–1937 list.

Zeno *Greek:* Hospitable. Also Zenas, Zenon.

Zenus This variation of Zeus, the chief of the Greek Olympian gods, is found on Puckett's 1800–60 list.

Zephaniah *Hebrew:* Precious to the Lord. Also Zepheniah.

Zimri Puckett's 19th-century find.

Zindel A variation of Alexander (see above) that means defender of humankind.

Zingo An unusual name found on Puckett's 1800–60 list.

Zinka An unusual name found on Puckett's 1936 list.

Zoltan *Hungarian:* Life. Rare.

Zuriel *Hebrew:* The Lord is my rock. Rare.

African

Names for Boys

Names they got from yearnings, gestures, flaws, wins, mistakes, weaknesses. Names that bore witness. Macon Dead, Sing Bird, Crowell Bird, Plate, Hagar, Ice Man, Muddy Waters, Jelly Roll, Fats, Leadbelly, Bo Didley, Peg Leg, Son, Shortstuff, Smokey Babe. By ancient customs for the next seven days there was but a single task with which Omoro would seriously occupy himself, the selection of a name for his first-born son. It would have to be a name rich with history and with promise for the people of his tribe—the Mandinkan believed that a child would develop seven of the characteristics of whomever or whatever he was named for.

—ALEX HALEY, *ROOTS*, 1977

Abam *Akan:* Third born after the twins.

Aban *Arabic:* An old Arabic name.

Abanu *Ibo:* I have joined the family.

Abasi *Swahili:* The stern one.

Abayomi *Yoruba:* Born to bring joy, or a ruler of people.

Abbas *Arabic:* A lion.

Abdalla *Swahili:* Servant of God.

Abdu *Swahili:* He worships God. Also Abdul. Abdul Alkalimat is an esteemed Malcolm X scholar and the author of *Malcolm X for Beginners.*

Abdullah *Arabic:* Servant of God. South African–born Abdullah Ibrahim lives in New York. A staunch opponent of apartheid, he is world-famous for his jazz piano renditions.

Abeeku *Fante:* Boy born on Wednesday.

Abegunde *Yoruba:* Born on a holiday.

Abeid *Swahili:* He is a leader.

Abejide *Yoruba:* Born in winter.

Abena *Yoruba:* He is pure.

Abi *Yoruba:* The royal guard.

Abiade *Yoruba:* Born to royal parents.

Abidugun *Yoruba:* Born before the war.

Abimbola *Yoruba:* Born rich.

Abiodum *Yoruba:* Born during the festival.

Abiola *Yoruba:* Honorable, born at the New Year.

Abiona *Yoruba:* Born on a journey.

Abioye *Yoruba:* Born during the coronation.

Abosi *Yoruba:* Life plant.

Abu *Swahili:* Nobility.

Abubakari *Swahili:* Noble. Abubakari, the brother of the great Mansa Musa of Mali, sailed for the New World in the 14th century, but never returned to Africa.

Abwooli *Uganda:* Catlike.

Acque *Hausa:* Meaning unknown.

Addae *Akan:* Beautiful as the morning sunrise.

Ade *Yoruba:* Royal.

Adeagbo *Yoruba:* He brings honor.

Adebamgbe *Yoruba:* Royalty has come to me.

Adebayo *Yoruba:* He came in a joyful time.

Adeben *Akan:* The 12th born.

Adeboro *Yoruba:* Royalty brings wealth.

Adedapo *Yoruba:* Royalty brings the people together.

Adegoke *Yoruba:* The crown has been exalted.

Adejola *Yoruba:* The crown passed through deep water.

Adelaja *Yoruba:* The crown settles a quarrel.

Ademola *Yoruba:* A crown is added to my wealth.

Adesola *Yoruba:* The crown honored us.

Adetokumbo *Yoruba:* Honor came from overseas.

Adewole *Yoruba:* Our crown has come home.

Adeyemi *Yoruba:* The crown suits him well.

Adigun *Yoruba:* He is righteous.

Adika *Ewe:* First child of a second husband.

Adio *Yoruba:* He is righteous.

Adisa *Yoruba:* He is precise.

Adjua *Akan:* He is noble.

Adofo *Akan:* The warrior.

Adom *Akan:* Help comes from God.

Adunbi *Yoruba:* Born to be pleasant.

Adusa *Akan:* The 13th son.

Afi *Yoruba:* Spiritual.

Afiba *Yoruba:* Born by the sea.

Agyei *Akan:* A messenger from God.

Agyeman *Akan:* The 14th son.

Agymah *Fante:* He will become an expatriate.

Ahmad *Arabic:* One worthy of praise. Bobby Moore was the birth name of TV sports commentator Ahmad Rashad.

Ahmed *Swahili:* Praiseworthy.

Aiyetoro *Yoruba:* Peace on earth.

Ajagbe *Yoruba:* He gets the prize.

Ajamu *Yoruba:* One who seizes possession after a fight, or he fights for what he wants.

Ajani *Yoruba:* One who takes possession after a struggle.

Ajayi *Yoruba:* Born facedown.

Ajene *Yoruba:* Truth.

Akabueze *Yoruba:* Support is paramount.

Akamafula *Yoruba:* May my work be rewarded.

Akanni *Yoruba:* He brings possessions.

Akelo *Acoli:* A son born after twins.

Akhenaton *Egyptian:* This pharaoh of Egypt was the first ruler in recorded history to believe in one God.

Akiiki *Uganda:* A good friend, or born to be an ambassador.

Akil *Arabic:* Intelligent, one who reasons well.

Akinkawon *Yoruba:* Bravery pacified them.

Akinlabi *Yoruba:* We have a boy.

Akinlama *Yoruba:* He possesses valor.

Akinlawon *Yoruba:* He is born to our family after his sisters, or his bravery will sustain them.

Akins *Yoruba:* He is a brave boy.

Akinsanya *Yoruba:* The hero avenges.

Akinshegun *Yoruba:* Valor conquers all.

Akinsheye *Yoruba:* Valor acts honorably.

Akinshiju *Yoruba:* Valor awakes. Akinshiju Ola is a dedicated journalist.

Akintunde *Yoruba:* A boy has come again.

Akinwole *Yoruba:* Valor enters the house.

Akinwunmi *Yoruba:* Valor is pleasing.

Akinyele *Yoruba:* Valor benefits the home.

Akna *Fante:* Born on Thursday.

Ako *Yoruba:* The first child is a son.

Akobundu *Yoruba:* Prudence is life.

Akono *Yoruba:* It is my turn.

Akou *Yoruba:* Wealth.

Akram *Arabic:* Most generous.

Akua *Fante:* Sweet messenger.

Akusa *Fante:* Born on Thursday.

Akwetee *Ga:* Younger of twins.

Alcoe *Hausa:* A person of poor quality.

Ali *Arabic:* Exalted.

Alimayu *Swahili:* God is honored.

Allee *Hausa:* A variation of the Arabic Ali.

Alonge *Yoruba:* A tall and skinny boy.

Amadi *Benin:* Sick at birth, or dedicated to God.

Ambakisye *Ndali:* God has been merciful.

Ambidwile *Nyakyusa:* God has convinced me.

Ambilikile *Nyakyusa:* God called me.

Ambokile *Nyakyusa:* God has redeemed me.

Ambonisye *Nyakyusa:* God has rewarded me.

Ameer *Arabic:* Commander, chieftain, or wealthy person.

Ametefe *Ewe:* Born after his father's death.

Amilcar *Carthagenian:* One worthy of praise. Amilcar was the father of Hannibal, the great leader of Carthage who took a squadron of elephants across the Alps and defeated the Roman army. Amilcar Cabral was the first president of Guinea-Bissau.

Amin *Arabic:* Faithful.

Amir *Arabic:* Populous. Amir Bey is a talented sculptor.

Amiri *Swahili:* Leader, ruler. The 1960s poet LeRoi Jones is universally known today as Amiri Baraka, a leading writer and activist.

Ampah *Ewe:* Trustworthy.

Anapa *Akan:* Born in the morning.

Anane *Akan:* Our fourth son.

Andalwisye *Nyakyusa:* God has shown me the way.

Andengwisye *Nyakyusa:* God has claimed me.

Andongwisye *Nyakyusa:* God has led me.

Angosisye *Nyakyusa:* God sanctified men.

Anika *Akan:* Goodness has come.

Animashaun *Yoruba:* He is generous.

Ankoma *Akan:* Our last born.

Antobam *Akan:* Your father died while your mother was pregnant, or the child did not meet the one who will take good care of him.

Anun *Akan:* Fifth-born son.

Anyabwile *Nykakyusa:* God has freed me.

Anyelwiswe *Nyakyusa:* God has cleansed me.

Aondochimba *Tiv:* God is above all things on earth.

Apara *Yoruba:* A child who comes and goes.

Apiyo and Acen *Acoli:* Names for twin sons.

Ara *Hausa:* The maker of honey.

Araam *Hausa:* Slender.

Ashaki *Yoruba:* Beautiful.

Ashon *Ga:* Seventh-born son.

Ashur *Swahili:* Born during Islamic month of Ashur.

Asim *Arabic:* Protector, defender. St. Louis native Jabari Asim is a young writer.

Asinia *Akan:* Stern.

Askia *Mali:* Askia Muhammad Toure, king of Songhay from 1493 to 1529, fought tradition to rule in the best interests of his people.

Asma *Arabic:* Bold. Also Azma.

Asudo *Ibo:* The year of peace.

Asukile *Nyakyusa:* The Lord has washed me.

Aswad *Arabic:* Black.

Ata *Fante:* Twin.

Atat *Somali:* One who brings sunshine. Also Atet.

Atiba *Akan:* He is born with understanding.

Atiim *Akan:* He is violent.

Atsu *Ewe:* Younger of twins.

Atta *Akan:* A twin.

Atu *Fante:* Born on Saturday.

Awotwe *Akan:* Eighth born.

Ayinde *Yoruba:* We gave praises and he came.

Ayize *Zulu:* Let it come.

Ayo *Yoruba:* Happiness.

Ayodele *Yoruba:* Joy has come.

Ayubu *Swahili:* Patience in suffering.

Azagba *Benin:* Born out of town.

Azibo *Ngoni:* Of the earth.

Azikiwe *Ibo:* Vigorous, healthy. Nnamdi Azikiwe was the first president of Nigeria.

Azizi *Swahili:* Precious.

Azubuike *Ibo:* Support is strength.

Baako *Yoruba:* The first-born.

Babafemi *Yoruba:* My father loves me.

Babatu *Yoruba:* He is a peacemaker.

Babatunde *Yoruba:* My father returns. Actor and dancer Babatunde is noted for his dramatic flair.

Babatunji *Yoruba:* My father returns again.

Badru *Akan/Swahili:* Born at full moon.

Badu *Akan:* The tenth-born child.

Bahati *West Africa:* Luck.

Bakari *Swahili:* Born with the promise of nobility.

Bakesiima *Uganda:* He has luck.

Balewa *Ewe:* He brings happiness.

Balla *Arabic:* Brave.

Balogun *Yoruba:* A warlord, or the chief of war. The late Kwesi Balogun was a political activist in the 1960s.

Balondemu *Musoga:* The chosen one.

Bamwoze *Uganda:* The child is spoiled.

Bandele *Yoruba:* Born away from home.

Banga *Shona:* Sharp as a knife.

Baraka *Swahili:* Blessed.

Baruti *Tswana:* Born to be a teacher. Baruti Bediako is a senior partner in the Bediako and Bektemba Accounting firm. His name was Tion Tanksley before he changed it.

Baye *Yoruba:* He is straightforward.

Bayo *Yoruba:* There is joy.

Becktemba *Ndebele:* He can be trusted. Also Bekitemba.

Bediako *Akan:* He overcomes obstacles.

Beedzi *Akan:* You came to eat. Also Beedzidzi. This name is given to a very sickly baby who was not expected to live, but survived nevertheless.

Behanzin *Dahomey:* He possesses strength and wisdom. Benhanzin Hossu Bowelle was the most powerful ruler in West Africa during the closing years of the nineteenth century.

Bejide *West Africa:* Born during the rainy season.

Bem *Tiv:* He is peaceful.

Bendo *Mende:* He seeks fame.

Beno *Nwera:* One of a band.

Betserai *Shona:* Born to assist.

Betta *Bobangi:* He will sustain.

Biboye *Ibo:* You are what I wish for.

Bisa *West Africa:* He is greatly loved.

Bloke *Yoruba:* He is a proud chief.

Bobo *Fante:* Born on Tuesday. *Hausa:* Be humble.

Bolewa *West Africa:* He brings happiness.

Bomani *Ngori:* A warrior.

Bongani *Ngori:* He sings with joy.

Boseda *Tiv:* Born on Sunday. Also Bosede.

Brenya *Akan:* I suffered before I got you. This name is given by parents who have lost previous children to death.

Bunwi *West Africa:* My gift.

Buyinza *Uganda:* God is mighty.

Bwagilo *Nyakyusa:* A source of things.

Bwana *Swahili:* Great master.

Bwerani *Ngoni:* Come child, you are welcomed.

Byakatonda *Uganda:* God owns everything.

Byansi *Uganda:* We come with nothing on the earth and we shall take nothing away from the earth.

Byarugaba *Uganda:* The giver's blessing.

Camara *West Africa:* Teacher. Author Camara Laye wrote *The African Child.*

Cara *Hausa:* He increases.

Cata *Mende:* A common plant.

Cazembe *Central Region:* A wise man is born. Cazembe Bektembe, the former Ken Starnes, is a senior partner in the Bektemba and Bediako Accounting firm.

Chabwera *Ngoni:* He has arrived.

Chafulumisa *Ngoni:* The swift one.

Changa *Central Region:* Strong as iron.

Changamire *Central Region:* Bright as the sun.

Chatha *Ngoni:* An ending.

Chatuluka *Ngoni:* A departure.

Chekandina *Yao:* Spicy.

Chenzira *Shona:* Born while his mother was traveling.

Chiamaka *West Africa:* God is splendid.

Chibale *Ngoni:* Kingship.

Chibeze *Ibo:* God is the king.

Chicha *Ibo:* Beloved.

Chidubem *Ibo:* May God lead me.

Chiemeka *Ibo:* God has done much.

Chigaru *Ngoni:* Hound.

Chihambuane *Bachopi:* Sweet potatoes.

Chijioke *Ibo:* God gives talent.

Chika *Ibo:* God is the greatest. This name may be used for boys or girls.

Chike *Ibo:* Power of God.

Chikosi *Ibo:* Neck.

Chikumbu *Yao:* Knife handle.

Chikwendu *Ibo:* Life comes from God.

Chilemba *Mwera:* Turban.

Chimanga *Ngoni:* Maize.

Chinelo *Ibo:* Thought of God.

Chinodu *Ibo:* God is the protector.

Chinua *Ibo:* God's own blessing. Chinua Achebe is an honored African novelist who is a professor of literature at the University of Massachusetts at Amherst.

Chinyelu *Ibo:* Invincible.

Chioke *Ibo:* A gift of god.

Chioma *Ibo:* The good God.

Chionesu *Shona:* A guiding light.

Chiosa *Ibo:* God of all. This is a unisex name that is used for boys or girls.

Chiumbo *Mwera:* A small creation.

Chuckwuemeka *Ibo:* Thank you, God. This

name may be used for boys or girls.

Chuckwuneru *Ibo:* God's work. This is a unisex name.

Chukwueneka *Ibo:* God has dealt kindly with us.

Chuma *Shona:* He brings wealth. *Ibo:* God's gift to you. Chuma Gault is the son of Charlayne Hunter-Gault and Ron Gault.

Chumachienda *Lomwe:* A dignitary is on his way.

Coblah *Ewe:* Born on Tuesday.

Coffie *Ewe:* Born on Friday.

Coley *Hausa:* He peddles small wares. Also Colee.

Comas *Mende:* He eats without sharing.

Commenie *Hausa:* He will exhort and persuade.

Commie *Ewe:* Born on Saturday. Also Comie.

Commo *Hausa:* He has returned.

Condy *Mende:* A sugar plum. Also Kondi.

Congo *Mende:* Reddish-brown. Also Kongo.

Coujoe *Ewe:* Born on Monday. The variations Cujo and Cudjoe appear among blacks in America in the early centuries.

Dab *Mende:* A small bird who weaves a nest in the grass.

Dada *Yoruba:* A boy child with curly hair.

Dage *Hausa:* Takes a firm stand. Also Dago.

Dakarai *Shona:* He brings happiness.

Damani *Western Region:* He is thoughtful.

Danjuma *Hausa:* Born on Friday.

Danladi *Hausa:* Born on Sunday.

Darweshi *Swahili:* He is like a saint.

Daudi *Swahili:* Beloved one.

Dawud *Swahili:* Beloved son.

Dedan *Swahili:* Town dweller, or he loves the city.

Deedum *Hausa:* Pitch-dark. Also Didum.

Dehkontee *Bossa:* Time will tell.

Dia *Mende:* He is a champion.

Diaba *Mende:* Cliff dweller.

Diah *Mende:* A small rice-eating bird. *Hausa:* Our offspring.

Diallo *Mende:* He is bold.

Diallobe *Central Region:* He is heroic.

Diarra *Mende:* A gift from God.

Dibia *Mende:* A healer is born.

Diliza *Zulu:* He destroys evil.

Dingane *Zulu:* He has needs. The great Zulu warrior Dingane, Shaka's successor, fought the Boers.

Dingiswayo *Zulu:* Dingiswayo was an able warrior who ruled all of Zulu land. Shaka was his protege.

Diop *Wolof:* Ruler, scholar. The late Cheik Anta Diop was a preeminent scholar and Egyptologist.

Djenaba *Western Region:* Affectionate.

E

Eba *Ngala:* He understands.

Ebere *West Africa:* He will show mercy.

Eberechukwu *West Africa:* God's mercy is here.

Ebi *Ibo:* Good thought. This name is used for boys and girls.

Ebiowei *Ibo:* A good, handsome boy.

Ede *Ibo:* Sweetness.

Edo *Ibo:* He is love.

Ego *Ibo:* Money.

Ehioze *Benin:* Born above the jealousy of others.

Eintou *West Africa:* He is a pearl.

Ejiikeme *Yoruba:* He will not use force.

Ekeama *Yoruba:* Nature is splendid.

Ekechukwu *Yoruba:* God's creation.

Ekundayo *Yoruba:* Our sorrow becomes happiness.

Ekwutosi *West Africa:* Do not speak evil against others.

Elel *Bobangi:* He comes like a cyclone.

Elowea *Hausa:* He comes like the dew.

Enaharo *Benin:* He shines like the sun.

Enobakhare *Benin:* The king's word.

Epatimi *Ibo:* A man of patience.

Erasto *East Africa:* He is a man of peace.

Ewansiha *Benin:* Secrets are not for sale.

Eze *Beni:* A king is born.

Ezeamaka *Bini:* A splendid king.

Ezema *Bini:* The senior chief. Legend holds Ezema was the first Bini man to grow oil palms.

Ezenachi *Bini:* The king rules.

Ezeoha *Bini:* The people's king.

Fadil *Arabic:* Generous.

Fance *Hausa:* To redeem.

Fanta *West Africa:* Born on a beautiful day.

Fara *Hausa:* Joy.

Faraji *Swahili:* He brings consolation.

Farhan *Somali:* One who brings happiness.

Farih *Hausa:* Bright light.

Fati *Yoruba:* He is robust.

Fatou Mata *Yoruba:* He is beloved by all.

Febechi *West Africa:* He will worship God.

Femi *West Africa:* He will love me.

Fenuku *Fante:* Born late, or a boy born after twins.

Fenyang *Tswana:* A conqueror.

Fifi *Fante:* Born on Friday.

Foluke *Yoruba:* This child is placed in God's hands.

Fouad *Arabic:* He comes from the heart.

Fudail *Arabic:* A child of excellent character.

Fulumirani *Ngoni:* Born on a journey.

Funsani *Ngoni:* Request.

G

Gahiji *Rwanda:* The hunter.

Gaidi Of unknown origin. Milton "Gaidi" Henry is a famed associate of Malcolm X.

Gaika *Zulu:* A gifted wood carver.

Gamba *Shona:* A warrior.

Gambo *Hausa:* A boy born after twins.

Ganyana *Uganda:* Born with the gift of patience.

Garai *Shona:* Be settled.

Gata *Hausa:* To be strong.

Gbolahan The origins of this name are not known. Gbolahan Okubadejo of Samuel J. Tilden High School in Brooklyn, excelled in health and medical studies. This valedictorian plans to attend Brown Unversity's program of liberal medical education.

Ginikanwa *Ibo:* What is more precious than a child?

Goah *Swahili:* Shield.

Goatsemodine *Tswana:* God knows.

Gogo *Nguni:* He is like grandfather.

Goredenna *Shona:* Black cloud.

Govan Of unknown origin. Govan Mbeki, a fearless opponent of apartheid.

Gowon *Tiv:* Rainmaker. Col. Yakubu Gowon, a Nigerian leader.

Gyasi *Akan:* Wonderful.

H

Habib *Arabic:* The beloved.

Habimana *Rwanda:* God exists.

Haji *Swahili:* Born during the month of pilgrimage to Mecca.

Haki *Arabic:* Wise judge. The 1960s Chicago poet Don L. Lee is now well-known internationally as Haki R. Madhubuti, writer and publisher of Third World Press.

Hakim *Arabic:* He is wise. Also Hakeem. Hakim has been a very popular name among African-American parents for several generations. Hakeem Olajuwon, a native Nigerian, is the center for the Houston Rockets. In January 1993, he turned 30, and in February he became a U.S. citizen.

Hakizimana *Rwanda:* It is God who saves.

Haleem *Arabic:* He is slow to anger.

Hamadi *Swahili:* Praised.

Hamid *Arabic:* Thanking God.

Hamisi *Swahili:* Born on Thursday.

Hamza *Arabic:* An important person out of history.

Hanif *Arabic:* True believer.

Hannibal *Carthagenian:* This ruler of Carthage is acknowledged as one of the greatest generals of all time. Hannibal Peterson is a well-known trumpeter.

Haoniyao *Swahili:* He doesn't see his own faults.

Harun *Arabic:* Exalted.

Hasani *Swahili:* Handsome.

Hashim *Arabic:* Crusher of evil.

Hassiem *Arabic:* He is strong.

Helal *Arabic:* Like the crescent.

Hondo *Shona:* He is prepared for war.

Husani *Swahili:* Handsome.

Ibrahim *Hausa:* My father is exalted.

Idi *Swahili:* Born during Idd festival. Idi Amin, the exiled former president of Uganda, is notorious for his brutal and deadly regime.

Idogbe *Yoruba:* Second born after twins.

Idowu *Yoruba:* Born after twins.

Ica *Bini:* The chief's necklace.

Ifeancho *Yoruba:* The desired child.

Ifeanyichukwu *Yoruba:* Nothing is impossible with God.

Ifoma *West Africa:* A lasting friend.

Ihechukwu *West Africa:* Light of God.

Ikechuckwu *Yoruba:* The strength of God.

Ikenna *West Africa:* Father's power.

Imarogbe *Benin:* This child is born to a good family.

Inaani *West Africa:* Who is left at home?

Ipyana *Nyakyusa:* Grace.

Iroagbulam *Ibo:* Let not enmity destroy me.

Irshad This is an African-

American variation of the Arabic Irshadi, which means to learn. Irshad Abdul-Haqq is the executive director of the Council on Legal Education Opportunity in Washington, D.C.

Ishaq *Arabic:* He laughed when he was born.

Issa *Arabic:* God is our salvation.

Isukanma *Yoruba:* May the future be bright.

Italo *West Africa:* He is full of valor.

Iyapo *Yoruba:* Child of many trials.

Jabari *Swahili:* He is brave. Jabari Asim is an aspiring poet and writer.

Jabulani *Ndebele:* Be happy.

Jafari *Swahili:* A creek.

Jahi *Swahili:* He has dignity.

Jaja *Ibo:* He is honored.

Jalaal *Arabic:* Majestic.

Jaleel *Arabic:* Illustrious. Jaleel White is an actor.

Jama *Somali:* One who brings people together (such as an elderman).

Jamaal *Arabic:* He is beauty. The variation Jamal is enormously popular among African-American parents, who for the most part prefer that spelling. Malcolm-Jamal Warner is an actor who starred on "The Cosby Show."

Jameel *Arabic:* Physically and morally attractive. Also Jamel. Jamel is intensely popular as a boy's name. However, black parents frequently use Jameel and Jamel as girls' names.

Janna *Hausa:* A cord used to fasten and decorate plaits on a woman's head.

Jaramogi *East Africa:* He travels often. Reverend Albert "Jaramogi" Cleague is a prominent minister and founder of the Shrine of the Black Madonna.

Jawanza *Central Africa:* This one is dependable. Author and lecturer Jawanza Kunjufu is an educator who has devoted his life's work to black boys.

Jawara *Hausa:* Peaceloving.

Jawhar *Arabic:* A jewel.

Jela *Swahili:* His father was in prison at birth. Jela is an excellent example of a name describing a child's circumstance at birth.

Jelani *Swahili:* He is mighty.

Jibade *Yoruba:* Born close to royalty.

Jimiyu *Uganda:* Born in a dry season.

Jojo *Fante:* Born on Monday. *Swahili:* This one is a storyteller.

Jongilanga *Southern Africa:* He faces.

Juma *Swahili:* Born on Friday.

Jumaane *Swahili:* Born on Tuesday.

Jumoke *Yoruba:* Everyone loves this child.

Jurodoe *Bassa:* Faithful.

Kadugala *Uganda:* He is very black.

Kafele *Ngoni:* He is worth dying for.

Kafuko *Uganda:* A child who follows a deceased brother or sister.

Kaga *Hausa:* The pick of the bunch.

Kahero *East Africa:* Conceived at home.

Kailugaru *Uganda:* He is very dark.

Kakuyon *Central Africa:* Maker of weapons.

Kala *West Africa:* Tall.

Kalif *Somali:* Holy Boy.

Kalindaluzzi *Uganda:* The well keeper.

Kalonji *Central Africa:* Man of victory.

Kamau *Ngoni:* Quiet warrior. Kamau Alexander was a forward with the Wichita State Shockers during the 1993 basketball season.

Kambui *East Africa:* Fearless.

Kambuji *Ngoni:* Goat.

Kamowa *Ngoni:* Beer.

Kanko *Hausa:* You are able to do.

Kanyama *Central Africa:* Guard.

Kapeni *Ngoni:* Sharp as a knife.

Karanja *East Africa:* Guide.

Karume *East Africa:* Keeper of the forest.

Kashka *Yoruba:* He is friendly.

Kasimu *West Africa:* Keeper of the forest.

Katamba *Uganda:* The chief.

Katayira *Uganda:* Not staying in one place.

Katorogo *Uganda:* The premature child.

Kaya *Akan:* This child is a laborer. This name is suitable for boys or girls.

Kayode *Yoruba:* He brought joy.

Kazandu *Zulu:* You are a young man.

Kazembe *Yao:* He is an ambassador.

Kazungu *Uganda:* A boy or girl who is very light-skinned.

Keambiroiro *Kikuyu:* Mountain of blackness.

Kefentse *Tswana:* Conqueror.

Kehinde *Yoruba:* The second born of twins.

Keita *Fulani:* Worshipper.

Kenyatta *Kikuyu:* A musician. Kenyatta is very popular.

Kereenyaga *Kikuyu:* Mountain of mystery.

Ketecumbeh *Mano:* Grow up and provide.

Ketema *East Africa:* From the valley.

Ketto *Hausa:* Sunrise.

Kgosie (HO sie) *Xhosa:* Born in South Africa and living in America on a British passport, Kgosie Matthews was campaign manager and the architect behind Carol Moseley Braun's successful bid for the U.S. Senate.

Khaalid *Arabic:* Durable, one who does not grow weak, or he remains strong even in old age. Also Akalid. Khalid Muhammad is a national representative for minister Louis Farrakhan and the Nation of Islam.

Khaldun *Arabic:* Eternal. Ibn Khaldun was a great traveler and scholar in North Africa.

Khalfani *Swahili:* He is destined to rule.

Khama *Botswana:* Khama, the good king of Bechauanaland, was so peace-loving that he surrendered his kingdom to his father, Sekohmi, who despised Khama's conversion to Christianity.

Khamisi *Swahili:* Born on Thursday.

Khari *Swahili:* Kingly.

Kiah *Bobangi:* Always.

Kiambu *Kikuyu:* This boy will be rich.

Kibumba *Uganda:* Creator.

Kifimbo *Swahili:* A very thin baby.

Kigongo *Luganda:* Born before twins.

Kimani *Swahili:* Sailor.

Kitaka *Central Africa:* Good farmer.

Kitwana *Swahili:* Pledged to live.

Kiyumba *Uganda:* Morning sun is sweet, but it becomes bitter in the afternoon.

Kizza *Luganda:* Born after twins.

Kobie *West Africa:* Warrior.

Kodjo *West Africa:* Humorous.

Kodwo *Twi:* Born on Monday.

Kofi *Twi:* Born on Friday. Kofi is enormously popular among black parents who prefer African names. Kofi Natambu is a poet/writer/publisher.

Kojo *Akan:* Born on Monday. *Yoruba:* Unconquerable.

Kokayi *Shona:* Summon the people to hear.

Koma *Bobangi:* Favorable, mature, perfect, proper.

Konata *Yoruba:* A man of high station.

Kondo *Swahili:* War. Zak Kondo has accumulated quite a following for his research on the life of Malcolm X.

Kondwani *Ngoni:* Joyful.

Kontar *Akan/Yoruba:* An only child.

Kopano *Tswana:* Union.

Koro *West Africa:* A golden child.

Kpodo *Ewe:* Elder of twins.

Kufere *Yoruba:* Do not forget.

Kufuo *Fante:* His father shared the birth pains.

Kunle *Yoruba:* His home is filled with honors.

Kwabena *Akan:* Born on Tuesday.

Kwacha *Ngoni:* Morning.

Kwada *Ngoni:* Night has fallen.

Kwadwo *Akan:* Born on Monday. Also Kwodwo, Kwadjo. Kwadwo Akpan of Washington, D.C., is an entrepreneur.

Kwakou *Ewe:* Born on Wednesday.

Kwame *Akan:* Born on Saturday. Also Kwamena. Kwame Nkrumah, the first president of the independent state of Ghana, was greatly admired by many African-Americans. Thus, Kwame endures as a very popular boy's name.

Kwasi *Akan:* Born on Sunday.

Kwayera *Ngoni:* Dawn.

Kwende *Ngoni:* Let's go.

Kweisi The exact language of this name is not known. Kweisi Mfume represents Maryland's Seventh Congressional District and is the chair of the Congressional Black Caucus for the 103rd Congress. Mfume says his adopted African name means conquering son of kings.

Kwesi *Akan:* Born on Sunday.

Lafe *Hausa:* Thin.

Lamburia *Ngoni:* Clean bush.

Landuleni *Ndebele:* One who finds greatness.

Lasana *Central Africa:* A poet of the people.

Lateef *Arabic:* Gentle, pleasant one.

Laze *Arabic:* Blaze.

Leabua *Sotho:* You speak.

Linhanda *Uganda:* Broadway.

Lishe *Hausa:* Born at midnight.

Lisimba *Yao:* The lion.

Lukman *Arabic:* A prophet is among us.

Lumo *Ewe:* Born face-down.

Lumumba *Bokango:* Gifted, brilliant. Patrice Lumumba was the beloved leader of the Congo.

Lutakkome *Nugwere:* Who talks much.

Lutalo *Luganda:* A warrior.

Luzige *Mugwere:* Locust.

Lwandeka *Mugwere:* Lost all relatives, left alone. A boy or girl's name.

M

Maajid *Arabic:* Honorable.

Maalik *Arabic:* Master. Malik is the version of this name preferred by African-Americans. Malik Chaka lives in Silver Spring, Md. A graduate of St. John's University, small forward Malik Sealy is blossoming in the NBA. Malik Spellman is a spokesman for Hands Across Watts, a group of former street gang members who organized the historic Kansas City peace talks.

Madzimoyo *Ngoni:* Water of life.

Magezi *Uganda:* A boy who is wise.

Magomu *Luganda:* Younger of twins.

Majeed *Arabic:* Noble. Jazz trombonist Majeed Greenlee has taught mu-

sic for many years at various New England colleges.

Makalani *Mwera:* One skilled in writing.

Makami *Hausa:* He seizes.

Malawa *Yao:* Flowers.

Mansa *Mali:* Mansa Kankan Mussa, king of Mali from 1312 to 1377, was a flamboyant leader and world figure.

Manu *Akan:* Born second.

Mapira *Yao:* Millet.

Masamba *Yao:* He leaves.

Mashama *Shona:* You are surprised.

Masibuwa *Yao:* Modern days.

Maskini *Swahili:* Poor.

Masomakali *Nyakyusa:* Sharp eyes.

Masud *Swahili:* Fortunate.

Matsimela *Sotho:* Roots.

Mawulawde *Ewe:* God will provide.

Mawuli *Ewe:* There is a God.

Mazi *Ibo:* Sir. Mazie is noted among contemporary African-American females.

Mbita *Swahili:* Born on a cold night.

Mbiya *Yao:* Money.

Mbizi *Lomwe:* To drop in water.

Menelek *Ethiopia:* Menelek II, king of Abyssinia from 1844 to 1913, is considered one of the great statesmen of African history.

Mensah *Ewe:* Third son. Ghanaian Joe Mensah is a polished performer of Ewe folksongs.

Mhina *Swahili:* Delightful.

Minkah *Akan:* Justice.

Molefi *Swahili:* The keeper of tradition. Molefi Asante is a highly regarded linguist and cultural historian. He is the chairperson of the African-American Studies Department at Temple University. Among his numerous books are *The Book of African Names* and *Afrocentricity: The Theory of Social Change.*

Mongo *Yoruba:* Famous.

Montsho *Tswana:* Black.

Mosegi *Tswana:* Tailor.

Mosi *Swahili:* Firstborn.

Moswen *Tswana:* Light in color.

Moyo *Ngoni:* Life, well-being, good health.

Mposi *Nyakyusa:* Blacksmith.

Mthuthuzeli *Xhosa:* Comforter.

Mtima *Ngoni:* Heart.

Mudada *Shona:* The provider.

Mugabe *Shona:* He is intelligent and quick. Robert Mugabe is the prime minister of Zimbabwe.

Muhammad *Arabic:* Worthy of praise. Muhammad Ali, former heavyweight champion of the world, was adored by a generation for his bravado and uncompromising integrity.

Muka *Bobangi:* We harvest.

Mukawano *Uganda:* A boy who is loved.

Musana *Uganda:* Born during the daytime.

Museveni *Uganda:* Museveni is the name given to the WWII African fighters in the Seventh Battalion of the British Army. It included men recruited from East Africa. Yoweri Museveni is the current president of Uganda.

Mwai *Ngoni:* Good fortune.

Mwamba *Nyakyusa:* Strong.

Mwanze *Swahili:* The child is protected.

Mwinyi *Swahili:* King.

Mwinyimkuu *Zaramo:* Great king.

Mwita *Swahili:* He summons the people.

Naamaa *Hausa:* Sweet herbs. Also Namon.

Naeem *Arabic:* Benevolent. Also Na'im. Na'im Akbar is a teacher and author.

Najja *Muganda:* Born after twins.

Nakisisa *Muganda:* Child of the shadows.

Nando *Mende:* A variety of okra.

Nangila *Abaluhya:* Born while parents were traveling.

Nangwaya *Mwera:* Don't trifle with me.

Nasib *Somali:* The lucky one.

Nassor *Swahili:* Victorious.

Ndale *Ngoni:* Trick.

Ndembo *Yao:* Elephant.

Ndidi *Ibo:* Patience.

Ndulu *Ibo:* Dove.

Ndweleifwa *Nyakyusa:* I came with the morning.

Ngoli *Ibo:* Happiness.

Ngozi *Ibo:* Blessing.

Ngunda *Yao:* Dove.

Niamke *Yoruba:* God's gift.

Nikusubila *Nyakyusa:* Hopeful.

Nkosi *Zulu:* Ruler. Author Lewis Nkosi's most notable novel is *Mating Birds.*

Nkuku *Yao:* Rooster.

Nkundinshuti *Rwanda:* One who likes his friends.

Nogomo *Central Africa:* He will prosper.

Nsekanabo *Uganda:* Boy who likes people, or boy who laughs with people.

Ntoko *Bobangi:* Professional ability, dexterity.

Ntoma *Bobangi:* Messenger.

Nuru *Swahili:* Born in daylight.

Nyamekye *Akan:* God's gift.

Oba *Hausa:* Father. *Bini:* Ruler. *Yoruba:* King. Professor Oba T'Shaka is an expert on the political legacy of Malcolm X.

Obadele *Yoruba:* The king arrives. Abubakari Obadele is a founder of the Republic of New Afrika, and a lecturer.

Obafemi *Yoruba:* The king likes me.

Obaseki *Benin:* The king's influence is far-reaching.

Obataiye *Yoruba:* King of the world.

Obawole *Yoruba:* The king enters the house.

Obayana *Yoruba:* The king warms himself.

Oboi *Acoli:* Second son.

Odai *Acoli:* Third son.

Ode *Benin:* Born along the road.

Odion *Benin:* Firstborn of twins.

Ogbonna *Ibo:* Image of his father.

Ogolu *Ibo:* He came at the right time.

Ogorchuckwu *Ibo:* Gift of God. This name is used for boys and girls.

Ojore *Ateso:* A man of war.

Ojuneku *Ibo:* The Lord has spoken.

Okang *Acoli:* First son.

Okanlawon *Yoruba:* Son born after several daughters.

Okechuku *Ibo:* God's gift.

Oko *Ga:* Elder of twins.

Okpara *Ibo:* First son.

Ola *Yoruba:* Wealth, riches. Ola has been an enormously popular girl's name since our arrival on these shores. In the created section you will see many names using this element.

Oladele *Yoruba:* Wealth arrives.

Olafemi *Yoruba:* Wealth favors me.

Olamina *Yoruba:* This is my wealth.

Olaniyan *Yoruba:* Honor surrounds me.

Olaniyi *Yoruba:* There is glory in wealth.

Olatunji *Yoruba:* Honor reawakens.   Michael Olatunji is a master drummer and teacher.

Olu *Yoruba:* Preeminent. Olu Dara is a versatile performer and musician with several albums to his credit.

Olubayo *Yoruba:* Highest joy.

Oluchuckwu *Ibo:* The handiwork of God.

Olufemi *Yoruba:* God loves me.

Olujimi *Yoruba:* God gave me this.

Olushola *Yoruba:* God has blessed.

Olutosin *Yoruba:* God deserves to be praised.

Oluwa *Yoruba:* Our Lord.

Oluyemi *Yoruba:* Fulfillment from God.

Omar *Arabic:* The highest. This name has been often used by black parents since the 1960s. Omar Clay is a percussionist with Max Roach's M'Boom.

Omolara *Benin:* Child born at the right time.

Omorede *Benin:* Prince.

Onipede *Yoruba:* The consoler is come.

Onyoka *Ibo:* Who is the greatest? A unisex name.

Oree *Bini:* Corncake.

Orji *Ibo:* Mighty tree.

Osagboro *Benin:* There is only one God.

Osahar *Benin:* God hears.

Osakwe *Benin:* God agrees.

Osayaba *Benin:* God forgives.

Osayande *Benin:* God owns the world.

Osayimwese *Benin:* God made me whole.

Osaze *Benin:* Whom God likes.

Osei *Fante:* Noble. Osei Tutu was the founder and first king of the Asante nation.

Othiambo *Luo:* Born in the afternoon.

Othieno *Luo:* Born at night.

Ottah *Urhobo:* Child thin at birth.

Owodunni *Yoruba:* It is nice to have money.

Oza *Bini:* Metal.

Ozoma *Ibo:* Another good one.

Paki *Xhosa:* Witness.

Petiri *Shona:* Where we are.

Pili *Swahili:* The second-born child. This name is

used for both boys and girls.

Preye *Ibo:* God's gift or blessing. Preye is used for both boys and girls.

Quaashie *Ewe:* Born on Sunday. The Qua phoneme is an extremely popular element in the current name-creating craze.

Rachiim *Persian/Arabic:* Seed of rulership. Musician Rachiim Ausar-Sahu is a bassist, composer, and choirmaster.

Ramni *Arabic:* He is wise.

Rashidi *Swahili:* Of good council.

Roble *Somali:* One who brings the rains.

Rudo *Shona:* Love.

Runako *Shona:* Handsome.

Runihura *Rwanda:* He smashes his enemies to bits.

Saabir *Arabic:* One who patiently endures hardships.

Saabola *Ngoni:* Pepper.

Saadiq *Arabic:* Faithful, a man of his word. Also Sadiq. Sadiq Muhammad is a writer and percussionist.

Sadiki *Swahili:* Faithful, sincere, a man of truth.

Salehe *Swahili:* Good, righteous.

Salim *Swahili:* Peaceful. Salim Salim was for many years the ambassador from Tanzania to the UN.

Samory *Sudan.* Also Samori. Samory Toure defied French expansionism in Africa. During an eighteen-year conflict with France, Samory continually frustrated the Europeans with his military strategy and tactics. Samori Marksman is a communicator and activist in New York City.

Sango *Bobangi:* Father.

Seba *Ngali:* To know, understand.

Sebahive *Rwanda:* Brings good fortune.

Sefu *Swahili:* Sharp as a sword.

Sekani *Ngoni:* Full of laughter.

Sekayi *Shona:* Full of laughter.

Sekhomi *Botswana.* Sekhomi was the father of King Khama of Bechuanaland. Despite Sekhomi's aversion to Khama's conversion to Christianity, his reign is distinguished by his desire to resist colonization and further technological advancement.

Sekou *West Africa:* Great warrior, fighter, leader. Sekou Toure is the beloved leader of Guinea.

Sentwali *Rwanda:* Brave one, or he is blessed with courage. Also Sentwaki.

Shaka *Zulu.* Shaka became king of all the Zulus in 1818. He united the people of South Africa against colonial control.

Shamba *Congo:* Shamba Bolongongo is called the African king of peace. He taught his subjects to "kill neither man, woman, nor child. Are they not the children of God and have they not the right to live?"

Shomari *Swahili:* Forceful personality.

Shumba *Shona:* Lion.

Simba *Swahili:* Lion. Simba Kenyatta was a participant in the National Urban Peace and Justice Summit, a nationwide meeting of gang members.

Sipho *Zulu:* A gift. Sipho Sepamla is a politically active poet.

Sipliwo *Xhosa:* A gift.

Siyolo *Zulu:* This is joy.

Solwazi *Swahili:* He is knowledge.

Sondisa *Shona:* Bring him near to us.

Sonigah *Bassa:* Boychild born on Sunday.

Ssanyu *Uganda:* He brings happiness.

Sudi *Swahili:* Good luck.

Suhuba *Swahili:* A good friend.

Sultan *Swahili:* Ruler.

Sundai *Shona:* Keep pushing forward.

Sundiata *Fulani:* Sundiata Keita was a 14th-century leader in the kingdom of Mali.

Sunna *Arabic:* Skillful man.

Sunni *Sudan.* Sunni Ali Ber, king of Songhay, led a small kingdom to become the most powerful empire in West Africa.

Suubi *Uganda:* He brings hope.

Tacuma *Central Africa:* He is alert.

Taharqa *Nubian:* At the age of 16, Taharqa led his armies against the invading Assyrians in defense of Israel. During his 25-year reign, Taharqa controlled the largest empire in ancient Africa.

Taiwo *Yoruba:* The elder of twins.

Talib *Arabic:* A seeker.

Tau *Tswana:* Lion.

Tenywa *Uganda:* Younger twin brother.

Thabiti *Mwera:* A true man.

Thankdiwe *Zulu:* Beloved.

Themba *Xhosa:* Hope.

Tichawona *Shona:* We shall see.

Toma *Mende:* Significant.

Tshepo *South Africa.* The meaning of this name is unknown. Tshepo Moyo, a South African student, was awarded a trip to the U.S. when he won an essay contest to celebrate the Day of the African Child.

Tumaini *Mwera:* Hope.

Tumwebaze *Uganda:* Let us thank God.

Tumwijuke *Uganda:* Let us remember God.

Tuponile *Nyakyusa:* We are saved.

Tusabomu *Uganda:* We pray thanks to God.

Twia *Fante:* Born after twins.

Tyehimba *Tiv:* We stand as a nation.

Uba *Ibo:* Wealthy.

Ubanwa *Ibo:* Wealth in children.

Uchachuckwu *Ibo:* God's sense, or God's plan.

Umi *Yao:* Life.

Unika *Lomwe:* Light up.

Useni *Yao:* Tell me. Useni Perkins is a teacher and author of children's books in Chicago.

Uuka *Xhosa:* Wake up.

Uwaboufu *Ibo:* The world is one.

Vuai *Swahili:* Savior.

Wabwire *Uganda:* Born at night.

Wafula *Uganda:* Born during the rain.

Wambuzi *Uganda:* Mr. Goat.

Wamukota *Abaluhya:* Left-handed.

Watende *Nyakyusa:* There is no revenge.

Weke *Ibo:* Born on Eke Market day.

Wemusa *Luganda:* Never satisfied with his possessions.

Yafeu *Fante:* He is bold.

Yahya *Swahili:* God's gift.

Yao *Ewe:* Born on Thursday.

Yawo *Akan:* Born on Thursday.

Yohance *Hausa:* God's gift.

Yoofi *Akan:* Born on Friday.

Yooku *Fante:* Born on Wednesday.

Yorkoo *Fante:* Born on Thursday.

Yusef *Arabic:* His power increases. This is a popular name among African-American parents who choose Afro-centric names. Yusef Lateef is an internationally famous jazz artist.

Yusuf *Swahili:* He shall add to his powers. Yusuf Salaam is a New York City teacher and journalist.

Yusufu *Swahili:* This one charms.

Zahur *Swahili:* Flower.

Zambga *Bossa:* Firstborn. Zambga Browne is a reporter for New York's *Amsterdam News.*

Zikusooka *Uganda:* Better to suffer early in life than later.

Zuberi *Swahili:* Strong.

Zuka *Shona:* Sixpence.

Newly Created

Names for Boys

You've got to have a name that appeals to the imagination . . . because it is a thing of the spirit.

—WOLE SOYINKA
THE TRIALS OF BROTHER JEROBOAM, 1973

If you are determined to give your baby son a name that is different and distinctive, consider this: Among his peers, six-month-old James Lewis Lipford may have the most uncommon first name after all.

A

Aadli

Aaric

Adarius

Adonal

Adren

Adrion

Ahkeel

Ajandu

Akeel

Akili

Alcee

Aldrefas

Aldwin

Alfornza

Algure

Aljevaes

Alzer

Aneal

Aneill

Anquan

Antar

Antewan

Antoyne

Antron

Antuan

Antuwain

Antwain

Antwaine

Antwan

Antwaun

Antwoin

Antwon

Antwone

Ardell

Ardril

Arealeius

Arthell

Artis

Artnell

Artreil

Artrell

Arvester

Ashkar

Atiba

Atiim

Audythe

Auggeretto

Autrell

Auvil

Avondre

Bahron
Barick
Barret
Barrick
Baryn
Bashawn
Basheer
Beakey
Benzell
Bermarr
Bernell
Bernerd
Beron
Bertral
Beshon

Blease
Bodell
Boheath
Bonell
Bradell
Bramdon
Brandell
Branell
Brazell
Brene
Breon
Breshaun
Bresheer
Briant
Brion

Brione
Brityce
Broshawn
Broshon
Bryan
Bryatt
Bryshaun
Bryton
Bubba
Burchell
Burdell
Burnard
Byshawn

C

Cabion
Calberto
Calray
Cantrell
Cardae
Cardale
Cardaryl
Carlan
Cartell
Carvon
Cashion
Catrell
Catron
Cavell
Cayo

Cebran
Cebron
Cedarian
Ceron
Chachona
Chaddrick
Chadric
Chadrick
Chandon
Chanod
Chantale
Charmyst
Charon
Charron
Charvoris

Charzell
Chimal
Chiquon
Chrome
Claudell
Cledis
Clidell
Clyvincent
Codell
Comar
Conall
Concey
Contrell
Cordy
Cutrell

D

Dachell
Dacian
Daheem
Dahvon
Dailyn
Dajaun
Dajshon
Dakarai
Dakary
Dalemetrius
Dalen
Daleron
Dalvin
Dalvis
Dalwyn
Damani
Damarius
Damek
Damiene
Damione

Damond
Damone
Danaris
Danarius
Danathan
Dankeis
Danmar
Dantes
Dantreil
Dantrell
Dantrelle
Danzell
Danzelle
Daquain
Daquan
DaQuenca
Daqwan
DaRell
Darence
Daria

Darold
DaRon
Darrelle
Darrian
Darshon
Dartavious
Dartel
Darvin
Dathan
Dathon
Datos
Datrell
Daurice
DaVar
Davar
Davarius
Davaron
Davarte
Davaughn
Davendra

Daverrell	Dekoven	Derod
Davon	Delandre	Deron
Davone	Delarno	Deryx
Davoris	Delawrence	Desean
Davron	Delmetric	Deseque
Dawan	Deloyd	Deshane
Dawayne	Delshawn	Deshaun
Dayquan	Delvernon	Deshawn
DeAndre	Demarcus	Deshay
Deandre	DeMario	Deshon
DeAnthony	DeMarkus	DeVanair
Deanthony	Demel	Devante
Deantony	Demerick	Devarius
Deatrice	Deming	Devenna
Deatrick	Demond	Devi
DeAundre	Demont	Devohn
Decasta	Demorris	Devone
Decory	Denaris	Devoris
Dedan	Denathan	Devron
Dedric	DeNeil	Deward
Deeward	Denisher	Dewayne
Defone	Denishu	Dionte
Deginald	Denorris	Diontray
Deivory	Denroy	Diquan
Dejava	Deontrae	Diquon
DeJay	Dequan	Diqwuan
DeJon	Dequann	Donal
Dejoshua	Dequinton	Donardo
DeJuan	DeRell	Dontay
Dekevin	Deric	Donte

Dontis	Dranell	Dushon
Dontonio	Drynell	Duwaymon
Dontrell	Duonne	Duwayne
Dontrille	Durance	D'Varius
Donyell	Durell	Dwan
Donzel	Durelle	Dwitt
DonZell	Durmon	Dwon
Donzell	Durod	
Dramahl	Duron	

Earld	Elquan	Etdrick
Earlonzo	Elyiah	Etube
Easmon	Emari	Euris
E Bron	Entric	Evric
Edrick	Ersell	Exree
Elmare	Ertis	

F

Farly
Feron
Ferrante
Ferrell
Ferrin

Flennord
Floribert
Fondale
Fontel
Fontell

Fonzell
Franshun
Freager
Fquira

G

Gadrick
Galvin
Gamal
Gamewell
Gamil
Gandale
Gandell

Gardell
Gardy
Garnell
Garon
Garran
Garrell
Garrod

Gaslyn
Gavan
Gavell
Gavon
Gaylan
Gaylin
Genaris

Gerodney   Gontrell   Gursharn
Gerrell   Gurshan   Gurshon

Haadee   Hari   Huel
Haiwan   Hassan
Hamal   Hitari

Ikarl   Ilbert   Imeen
Ikeam   Ildefonso   Imen
Ikee   Ima   Issa

J

Jabali	JaJuan	Jaramagi
Jabari	Ja'Karl	Jareem
Jabrell	Jalann	Jarel
Jabrill	JaMar	Jarmar
Jabron	Jamar	Jarmell
Jabulani	Jamarcus	Jarnell
Jacari	Jamard	JaRon
Jacarius	Jamari	Jaron
Jacori	Jamario	Jarone
Jacquan	Jamarius	Jarrof
Jacqueese	Jamarr	Jarvoris
Jada	Jamarvis	Jashan
Jadarius	JaMel	Jashon
Jadaryl	Jamell	Jathan
Jadon	Jamichael	Jathon
Jaha	Jamil	Jatravis
JahDey	Janard	Java
JahDoy	Janasfa	JaVar
Jahmar	Janorris	Javarius
Jahvaughn	Jaquan	Javaron
Jahvon	Jaquon	Javarous

214

Javarta
Javhar
Javon
Jawan
Jawon
Jawuan
Jawwan
Jayice
Jemel
Jemelle
Jenner
Jeray

Jermal
Jermall
Jermel
Jermell
Jeron
Jerrick
Jerrod
Jeshaun
Jevohn
Jevon
Jigness
Jolon

Jontrell
Jovontue
Jubarry
Juelian
Juneal
Junell
Jurall
Jurrell
Juvon
Juvone
Juwon

Kadarra
Kadrick
Kafhif
Kaheem
Kai-Jana
Ka Juanis
Kalama
Kalan

Kaleem
Kali
Kalief
Kalmus
Kalonji
Kamar
Kamishion
Kapena

Kapree
Karee
Kareel
Karmeeleyah
Karneil
Karnell
Kartrell
Karun

Kashon	Kelechi	Kennol
Kasonde	Kelepi	Kennon
Kasra	Kelis	Kennyatt
Kassa	Kellon	Kenroy
Katarius	Kelson	Kentavis
Katray	Kelton	Kenyon
Katrell	Keltron	Keon
Kavon	Kelvis	Keondre
Kayesean	Kelwood	Keondric
Kaylan	Kemal	Keontae
Kayron	Kemar	Kerek
Kayvon	Kempton	Keron
Kcey	Kenard	Kerron
Kchebe	Kenardo	Kesson
Keba	Kenari	Kethus
Kedron	Kenarri	Ketori
Keel	Kenawa	Ketric
Keelan	Kendale	Kevron
Keetron	Kendra	Keymetrius
Keetun	Kendrall	Keyontay
Keeven	Kendrayle	Keyrn
Kejuan	Kendrell	Khalique
Kelan	Kendron	Khambreal
Kelcy	Kendryl	Khambrell
Keldon	Keneef	Kharman
Keldrain	Kenin	Khemara
Keldrick	Kenji	Khemra
Kela	Kennan	Kiande
Kele	Kennet	Kibian
Kelean	Kennis	Kishahn

Kiwame	Kool	Kumar
Kiwane	Korey	Kydell
Kiyamm	Korie	Kyron
Kleedis	Kovey	

Laartis	Lajuan	Lapreece
Labar	Lakendric	Laprell
Labarius	Lakendrick	La Prese
LaBradford	Lakim	Laquan
Labrando	Lakista	Laquavis
Labrawn	Lamarcus	Laquenton
Lacatron	La Mare	Laquon
Ladall	Lamario	La Ray
Ladaniel	Lamaris	Larmar
Ladarian	Lamark	Larmel
LaDarrell	Lamarque	Larmell
La Derek	Lamarr	La Rocque
Ladexter	Lameek	Larod
Ladrius	Landell	La Ron
Lafonzo	LaNeil	Larome
La Jack	Lanorris	Laron
Lajavon	Lanue	Larrick
La Juan	Laphonso	Lashajuan

Lashaud	Le Baron	Leshon
La Shawn	Lebaron	Le Torre
Lashon	Lebert	Letrell
Lashwan	Lebryan	Letrone
Lathaniel	Ledale	Levan
Latrell	Ledon	LeVeldro
Lavall	LeeVeil	LeVon
Lavalle	Lefarris	Levoris
La Vance	Legrant	Lewin
Lavar	Lekendric	Londone
La Vaughn	Lemar	Lonell
Lavaughan	Lemarcus	Lonnell
La Vell	Lenaris	Lontay
Lavell	Lenear	Lossie
La Vonte	Lennard	Lovell
Lavoris	Lenneal	Lurance
La Waan	Lenorris	Luron
Lawanza	Leondris	Lyeneil
LaZelle	Lequan	Lyndell
Lazerick	Le Ron	Lynell
LeAndre	Leshawn	Lynntrell

M

Maclovio

Makal

Malique

Malton

Malvin

Maneet

Manice

Maniel

Manoj

Marcel

Marcell

Marceo

Marcnell

Marcum

Mardel

Marek

Marice

Marius

Markeis

Markeith

Markell

Markis

Marklon

Markus

Marnell

Marqell

Marquel

Marquell

Marquero

Martron

Martynas

Marvell

Marwan

Marzarius

Marzell

Mathan

Maurico

Maurisha

Mawubi

Medardo

Mekell

Mellover

Meltonio

Menyell

Merican

Michon

Mikell

Mikka

Minica

Mi-Quane

Mishaun

Mishawn

Monitirius

Montarius

Montavis

Montay

Monterrio

Montrale

Montrell

Moran

Mystik

N

Nabila	Nastas	Nethanel
Naeem	Natavius	Netrho
Nafese	Nathon	Newstell
Nafife	Natione	Nichonar
Nafis	Navid	Nihad
Nafius	Navpaul	Nimbo
Naftali	Navrattan	NiNie
Nahun	Nazir	Nitron
Najee	Nedrjick	Nizel
Nande	Nefta	Noberto
Nandel	Negele	Noeman
Nartavious	Nemanya	Nohan
Nartavleon	Nenad	Norvel
Narvel	Nerone	Norward
Naryan	Neshan	
Nashon	Netavius	

O

Obra
Obsner
Ochiel
Odonovan
Ofa
Olabese
Oldine
Omkar

Omm'A
Omo
Ondre
Ontriel
Onufre
Ordell
Orell
Orencio

Orien
Orren
Otus
Ovieh (Ova)
Ozell
Ozkan

P

Paris
Parmell
Parnell
Parron
Parshwa
Patrique

Peabo
Percell
Percelle
Pervires
Pharis
Pherleskis

Phozia
Pradel
Prashaun
Purnell

Quadaryl
Quadell
Quadry
Quame
Quandale
Quanell
Quantay
Quantelle

Quantrell
Quashawn
Quendell
Quenell
Quentrel
Quenzell
Quinard
Quindale

Quindell
Quinnell
Quinntal
Quinshun
Quintae
Quintrell
Quinzell
Quonah

Rachamin
Rachard
Rachid
Radell

Rafique
Rahakeem
Raheen
Rainell

Raishard
Raishawn
Rajev
Raleek

Ramard
Ramel
Ramell
Rami
Ramond
Ranarde
Randelson
Ranique
Rashad
Rashand
Rashaun
Rashawd
Rashel
Raskessa
Ravelnel
Raydell
Rayfus
Raynal
Raynel
Raynell
Rayshawn
Rayshon
Rayvon
Rell
Renardo

Rendell
Renel
Renell
Renique
Reshaud
Reshawn
Revelle
Reynell
Rhondall
Rhondell
Ricardel
Rimani
Riordran
Rochid
Rodell
Rodjo
Rodnell
Rodwell
Ronale
Rondall
Rondel
Rondell
Rondrell
Ronel
Ronell

Ronelle
Ronnel
Ronnell
Rontarius
Rontravis
Ronyell
Rosscil
(row sell)
Roszell
Rowell
Roydell
Royshan
Rucel
Rudell
Rudelle
Ruel
Rukidi
Rumeal
Ruthren
Ruwan
Ryad
Rydell
Rynell
Ryshawn

S

Sabino	Santelle	Shamarr
Sabre	Saquan	Shamaul
Sabrea	Sa Sha Ron	Shameer
Sabron	Saun	Shamel
Sadale	Savino	Shamele
Sadarius	Schemel	Shamell
Sadayo	Seandell	Shamik
Saderick	Sebon	Shammah
Sakal	Sedell	Shammel
Sakorey	Sedric	Shanden
Samar	Sedrick	Shanene
Sametrius	Selvin	Shantae
Samier	Sequana	Shaquai
Samiuela	Servando	Shaquon
Samnil	Serville	Shariff
Samora	Sethan	Sharima
Sanak	Shadron	Sharis
Sande	Shafarr	Sharone
Sandu	Shahif	Sharvelle
Sanjay	Shakeem	Shaumbee
Santana	Shamari	Shawndall

Shawnden
Shawnelle
Shawntae
Shawntell
Shawon
Shayan
Shazzon
Sheldron
Shemmill
Shemnill
Shenal
Sherif
Sherlon
Shermarl

Sherod
Sherrod
Sherron
Shevon
Shimichael
Shirmef
Shomari
Shon
Shondale
Shondel
Shonntay
Shontae
Shontarious
Shundell

Shylow
Siddell
Sirroan
Slaye
Sonnell
Stantell
Stefon
Sulaye
Surnell
Swakemyua
(swa key mia)
Symone
Syntyron

T

Taahron	Tajuan	Tasheed
Taari	Takeef	Tashon
Taaryon	Tamal	Tauheen
Tabari	Tamar	Tauris
Tabarus	Tamarcus	Taurmel
Tacari	Tamario	Tavar
Tacaris	Tamaris	Tavaras
Tacory	Tamarius	Tavarri
Tacovi	Tamarr	Tavarris
Tadarias	Tanzel	Tavars
Taddius	Taquan	Tavarus
Taeron	Tarell	Tavio
Tafarere	Tarelle	Ta Von
Tafari	Tariq	Tavon
Tafarie	Tarnorris	Ta'Vonne
Tafton	Tarsheen	Ta Vonte
Taharqua	Tarthell	Tavores
Taheer	Tarvaris	Tavoris
Tahkai	Tarvon	Tavorius
Tahron	Tarvoris	Tavorris
Tahshawn	Tashee	Tavuris

Tawara	Termarcus	Therron
Tawrence	Termayne	Thurl
Tayquere	Teron	Tierre
Tayron	Terraye	Tikori
Tchaka	Terreal	Tikshaud
Tebais	Terrelle	Timaris
Tedric	Terrill	Tiombe
Tedrick	Terron	Tion
Tedrin	Terrone	Tiquan
Tedron	Terrynce	Tivon
Teedray	Terryon	T Jae
Teejay	Tervarius	Toddrell
Tefari	Teryl	Tolani
Tehuti	Tetric	Torell
Telbert	Tevaris	Toris
Tellis	Tevarus	Tradale
Telvin	Tevon	Trajan
Temarcus	Tevoris	Tramaine
Tendayi	Tezeell	Tramayne
Tendi	Thabo	Travell
Tenkera	Thamar	Travelle
Tenorris	Thamonn	Travior
Tenqualus	Thara	Travon
Teodoro	Tharon	Travontae
Teodross	Theandre	Travor
Teon	Theapolis	Travoris
Terelle	Thehandre	Travorus
Teric	Themis	Traychel
Terick	Theodario	Traynard
Termaine	Theroni	Trayon

Trayshawn	Trevel	Tyquan
Trechard	Trevelle	Tyree
Tredel	Trevis	Tyreece
Tredell	Trevonn	Tyreef
Trelonnie	Trevoris	Tyreel
Tremell	Trevorus	Tyreen
Tremelle	Treymane	Tyrelle
Trenard	Tristan	Tyren
Trendon	Troychel	Tyrenzo
Trendun	Turell	Tyrill
Trennard	Turi	Tyrin
Trenttonio	Turrell	Tyriq
Treon	Tyhim	Tyrrell
Trevares	Tyji	Tyshawn
Trevaris	Tyjuan	Tyshon
Trevaughn	Tylon	Tywan

Udell   Undrea
Umar   Urell

Vanard   Varnell   Vernell
Vandale   Vaushon   Vershawn
Vandy   Vendell   Vidal
Vanshawn   Verdell   Vondae
Vantrell   Vernal   Voshon
Varmar   Vernall

W

Wabon
Wadale
Wadell
Wadsin
Waheed
Wakeem

Wakell
Waldale
Waleed
Wamoth
Wanell
Warya

Waynell
Wellman
Wilman
Wondell
Wydell
Wykeen

Y

Yakeen
Yanell

Yarnell
Yavari

Z

Zachari
Zachory
Zadri

Zandrae
Zaquan
Zarick

Zemarr
Zentil
Zeshawn

Names
for Girls

Traditional American

Names for Girls

When I left the house of bondage I left everything behind. I wasn't going to keep nothing of Egypt on me, an' so I went to the Lord an' asked him to give me a new name. And he gave me Sojourner because I was to travel up and down the land showing the people their sins and bein' a sign unto them. I told the Lord I wanted two names 'cause everybody else had two, and the Lord gave me Truth, because I was to declare the truth to the people.

—SOJOURNER TRUTH
NARRATIVE OF SOJOURNER TRUTH, 1850

Note: *You'll also notice some created names as you read through the European based names. These are names that have become more common and widely enough used to be included here.*

A

Abarena This unusual name found among African-American females in 1899 may be related to Abarrane, the feminine version of Abraham. It may be an African-American version of Abina, meaning born on Thursday, from the Akan people of Ghana.

Abb This highly unusual first name appears among free black names of the 19th century.

Abba A very rare first name, found among 19th-century free black women.

Abbey *French:* A diminutive for Abigail (see below). Also Abbie, Abby, Abbe. Abbey is highly recognizable because of the contributions of singer, actress, and poet Abbey Lincoln.

Abda *Hebrew:* A masculine name found in 1 Kings 4:6. Abda was a Levite. Abda Bussion is a college student.

Abiah This highly unusual name of the 19th century became obsolete during the 20th.

Abigail *Hebrew:* My father rejoices. Also Abigal (which some sources claim to be the original Hebrew spelling), Abagail, Abigale, Abbigale, Abbygail, Abigal. The biblical Abigail of 1 Samuel 25 stops King David from shedding blood.

Abrena This apparent African-American creation appears in the 1920s, but its use was never widespread. It perhaps draws from Abra, sometimes considered the feminine form of Abraham.

Abriana *Italian:* The feminine form of Abraham.

Acubeth An unusual name employed by free black women in New England during the 19th century.

Ada *German:* Happy, prosperous. Also Aida. With the assistance of Thurgood Marshall and the NAACP, Ada Lois Sipuel broke the color bar and gained admission into the University of Oklahoma Law School in 1949. Born in Chickasha, Okla., she was the first black to attend the university. Ada S. McKinley in 1919 founded the Southside Settlement House in Chicago. This first settlement house for blacks with a black staff is now named McKinley House for its founder. The beautiful Aida Overton Walker was a pioneer entertainer.

Adah *Hebrew:* Adornment. Adah Issacs Menken was an actress from Louisiana who lived and worked in Paris until her untimely death in 1868.

Adaline A variation of Adeline (see below).

Adamina *French:* The feminine form of Adam. Rare.

Addie This diminutive for Adelaide and other names beginning with Ade was quite popular among African-American parents for several generations. Also Addy. Women's rights activist Addie W. Hunton was a primary organizer of the Fourth Pan-African Congress held in New York City in 1927.

Adela A little-used short form of Adelaide (see below). Also Adella, Adelia. Adella Hunt Logan (1863–1915) was an indomitable supporter of a woman's right to vote and of the education of blacks.

Adelaide *German/French:* Nobility. Adelaide Sanford, a member of the New York State Board of Regents, has devoted her life to improving educational standards for black children. Born in 1900, Adelaide Washington is a highly respected Gullah resident in South Carolina.

Adele *German:* Noble. Also Adelle, Adellah, Adell.

Adeline One of the numerous adaptations of Adelaide (see above) so popular during the late 19th and early 20th centuries. Also Adaline, Adelina.

Adelphi *Greek:* Of a masculine connotation, Mount Adelphi is where the Greek oracle resided. However, it is noted among 19th-century black female names.

Adelphia A version of Adelphi (see above) found in the early 20th century.

Adesta A rare name appearing in Puckett's index of unusual black female names.

Adina *Hebrew:* Noble. *French:* Adornment. Also Adeana, Adine.

Adira *Hebrew:* Noble, powerful.

Adlena A rare name and a testament to African-American naming creativity in Puckett's index of unusual names.

Adona The feminine of Adonis, the handsome young man of Greek mythology who won the love of Aphrodite, the mythical goddess of love. Also Adonia.

Adoncia *Spanish:* Sweet.

Adorna *English:* To adorn.

Adrana This name appears to be of recent invention. Also Adrena, Adrenia.

Adrienne *Latin:* Dark one; the feminine form of Adrian. Also Adriana, Adrianne, Adriene. Adrienne Ingrum is a publisher and vice-president who lives in Harlem.

Aesha A common African-American spelling variation of the Swahili Aisha which means life, prosperous. Also Aiesha.

Affee This unusual 17th-century African-American female name is said to have African origins.

Affie Affic is first noted in the early 20th century.

Agatha *Greek:* Good. The Christian St. Agatha was a third-century virgin martyr.

Aggy A nickname for Agnes (see below) or Agatha (see above) used as a given name by free black parents of the 17th and 18th centuries. Also Aggie. Athlete Aggie Harrison is a triple jumper for Texas A&M University.

Agnes *Greek:* Pure, virginal.

Aileen *Irish:* Light. Also Ayleen. Aileen Clark Hernandez is a noted labor relations specialist and women's rights advocate. In 1966, she founded her own public relations and management firm.

Ailese Noted among 17th- and 18th-century free black women.

Aimee *French:* Beloved. This French version of Amy (see below) is found among Haitian-Americans.

Airlessa Noted on Puckett's 19th-century list, Airlessa sounds like an African-American invention.

Airzena Clearly an African-American invention, this name is found on Puckett's 19th-century list.

Aisey This highly unusual name appears in Washington, D.C., among black females during the 18th century.

Aisula Another Puckett pearl, Aisula resonates with African vibrations.

Alabama Found among female names in this state on Puckett's 1877–1937 list.

Alair *Greek:* Cheerful.

Alana *French:* A feminine form of Alan. Also Alanna, Allanna, Allena, Alayna. Its use is first noted in the 20th century and is a favored name of black American parents.

Alandra *Spanish:* A form of Alexandra.

Alanza A feminine form of Alonzo.

Alaundra Alaundra Carter lives in San Diego.

Alazanah Noted in the 1920s.

Albenia This early 20th-century African-American invention never received widespread use.

Alberta *German:* Noble shining; the feminine form of Albert. Alberta has endured as a favored name. At the tender age of 12, Alberta Hunter began her career as a blues singer in 1907 Chicago. She retired in 1954 to care for her mother and study to become a practical nurse. After working as a nurse for 20 years, the indefatigable Hunter resumed her singing career and recorded an album at age 83.

Albertha A popular spelling variation of Alberta (see above).

Albertina This feminine form of Albert has been favored by black parents since the 19th century. Albertina Waller, gospel vocalist, is noted in the New York *Amsterdam News.* Albertina Sisulu is the wife of Walter Sisulu, a South African patriot.

Alcenia Found on Puckett's list of black female names of the late 19th and early 20th centuries, Alcenia appears to be a variation of Alcina, who in Greek mythology is a sorceress ruler over a magical island.

Aldara *Greek:* Winged gift.

Aldezena An unusual name found among free black women in the Washington, D.C., area, in the 18th century.

Aldia Collected in *Black Names in American.*

Aldina *German:* Old. Also Alda, Aldine, Aldyne, Aleda.

Aldira *Hebrew:* Noble, mighty. Found in Puckett's collection, Aldira has never been widely used and has been largely neglected in the latter 20th century.

Aldona *German:* The old one.

Aldonia Noted by Puckett.

Aldonza *Spanish:* Sweet.

Aldora *English:* Noble gift.

Aleana This unusual name may be related to Alena, called by one source the Russian variation of Helen (see below) and by another a diminutive of Magdalena, but its origin is not clear. Also, Alenna, Alennia. It appears in Puckett's collection of the 1920s.

Aleda The origins of this contemporary creation are unclear and disputed. One source describes it as a form of Alda.

A'Lelia This lovely name represents another early indication of our fancy for name elaboration. A'Lelia Walker, the famous daughter of Sarah Breedlove McWilliams Walker, widely known as Madame C. J. Walker, was a patron of the arts during the Harlem Renaissance of the 1920s.

Aleta *Greek:* Footloose.

Aletha *Greek:* Truth. Also Alethea, Aleethia, Alethia, Alithia. Aletha and Alethea are perhaps the most popular versions of this name, which has been long favored by African-American parents.

Alexa A feminine form of Alexander. Born in Lansing, Mich., Alexa Canady is a double first. She was the first female and the first black neurosurgical resident at the University of Minnesota.

Alexis *Greek:* Defender. Originally a boy's name, it is now exclusively used for girls. Alexis DeVeau is a poet and author.

Alfre A diminutive for Alfreda (see below). Actress Alfre Woodward played Winnie Mandela in the HBO biopic about the struggle of Winnie and Nelson Mandela to overcome apartheid.

Alfreda The feminine form of Alfred. Also Alfreeda.

Alice *German:* Noble. Also Alecia, Alicea, Alicia. Alicia is perhaps the most often used form. Poet, essayist, and novelist Alice Malsenior Walker is by far our most famous and well-received Alice. She has won the Pulitzer Prize for fiction and the American Book Award. Alicia Hastings became chairperson of the Department of Physical Medicine and Rehabilitation at Howard University in 1967. Physician Alice Woodby McKane, with the assistance of her husband, founded the first school for black nurses in southeast Georgia. Community activist Alice Harris was a 1993 *Essence* Awards recipient. In 1948, when she won the high jump, Alice Coachman became the first black woman to win an Olympic Gold Medal.

Alina *Slavic:* A variation of Helen (see below).

Alisha This variation of Alice is enormously popular among black parents. The drama of the spelling quite likely has origins in the black penchant for the distinct.

Alison This variation of Alice (see above) is surging in popularity. Also Allison. Allison Brown is a student in Detroit.

Aljenae Aljenae Elizabeth Wilson's parents combined the names of her father (Alvin), her mother (Jean), and her father's uncle (Nathan). She is an elementary school teacher and mother of three in Highland Park, Mich.

Allene This form of Alice (see above) has been very popular but is now neglected. Also Alene, Allena.

Alma *Latin:* Born with a giving nature. This name has been well-used by African-American parents. Alma Thomas is a highly touted educator and artist.

Almarine *German:* Work ruler. Rare.

Almeda *Latin:* One who is focused and achieves.

Almeta This variation of Almeda (see above) first appeared among early 20th-century African-American women. Also Almetta. Almetta appears among contemporary women.

Almira *Arabic:* Princess, exalted.

Almitra The woman who touched the heart of the prophet in Kahlil Gibran's *The Prophet*. Rare. Almitra Dye is a young housewife and student in Detroit.

Alona *Hebrew:* Strong as an oak tree.

Alphonsine This feminine version of Alphonso was found among black females in Georgia, 1899.

Alta *Latin:* Elevated, lofty. Actress Alta Harrison was a key member in Detroit's theater movement.

Altamase This unusual variation of Alta (see above) appears confined to the black experience. Also Altamese.

Altha This apparent black variation of Alta (see above) appears on Puckett's 1936 list. Unusual.

Althea   *Greek:* Wholesome, or with healing power. Also Althia. Raised in Harlem and educated at the historically black Florida A&M University, Althea Gibson was the first black to compete successfully in major international tennis play. Althea T. L. Simmons is the chief congressional lobbyist of the NAACP.

Altonia   Altonia is found in Puckett's index of unusual names.

Altoria   This name in Puckett's index sounds like an African-American invention. Rare.

Altovise   Altovise Davis, the wife of the late Sammy Davis Jr., was a former Broadway dancer.

Alva   *Hebrew:* Brightness. Used mainly for boys in white families, but seen more among girls in black families. Although it occurs over generations, Alva is not in widespread use.

Alvena   Feminine version of Alvin. Also Alvenia.

Alverda   This name resonates with African-American sound approaches to names.

Alvira   This invention appears in 1936 according to Puckett's list.

Alzarah   An odd name of the late 19th and early 20th century in the South.

Alzera   An unusual name appearing on Puckett's early 20th-century list.

Alzetta   Alzetta Latrice Bozeman is a member of the class of 1993, Spelman College.

Alzora   Several variations of this name appear among blacks during the early 20th century. Regular use was apparently short-lived.

Amanda   *Latin:* Worthy of much love. Before her death in 1957, pharmacist Amanda Victoria Gray Hilyer operated her own drugstore in Washington, D.C., for many years. Her cultural, social, and political activities made her a pillar of the community. Amanda Berry Smith was a renowned missionary and evangelist who served on four continents.

Amaretta   Noted in the 1700s.

Amarillis   An unusual name employed by free blacks in New England during the 18th century. It could be a spelling variation of Amaryllis, a shepherdess in the poems of the poet Virgil. It means fresh.

Amber   *French:* A semiprecious gem of the golden-brown or amber hue. Although not widespread, Amber has been used regularly by black parents.

Amelia   *German:* Industrious, one who strives to accomplish. The Spanish version is Amalia.

Amertine   Found among early 20th-century names listed by Puckett.

Amia   This unusual form of Amy (see below) is found among 18th-century black families.

Amy   *Latin:* Beloved. Also Ammie.

Ana   A Spanish form of Anna.

Anaka   With tones of Africa, Anaka appears on Puckett's 18th-century list. Also Anaca, Anaky, Aneca, Anecky, Annaka. It may be related to the Hausa Anika, which means sweet face. Anaka Brown lives in Highland Park, Mich.

Anastasia   *Greek:* Resurrection. Also Annastasia, Anastashia.

Anderia   Here, Andrea (see below) becomes An Dee Ria.

Andrea   *Greek:* A man's woman. *Latin:* Womanly. Also Andra, Andria.

Aneesha   Newly created. Aneesha Hardin is a student at South Bronx Job Corps Center in New York.

Angela   *Greek:* Messenger; the feminine form of Angel. Angels are considered messengers of God. Activist, educator, and author Angela Davis graduated magna cum laude from Brandeis University in 1965. Angela Bofill is a famous jazz singer.

Angelica *Latin:* Like an angel. Also Agelika, Angelique. Angelique Ray attends Heritage Hall High School, in Oklahoma City.

Angeline This form of Angela (see above) was favored by black parents in the early 20th century. Also Angelina, Angelena.

Angelois A blend of Angela (see above) and Lois (see below).

Anika Anika Poitier is the daughter of actor and producer Sidney Poitier.

Anilesa Anilesa may be a variation of the German Anneliese, a combination of Ann (see below) and Liesa. Also Anna Lisa, Annelisa, Annelise.

Anissa Anissa Rena Cooke graduated from Howard University magna cum laude, class of 1993.

Anita *Spanish:* A diminutive for Ann (see below). Also Anitra. Oklahoma University Law School professor Anita Hill is a famous bearer of this name. Dancer and actress Anita Bush founded the first major African-American dramatic company. The Anita Bush Players gave Harlem audiences a taste of Broadway and provided work for black actors. Pop singer Anita Baker appeared on the 1993 *Essence* Awards show at Madison Square Garden in New York City.

Ann The English version of the Hebrew Hannah, which means grace. Also Anna, Anne, Annie, Anny. All forms of this name have been enormously popular among black parents as a girl's name. Annie M. Turnbo Malone was a business executive and philanthropist. Anna Julia Cooper, whose 106 years spanned from slavery to the civil rights movement, dedicated her life to higher education for blacks. Activist and author Anna Arnold Hedgeman was a tireless and famous social worker whose life work was social justice. Annie Wealthy Holland (1871–1934) was an illustrious teacher who ably assisted her students in rural North Carolina. Humanitarian Anna Elizabeth Lewis Hudlum devoted her life to uplift African-Americans in Chicago. Ann Lane Petry is the author of *The Street*.

Annala Ann is used as a prefix for several names. This appears to be an African-American variation on the theme, found in Puckett's collection.

Annaritta An apparent African-American invention noted on Puckett's list.

Annette A French form of Ann. Also Annetta.

Annis *Greek:* Whole, complete.

Annulette A name found on Puckett's 1933 list.

Anona *Latin:* The Roman goddess of the harvest. Also Anonna.

Antoinette *Latin:* Priceless; a feminine version of Anthony. Also Antonia.

Apphia A name employed by free blacks in New England in the 18th century.

April *Latin:* Opening up or born in April. This lovely spring month is regularly used as a girl's name. Single mother April Rhone is a businesswoman. Her company, Afri-Concepts, is located in Dallas.

Aqualyn Aqualyn Yhane Laury is a Spelman College graduate.

Araminta Invented by an 18th-century British playwright, this very unusual name is noted among turn-of-century black women. Rare.

Arberta An African-American variation of Alberta.

Arcadia *Greek:* Happiness. Also Arcada.

Ardella *Latin:* Ardent with enthusiasm. Ardelia and Ardell are forms of the name found among black schoolgirls, 1877–1937.

Arenia The origins of this unusual name quite probably lie in black invention. Arenia Conelia Mallory was founding president of Saints Junior College, Lexington, Ky.

Areta *Greek:* Virtue.

Aretha This variation of Areta (see above) is found almost exclusively among blacks. Aretha Franklin grew up singing in her father's church in Detroit. Dubbed the queen of soul, she has achieved world renown and adulation.

Ariadne *Greek:* Chaste. Also Ariana, Arriana.

Arilla An unusual name found among 18th-century black women in Washington, D.C.

Arizona This western state's name is found on Puckett's 20th century list for females.

Arlene *Latin:* Strong, womanly. Also Arline.

Arlyn Arlyn Traylor is the daughter of Lynda Gunn, a model who posed for Norman Rockwell. Arlyn's mother is the little girl in Rockwell's "The Problem We Will Live With."

Arminta Noted in the early 20th century.

Arnell The feminine form of Arnold.

Arrenia An 18th-century black woman's name.

Arsula An invention that sounds like a blend of the European and the African.

Artemisia In Greek mythology, Artemis was the goddess of the moon, of hunting, and of wild animals. This is also the name of a sagebrushlike plant found in dry regions. Artemisia E. Dinwiddie was a wife and mother of five.

Artesia An unusual name found on Puckett's list.

Arthurene A feminine form of Arthur. Also Arthurine.

Artu Noted among unusual names in the early 20th century.

Arva Arva Quester Blackwood is a member of the class of 1993, College of New Rochelle.

Ashanta A variation of Ashanti, the name of a West African ethnic group. Also Ashante, Ashaunta, Ashuntae.

Athena *Greek:* Wisdom. Also Athenia. Rarely used.

Audreen A form of Audrey (see below). Audreen Ballard is an editor.

Audrey *English:* Noble strength. Also Audra, Audre. Poet, essayist, and librarian Audre Lourde displayed noble strength in her battle with cancer.

Augusta *Latin:* Exalted; feminine version of Augustus. Librarian Augusta Alexander Baker received many awards for her work in the field of children's literature. In 1953, she became the storyteller specialist for the prestigious New York Public Library system. Augusta Christine Savage is widely acclaimed for her intense and serious sculpture.

Augustena An elaboration of Augusta (see above), noted in Augusta, Ga., in 1899.

Aurelia *Latin:* Golden.

Aurora *Latin:* Roman goddess of dawn.

Autherine This unusual name sounds like an African-American invention. Autherine Lucy was the first black person ever admitted to a white school or university in the state of Alabama.

Autree A variation of Audrey (see above). An unusual name among schoolgirls in 1877–1937.

Ava *Hebrew:* Like a bird.

Avis *Latin:* A bird.

Avonia Found among free blacks in the 18th century.

Ayesha A popular variation of the Swahili Aisha, which means life. Also Ayiesha, Ayeisha, Ayisha.

Ayanna Also Ayana, Ayania, Ayannia. Ayanna Ragin is one of *Ebony* magazine's 1993 Top High School Seniors. A senior at Benjamin Franklin High School in New Orleans, Ayanna plans to pursue a career as a writer.

Azalia Azalia Hackley was a foremost librarian and collector of African-American artifacts.

Azalie This name sounds like a variation of the once-popular Hazel Lee.

Azania This is the name given to South Africa by the indigenous people. Here it is used as a girl's first name.

Azarene Name found among unusual schoolgirl names, 1877–1937.

Azariah *Hebrew:* Whom God helps. In the Old Testament, 28 different men are called Azariah. Although in Hebrew it is a male name, Azariah is noted among female names in Puckett's collection.

Azeline Noted among schoolgirls, 1877–1937.

Azie Name in Puckett's index of unusual names. In 1977, Azie Taylor Norton became the 36th treasurer of the U.S., the first black woman in that position.

Azuba This unusual name is found among free black names in New England during the 18th century.

Babette A diminutive for Barbara (see below). Rare.

Balenda Balenda Lavelle Nelson is a member of the class of 1993, Howard University.

Ballencia This variation of Valencia (see below) appears among unusual schoolgirl names.

Barbara *Greek:* Barbarian, foreign. The enormous popularity of this given name is seen in the large number of outstanding African-American women who answer to it. The elegant Barbara Summers, model turned writer, is the editor of *I Dream a World: Portraits of Black Women Who Changed America,* and the author of *Nou-*

velle Soul, a collection of contemporary short stories.
Barbara Chase-Riboud, sculptor, writer, and poet, has
lived in Paris since 1961, where she has achieved international acclaim for her contributions to the fine arts
and literature. Reverend Barbara Clementine Harris became the first woman bishop in the Episcopal church on
Feb. 12, 1989. The formidable Barbara Jordan, U.S.
Representative, outstripped her own stellar record of
achievement when she spoke on the duty of public officials. Barbara J. Wilson is the CEO of Ferndale Honda,
Inc., in Ferndale, Mich.

Barnetta   This unusual name is another indication of the
African-American flair for drama in naming their children, especially girls.

Bathsheba   *Biblical/Hebrew:* Daughter of an oath. In the
Old Testament, Bathsheba is a wife of King David and
the mother of King Solomon. Found among free black
names 1800–60. Rare.

Beah   The origins of Beah are not known. Actress Beah
Richards was born in Vicksburg, Miss. in 1926.

Beata   *Latin:* Blessed happy one.

Beatrice   *Latin:* She brings happiness. Also Beatryce. Favored by black parents over several generations,
Beatrice remains in steady use. Beatryce Nivens is the
author of *The Black Woman's Career Guide.*

Becae   Name found in Puckett's list, "In the Beginning:
1619–1799." Also Beck, Bek.

Becki   A diminutive for Rebecca (see below). Also
Becky. Regularly used as a given name.

Beda   *English:* Warrior maiden.

Bedelia   *Irish:* Strength.

Bela   *Czech:* White. Also Belalisa.

Belessa   This appears to be a variation on Belle (see below) confined to black parents. It was first noted in the
19th century.

Belinda   Sources describe Belinda as of uncertain origin, having English upper-class connotations, and used by Alexander Pope in *The Rape of the Lock*. One source says it derives from the old Spanish Bellalinda, which means beautiful. Belinda appears on Puckett's list of free black names, 1800–60.

Bellah Found in the 19th century. Also Bella. Accountant Bella Marshall is a Detroit city official.

Belle *French:* Beautiful. Also Bell. Never widely used by black or white families it is most often heard in the phrases "belle of the ball" or "Southern belle." The highly respected black intellectual Bell Hooks is the author of *Ain't I A Woman*. Hooks used the title of Sojourner Truth's famous speech to distinguish her book.

Belzara A distinctive African-American variation on Belle (see above), appearing in the 19th century.

Belzora An unusual 19th-century listing.

Bemshi Bemshi Shearer explains that her father coined her name from a jazz song, "Bemsha Swing." She is a jazz singer living in New York.

Bena *Hebrew:* Wise; a feminine form of Ben.

Benilde Benilde Little is a writer.

Benita *Latin:* Blessed.

Bera *German:* Of the bear.

Berdine *German:* Bright maiden.

Berit *Scandinavian:* Magnificent.

Bernadette *French:* Courageous as a bear; a feminine form of Bernard. Also Bernadeena, Bernadene, Bernadett, Bernadetta, Bernadina, Bernadine, Berneta, Bernetta, Bernette, Bernita. In 1990, when Rick Pitino, head coach of the famed Kentucky Wildcats college basketball team, hired Bernadette Locke-Mattox, she became the first woman ever named to the coaching staff of a men's major college basketball team. A graduate of Detroit's Northeastern High School and Michigan State Normal College, Bernadine Newson Denning has dedicated her life to improving the quality of education in public schools.

Berndella Noted in the 19th century.

Bernice *Greek/Latin:* She who brings victory. Also Bernelle, Bernetta, Bernette. This name enjoyed widespread popularity until the recent surge of inventions. Bernice J. Reagon is a civil rights activist and singer who organized Sweet Honey in the Rock, a folk-music group that has sung its political message around the world.

Berta A black variation of Bertha (see below).

Bertha *German:* Bright. This once-popular name has been neglected in the latter half of the 20th century.

Berthana This adaptation of Bertha (see above) appears on Puckett's 1800–60 list. There is no evidence of its use in the 20th century.

Berthelle Found on Puckett's 19th-century list, this unusual name resonates with sounds preferred by African-Americans of that period.

Berthena This variation on Bertha (see above) is another example of our preference to embellish or extend sounds.

Bertie A nickname for various names ending in bert, sometimes used as a given name.

Bertie Mae This two-name combination was popular at the turn of the century, but two-name combinations never made it out of the 1950s and are rare in the 1990s.

Bertina *German:* Shining bright.

Bertlina A variation of Bertha (see above) noted in southern cities in 1899.

Beryl *Greek:* This sea-green jewel was an emblem of good fortune. Beryl Banfield is a noted educator and consultant in New York City.

Bess *Hebrew:* Consecrated to God. Also Bessie, Bessy, Bessye. These diminutives for Elizabeth (see below) have obtained first-name status. Bessie Blake is the dean of the School of New Resources, College of New Rochelle. Bessye Banks Bearden, mother of the famed artist Romare Bearden, was nationally known for her work in the Democratic Party. Empress of the blues Bessie Smith is credited with blending African and Western styles of music. Bessie Coleman was the first black woman aviator. Quite a few distinguished women have answered to Bessie.

Beth *Hebrew:* This diminutive for Elizabeth (see below) is often employed by white families. Although regularly used, it occurs less frequently among black families.

Betsy One of the several diminutives for Elizabeth (see below). Betsy is seldom used by black families.

Betty This diminutive for Elizabeth (see below) has enjoyed long-standing extensive popularity. Recently it is most often seen in combination with other names: Betty Jean, Betty Ann, Betty Jo, Betty Lou. It appears on Puckett's list of names most often used among free black women in the South, 1619–1799, as Betty, Bett, and Bette. The parents of Betye Saar gave an unusual spin to the more common spelling. Saar is an award-winning artist and educator. College administrator Betty Shabazz is the widow of Malcolm X.

Beulah *Hebrew:* She who is to be married. Following the negative stereotyping perceived by black parents in the TV show portraying Beulah as the maid, the name has been totally neglected since the late 1950s.

Beverly *English:* Dweller at the beaver meadow. This name has enjoyed sustained popularity among black parents. Beverly Johnson was the first black model to appear on the cover of *Vogue.* Beverly Chapital is a psychologist and counselor in New Orleans.

Bianca *Italian:* White.

Biddy The courageous Biddy Mason overcame the horrendous hardships of slavery. Although she was not allowed to speak, because blacks were not permitted to testify against whites, Biddy won the freedom of her family in the California court system on Jan. 21, 1856.

Named Bridget (see below) at birth but called Biddy all of her life, this strong woman distinguished herself as a skilled nurse and midwife. She used the skills she learned in slavery to serve the citizens of Los Angeles and became one of the first black women to own property there.

Billie   *English:* Resolute, has willpower. This is the feminine version of Billy, which is a diminutive for William. Born Eleanora Fagan, Billie Holiday embarked on a fabled career as a jazz singer that was marked by triumph and tragedy.

Binah   This name resonates with African origins. Similar to the popular Benta of Senegal, Binah appears on Puckett's list "In the Beginning, 1619–1799."

Birdie   *English:* Little birdlike one. Also Birdia.

Blanche   *French:* The fair, white one. Blanche Calloway is the sister of the great entertainer Cab Calloway. For a period, she was the lead vocalist for his dance band. In 1930, Blanche Calloway formed her own band, becoming the first woman to lead an all-male band.

Blossom   *English:* Fresh, springlike, lovely.

Bobbie   This pet form of Roberta (see below) is used regularly but infrequently. Also Bobbi. Bobbie Jo and Bobbie Lee are popular two-name combinations. Bobbi Kristina Brown is the infant daughter of soul superstars, Bobby Brown and Whitney Houston.

Bohemia   A most unusual name appearing among free blacks in the 17th century.

Bonelle   An African-American variation of Bonnie (see below).

Bonita   *Spanish:* Good, pretty.

Bonnie   *Scottish:* The good one, fair of face.

Brandi   This variant of Brandy is well-liked by black parents.

Brenda   *German:* Firebrand. This name has enjoyed enormous popularity among black parents.

Brenna *Irish:* Raven maid.

Bria The origins of this name are not clear, but it appears to be a recent invention. Bria Murphy is the daughter of Eddie and Nicole Murphy.

Briana Derived from the masculine Brian. Also Briane, Briann, Brianna, Brianne. Brianna Sabrae Green lives in New York City.

Bridget *Irish:* Strong, protective power. Appears in the early 17th century. Used regularly but infrequently.

Brie *French:* A region famous for its cheese of the same name.

Brina Brina may be related to Breanna or it could be an independent invention. One source describes the name as Slavic, meaning defender.

Brooklynne The feminization of New York's most famous borough may imply that the daughter was conceived there. Thus she is Brooklyn's child.

Brunella *French:* Little one with brown hair.

Burdelle An unusual name that resonates with sounds of an African-American invention.

Calandra *Greek:* Lark.

Caledonia *Latin:* From Scotland; Caledonia is an ancient name for Scotland. Also Caldonia. Popular among black parents in the deep South around the turn of the century, Caldonia bit the dust with the popularity of Louis Jordan's song "Caldonia, What Makes Yo' Big Head So Hard?"

California The name of one of our loveliest and most popular states is found among the unusual names of schoolgirls by Puckett.

Calvetta A 1993 *Ebony* Bachelorette, Calvetta Phair is a financial planner in Seattle.

Camelia *American:* A flower. Popular during the period of flower names (Violet, Rose, Iris) that started at the turn of the century and faded near the middle.

Camera Camera Ashe is the daughter of Jeanne and Arthur Ashe. Her mother is a highly respected photographer.

Camille *Latin:* Young ceremonial attendant; the name is said to refer to the beautiful virgin girls who participated in a Roman pagan religious ceremony. Also Camilla. Philanthropist Camille Cosby is the wife of comedian Bill Cosby.

Candace *Latin:* Glitter, glowing white. Also Candice, Candis, Candee, Candy, Candi, Kandy, Kandi. The spelling Candis first appears among free black names in the 19th century. Candace was the name of an ancient Ethiopian queen. Candace "Candy" Shannon is a broadcaster in Washington, D.C.

Canzata An African-American invention. Canzata Smith lives in Tulsa, Okla.

Cara *Latin:* Darling.

Caralee An African-American variation of Cara (see above) appearing on Puckett's list.

Caresse *French/Latin:* Dear one. Also Carissa, Caresa, Caressa, Carisa, Charissa, Karis, Karisa.

Carina *Italian:* Dear little one.

Carita *Latin:* Beloved.

Carla The feminine form of Carl. A fashionable name among black parents.

Carlease Found in Puckett's collection of unusual names.

Carlene Variation of Carla (see above) in regular but infrequent use among black parents. Also Carleen.

Carleta This variation of Carla (see above) is seen in Puckett's collection.

Carlodena A variation of Carla (see above) appearing in Puckett's index of unusual names.

Carlotta This Italian form of Carla (see above) is found among African-Americans.

Carmen *Latin:* A song. Carmen McRae is a famous jazz singer who has enchanted audiences around the world.

Carnella The origins of this name appear to lie in African-American creativity. Reverend Carnella Barnes committed her ministry to the aid of senior citizens.

Carnetta This name, an apparent invention, appears on Puckett's list of unusual names.

Carol *Latin:* From Carola; strong and womanly; a feminine form of Carl and Charles, as well as a diminutive for Caroline (see below). Also Carel, Carey, Carole, Carley, Caryll. Appearing about 100 years ago, it is now an enormously popular first name among both black and white parents. Broadcast journalist Carole Simpson is an anchor for ABC.

Caroline *Latin:* Little, womanly one; a feminine form of Carl and Charles. Also Carolina, Caraleen, Caraleena, Caralyne, Caralynn, Carolyn. The name was found among 18th-century free black names. Caroline Virginia Still Anderson was a prominent physician in Pennsylvania from 1878 until her death in 1919. Carolyn Robertson Payton was the first black woman director of the Peace Corps.

Carrie This diminutive for Carol (see above) has taken on first-name status. Also Carrey, Carie, Cari. In 1987, Carrie Saxon Perry became the first black woman mayor of Hartford, Conn.

Casey *Irish:* Watchful. Also Cacey, Cacie, Casi, Casie.

Casina This unusual 18th-century name may have origins in the Greek Cassia, which means cinnamon.

Cassandra Cassandra is the unheeded prophet of Greek mythology who warned the Trojans against accepting the wooden horse. Also Casandra. Called by some a name of doom and gloom, the elegant-sounding Cassandra is found among 18th-century free black names. Critics call vocalist Cassandra Wilson innovative and experimental in her approach to jazz.

Catherine *Greek:* Pure one. Also Catherina, Caitrona, Caity, Catti, Catarina, Catarine, Cathaleen, Cathleen, Cathryn, Catryna. The history of this name is deep and full of luster. With phonetic variations, the name is found in every Western country as well as among 18th-century free black women. Catti is a sculptor who works in mixed media. Catherine Elizabeth Sarita McKinley is a writer and aspiring literary agent.

Cecilia *Latin:* Blind, dimly sighted one; a feminine form of Cecil. Also Cecelia, Celia, Cissie. In modern times, the name is associated with music, since St. Cecilia is the patron saint of music. Cecelia Adkins is the executive director of the Sunday School Publishing Board of the National Baptist Convention, USA. Cecilia Roberts is the chief executive of Majestic Life Insurance Co. of New Orleans, the 15th largest black-owned insurance company in the nation.

Cecily A form of Cecilia (see above) found among 18th-century free black names. Also Cicely. Actress Cicely Tyson won widespread critical acclaim for roles in the movie *Sounder* and the TV production *The Autobiography of Miss Jane Pittman.* Cicely D. Cooper is advertising coordinator for *Emerge.*

Cedrice Newly created. Cedrice Nichole Davis graduated magna cum laude, class of 1993, Howard University.

Celeste *Latin:* Heavenly. Also Celina, Celestine. Celestine Strode Cook is a well-known business executive and civic leader in Houston and New Orleans.

Celina Also Celena. Appearing early in the 20th century and remaining in fair use.

Chalina *Spanish:* A diminutive for Rosa (see below).

Chana *Hebrew:* A variant of Hannah (see below).

Chanda Chanda Rubin, age 17, has emerged as a star tennis player at Acadinana High School in Cody, La.

Chandelle *French:* Candle. Also Candel.

Chandra *Hindi:* Of the moon. Chandra is experiencing a surge of popularity among black parents.

Chanel *French:* Canal.

Chante Chante Moore is a pop singer of ballads.

Chantel *French:* Singer. Also Chantelle, Chantell, Chauntel, Chantal, Chantalle, Chantrell, Chante, Chantay, Chantae, Chanta, Chaunte. Variations of this name are especially popular among contemporary black parents. Chante Moore and Chantay Savage are hot R&B singers.

Charcey Charcey Glenn is the mother of NBA superstar Charles Barkley.

Charity *Latin:* Benevolent, loving thy neighbor. One of the three cardinal virtues used as names (along with Faith and Hope), Charity is found among 18th-century free black names. Of the once popular virtue names (Chastity, Fortitude, Humility, Mercy, Obedience, Temperance), the three cardinals remain in regular use.

Charla A feminine form of Charles.

Charlayne A feminine form of Charles with high-fashion character. Charlayne Hunter-Gault is an anchor on the "McNeil/Lehrer Report," a nightly TV news show. Hunter-Gault in her recent autobiography details how her determined commitment to pursue a career in journalism spearheaded the integration of the University of Georgia. In 1961, she and Hamilton Holmes became the first black students to attend that university.

Charlemae A combination of Charles and Mae (see below), probably the names of the parents. Librarian and storyteller Charlemae Hill Rollins opposed racial stereotypes in children's books and was widely recognized as an authority on black literature.

Charlene   A feminine form of Charles. Also Charlena, Charleana, Charleene, Charline, Charleena, Charlaine, Charlayne, Charlita, Charlisa, Chardae. The name has been well used by black parents. Charleana Horne lives in Detroit.

Charleszetta   This feminine form of Charles appears to be used exclusively by black parents. Its fashionable use until mid-century attests to the popularity of Charles as a boy's name, since girls with this name were most often named for their fathers. Reverend Mother Charleszetta Waddles of Detroit, a humanitarian of extraordinary courage, has operated her Perpetual Help Mission for nearly 40 years. Her sole goal is to assist the poor and deprived.

Charlotte   *French:* Womanly, petite. Also Carlotta, Charlotta. Charlette represents a spelling of the name sometimes employed by black parents. Charlette Hargrove is a high school basketball player in North Carolina. In 1928, Charlotte Hawkins Brown was the first black woman to be elected to the 20th Century Club of Boston. Charlotte Forten Grimke, of the famed Forten and Grimke families, like numerous members of her family, dedicated her life to the welfare of African-Americans. In 1862, when she arrived on St. Helena, an island off the coast of South Carolina, she was one of the first black teachers for the newly freed slaves.

Charmaine   *French:* Fruitful orchard. Also Charmayne, Charmian, Charmine.

Charshee   Charshee McIntyre is a professor of black studies at Old Westbury College in Long Island, N.Y.

Chastity   *Latin:* Pure, innocent. One of the virtue names so popular at the turn of the century.

Che-Lin   Che-Lin Aldridge of Atlanta was named for Che Guevara, the Cuban revolutionary, and Lin Piao, the Chinese patriot.

Chelsea *English:* Landing place on the river; a popular district in London. Appears on Puckett's list of unusual names among free black women 1800–60. Chelsea is experiencing enormous popularity among white parents in the 1980s and 1990s, particularly since the Clintons entered the White House with their daughter, Chelsea. The name has been used regularly but infrequently by black parents.

Cherry *English:* A diminutive for Charity (see above). Also Cheri, Cherrie.

Cheryl *American:* Also Cheryll, Sheryl. First used in the 1920s, coming into high fashion in the 1940s and 1950s. Enormously popular among black parents of the 1950s. Cheryl Woodruff and Cheryll Y. Greene are editors extraordinaire.

Chessa *Slavic:* At peace. Also Chesna.

Cheyenne The name given to a cultural and ethnic group of Native Americans who lived on the great western plains. Rare.

Chia An unusual name appearing on Puckett's list of names in Washington, D.C., 1800–64.

China This name of the country in Asia is infrequently used by black parents as a girl's name. Also Chynna, Chyna.

Chinyere Chinyere Jo Sims is a member of the class of 1993, Howard University. Chinyere Neal is a broadcaster in Detroit.

Chissa An unusual name found in Washington, D.C., among free black women during the 1800s.

Chloe *Greek:* Young fresh blossom. Appearing among free black women as early as 1700, it is used regularly but infrequently.

Christie Diminutive for Christine (see below). Also Christy, Christi.

Christine *French:* A feminine form of Christian. Also Christiana, Christina, Christeen, Christen, Kristin.

Cindy   Diminutive for Cynthia (see below). Also Cindi.

Cissie   A pet form of Cecily (see above). Singer Cissie Houston is Whitney Houston's mother.

Clara   *Latin:* Brilliant. Also Claire, Clarette. As a brigadier general, Clara Adams-Ender is the highest ranking nurse in the U.S. Army. Clara Stanton Jones was the first African-American to serve as director of the Detroit Public Library. Clara Mae Ward replaced her mother as the leader of the famous gospel group, the Ward Singers. Clara Taylor Reed is the chief executive of Mid-Delta Home Health, Inc. Clara McBride Hale, our beloved Mother Hale, was in a class by herself. During her lifetime, she was mother to hundreds of children. *I Dream a World* reports that when President Ronald Reagan cited Mother Hale as an American hero for her work with the babies of drug-addicted mothers, she responded, "I'm not an American hero. I'm a person who loves children."

Clarice   *French:* Little brilliant one. Clarice Taylor is an actress.

Clarissa   This English form of Clarice (see above) is found among free black women during the 1700s. "Solace," a poem by Clarissa Scott Delaney, has been published in many anthologies.

Claudette   A variation of Claudia (see below). Claudette, the former wife of singer Smokey Robinson, was his childhood sweetheart.

Claudia   *Latin:* Lame; a feminine form of Claude. Claudius was a famous Roman family known for its magnanimous attitude toward its captives. Claudia Haywood, a student at Rice University, won the 1993 NCAA championship for her performance in the long jump contest.

Claudine   A variation of Claudia (see above).

Cleareater   Cleareater Long lives in Highland Park, Mich.

Cledie   Cledie Taylor is an arts advocate in Detroit.

Clementia *Latin:* Calm, merciful.

Clementine This feminine form of Clement was found during the 1700s among free black women. However, its use has remained infrequent. Folk artist Clementine Hunter continued painting until she was 102 years old. At birth, she was named Clemence.

Cleona Found in Puckett's index of unusual names.

Cleopatra *Greek:* Father's glory. Cleopatra was a famed queen of Egypt. Rare.

Clotilda Also Clotilde. Clotilda F. Charlot is a member of the class of 1993, Howard University.

Clydena Found among schoolgirls in the late 19th and early 20th century, this name sounds like an invention.

Clymenza Perhaps this unusual name is a variation of Clymene, who in Greek mythology is the mother of At-las.

Colette *French:* Victorious army; a diminutive for Nicolette. Also Collette.

Colleen *Irish:* Maiden. Also Coleen, Collene, Collena, Colene.

Comfort *French:* To comfort. A popular Puritan name found among free black women of the 18th century.

Concordia *Latin:* Harmony.

Condoleezza Sovietologist Condoleezza Rice was recently appointed provost at Stanford University.

Conney According to Puckett, this name has an African background. Also Conny.

Connie Diminutive for Constance (see below). Also Conny. The name has enjoyed widespread use among black parents as an independent name.

Constance *Latin:* Steadfastness. Constance Baker Motley is a senior judge for the Southern District of New York. Constance Weaver is the editor of *Class* magazine.

Conswella A phonetic spelling of Consuelo, which means consolation in Spanish. Also Consolata,

Consuela, Chelo. Conswella Sparrow is an outstanding member of her high school basketball team, in Shelbyville, Tenn.

Cora *Greek:* Maiden; from Kore, who in Greek mythology was the maiden daughter of the goddess Demeter. Also Coralee, Cora Mae. Born in Charlotte, N.C., lawyer and civic leader Cora T. Walker practiced law in Harlem for more than 20 years.

Coral *Latin:* A semiprecious growth under the sea. Coral reefs are popular vacation spots.

Cordelia *Welsh:* A jewel from the sea. Also Cordella, Cardella. In Welsh legend, Cordelia was the daughter of King Lear. H. Cordelia Ray is a poet.

Coretta This variation of Cora (see above) is highly recognizable because of the leadership of civil rights activist Coretta Scott King, the widow of Martin Luther King.

Corla Chicago teacher Corla Wilson is heralded by the New York *Amsterdam News* for reclaiming cast-away children branded disruptive, disabled, or dysfunctional. This dedicated teacher received a 1993 *Essence* Award.

Corliss *English:* Good-hearted, carefree. Corliss McAfee is an accountant.

Cornelia *Latin:* A cornell tree, queenly; a feminine form of Cornelius. Also Cornella.

Corrinne A variation of Cora (see above). Also Corine, Corena, Corina, Corinna, Corynne, Corryn, Coryn.

Courtney *English:* Court dweller; the surname of an aristocratic British family from Courtenay in France. This masculine name is now more often seen among girls.

Crecia Perhaps a short form of Lucretia (see below), this name appears on Puckett's list of unusual female names of the 19th century. Puckett also lists the variation Crecy.

Creola *Spanish:* Dark-skinned one.

Cressa Unusual female name of the 19th century.

Crissina An apparent recent invention appearing among black women in Washington, D.C., in 1863.

Crystal *Latin:* Beautiful, like the transparent quartz of the same name. College student Crystal Irving performed like a star in the Sun Classic Track and Field meet in 1993.

Cudell This unusual name, which appears in Puckett's index, certainly resonates with the sounds of African-American coinage.

Cutrena Found in Puckett's index of unusual names. Could be a phonetic spelling of Katrina.

Cynthia *Greek:* The moon. In Greek mythology, Cynthia was one of the names for Artemis or Diana, the moon goddess.

Cyrena In Greek myth Cyrene was loved by Apollo.

Cyrilla *Greek:* The feminine version of Cyril.

Dacia *Greek:* From Dacia, a province in ancient Roman.

Dahlia *Swedish:* Valley. Also Dalia. The dahlia, a perennial plant with very large flowers, is named for A. Dahl, an 18th-century Swedish botanist. Unlike other flower names such as Rose and Iris, it was never in widespread use among black parents.

Daisia From Puckett's index of unusual names.

Daisy *English:* Eye of the day. An enormously popular 19th-century flower name. In French, this miniature symbol of the sun is called Marguerite. Thus, Daisy was often used as a nickname for Margaret (see below). As a given name, Daisy is neglected today. The prodigious political activist and champion of black rights Daisy Lampkin served as field secretary for the NAACP from 1927 to 1947. Based in her hometown of Pittsburgh, she served on the board of directors of the NAACP until her death in 1965. Daisy Elliott, a delegate to the state's constitutional convention, wrote the civil rights portion of Michigan's new constitution.

Dakota *Native American:* Friendly ally. The western states North and South Dakota are named for the Dakota branch of the great Sioux nation. The melodic voice of singer Dakota Staton has sustained her popularity for a generation.

Dale *English:* From the valley. Dale is most often used as a boy's name, but is sometimes employed as a girl's name.

Dallas *Scottish:* From Dallas, a village in Scotland. The city of Dallas was named for G. M. Dallas, a U.S. vice-president. First noted by Professor Puckett, the use of interesting place names is a growing contemporary practice as parents seek to distinguish their children's names.

Dana *English:* From Denmark. In Scandinavian mythology, Dana is the mother of the gods. Although traditionally considered a boy's name, it is used almost exclusively for girls in America among both black and white families.

Danette A feminine version of Daniel. Also Danita.

Danielle *Hebrew:* God is my judge; a feminine version of Daniel. Also Danyel. Danyel Mitchell of Louisiana State University is the 1993 NCAA outdoor discus champion.

Danula Found among Puckett's unusual schoolgirl's names, and apparently related to Daniel.

Daphna This variation of Daphne (see below) is found among free black names of the 1700s.

Daphne *Greek:* Laurel or bay tree. In Greek mythology, when the nymph Daphne attempted to flee the amorous advances of Apollo, she was turned into a laurel tree. Found among free black names of the 1800s. Daphne Muse is a writer.

Dara *Hebrew:* House of wisdom or compassion. In the Bible a male name, but in modern usage almost exclusively found among girls.

Darcy *Irish:* Dark. Also Darcie, Darcey. Darcy Aldridge lives in Atlanta.

Darice *Greek:* Wealthy; a feminine form of Darius. Darice LaRee Butler is a member of the class of 1993, Howard University.

Darnella This female version of Darnell is found in Puckett's list of 1877–1937.

Darlene *English:* Dearly beloved, darling. Also Darline, Darla, Darleen, Darlena, Darlina, Darleena, Darleane.

Darthula Found on Puckett's index of unusual names.

Dashaland Dashaland Brown is a student at the South Bronx Job Corps Center in New York.

Dasia *Hebrew:* The law of the Lord.

Davette A feminine form of the enormously popular David.

Dawn *English:* The first light of the morning sun. Also Dawnn. Singer and actress Dawnn Lewis was one of the original cast members of "A Different World" and "Hanging With Mr. Cooper."

Daya *Hebrew:* Like a bird.

Dazell This unusual name is found on Puckett's list of 1877–1937.

Dearie A name noted among contemporary schoolgirls in South Carolina.

Debbie A diminutive for Deborah (see below). Also

Debby, Debbi, Deb. Debbie Ann Parris of LSU won the 1993 NCAA 400-meter hurdles.

Deborah *Hebrew:* To speak kindly; an Old Testament prophet. Also Devorah, Devora. Deborah "Debbie" Allen is a versatile performer whose artistic accomplishments include acting, producing, writing, directing, singing, and dancing. Adventurous and courageous, Deborah Sampson distinguished herself as a soldier in the Continental Army during the American Revolution. With the assistance of Paul Revere, Sampson is believed to be the first woman to draw a soldier's pension.

Debra A variation of Deborah (see above).

Decia *Latin:* Tenth.

Deidre *Irish:* Sorrow, compassion.

Dejeurnetta Dejeurnetta Marie Rucker is a member of the class of 1993, Howard University.

Deka *Greek:* Tenth.

Delena Noted by Puckett in 1877–1937.

Delfina *Greek:* Delphi, the seat of the Pythian oracle in Greek myth, derived its name from Delphis, the Greek word for dolphin. The implications of the name are complex. For the Greeks Delphi represented the womb of the earth. Many contemporary sources describe it as a flower name, since the delphinium gets its name from its dolphin shape. In any case, it means calm, serene, loving, like the gentle dolphins of the sea. Also Delfine, Delphina, Delphine. In long-standing use by black parents.

Delia *Greek:* Visible. In Greek myth, Delia was one of the names of Artemis, the mythical goddess of the moon who was born on the isle of Delos. The name appears in the 1800s.

Delilah *Hebrew:* Gentle. In the Old Testament, Delilah betrayed Samson. The name was found among free black women in the early 1800s but is rare today. Journalist Delilah Leontium Beasley (1867–1934) was a one-woman crusader in her effort to document the history of blacks in California. In her biography, *Delilah Leontium Beasley: Oakland's Crusading Journalist,* Lorraine J. Crouchett depicts what is known of her history. Delilah Jackson is a tireless advocate for the arts in New York City.

Delita Noted in Puckett's list of unusual schoolgirls' names.

Della This pet form of Adele (see above) or Adela (see above) is now well-established as a name in its own right. Della Reese is a well-known singer. She was born Deloreese Patricia Early.

Delois This name found among Puckett's unusual schoolgirl names is quite probably an African-American variation of Delores (see below), itself a variation of Dolores (see below). Or it may represent our fondness for De as a prefix.

Delora *Latin:* From the seashore.

Delores A variation of Dolores (see below). Also Deloris.

Deloria This name appearing on Puckett's list of unusual schoolgirls' names is probably a variation of Delora (see above).

Delozier Documented in the 1800s.

Delpha *Greek:* Dolphin. Also Delphi, Delphia. Appears among free black women during the 1800s.

Delphine The French form of Delfina (see above). Also Delphena, Delphene.

Delta *Greek:* Fourth. This fourth letter of the Greek alphabet represents the name of a fourth daughter.

Demetria *Greek:* Fertility.

Dena *English:* From the valley; a feminine version of Dean.

Denise *Greek:* From Dionysus, Greek God of wine; a feminine version of Dennis. Denise Rollins works with various arts foundations in Washington, D.C.

Denolyn Denolyn Carroll is managing editor for *Class* magazine.

Dequilla This name is found on Puckett's 1877–1937 list.

Desdemona *Greek:* Tragic, cruel. In Shakespeare's *Othello,* Desdemona is a tragic heroine falsely accused of adultery. In a fit of jealous rage, her husband murders her.

Desery Desery F. Greene is a student at the South Bronx Job Corps Center in New York.

Desiree *French:* Greatly desired.

Deska Deska Ann Gaskins-Perry graduated from Howard University in 1993.

Dessa The origins of this unusual name are not clear. *Dessa Rose* is the title of Shirley Anne Williams's highly acclaimed historical novel.

Dessie An unusual name appearing on Puckett's 1877–1937 list.

Detroit This rare usage of the name of the largest city in Michigan is documented among contemporary women in South Carolina.

De Vera This name appears to be another indication of our preference for the De prefix. Found on Puckett's 1877–1937 list.

Devona *English:* From Devonshire.

Devora A variation of Deborah (see above).

Dewilda This name is unquestionably an invention. It appears on Puckett's 1877–1937 list.

Dewonda A customer service representative for a major multinational corporation explained from her Atlanta base that her father tried to name her "The Wonderful." The doctor convinced him to call her Dewonda. The Wonderful is documented by Puckett as a female given name.

Diamond *Greek:* Brilliant. This name of a precious gemstone is infrequently employed as a girl's name, perhaps to emphasize just how much a little girl means to her parents.

Diana *English:* Divine. Also Deanna, Dianna, Dionna. Diana was the mythological Roman goddess noted for her beauty and swiftness. Superstar Diana Ross is loved around the world. As a child in Detroit, Diane—as she was then known—sang in the Olivet Baptist Church choir where her parents and siblings also sang.

Diane *French:* Divine. Also Diahann, Diahanne, Dyann, Dyanne. Diane has been quite a fashionable name for African-American girls for several generations. Singer and actress Diahann Carroll was born in 1935 in the Bronx, N.Y. Her performance in school plays and the church choir won the 10-year-old a Metropolitan Opera scholarship for singing lessons.

Dianna This version of Diana (see above) was found among free black women in the 1700s.

Dinah *Hebrew:* Judged and avenged. Also Dina, Dynah. In the Old Testament, Dinah is Jacob's only daughter. The name appears on Puckett's list "In the Beginning: 1619–1799." Black and white music aficionados consider Dinah Washington one of the greatest blues singers of all times. The young Dinah, who answered to Ruth Lee Jones, was tutored in music by her mother, the pianist at St. Luke's Baptist Church.

Dinora *Spanish:* A form of Dinah (see above).

Dionne In Greek myth, Dione was the wife of Zeus and the mother of Aphrodite. Also Dionna, Diona, Diondra. Singer Dionne Warwick achieved international recognition as a song stylist when she teamed up with composer Burt Bacharach. Warwick's renditions of Bacharach's music and Hal David's lyrics achieved international recognition for this musical triad. Like most black singers, Warwick developed her musical abilities singing in church.

Divina *Hebrew:* Greatly loved one. Also Devinia, Davina.

Dixie This English surname is most often used to refer to the Southern states, or those states below the Mason-Dixon Line.

Djuana Microbiologist Djuana G. Davis lives in Morrisville, N.C. She was selected as a 1993 *Ebony* Bachelorette.

Dolly A short form of Dorothy (see below) sometimes used as an independent name.

Dolores *Spanish:* A favored name honoring the Virgin Mary, Mater Dolorosa, Our Lady of Sorrows.

Dominique *Latin:* Belonging to the Lord. This spelling of the Latin Dominica, a name for girls born on Sunday, is the most popular among both white and black American parents.

Donella *Irish:* Dark-haired girl.

Donna *Italian:* Lady; a feminine form of the Latin word for Lord. Donna has been well-used by black American parents. Donna Tyler is an assistant dean.

Dora *Greek:* A gift. Dora enjoyed widespread use until the recent preference for invented names.

Dorcas *Greek:* Charitable.

Dorcey This variation of Dorcas (see above) is used infrequently.

Doreen *French:* Gilded. Found in regular use among black parents.

Doretha *Greek:* Gift of God. Also Dorethae.

Dorinda An 18th-century invented name believed to be first used in Farquhar's play *The Beaux Stratagem,* in which Dorinda is the daughter of Lady Bountiful. It appears on Puckett's 1920 list.

Doris *Greek:* Bountiful, from the sea. Mentored in her teen years by librarian Charlemae Hill Rollins, Doris Saunders went on to distinguish herself as a journalist and publishing executive. She was born in Chicago to Alvesta Stewart Evans and Thelma Rice Evans. Doris L. Wethers was born in Passaic, N.J. Throughout her career, this pediatrician has tirelessly fought to combat sickle-cell anemia.

Dorothea Dorothea Jaxson is a teacher, dancer, and choreographer in New York City.

Dorothy *Greek:* Gift of God. First documented among free black women during the 1800s, Dorothy has remained in fashion. In 1919 in Philadelphia, Dorothy Brown's unmarried mother had no alternative but to place her 5-month-old daughter in an orphanage. Of a most determined spirit, Brown became the first black surgeon to practice in the South. A staunch women's rights activist with international affiliations, the indefatigable Dorothy Height in 1957 became president of the National Council of Negro Women, founded by Mary McLeod Bethune. Opera singer Dorothy Maynor is the founder of the Harlem School for the Arts. Many distinguished African-American women have lived up to the virtuous meaning of Dorothy.

Dovie An unusual name of obscure origins.

Drucilla *Latin:* A Roman family name. Also Drusilla. Appears on Puckett's list of unusual names.

Drunetta Collected by Puckett, 1877–1937.

Dulcie *Latin:* Sweet one.

Earlene *German:* Shield; a feminine form of Earl, a title of nobility. Also Earline, Earlean, Earleen, Earlina, Earlene, Earline, Earlene, Erlene, Erlina, Earlinda. Long a favorite among black American parents, now fading from use.

Earlie   Diminutive for Earlene. Also Early. Early Mae is a once-popular double name.

Earmine   The origins of this unusual name are not clear, but it appears to be an African-American invention.

Earsel   From Puckett's index of unusual names.

Eartha   *English/German:* The earth. Also Ertha. Rare. Orphaned at age 6, entertainer Eartha Kitt was moved by her aunt from Columbia, S.C., to New York City. At age 16, she auditioned for Katherine Dunham's dance troupe. The rest is history; Kitt is internationally renowned. Eartha White epitomizes the proverb, "Blossom where you are planted." In her 94 years, she made many stellar contributions to her hometown, Jacksonville, Fla.

Earthalee   This combination is a distinctively African-American blend.

Easter   *English:* Born at Eastertime. Although noted by Puckett, it is rarely used.

Ebony   *Greek:* Black; the name of a rare type of black wood. Also Ebonee, Eboni. *Ebony* is our most popular commercial magazine. Ebony Jo Ann is a jazz singer. Eboni Green was a 1993 New York Public School Athletic League champion. A student at Paul Robeson High School, she is an outstanding track and field competitor.

Edana   *Irish:* Ardent.

Eddie   This diminutive for Edward is a boy's name sometimes used for girls. Rarely used alone, it is most often seen in combinations such as Eddie Mae, Eddie Jean.

Edeline   *German:* Of good cheer; a variation of Adeline (see above).

Edina   *English:* Prospering and happy.

Edisa   Edisa Weeks of Brooklyn is a dancer.

Edith   *English/German:* Rich gift. Edie and Edy are diminutives. In the field of jurisprudence, Edith Sampson holds an impressive list of firsts. Physician Edith Irby Jones, a native of Conway, Ark., was the first black student admitted to the University of Arkansas. At the 1964 Olympic Games, Edith McGuire Duvall set an Olympic record in winning the 200 meters.

Edlyn *English:* Little princess. Rare.

Edmonda *English:* Prosperous protector; a feminine form of Edmund. Also Edmunda.

Edmonia Edmonia Lewis was one of the earliest black women to win fame as a sculptor. She worked in marble.

Edna *Hebrew:* Rejuvenation. Also Ednah.

Ednelia An unusual name listed among Puckett's schoolgirls' names.

Ednola Collected in *Black Names in America.*

Edra *Hebrew:* Powerful.

Edria *English:* Powerful, prosperous. Also Edrea.

Edris *English:* Wealthy, powerful; a feminine version of Edric.

Edvenie An unusual name documented by Puckett in his list of schoolgirls' names.

Edwina *English:* Wealthy friend; a feminine version of Edwin. Also Edweena, Edwena, Edwyna. Rare. Edwyna G. Anderson is noted in the New York *Amsterdam News* as the first black chairperson and the first woman chair of the Pennsylvania Electric Association.

Edwonia Documented by Professor Puckett.

Effie *Greek:* Well-spoken. This short form of the now obsolete Euphemia came into regular use around the turn of the century. Popular combinations were Effie Jean and Effie Lee. Its use has faded since the 1950s. Librarian Effie Lee Newsome wrote children's literature.

Egypt This name for a country in Africa is used by parents who wish exceptionally unusual names for their girls. Rare.

Eileen   *Irish:* Brilliant, shining light; a form of Helen (see below). Also Eilene, Eilena, Eileene, Eila, Ilene.

Eirene   *Norse:* Peace.

Elaine   *French:* Bright light; a form of Helen (see below), Helaine in French. Also Elaina, Elane, Elayna, Eleana. In the tales of King Arthur, Elaine is the mother of Galahad.

Elana   *Hebrew:* A tree. Also Ilana.

Elberta   *English:* Highborn; a feminine version of Elbert. Also Elbertha. These names have been used by black parents for several generations.

Eldessa   An unusual name listed by Puckett.

Eldora   *Spanish:* Gift of the sun. Used occasionally.

Eldra   Listed in *Black Names in America.*

Eleanor   The origins of this name are disputed. The most often reported root is said to lie in the Greek Helen (see below). Also Eleanora, Eleanore, Elinor. Eleanor I. Franklin was valedictorian of her class at Carver High School in Monroe, Ga. She went on to become a widely recognized endocrinologist and the first woman medical administrator at Howard University Medical College. Eleanor Holmes Norton is the first woman to be elected mayor of Washington, D.C.

Elena   A Spanish form of Helen (see below).

Eleni   *Greek:* Light. Eleni is a popular modern form of Helen (see below) in recent use by both black and white parents.

Elektra   *Greek:* Shining bright. Also Electra. It is no wonder that this name is not often used. It is generally associated with Greek tragedies that involve incest, murder, and vengeance.

Elester   This unusual name is documented on Puckett's list of names for schoolgirls.

Elise   *French:* Pledged to God; a short form of Elizabeth (see below). Also Elisa, Elissa.

Elisha An early citing of this alternate spelling of Alicia occurs in Puckett's 1800–60 list.

Elizabeth *Hebrew:* Consecrated to God. Also Elisabeth, Lizabeth. Elizabeth has enjoyed enormous popularity among black parents. Elizabeth Haynes, a sociologist and social worker, was the first black secretary of the national YWCA. She is the author of the celebrated *Unsung Heroes*. Elizabeth Catlett is a famous sculptor. Her work in marble, wood, and terracotta has been exhibited at many prestigious museums, including the Museum of Modern Art. Elizabeth Taylor Greenfield was born in Natchez, Miss., in 1809. Upon hearing Elizabeth's lovely singing, a Quaker woman took her to Philadelphia for training. Known as the Black Swan, Greenfield sang at Buckingham Palace at a command performance before Queen Victoria. Elizabeth Prophet was an outstanding educator and sculptor. Elizabeth Keckley was dressmaker and friend to Mary Todd Lincoln, wife of President Abraham Lincoln. Educator Elizabeth Duncan Koontz was the first black person elected president of the National Education Association. Artemisa Elizabeth Baker Dinwiddie was a schoolteacher, wife, and mother of five.

Ella *German:* Complete. Some sources report Ella as a short form of Eleanor (see above) and Ellen (see below). Also Ella Mae. Jazz singer Ella Fitzgerald, called the queen of scat by some and the first lady of song by others, is one of the most gifted singers of all times. Although she remained in the background, community organizer Ella Baker was a leading architect of the civil rights movement. Ella Shepphard Moore was an outstanding member of the fabled Fisk Jubilee Singers. On their first tour in 1871, the singers raised $20,000, a huge sum at the time.

Ellabelle Found on Puckett's list documenting unusual names among schoolgirls.

Ellen *Greek:* Bright light, brilliant; a form of Helen (see below).

Ellenae   Ellenae L. Henry-Fairhurst is chief executive of Huntsville Dodge Inc., Huntsville, Ala. Her company is one of the Black Enterprise 100 Auto Dealers.

Ellice   *Greek:* Jehovah is God; a feminine form of Elias.

Elma   *German:* God's protection. Some sources report its origins in the Greek Elmo, which means amiable.

Elmetta   This variation of Elma (see above) resonates with the sounds of an African-American creation. It appears on Puckett's 1920 list of female names. Rare.

Elmina   An African-American variation of Elma (see above).

Elmira   *English:* Noble, famous, aristocratic. Also Elmyra. Used occasionally by black parents.

Elnora   A form of Eleanor (see above). Also El Nora, Elnoria. This name has enjoyed widespread use among black parents. Popular in the first half of 20th century, it is neglected today.

Eloise   *French:* Renown in battle; a form of Louise (see below). Also Eloisa.

Elreta   An African-American invention. Elreta Alexander Ralston of Guilford County, N.C., was the first black woman elected to a judgeship by popular vote.

Elsa   *German:* This short form of Elizabeth (see above) is rarely used by black parents.

Elsie   A form of Elizabeth (see above). Elsie Washington is a writer. Elsie Carrington is a nurse.

Elva   The meaning of this name is unclear, although sources agree that its origins are Irish.

Elverta   Collected by Puckett.

Elvina   *English:* Noble friend. Also Elvinia. Occasionally used by black parents.

Elvira   *Spanish:* Meaning unknown.

Elvita   An unusual name found among black American girls. Elvita Reed is a college student.

Elza   The origins of this name are not clear. It appears to have come from the Portuguese. The wife of the Brazilian philosopher Paulo Freire, the author of *Pedagogy of the Oppressed,* is named Elza. It is also sometimes found among Spanish speakers. Its use by black parents is extremely rare.

Elzara Noted in 1877–1937 by Puckett, this variation of Elza (see above) is quite likely an African-American creation.

Elzena This unusual name is documented on Puckett's list of names among schoolgirls. Also Elzina.

Emanuele *Hebrew:* God is with us. Also Emmanuelle, Emanuelle, Emanuella.

Emily *Latin:* Industrious, striving. Occasionally used by black parents.

Emma *German:* All embracing, whole, complete. Also Emma Joyce, Emma Lee, Emmy. Emma Frances Merritt is an educator.

Emmaline *German:* Hardworking. Also Emeline, Emmalyn, Emmalee, Emmeline, Emilyn. Emilyn Brown is a college student.

Emmie Boasting a 3.0 grade average, Emmie Reed picked up three degrees during commencement exercises at the University of California, 1993. According to *Jet,* this outstanding student received bachelor's degrees in political science, social science, and legal studies. Named for her father, Emmit Reed Jr., Emmie credits her success to his guidance.

Enid *Welsh:* Life, spirit. Enid has been quite fashionable among black parents.

Enola A Native American name of uncertain meaning. Enola Gay was inscribed on the plane from which the atomic bomb was dropped on Japan.

Enolia Enolia Pettigen McMillan was the national president of the NAACP from 1985 to 1989.

Enrica *Spanish/Italian:* Rules her home.

Ensa Ensa Cosby is the daughter of Bill and Camille Cosby.

Era An extraordinarily rare name, Era is probably of recent coinage. Journalist Era Bell Thompson rates among the most important contributors to African-American journalistic history. She capped a spectacular career as international editor of *Ebony*.

Erica *Scandinavian:* Rules forever. Also Erika, Ericka. Erika Huggins was a leader of the Black Panther Party.

Erika Erika Cosby, a daughter of Bill and Camille Cosby, received her master's degree in fine arts from the University of California at Berkeley.

Erin *Irish:* A poetic name for Ireland. This boy's name now almost exclusively reserved for girls is infrequently used by black parents.

Erlina Found in Puckett's list of free black names, 1800–60.

Erma *German:* Universal. Also Irma. Singer Erma Franklin is a sister of Aretha.

Ernesta *German:* Purposeful, intent; a feminine form of Ernest. The success of entrepreneur Ernesta Gertrude Bowman Procope epitomizes the meaning of her name. She is the founder of the nation's largest black-owned insurance brokerage agency, E. G. Bowman Co.

Ernestine *German:* Determined. Also Ernestina, Erna, Earnestine.

Ersa Ersa Hines Poston has held many government positions in New York state.

Eslanda Eslanda "Essie" Cordoza Goode Robeson was the wife of Paul Robeson. The product of a long line of high achievers, she was an accomplished chemist and anthropologist. She was also a human rights activist and a writer.

Essie This diminutive for Esther (see below) has enjoyed first-name status among black parents for several generations.

Estella *Latin:* A star. Also Estelle.

Ester This variation of Esther (see below) is found among contemporary South Carolina schoolgirls.

Esther *Persian:* Star. This biblical name can be traced through the Latin, Greek, and Hebrew to Persian. Esther Gordy Edwards, sister of Berry Gordy, played a key role as an executive in the companies that formed the Motown organization.

Ethel *German/English:* Noble. Ethel has been well-used by black parents. Ethel Waters, a child of poverty, overcame many obstacles to pursue an acting career.

Ethiopia The name of this country in Africa has on rare occasions served as a first name for girls.

Etolia This apparent creation was found among high school girls in the 1950s.

Etoria The roots of this name seem to lie in African-American invention. It can be traced back several generations in the Will Franklin Martin family of Nashville.

Etta *German:* Happy. Often seen as Etta Jane. Etta James is a noted blues diva.

Eudora On Puckett's list of unusual names of schoolgirls.

Eugenia *Greek:* Wellborn; a feminine form of Eugene. Also Eugena, Eugina.

Eulalie *Greek:* Sweet-spoken. Also Eulalia, Eula, Eulalee, Eulah, Eulia. Eula Bell and Eula Mae were popular combinations in the early part of the century. Eulalia Bass is a member of the Little Rock Missionary Baptist Church. Eulalie Spence was a prolific playwright and theater critic.

Eulania One of Puckett's pearls.

Eulene Found on Puckett's index of unusual names.

Eunice *Greek:* Joyful, victorious conqueror. Eunice W. Johnson is secretary-treasurer of *Ebony* and director of Ebony Fashion Fair.

Eurcelyn As for so many of the names found in *Black*

Names in America, the origins of this unusual name probably lie in the African-American penchant for name invention.

Eurena   Noted by Puckett.

Eva   *Hebrew:* Living one. Eva Alberta Jessye, music director for the first all-black motion picture, *Hallelujah,* studied at Langston University and taught music in Muskogee, Okla.

Evalina   Noted in the 1920s. Evalina Jones lives in San Pedro, Calif.

Evangeline   *Greek:* Good news. Also Evangelina.

Evashti   An African-American creation.

Eve   *Hebrew:* Life. Also Evie, Evita, Eva. Although Eve is occasionally used by black parents, Eva has been the far more popular form of this name.

Evelina   *French:* Hazelnut. Also Eveline.

Evelyn   *English/French:* The meaning of Evelyn is not known. Originally a surname and then a boy's name, it is now widely used as a girl's name. Actress Evelyn Prer was a member of the Lafayette Players during the Harlem Renaissance.

Evette   *French:* A variation of Yvette (see below); a diminutive for Yvonne (see below).

Evona   Found in Puckett's index of unusual names.

Evonne   *French:* Archer's bow; a variation of Yvonne (see below). Also Eyvonne.

Evora   Found in Puckett's index of unusual names.

Ezzetta   Found in Puckett's index of unusual names.

Facilla Found in Puckett's index of unusual names.

Faith *Latin:* Ever true. With its roots in the Bible, Faith appears among free black names, 1800–64. A virtue name, Faith has remained quietly fashionable well into the 20th century. Literary agent Faith Hampton Childs is growing in stature and reputation. Faith Ringgold is an outstanding artist.

Fancy This word with its positive connotation of whimsical imagery enjoyed a brief period of popularity. Also Fancy May.

Fanny This diminutive for Frances (see below) has often served as an independent name among black women. Also Fannie. It first appears on Puckett's 1619–1799 list and has remained in frequent use until quite recently. Fannie May and Fannie Lou were popular combinations when Fannie was in vogue. In Montgomery County, Miss., Fannie Lou Townsend felt the heavy hand of economic and racial oppression at the tender age of 6. Following the ruthless poisoning of her father's livestock by a jealous white neighbor, she joined the family in the cotton fields. Later, she was known to a generation of civil rights activists and political organizers as Fannie Lou Hamer. According to *Notable Black American Women,* "Hamer's life was a reflection of the continued abuse, pain and suffering" inflicted upon Mississippi's black citizens. Nevertheless, possessing a courageous, indomitable spirit deeply rooted in the Bible, Hamer drew national attention when, as a leader of the Mississippi Freedom Democratic Party, she challenged the 1964 National Democratic Convention. Her tireless struggle for human and civil rights stands as a monument to all who love freedom.

Fataque   This early evidence of an attraction to the que sound appears on Puckett's index of unusual names.

Fatima   *Arabic:* Fatima was a daughter of the prophet Muhammad. The original meaning of Fatima is not known. Found in Puckett's index of unusual names.

Fatrice   An apparent invention appearing in Puckett's index of unusual names.

Faucette   A gem collected by Puckett.

Faustine   *Latin:* Fortunate, auspicious; a feminine version of Faust. Also Fausteen, Faustina. Found among unusual names of schoolgirls, 1877–1937.

Fawn   *French:* Young deer.

Fay   *French:* Fairy. *English:* Related to faith. Also Faye, Fayette.

Feeby   This phonetic spelling of Phoebe (see below) appears on Puckett's 1619–1799 list.

Felicia   *Latin:* Lucky. A popular name among both British and white American parents through the 18th century, Felicia appears on Puckett's 1877–1937 list. Felicia Toney Williams is the first black woman to serve on the Second Circuit Court of Appeals in Louisiana.

Felicity   A form of Felicia (see above). Felicity de Jager is a ballerina who performs with the Dance Theatre of Harlem.

Fenella   *Irish:* White shoulder.

Fern   *English:* A plant name used as a given name.

Fifi   *French:* A diminutive for Josephine (see below).

Flettene   Flettene Parks Neal works as a creative director.

Flemmie   Flemmie Kittrell was a noted educator and nutritionist who dedicated her entire career to improving family welfare and nutrition.

Flora *Latin:* Flower. Appears on Puckett's 1619–1799 list.

Florastine A variation of Flora (see above). Also Florestine. Florestine Purnell is managing editor of *Emerge.*

Florence *Latin:* Flourishing, blooming, prospering. Also Florynce. Appearing in Puckett's collection, 1877–1937, Florence has been a popular choice among black parents as a girl's name. Florence Mills was the preeminent black woman entertainer during the Harlem Renaissance. Olympian and Gold Medalist Florence Griffith-Joyner is internationally adored as a world-class sprinter and noted for her elegant running costumes. She brought glamour to track and field. Flo-Jo, as she is affectionately called by fans, is the sister-in-law of Jackie Joyner-Kersey.

Florenza A purely African-American variation of Florence (see above). Appears on Puckett's 1936 list.

Florette Variation of Flora (see above) appearing in *Black Names.* Also Floretta, Floria.

Florida The name of a state filled with sunshine and flowers. Florida Ruffin Ridley is a social worker and clubwoman.

Florinda An unusual name appearing on Puckett's 1877–1937 list.

Florine A variation of Flora (see above) and Florence (see above). Also Florene, Florie, Florina, Florrie. They appear on Puckett's 1877–1937 list, and are still used.

Flossie A diminutive for Florence (see above) infrequently used by black parents as a given name.

Flozell A new creation appearing in 1920.

Fontana A variation of Fontanne (see below) appearing in 1936.

Fontanne *French:* Spring, fountain.

Fortune *Latin:* Good fate, good destiny. This name of hope appears among 19th-century free black women.

Fquira Fquira Johannes is a student at the South Bronx Job Corps Center in New York.

Frances *Latin:* From France; a feminine form of Francis. It appears on Puckett's 1619–1799 list and remains in use. Frances E. W. Harper is the author of *Iola Leroy*. Noted child psychiatrist and educator Frances Cress Welsing is famous for *The Cress Theory of Color-Confrontation and Racism.*

Francina A version of Frances (see above). Also Francine, Francene, Francesca, Francetta, Francette, Franchesca. Francina and Francine appear in Puckett's collection, 1877–1937.

Frankie This diminutive for Frank or Frances (see above) appears among free black names, 1619–1799. Frankie Yarrell is a student at Marymount College, Tarrytown, N.Y.

Freda *German:* Peaceful. Also Freada, Freeda, Freida, Frieda. In regular use. Freda Payne is one of the countless pop/soul singers from Detroit.

Freddie A diminutive for Frederica (see below). Also Freddi. In rare use as a given name.

Frederica *German:* Peaceful ruler. Also Fredericka, Frederique. Occasionally used by black parents. Fredericka Washington, whose skin was so light that she could pass for white, said, "I am a black woman and I am proud of it." This talented dancer and actress founded the Negro Actors Guild of America. Born Fredericka Carolyn Washington in Savannah, Ga., she was nicknamed Fredi by her mother.

Fredonia This adaptation of Fred appears in 1933. Fredonia Nunley was a popular high school music teacher and church choir mistress during the 1950s in Oklahoma.

Freetta This phonetic spelling of Fredda appears among contemporary schoolgirls.

G

Gabriella *Italian:* God is my strength; a feminine form of Gabriel.

Gabrielle *French:* God is my strength.

Gail *English:* Joyful, lively one. It is derived from Gay, which means lighthearted, happy. Also Gayle. Gail is an enormously popular choice for girls. A woman of Olympian stature, Gail Devers was the recipient of a 1993 *Essence* Award for overcoming a crippling disease to win a Gold Medal at the Barcelona Games.

Gale *Norse:* Singer. More often used for boys.

Galiana Legend holds that this is the name of a Moorish princess for whom an elegant palace was built during the Moorish occupation of Spain.

Galina A Russian form of Helen (see below).

Gay *French:* Bright, lighthearted. Also Gaye. This name has been well-used by black parents. Gaye is now the preferred spelling, probably due both to the gay rights movement and to the recent preference for flair and drama in spelling.

Gayleen Variant of Gail (see above). Also Gayline.

Gaylynn Gaylynn McKinney is a percussionist with the all-women band Straight Ahead.

Gaynelle A variation of Gay (see above) found in Puckett's collection.

Geneva *French:* The juniper tree. Geneva Smitherman is a linguist.

Genevieve The origin of this name is not clear. It is said to come from the German or French, in which case it means of the race of women. However, if it comes from the Irish, it means fair one. Rare.

Genora An unusual name appearing in Puckett's 19th-century collection.

Georgene Appearing on Puckett's unusual schoolgirls' names list, Georgene is possibly a blend of parents' names.

Georgette A form of Georgia (see below).

Georgia *Greek:* A farmer; a feminine version of George. Also Georgiana, Georgianne, Georgina. Georgia Davis was a successful business executive in Louisville, Ky. until her election to the Kentucky State Senate in 1967.

Geraldine *German:* Rules by the spear; a feminine version of Gerald. Also Geraldene, Geralda, Geraldyn. Geraldyn "Gerri" Hodges Major was born in Indiana in 1894. She died in New York Hospital at age 90 in 1984. Counted among the earliest African-American journalists, she wrote numerous articles for *Ebony* and *Jet.* Notice that the spelling of her name is early evidence of an African-American desire to elaborate and distinguish names. Geraldine Pindell Trotter, in partnership with her husband, Monroe Trotter, played a leading role in the equal rights struggle.

Geralyn Also Gerlene, Gerlina, Gerline, Gerlean. Geralyn appears on Puckett's list of unusual schoolgirls' names.

Geralynne A variation of Geraldine (see above).

Gerelda Gerelda L. Dodd is the chief executive of Integrated Steel, Inc.

Germaine *German:* From Germany.

Geronda Geronda Vertosha Carter is a Spelman College graduate.

Gertrude *German:* Spear maiden. Gertrude Malissa Nix Pridgett Rainey was the real name of the famous blues singer Ma Rainey. Gertrude Bustill Mossell (1855–1948) was a distinguished journalist, educator, and champion of women's rights.

Gilberta *German:* Illustrious pledge; a feminine form of Gilbert.

Gilda *English:* Golden one.

Gina A diminutive for Regina (see below).

Ginger *English:* This nickname for Virginia (see below) was popularized as an independent name by the actress Ginger Rogers. Occasionally used by black parents.

Ginny A nickname for Ginger (see above).

Gladys *Latin:* Lame; a variation of Claudia (see above), which comes from Claude.

Glenda *Welsh:* Fair and good. Also Glinda. Enormously popular in latter half of 20th century among black parents.

Glenis Unusual variation of Glynis (see below). Also Glinis. Both are found on Puckett's list.

Gloria *Latin:* Glory, glorious. A very fashionable name. The efforts of Gloria Richardson during the 1960s were key to the desegregation of Cambridge, Md. Gloria Foster is a highly respected actress.

Glycine An unusual name appearing on Puckett's 1877–1937 list.

Glynice Glynice L. Coleman is vice-president of R&B promotions, EMI Records Group, North America.

Glynis *Welsh:* Small valley. Also Glennis.

Golda *English:* Gold.

Goldie A popular diminutive for Golda (see above).

Gonzola Appears on Puckett's list of unusual school-girls' names.

Grace *Latin:* Graceful, attractive one. In 1966, educator Grace Townsends Hamilton became the first black woman to be seated in the Georgia legislature. Grace Ann Bumbry is an opera diva.

Gretchen The German form of Margaret (see below). Rare.

Gussy A feminine version of Gus that appeared in the 19th century. Also Gussie.

Gwendolyn *Welsh:* Fair. Also Gwendolen. Gwendolyn Brooks is the poet laureate of the state of Illinois. She won the first Pulitzer Prize ever received by an African-American.

Gynell A name collected by Puckett.

Hadara *Hebrew:* Adorned with beauty, honored.

Haddie The origins of this name are not clear. It is perhaps a variant of Hattie (see below).

Hadessa In the Bible, Hadassah, a myrtle tree, is the Hebrew name of Esther (see above). It appears on Puckett's index of unusual names.

Hadley *English:* From the field of heather. Rare.

Hagar *Biblical/Hebrew:* Forsaken stranger. In the Old Testament, Hagar is the Egyptian handmaiden of Sarah. Although it appears among free black names in the 19th century, there is no evidence of its use in the 20th century.

Halle A variant of Holly (see below). In 1891, Halle Tanner, as resident physician of Tuskegee Institute, was the first woman physician ever admitted on examination to practice medicine in Alabama. Selected by Booker T. Washington to serve at his institute, she was a member of the prestigious Tanner clan of Philadelphia. Halle Berry is an actress.

Haley *Irish:* Ingenious.

Hallie The feminine form of Hal, the diminutive for Harold. Also Halli, Halley. The career of educator Hallie Brown, an accomplished elocutionist, has been punctuated with achievement.

Hallique Appearing in Puckett's index of unusual names, Hallique is noted among contemporary schoolgirls in South Carolina.

Hannah *Biblical/Hebrew:* Graceful, merciful. Hannah Elizabeth Byrd was the first African-American woman magistrate in Pennsylvania.

Harlene *English:* From the meadow of the hares; a feminine version of Harlen. Also Harleen, Harlee, Harlie.

Harmony *Latin:* Harmonious, fitting.

Harriet *French:* Ruler of the estate. Also Harriett, Harriette. Harriet Michel is executive director of Minority Suppliers, a New York–based organization that performs as an advocate for minority entrepreneurs and businesses. Harriet Gibbs Marshall was the first black to graduate from the Oberlin Conservatory of Music. Abolitionist Harriet Tubman is perhaps our most historical and famous Harriet. She is called the Moses of her people, for her legendary feats. Among her many triumphs during a life of brutal hardships were her numerous trips into the bowels of slavery to lead more than 300 people out of bondage. Activist Harriet Forten Purvis of the prominent Forten family was also a staunch abolitionist. Harriette Cole is fashion editor for *Essence.*

Hattie A diminutive for Harriet (see above), which has taken on first-name status. Hattie Winston is a consummate actress.

Havenia An unusual name found in Puckett's index.

Hazel *English:* The hazelnut tree. Early Europeans viewed the branch from the hazelnut tree as an insignia of rulership. The enormous popularity of the name Hazel has endured. Hazel Scott, the first wife of Adam Clayton Powell Jr., was admired for her piano playing and singing, and respected for her social activism. Actress and singer Hazel Bryant, formerly of Zanesville, Ohio, has been successful in New York theater. Hazel Harrison was a well-known concert pianist in Europe. Hazel Ann Marable, wife, mother, and business manager for her husband's prolific writing career, is a source of strength to her family. Manning Marable, an outstanding college professor, extolled his wife's virtues in the "Brother" column of *Essence.*

Hazeline   A variation of Hazel (see above) found in Puckett's index of unusual names.

Heather   *English:* A flower name referring to the heather. The purple heather bush is said to symbolize beauty, and the white blossom protects against danger.

Hedda   *German:* Strife in battle.

Hedy   *Greek:* Sweet.

Heidi   *German:* Noble and cheerful. Found in Puckett's 18th-century list as Heide.

Helen   *Greek:* The bright one. Also Helena, Helene. In Greek mythology, the abduction of Helen, the daughter of the god Zeus, lead to the Trojan Wars. The popularity of this name has endured over several generations.

Helga   *English:* Holy one. The incomparable Helga Rogers, wife of the esteemed researcher J. A. Rogers, continued to publish her husband's books after his death.

Hellena   This variant of Helen (see above) appears in Puckett's list of unusual schoolgirls' names.

Heloise   *French:* Famous in war; a form of Louise (see below).

Henriene   A feminine form of Henry noted in Puckett's index of unusual names. Also Henrienne.

Henrietta *German:* Ruler of the house; a feminine form of Henry. Henrietta Vinton Davis (1860–1941) was a noted elocutionist.

Henr'ta Henr'ta Heysha lives in New York.

Hermenia An unusual name appearing in Puckett's 1877–1937 list.

Hermione *Greek:* Earthly. Hermione Brooks is a promoter.

Hermosa *Spanish:* Beautiful.

Herrita Herrita L. Stokes lives in Prairieville, La.

Hesper *Greek:* Evening star.

Hester *Greek:* A star; a form of Esther (see above).

Hetty A form of Harriet (see above). Hetty Jones is a writer.

Hilary *Greek:* Cheerful. Also Hillary.

Hilda *German:* Battle maid. Hilda O. Fortune is an educator and author.

Hildegarde *German:* Battle stronghold. This is a rare choice among black parents.

Holly *English:* Holly tree, holy. Also Holli, Hollie. When two-name combinations were fashionable, Hollie Mae was quite popular. It appears today among schoolgirls. Holli Hyche of Indiana State University won the 1993 NCAA 100- and 200-meter championship for both indoor and outdoor track and field competition.

Honey *English:* Sweet one. Rare as a given name, most often used as a pet name.

Honora *Latin:* Honorable.

Hope *English:* Faith, trust. Hope is a popular choice. Hope Clark is in much demand as a choreographer.

Hortencia *Spanish:* Garden; a form of Hortense (see below).

Hortense *Latin:* Of the garden. Hortense Spillers is a highly accomplished educator and author.

Hurleen   Hurleen Hardaway was a student at Wayne State University.

Huvena   Huvena Hamptom says her father, Hubert, gave her this name.

Hyacinth   *Greek:* The purple hyacinth flower.

Hytorria   An unusual name collected by Puckett.

Ianatha   A variation of Ianthe (see above). Also Iantha, Ianthia. All are found on Puckett's 18th-century list.

Ianthe   *Greek:* Violet flower. Also Ianthina, Janthina.

Ida   *German/English:* Industrious, prosperous, happy. Mount Ida in Crete is often mentioned in Greek mythology. According to myth, Jupiter was concealed there as a baby. Also Idalina, Idaline, Idetta, Idette, Idalou, Idamay. First appearing on Puckett's 1877 list, Ida, very fashionable in early 20th century, is used less frequently today. Political activist Ida B. Wells Barnett left a legacy punctuated with achievement. This staunch antilynching crusader excelled as a journalist, social activist, clubwoman, lecturer, wife, and mother.

Idalette   A variation of Ida (see above) noted in *Black Names in America.*

Idalia   *Greek:* Behold the sun.

Idata   Idata Gurley is a member of the Little Rock Missionary Baptist Church.

Idelia This form of Idelle (see below) is noted among unusual names of schoolgirls by Puckett.

Idella This form of Idelle (see below) is found among free black names in 1877.

Idelle *Irish:* Bountiful. Also Idelisa.

Idena A Puckett gem.

Idina *English:* From Edinburgh, Scotland.

Idonia This name appears on Puckett's list, 1877–1937. Sources link it to Iduna (see below).

Iduna *Norse:* Loving one. In Norse mythology, Iduna kept the golden apples of youth. Also Idunna.

Iesha Iesha Precious Fields is a Howard University graduate.

Ietta This gem is noted in Puckett's collection.

Ifella Puckett notes this name among unusual names for schoolgirls.

Ikella Found in Puckett's index of unusual female names.

Ilana *Hebrew:* Tree.

Ilene *Irish:* Light; a variation of Eileen (see above); the Irish form of Helen (see above). Also Ilean, Ileen, Ileene.

Ilia A Puckett pearl.

Imena Found on Puckett's 1877–1937 list. Imena resembles the Swahili Amina.

Ilsa *German:* Noble maiden. Also Elsa.

Imogene While sources agree that Imogene comes from Latin, there is disagreement over its meaning. It is said to mean last born, image, and innocence. Also Imogen.

Ina *Latin:* Mother; a suffix added to masculine names to create a feminine version: Georgina, Edwina.

Inabel Inabel Burns Lindsay was a noted social worker.

Inda This name appears on Puckett's 1899 list.

Inell Most likely an invention, Inell appears among Puckett's unusual names among schoolgirls.

Inetha Noted on Puckett's index of unusual names, Ineatha appears among contemporary high school girls.

Inetta Noted in 1899.

Inez *Spanish:* Pure. Popular for the better part of the 20th century, Inez appears among contemporary schoolgirls. In tandem with Carvel Simmons, Inez Simmons is CEO of the Cincinnati-based Simmons Enterprises, Inc.

Inger *Scandinavian:* Beautiful. Sprinter Inger Miller is a top NCAA competitor. The daughter of Lennox Miller, a two-time Olympic medalist, Inger is now a star in her own right.

Ingrid *Scandinavian:* Beautiful.

Iola *Greek:* Violet-colored cloud of dawn. In Greek myth, Iola was a princess captured by Hercules.

Ioma The origins of this unusual name are not clear. Also Iomah. Reverend Ioma Murray leads a small congregation in Harlem.

Iona *Greek:* Violet. Also Ionia. Ionia Rollin Whipper, a physician and religious leader, founded a home for unwed mothers in Washington, D.C.

Ione This version of Iona (see above) is found among contemporary high school girls.

Irene *Greek:* Peace; Eirene was the Greek goddess of peace. Also Irena, Irina. Irene is a very popular name among black parents. Singer Irene Reid wooed a generation with her blues and jazz sounds. Irene Diggs is a noted anthropologist.

Iris *Greek:* The rainbow, a flower. The mythical Greek goddess Iris represents the rainbow.

Irma *German:* Noble one.

Irvette *English:* Sea friend; a feminine version of Irving.

Isabel *Spanish:* Consecrated to God. Also Isabelle.

Isabella This English variation of Isabel (see above) is found among free black names, 1800–60. Isabella was Sojourner Truth's name before she changed it.

Isadora *Greek:* Gift of Isis, the principal goddess of ancient Egypt.

Isletta The lyrical Isletta is an apparent African-American invention appearing in Puckett's collection of unusual names of schoolgirls.

Itenia Appears among Puckett's list of unusual schoolgirls' names.

Ivana This Slavic feminine of John is found among free black women of the 19th century. Also Ivanna.

Ivanetta A feminine version of Ivan, found in Puckett's index of unusual names.

Ivanona This feminine variation of Ivan appears in Puckett's index of unusual female names.

Ivory *Latin:* Precious substance obtained from the tusk and teeth of slaughtered elephants. Also Ivoreen, Ivorine. The demand for ivory plays a large role in causing the great elephant herds of Africa and Asia to become endangered.

Ivy *English:* A vine, a climbing plant. Appears among free black women, 1800–60.

Izell Appears in Puckett's list of unusual names of schoolgirls.

Izetta Appearing on Puckett's index of unusual names, Izetta is found among contemporary high school girls.

Izola This African-American invention appears among Puckett's unusual names for schoolgirls.

Jackie This short form of Jacqueline (see below) is regularly used as an independent name. Jackie Joyner-Kersey has won a Gold Medal in the Olympics and all the major athletic games. Many consider her one of the best athletes in the world. Jackie Jackson is Reverend Jesse Jackson's wife.

Jacqueline *French:* Protect. The name Jacqueline is traced to the Hebrew Jacob, meaning to supplant. Jacques is the French form of Jacob or James, names that have illustrious biblical histories. Also Jaclyn, Jacklynn, Jackleen, Jaclynn, Jakleen, Jaklyn, Jacquelin, Jacquelyn, Jacquelyne, Jacquelynn, Jacqualine, Jacqualyn, Jacquelynne, Jacquelina, Jacqueleen. The high-fashion Jacqueline is in consistent use by black parents. Jacquelyne Johnson Jackson is a noted sociologist. Junior high school student Jacqueline Brett Segue, of Grosse Pointe Academy, is called an all-around student by her teachers and peers. She excels in both academics and athletics.

Jada Jada Pinkett is an actress.

Jamaica The name of the Caribbean island has been used as a given name. Jamaica Kincaid is a stylish novelist.

Jametrice The *Charlotte Observer* describes Jametrice Glisson as a Gullah storyteller.

Jamie *Scottish:* A diminutive for James. In regular use as a feminine name for about 30 years. Occasionally used by black parents.

Jamila   Jamila Wideman is an outstanding basketball player at Amherst Regional High School, Amherst, Mass.

Jamilla   Jamilla is the Arabic word for beautiful.

Jan   *Hebrew:* The Lord is gracious; a feminine form of John.

Jana   A variation of Jan (see above). Also Janna. Jana Dilworth lives in Oak Park, Mich.

Jane   *Hebrew:* The Lord is gracious; a feminine form of John. Jane outstripped Joan as a favorite female version of John in the 16th century. It appears among free black names in the 1700s. Of enduring popularity until very recently, Jane has been widely used. Jane M. Bolin, who liked to be known as Mrs. Walter P. Offutt Jr., was appointed in 1938 as judge of the Domestic Relations Court of New York City by Mayor Fiorello LaGuardia. She was the first black woman judge in the United States. Nurse Jane Edna Hunter, a staunch advocate of self-help, devoted her life to improving the quality of life for black women. She was founder and director of the Phillis Wheatley Association in Cleveland. Poet Jayne Cortez dazzles audiences with her socially relevant verse chanted to the music of her jazz combo.

Janel   Appears among contemporary college students.

Janet   This form of Jane (see above) has had sustained and enormous popularity. Dancer Janet Collins distinguished herself on the stages of Los Angeles and Broadway. Janet Hubert-Whitten played Aunt Vivian on "The Fresh Prince of Bel-Air" hit television show. Superstar Janet Jackson, sister of Michael, is a top pop artist.

Janette   Also Janetha, Janetta. Noted in 1877–1937. Janette Stephens is a student at Marist College, South Bronx campus, New York.

Janice   A variation of Jane (see above). Also Janece,

Janique, Jannice, Janyce, Janis. Janice E. Powell lives in Manhattan. Janis Ahmed lives in Corona, N.Y.

Janie   A form of Jane (see above). Occasionally used by black parents, sometimes in two-name combinations such as Janie May. Janie is perhaps best known for its presence in Zora Neale Hurston's classic, *Their Eyes Were Watching God.* The heroine, Janie Crawford, defies tradition in her search for identity.

Jannon   Jannon Roland is a remarkable basketball player for Urbana High School in Urbana, Ohio.

Jara Lee   An unusual two-name combination appearing in Puckett's index.

Jarena   The origins of this name appear to be rooted in African-American creativity. According to *Notable Black American Women,* Jarena Lee was a 19th-century evangelist and itinerant preacher who published two autobiographies: *The Life and Religious Experience of Jarena Lee* and *Religious Experience and Journal of Jarena Lee.*

Jasmine   *English/French:* A flower. This exotic flower name has its roots in the Persian Yasemin and the Arabic Yasamin. Rare.

Jaylaan   Jaylaan Ahmad-Llewellyn lives in East Hampton, N.Y.

Jean   *Latin:* Jean became popular in Scotland, but its roots lie in the Latin Johanna, which is the feminine form of Johannes. The French Jehane grows out of this Latin form of John. Also Jeanna, Jeanne, Jeannie, Jeanetta, Jeanette, Jeannette. In the mid-19th century, Jean upstaged Jane (see above) in Scotland as a preferred female version of John. It appears among free blacks in the United States in the 1700s. Until the recent outbreak of created names, Jean was a frequent selection. Librarian Jean Blackwell Hutson held the position as chief of the Schomburg Center for Research in Black Culture, New York Public Library, from 1972 to 1980. Jeanne Moutoussamy-Ashe, the widow of Arthur Ashe, is a distinguished photographer and the author of *View Finders: Black Women Photographers.*

Jeannine A popular contemporary form of Jean (see above) occasionally used by black parents.

Jelena A Russian variation of Helen (see above).

Jelette Appears in Puckett's index of unusual names.

Jemima *Hebrew:* Little dove; one of the three daughters of Job. Jemima appears among free black names, 1800–60. An often-used name among black parents until the General Mills company presented its Aunt Jemima products. Many black parents were offended, calling the use stereotyping. Today Aunt Jemima's image has been cleaned up, but the name retains an element of reproach.

Jenelle A Puckett find.

Jenesa Vibrating with African-American rhythms, Jenesa is found among Puckett's unusual names of schoolgirls.

Jennett This unusual form of Jeannette appears among free blacks in the 1700s.

Jennifer *Welsh:* White, fair, yielding. Also Jenna, Jennie, Jenny, Jinny. It appears on Puckett's list in the 1700s, along with its variations. Singer Jennifer Holiday won a Tony Award for her performance in *Dreamgirls.*

Jense This name appears in Puckett's list in 1920.

Jeralyn A variation of Geraldine (see above) appearing in Puckett's 1800–60 list.

Jereline This unusual name occurs among free blacks in Washington, D.C., 1863–64.

Jerusha *Hebrew:* Married. Also Jerrusha, Jerussia. Jerusha appears in the 18th century and remains on Puckett's lists through 1937.

Jessica *Hebrew:* Wealthy; Yishay in Hebrew, Iscah or Jesca in the Old Testament. Sources agree that Shakespeare coined Jessica for Shylock's daughter, a young Jewish woman in *The Merchant of Venice.* Used by black parents since the early 20th century.

Jessie Pet name for names beginning with Jess. Also

Jessye. Sometimes employed by black parents for girls. Diva Jessye Norman is an opera singer extraordinaire.

Jestine   Also Jestina. Jestine appears on Puckett's list of names in southern cities, 1877–1937.

Jetaime   This unusual given name documented in the New York *Amsterdam News* means I love you in French.

Jetta   *English:* From jet, an intensely black stone. Jetta appears on Puckett's early list.

Jettie   Appears on Puckett's 1877–1937 list. Rare.

Jewel   *English/French:* A precious gem. Also Jewell, Jewelle. Occasionally used by black parents. Jewell Jackson McCabe is the founder of the National Coalition of 100 Black Women.

Jewette   Appears on Puckett's 1877–1937 list. Unusual.

Jill   *Latin:* Youthful; a diminutive for Gillian, which is rooted in the Latin Juliana. Employed regularly, but infrequently. Jill Nelson is the author of *Volunteer Slavery: My Authentic Negro Experience*. Jill Brown is an airline pilot.

Jimelle   This feminine variation of Jim appears on Puckett's index of unusual names.

Joan   *Hebrew:* The Lord is gracious; a feminine form of John that predates Jane (see above). Joan Murray was the first black woman to report the news on TV. Joan B. Johnson is the chief executive of Johnson Products Co., a hair-care products manufacturer in Chicago.

JoAnn   A variation of Joan (see above) and Jane (see above). Also Joanna, Joanne. African-American parents have demonstrated a preference for names beginning with the prefix Jo. Like De, Le, and La, Jo is an often used prefix in created names. Joanne Powell was a member of the founding team of *Emerge*.

Jocelia   Appears in Puckett's index of unusual names.

Jocelyn   *English:* A blend of Joyce (see below) and Lynn (see below). During the Middle Ages, it was a male name. M. Jocelyn Elders was nominated by President Clinton as the new U.S. surgeon general. A first.

Jodelle A French surname sometimes used as a given name.

Jodie A diminutive for Judith (see below). Also Jody.

Joella *Hebrew:* Jehovah is the Lord; a feminine form of Joel. Also Joelle.

Johanna *Hebrew/Latin:* God is gracious; a feminine form of John. Also Johannah. Appears in Augusta, Ga., in 1877.

Johnalee A feminine variation of John appearing in Puckett's index of unusual names.

Johnelle The popularity of John as a first name for males is reflected in the large number of feminine variations of the name. One assumes that these girl babies were named after fathers, uncles, or grandfathers.

Johnese A feminine version of John found in Puckett's lists.

Johnetta An enormously popular variation of John. Also Johnita, Johneline, Johnice, Johnsie. Anthropologist Johnetta B. Cole is the first black woman president of Spelman College, historically a black women's college in Atlanta.

Johnnie The spelling Johnnie is said to be the feminine version of Johnny. The popular name Johnnie Mae of the early 20th century appears among contemporary schoolgirls.

Joie *Portuguese:* Joie Lee is Spike Lee's sister.

Jolene A well-established name of uncertain origins, Jolene appears to be a 20th-century creation.

Jonell Jonell Nash is food editor for *Essence*.

Josephine *Hebrew:* She will add; a feminine version of Joseph. Frequently used for girl babies in black homes, since the 1800s, Josephine remains a popular choice. The legendary entertainer Josephine Baker spent the later years of her life adopting and caring for orphaned children. Josephine Harreld is a noteworthy musicologist.

Joy *Latin:* Joyful. Occasionally employed by black parents. Joy Cain is parenting editor of *Essence.*

Joyce *Latin:* Joyous. A very fashionable choice for much of this century. New York City's former first lady is Joyce Dinkins.

Juanita *Spanish:* God is gracious; the feminine of Juan, the Spanish form of John. Quietly fashionable. Juanita E. Jackson was the first African-American woman to graduate from the University of Maryland Law School. This notable organizer was appointed special assistant to the secretary of the NAACP in 1935. Born in Wewoka, Okla., in 1919, Juanita Kidd Stout became the first elected black woman to sit on the bench in Philadelphia. Juanita Jordan, wife of NBA superstar Michael Jordan, says their daughter Jasmine Mickael has Michael wrapped around her finger.

Juda On Puckett's list of unusual names found among free blacks in New England, 1830.

Judia An unusual form of Judy (see below). Judia Jackson Harris was an outstanding educator in her home state of Georgia.

Judith *Hebrew:* Jewess. In the Old Testament, Judith is the wife of Esau. This stylish name has been used by black parents. The beautiful and elegant ballerina Judith Jamison served as the principal dancer of the highly esteemed Alvin Ailey Dance Company, which she now leads.

Judy A diminutive for Judith (see above). Listed among free black female names found in the 1700s, Judy has endured as a popular choice. Judy Richardson is a documentary producer.

Juelda Also Junella. Juelda appears on Puckett's 1933 list. This unusual name resonates with certain African-American sound preferences.

Julet Appears among free black women in the 1700s.

Julia *Latin:* Youthful; a feminine version of Julius. Also Julie, Juliana, Juliet, Julienne, Juliette. Appearing in the 1800s, the elegant name Julia has been used by black parents for many decades. Julia Martin is a noted chemist. Downtown Julie Brown is a popular MTV video jock. Julia W. Taylor is the CEO of Mechanics and Farmers Bank, which is listed among the BE 100s.

June This sixth month of the year is associated with the beauty of spring and early summer. Also Junetta. June Jordan is an outstanding poet and essayist.

Justine *French:* Fair, just, upright. Also Justina.

Kadija A variation of the popular Arabic Khadijah. Kadija George is a writer.

Kai (kye) *Hawaiian:* A place name meaning sea or seawater. Also Ky. Gerri Kai Jackson is a student at Emory University. She prefers to be called Kai.

Kaila *Hawaiian:* A flower crown.

Kaitlin *Irish:* Also Caitlin. A phonetic spelling of Catherine (see above).

Kala *Hindu:* Black. Preschooler Kala Paunice Patton Morgan lives in Elizabeth, N.J.

Kalani *Hawaiian:* The sky chief.

Kalei *Hawaiian:* The flower wreath.

Kalen Kalen Tubridy is an outstanding member of the

girls' basketball squad of Townsend Harris High School, New York City.

Kali *Sanskrit:* Energy. Kali Grosevenor, like her mother, Verta Mae, is an accomplished writer and poet.

Kalifa *Somali:* Chaste, holy.

Kalina An unusual name appearing in Puckett's collection. One source attributes Kalina to Polish as a flower name.

Kalinda An unusual variation of Linda (see below), noted in the 19th century. This blend showcases our fascination with the Ka sound.

Kalisa Kalisa Nicole Clifton graduated magna cum laude from Howard University, class of 1993.

Kallie The origin of Kallie is not clear. It is perhaps a variation of Kelly (see below).

Kansas This name of a midwestern state appears among unusual names for schoolgirls collected by Puckett.

Kara *Latin:* Beloved, sweetheart. One source says it means precious jewel in Vietnamese.

Karen A Danish form of Catherine (see above), which in Greek means pure. Also Karyn. A fashionable, often-used name found among contemporary black women. Karen J. Halliburton is the director of information for *Essence.* Karen Lynn Simily of Oklahoma City is an active mother of three. Karyn White is a popular singer.

Karine This variation using Ka appears on Puckett's list of unusual schoolgirls' names.

Karma A Hindu, Buddhist word that describes a religious concept used as a name. Karma Lowe ranks in the top percentile of the 1993 senior class at Booker T. Washington Senior High School in Houston.

Kata Appears among free black names, 1800–60.

Kate This diminutive for Catherine (see above), the pure one, appears among free black names, 1700–1800.

Katherine *Greek:* An alternate spelling of Catherine. Also Katharina, Katharine, Katherina, Kathryn. This sophisticated name with its roots in antiquity first appears on Puckett's 1877–1937 list. Katherine Brown lives in Highland Park, Mich. Katherine Boyd is a promising writer and actress. Anthropologist Katherine Dunham redesigned the art of modern dance when she introduced African and Caribbean rhythms and movements to the American stage.

Kathleen An Irish form of Katherine (see above). Also Kathaleen, Kathlena, Kathleena, Katrina. Kathleen Battle is a fully ascended opera star.

Kathy A popular diminutive for Katherine (see above), now often used as an independent name. Also Kathe, Kathi. Kathe Sandler is a filmmaker.

Katia An unusual form of Kate (see above). Katia Stansberry was cocaptain of the girls' swim team and the speech team president at Denver's Montbello High School.

Katie A diminutive for Katherine (see above) infrequently used as an independent name.

Katrea Katrea Valencia McKinnis is a member of the class of 1993.

Katriane A Russian form of Katherine (see above). Also Katalina.

Katrine A Scottish form of Katherine (see above).

Katurah Katurah John-Sandy is the daughter of publisher Rene John-Sandy, founder of the popular *Class* Magazine, which caters to Caribbean-Americans.

Katy A diminutive for Katherine (see above).

Kay A nickname for Katherine (see above) or Karen (see above).

Kayla Kayla Gray is a photographer noted in *Black Beat* magazine.

Keisha This name could wind up winning the all-time popularity contest. Keisha is a hot name all around the country. Its sound patterns are heard again and again in various forms. Keisha I. Freeland lives in the South Bronx, N.Y.

Kelly *Irish:* Battle maid; an Irish surname and boy's given name that has become popular as a girl's name. Also Kelli. Kelli Jones is curator at Jamaica Art Center in Queens, N.Y. Kelli Jennings of Chicago is an officer in the naval reserve. Kelly Alexander is a successful model.

Kendra Kendra La Shonne Floyd graduated from Spelman College, class of 1993.

Kenitra Kenitra Sybelle Boone is a member of Howard University's class of 1993.

Kerensa *Cornish:* Beloved.

Kerry *Irish:* Dark one. Also Kerrie, Kerri, Keri, Kerie, Keree, Kerrey, Kerry Ann, Kerryann, Kerryanne.

Kesabi Kesabi La Grace Dabney graduated from Howard University in 1993.

Kessiah This spelling variation of Keziah (see below) appears among freed blacks in Washington D.C., 1863–64.

Keziah *Hebrew:* In the Old Testament, Kezia is one of the daughters of Job. Appears among free black names, 1700–1800.

Kia Newly created. Kia Monique Sweeney is a schoolgirl. Kia Noel Marie Brown is a preschooler.

Kim A diminutive for Kimberley (see below) often used as a given name. Kim Weston was a popular singing star of the 1960s and 1970s. Actress Kim Coles, formerly of "In Living Color," stars in a TV show called "Living Single" with Queen Latifah.

Kimberley *English:* From the royal meadow. Also Kimba, Kimber, Kimberlee, Kimberly, Kimblyn. The history of this surname is traced to a diamond-mining town in South Africa named for Lord Kimberley. It is said that many young British boys were given the name to honor their fathers who fought in Kimberley during the Boer War. Since the 1940s, its use in the U.S. has been confined to girls. During the 1960s, Kimberley experienced a surge of popularity in black families. Kimberly Knight is an associate editor of *Essence.*

Kimmie A diminutive for Kimberley (see above), appearing in Montgomery, Ala., 1877–1937, well before Kimberley became fashionable among black parents.

Kinshasha This sassy name is based on Kinshasa, the capital of Zaire. When asked about the spelling of her name, Kinshasha Holman Conwell remarked that she had spelled it "my own black way." Her statement captures the spirit of much of our naming history. Conwell is executive director of the Studio Museum in Harlem.

Kirsten *Scandinavian:* A form of Christine (see above).

Kissie A diminutive for Keziah (see above) appearing in Augusta, Ga., in 1899.

Kitra *Hebrew:* Crowned one.

Kitty A short form of Katherine (see above) and Kathleen (see above). Kitty Green owns the Gullah House Restaurant.

Kizzie This diminutive for Keziah (see above) was popularized in Alex Haley's *Roots.* The variation Kizzy appears among free black names, 1800–60.

Koma Perhaps rooted in Africa, Koma is noted in Puckett's index of unusual names.

Kometa Appears in Puckett's index of unusual names.

Kozelle This unusual name appears in Puckett's index.

Kristen A form of Christine (see above).

Kristina Alternate spelling for Christine (see above). Also Kristine. Kristine Hunter is a novelist.

Kristy A diminutive for Kristine sometimes employed as a given name. Kristy Gaines is a member of the class of 1993.

Kurtheelia Noted in the 19th century.

Kutha An unusual name found in Puckett's index.

Kweli Kweli Imara Archie attends Spelman College.

Kyeeniah Kyeeniah Nix is a student at Hunter College, New York City.

Kyla A feminine form of Kyle.

Kyra *Greek:* Lady; a title of respect.

La Puckett documents an early preference for the La phoneme in these names: La Blanche, La Dora, La Eunice, La Fay, La Jeune, La Perle, La Rossie, La Rue Forrest, La Tausca, La Vada, La Verne, La Zora.

Laetitia A spelling variation of Letitia (see below) found among free black names, 1800–64.

Lafiette Dedication and determination allowed 18-year-old Lafiette Denise Wells to survive the New York homeless shelter system, graduate from high school, and win a scholarship to college.

Lahalia This rhythmical use of La was noted in 1877–1937.

La June Noted by Puckett among unusual names of schoolgirls, 1877–1937, La June is an early documentation of the use of today's enormously popular La and Le prefixes to create distinct names.

La Keya La Keya Williams of Jamaica High School is a track and field champion in the New York Public School Athletic League.

Lana Sources disagree on the origins of Lana, which appears among free black women in the 1800s. Some claim it is a form of Alana (see above), which is itself a form of Helen (see above). Others say it comes from the Latin and means wool. Most agree it was popularized by actress Lana Turner.

Laney This unusual given name is found among free black women during the 19th century.

Lanieash Lanieash Lloyd is a West Indian American who lives in Queens, N.Y.

Lannah A phonetic spelling of Lana (see above) noted among 19th-century black women.

Laquiana Soloist Laquiana Fallin attends Spelman College.

Lara *Latin:* In Roman mythology, Lara is a nymph who loses her tongue to Jupiter for her betrayal of Juno.

Larissa *Greek/Latin:* Cheerful. In use only since the 1960s, Larissa is said to come from the Latin Hilarius.

Latia Latia Curry of New York's Peter Stuyvesant High School is a track and field champion.

Latiffah An African-American spelling variation of the Arabic Latifah, which connotes gentle kindness. Rap artist Queen Latifah has given this name new currency.

La Toya Perhaps the controversial La Toya Jackson of the famed Jackson family can be credited with the proliferation of this name. *The Diary of LaToya Hunter: My First Year in Junior High* by LaToya Hunter won this 12-year-old a review in the pages of the *New York Times.*

Latrice Latrice George was a 1993 recipient of a Project Excellence scholarship. Founded by Carl T. Rowan, the fund, during its sixth annual dinner honoring academic excellence, awarded 80 gifted black Washington, D.C., area high school seniors scholarships totaling $1.3 million.

Laura *Latin:* Laurel; a feminine form of Laurus. In

Rome, the leaves of the laurel tree were used to fashion a crown for the honored. Also Lauri, Laurie. Appearing among black women in the 1800s, Laura has enjoyed consistent use. In 1924, Laura Wheeler Waring won a Cresson Memorial Scholarship and attended the Grand Chaumiere in Paris. Her oils, watercolors, and pastels primarily depict African-American life.

Lauraine   A variation of Lorraine (see below).

Lauranell   A variation of Laura (see above) found among modern schoolgirls.

Laureen   A variation of Laura (see above). Also Lauren, Laurina, Laurene, Loren.

Lauretta   A variation of Laura (see above).

Laurice   A variation of Laura (see above).

Lavada   Appears in Puckett's collection.

Laveda   *Latin:* Purified, cleansed. Also Lavella, Lavelle, Lavetta, Lavette.

Laverne   *Latin:* Laverna was the Roman goddess of thieves and liars. Some sources mistakenly report it as Spanish for green. Also La Verne, Lavern, Leverne. Lavern Baker was a top soul singer of the 1960s.

Lavinia   *Latin:* Lady from Rome.

Landonina   One of several names noted as unusual female names appearing in Washington, D.C., 1800–64.

Lavonia   A feminine form of Lavon.

Leah   *Biblical/Hebrew:* Weary. One of the 50 most frequently used free black female names, 1800–64.

Leala   *French:* Loyal, faithful. Also Layla.

Leandra   Feminine form of Leander, which in the Greek means lion man.

Leanell   Appears in Puckett's index of unusual names.

Leanetta   An interesting name appearing in Puckett's collection.

Leanna   *Irish:* Loving. Also Leanne, Leana, Leeanne. Found in Augusta, Ga., 1877.

Lee Jean A two-name combination found among contemporary schoolgirls.

Lehannah Appearing in 19th century, early evidence of our strong and enduring attraction to the prefix Le, which, like La, is presently enjoying a volcanic burst of creative activity.

Leila *Arabic:* Dark as night, chaste, affectionate. In Persian mythology this black beauty is a heroine. Also Layla, Laila, Leela, Lela, Lelia.

Leksha Leksha Fullmore is a basketball player and high school student.

Lemona Appears in Puckett's lists, 1877–1937.

Lena *Latin:* She who allures. Reported by some sources as a diminutive for names such as Helena and Selena. Appears among black women in Augusta, Ga., 1877. The exquisite, alluring Lena Horne, the grand dame of entertainment, has dazzled, charmed, and delighted audiences around the world as a song stylist and bona fide beauty.

Lenora *Greek:* Bright, shining light; a form of Eleanor (see above). Also Leonora, Lenore, Leora.

Leola For the black community, one wonders if this is a form of Leona (see below) as some sources report it, or a blending of Le and Ola. Leola Jeffries is the mother of Leonard Jeffries, who has chaired the Black Studies Department of City College of the City University of New York from its inception in 1972.

Leona *Latin:* Lionness; a female version of Leon. Also Leonia, Leonie.

Leontine A feminine version of Leon. Also Leontyne. Leontine appears on Puckett's 19th-century list. Leontine Kelly was the first black woman to be elected bishop in the Methodist Episcopal church. Leontyne Price, grand dame of black divas, sits atop a pinnacle of success. Influenced by Marian Anderson, Price has authored a list of firsts and presided over a star-studded career. One critic proclaims her "a prima donna assoluta."

Leria This unusual name appearing in the 1600s displays African-American rhythmic sounds.

Lerona Lerona is found in Puckett's collection of unusual names among schoolgirls.

LeShiryl LeShiryl is a medical technician in Detroit.

Lessie Appears among Puckett's unusual names.

Lestine Found among Puckett's unusual names for schoolgirls.

Leta *Latin:* Glad.

Letha *Greek:* Forgetfulness. Also Lethea, Lethia. Appears among free blacks in Washington, D.C., 1863–64 as Lethea.

Letitia *Latin:* Joy. Also Letetia, Leticia, Liticia. Letitia Brown is a well-known educator and historian.

Lett A diminutive for Letitia that appears during the 1600s. Also Letty. Letty Redley is a teacher in Michigan.

Levana *Latin:* To rise.

Levina *English:* A flash of bright light. Also Levinia.

Levira This name appearing on Puckett's 1877–1937 list resonates with the sounds of an African-American invention.

Levisa An unusual name appearing in the 19th century.

Levita An apparent invention found among 19th-century black women.

Lexie Lexie Elmore is a county supervisor in McComb, Miss.

Liana *French:* To wrap around; a vine found in tropical forests.

Lieta Lieta Williams dropped back in and at age 20 obtained her high school diploma from the New York City Housing Authority's Alternative High School Program.

Lila A variation of Leila (see above). Also Liela, Liella.

Lillian A highly favored version of Lily (see below).

Jazz pianist Lillian Hardin Armstrong was a peer of Jelly Roll Morton and Louis Armstrong. Attorney Lillian Burke was the first black woman elected to the Ohio bench.

Lily *Latin:* A flower. Also Lila, Lillie, Lily Jean. Appearing in the 19th century, this sweetly lyrical name has been used by black parents. Lily White Baker's granddaughter is Lily Jean Russell.

Lina A diminutive for names such as Adelina, Angelina, Emelina, Carolina. Also Linah. Appears in the 19th century as an independent name among black women.

Linda *Spanish:* Pretty. In Old German, Linde was a popular feminine suffix that meant wise as a serpent. In English, Linda is often viewed as a diminutive for Belinda, Malinda, or Melinda. Also Lin, Lindi, Linn, Lynda, Lynde, Lyn, Lynn, Lynne. Appearing in the 1800s, Linda has enjoyed immense popularity, but is somewhat less fashionable in the face of the current creation mania. Linda Johnson Rice is president and chief operating officer of *Ebony*.

Lindsay *Scottish/English:* From the linden tree grove. Also Lindsey, Lynsey. This surname, once predominantly a boy's name, is now more often seen as a girl's name.

Linette A variation of Lynette (see below). Also Linnetta.

Lisa *Hebrew:* Pledged to God. A popular diminutive for Elizabeth (see above), which is now an immensely successful given name among both black and white parents. Lisa Kennedy is an editor at the *Village Voice*.

Litha An apparent invention appearing in the 19th century.

Liza A diminutive for Elizabeth (see above) sometimes used as an independent name.

Lizzelle Also Lizzell. Unusual names in Puckett's index.

Lizzerine Name collected by Puckett.

Lobertha An African-American invention of the 19th century.

Lois Considered by most as a variation of Louise (see below), Lois in the New Testament is Timothy's grandmother, 2 Timothy 1:5.

Lola A diminutive for Dolores (see above) now best known as an independent name. Lola Falana was a top dancer before being stricken with multiple sclerosis.

Lonia Appears in Puckett's index of unusual names.

Lonnetta The origins of this name are not clear. Also Lonette, Lonnette. Actress Lonnette McKee starred in Spike Lee's *Jungle Fever.*

Lonteshia This unusual name reflecting popular modern sounds appears in Puckett's index.

Lonzella Found in Puckett's list of unusual names of schoolgirls.

Lonzetta Found in Puckett's index of unusual names.

Lora Until the 14th century, Lora was the common spelling for Laura (see above).

Lorelei *German:* Lures ships to the rocks.

Lorena Variations of Laura (see above). Also Lorene, Lorenia, Loreen, Lorenna, Lorrina. While Lorena appears in Georgia, Lorene appears in Oklahoma, 1877–1937. Lorena is occasionally used by black parents.

Loretta A 19th-century variation of Laura (see above). Loretta Boyd resides in Detroit.

Lori A variation of Laura (see above). Also Loris, Loriel.

Lorna *Scottish:* From the place name Lorn. Associated with cookies in America.

Lornella Appears in Puckett's index of unusual names.

Lorraine *French:* From Lorraine, an eastern province in France. Playwright Lorraine Hansberry won the New York Drama Critics Award for *A Raisin in the Sun.* Lorraine Hale has played a key role in Hale House. Her mother, Clara McBride Hale, founded this home for babies of drug-addicted mothers in 1973. In addition to raising Lorraine and Nathan, by 1969 Mother Hale had raised 40 children. Lorraine Hale continues to administer Hale House.

Lottie *French:* Little woman. Also Lottie May. Popular around the turn of the century.

Lou This short form of Louise (see below) is rarely used independently. It is most often seen in combinations: Louann, Louanne, Louella, Louetta, Louvetta, Luann, Luanne, Loulou, Betty Lou, Sarah Lou, Jenny Lou.

Louisa A form of Louise (see below) appearing among free black women, 1800–60.

Louise *French:* Famous warrior; a feminine form of Louis. Actress Louise Beavers (1902–62) is known worldwide for her work in Hollywood. Critics accused her of fostering stereotypes in playing the roles of obsequious maids and mammies. She viewed it as honorable work.

Lourane This unusual name appears in Augusta, Ga., in 1899.

Louvenia Also Louvennia, Luvenia. First appearing on Puckett's list in the 19th century, Louvenia appears among contemporary black women and schoolgirls. Louvenia Ward of New York says the name has been in her family for many generations.

Lovie Also Lovey. These names which connote love and affection appear in the 19th and early 20th century for a brief period of popular use. Lovie Mae is found among contemporary schoolgirls. Lovie Austin was a tantalizing blues singer.

Lozetta Lozetta is quite likely an African-American variation of Loretta (see above).

Luberta An African-American invention occasionally used today. Also Lubertha.

Lucena An unusual name appearing among black women in the 19th century.

Lucetta A form of Lucy (see below).

Lucia *Latin:* Light.

Lucille *French:* Light. Also Lucilla. Lucille Armstrong was the great Satchmo's last wife.

Lucinda *Latin:* Light.

Lucretia *Latin:* Wealth. Also Lucretta. Noted by Puckett in 1800–60, Lucretia is found among contemporary schoolgirls.

Lucy *Latin:* Light. Also Lucie. Lucy enjoyed popularity among black parents during the early 20th century. In 1894, Lucy Crump Jefferson opened a funeral home that was the first black business in Mississippi. Lucy Diggs Slowe (1885–1937) was a well-known educator.

Ludeen This apparent invention appears among schoolgirls, 1877–1937.

Ludella Also Ludelle. These names appear among schoolgirls, 1877–1937.

Ludessa This name feels like an African-American invention. It appears in Puckett's collection of unusual black names.

Ludina Also Ludine. These names from 1877–1937 document a fondness for Lu as a phoneme.

Luellen A popular use of Lu.

Luetta A variation of Lou (see above).

Lugenia This rarefied combination of Lou (see above) and Gene apparently grows directly out of the African-American lexicon. Lugenia Burns Hope (1871–1947) amassed an impressive record in her tireless work to bring equality to African-Americans.

Lula Also Lula May. Lula appears in Puckett's list of names in southern cities, 1877–1937. Quite popular in the early 20th century.

Lunetta This use of Lu appears in the 1920s.

Lura A phonetic variation of Laura (see above) sometimes used by African-Americans. Also Luette, Lurlene, Lurline.

Lurlene This form of Lorelei appears in Puckett's collection. Also Lurline, Lurleen. Lurlene Hunter was a sultry songstress in the 1960s.

Lyda This name is perhaps related to Lydia (see below) or is a result of black invention. Lyda Moore Merrick holds an impressive list of awards and achievements. She founded the first Braille magazine for blacks in 1952.

Lydia *Greek:* A woman from Lydia, a region in Asia. Appearing in the 1600s, Lydia is noted as one of the 50 most often used names of free black women of the period. Occasionally used today.

Lynette *Welsh:* Idol, icon. Also Lynetta, Lynnette.

Lynn A diminutive for Linda (see above), which has become a name in its own right. Also Lynnell. Lynn Wilder is the daughter of Governor L. Douglas Wilder of Virginia.

Lyzola An unusual name appearing in the late 19th century that sounds like a recent invention.

Mabel *Latin:* Lovable. Introduced as a diminutive for Amabel, the use of Mabel goes back to the 1700s. However, its popularity waned as we moved toward the cities. Mabel Smith is a counselor at District Council 37 in New York City.

Mabelia   This variation of Mabel (see above) appears in Puckett's index of unusual names.

Macedonia   The use of this name of an ancient country in Southern Europe as a girl's name is extremely rare. However, it appears among free blacks of the 1700s.

Macey   Found in contemporary South Carolina.

Madeline   *Greek:* Magnificent. Also Madelaine, Madeleine, Madalena, Madelle. Madeline, an early spelling variation of Magdalene, quickly gained popularity. Over the centuries there have been numerous spelling variations, representing various sound preferences. In the Greek, where the name originates, it was a place name for one who came from Magdala, a town on the Sea of Galilee, the birthplace of Mary Magdalene. The name was introduced into Great Britain through the French Madeleine.

Madena   Resembling Madonna, Madena is found among black women of the 19th century.

Madesta   The origins of this unusual, lyrical name appear to be rooted in African-American invention.

Madge   *Greek:* A pearl. Originally a diminutive for Margaret (see below), Madge is infrequently employed as a given name.

Madie   Also Madey. Documented in Arkansas in 1936, Madie is in regular but infrequent use.

Madonna   *Latin:* My lady. Used almost exclusively by devout Catholic families, Madonna appears in Puckett's index. The controversial superstar Madonna has probably put the name out of reach for most parents.

Madora   A form of Medea (see below). Also Medora.

Mae   An alternate spelling of May (see below). Mae C. Jemison was the first black woman astronaut.

Maecile   An example of the African-American attraction to Ma as a prefix.

Maedell A blend appearing in Puckett's index of unusual names.

Maelyne A variation of May (see below).

Magalina A variation of Magdalina (see below). Also Magilene.

Magdalina *Hebrew:* Megdal, a high tower. Also Magdaline. The ancient Greek town of Magdala was cited as magnificent because of its location by the sea and its high tower. Mary Magdalene renounced her sins at the feet of Jesus Christ. Although it appears on Puckett's early list, given its sacred connotations, Magdalina is rarely used.

Maggy This form of Maggie, a diminutive for Margaret (see below) and Magnolia (see below), appears among free blacks in the 1700s.

Magnolia *French:* The magnolia tree, adored for its large fragrant flowers, was named for the French botanist Pierre Magnol. For a short time Magnolia flourished as a high-fashion name. But its use may have been truncated by an unfavorable association with southern plantations.

Mahala *Hebrew:* Tenderness. Also Mahalah, Mahalian, Mahelia.

Mahalia Mahalia Jackson distinguished herself as the greatest gospel singer in the world, and she virtually embodied African-American sacred music.

Mahogany The great mahogany trees of the Brazil rainforest are known around the world for their hard, reddish-brown wood. Mahogany appears as a female name in the 19th century. Recall the eponymous character from the film *Mahogany,* starring Diana Ross.

Maia *Greek:* Mother. In Greek mythology Maia, the daughter of Atlas, is the mother of Hermes, the god of cunning who is identified with the planet Mercury. In Roman myth, the month of May was named after this goddess of spring and growth.

Maida *English:* A maiden.

Maizie   Appears in Puckett's index of unusual names. Mahazie and Mazie appear among contemporary black women, while Maizie Zonetta is found earlier.

Majenta   Listed in Puckett's index of unusual names.

Majesta   *Latin:* Dignity, majesty. Also noted in Puckett's index as Majester.

Maleatha   Also Maletha. Maleatha is in Puckett's index of unusual names.

Malena   A variation of Madeline (see above). Also Malina. Malena is found among 18th-century free black women.

Malinda   *Greek:* Gentle. Also Malinde, Melinda.

Maliqua   This name represents a variation of Arabic and Swahili phonemes.

Malissa   A variation of the popular Melissa (see below). Malissa Drayton is a fashion editor.

Malta   Noted in the index of unusual names, this place name is evidence of our attraction to pretty sounds.

Malva   *Greek:* Delicate, slender. *Latin:* Mallow flower. Also Malvina, Melva, Melba.

Mamie   Originally a diminutive for Margaret (see below), Mamie has been well-used by black parents as a girl's name. Mamie Smith is credited with recording the first blues song.

Manetta   A contemporary American invention said to come from Manatee Pocket, a section of Salerno, Fla.

Manette   A diminutive for Marion (see below).

Magena   *Hebrew:* Melody. Also Mangina.

Mansi   *Hopi:* Plucked flower.

Manuela   *Spanish:* God is with us; a feminine form of Emmanuel.

Maquisha   Maquisha Walker is an outstanding basketball player for Athens High School, Athens, La.

Mara   *Hebrew:* Bitter; an early form of Mary (see below).

Marcelite Marcelite J. Harris is a brigadier general and vice-commander of the Oklahoma City Air Logistics Center at Tinker Air Force Base.

Marcella *Latin:* Belonging to Mars; a feminine form of Marcellus. Also Marcela, Marcelle, Marcellina, Marcelline, Marchella, Marchelle, Marcile, Marcille, Marcy. Marchelle Payne is a triple jump competitor for the University of Maryland.

Marcenia A variation of Marcia (see below). Also Marcena, Marcene, Marcine.

Marcia *Latin:* Warlike; a feminine form of Mark. Also Marsha, Martia. Marcia Caster is a writer. Recently named editor of *Ms.* magazine, Marcia Anne Gillespie was at one time the editor of *Essence.*

Mardell *English:* From the meadow near the lake.

Mareda Collected by Puckett.

Marelda *German:* Renowned battle maid.

Marenda Also Marinda, Meranda. Documented among 19th-century black women.

Maresa A variation of Marissa.

Maretta *American:* A contemporary invention said to combine Martel and Izetta (see above).

Margaret *Greek:* A pearl. Also Margareta, Margarete, Margaretha, Margaretta, Margarita, Marge, Margot. Enormously popular over the centuries among English-speaking families, Margaret and Margrete are documented among free black women in the 1700s. Margaret Morgan Lawrence is a lauded psychiatrist. The renowned poet and educator Margaret Walker is the author of *Jubilee,* a historical novel loosely based on her grandmother's legacy. Margo, a variation of Margaret, is documented in Pine Bluff, Ark., in 1936.

Margarite A variation of Margaret (see above) appearing in 1936.

Margella This variation of Margaret (see above) appears in Washington, D.C., 1863–64.

Margie A diminutive for Margaret (see above) sometimes employed as an independent name.

Marguerite With its high-fashion tone, Marguerite appears among college students in 1930. It is the name of Harry Belafonte's first wife.

Maria This Latin, French, Italian, Spanish, and Swedish form of Mary (see below) appears among free blacks in the 1600s. Maria Louis Baldwin (1868–1922), affectionately called Mollie, was a distinguished educator in Cambridge, Mass.

Mariah A form of Maria (see above) appearing in the 1700s.

Marian A compound of Mary Ann documented in the 18th century. Also Mariane, Marianne. Perhaps our most celebrated Marian is Marian Anderson, the great lady of song. Her unusual contralto, trained in the church choir, captivated audiences the world over and forged the way for today's spate of divas. In 1965, Marian Wright Edelman became the first African-American woman admitted to the bar in Mississippi. A steadfast advocate for the poor and especially the children of the poor, Edelman founded the Children's Defense Fund in 1973.

Maribel A popular, modern combination of Mary (see below) and Belle (see above).

Marie This French version of Mary (see below) was also the early form of the name in England. Also Maree. With deep roots in African-American naming practices, Marie has long been in vogue. The indomitable, indefatigable Marie Elizabeth Dutton Brown is called the godmother of blacks in book publishing. Hired as a senior editor at Doubleday Anchor Press in the late 1960s, the boom days of affirmative action, she was one of the first black women to hold such a position. There she shepherded many black-themed books into publication and nurtured a generation of new writers. Her literary agency, Marie Brown Associates, offers literary and marketing services to writers and publishers. A patron of black arts and culture, Brown is especially supportive of young writers.

Mariel A Dutch form of Mary (see below).

Marietta A French form of Marie (see above).

Marilyn A frequently employed variation of Mary (see below). Also Marelyn, Merilyn.

Marion *French:* A diminutive for Marie (see above) found among free blacks in the 1800s.

Marire This lyrical name appears among Puckett's unusual schoolgirls' names.

Maris *Latin:* Star of the sea. Also Marise, Marisa, Marissa, Maritza, Merissa.

Marita *Latin:* Married woman. Marita Golden is a vastly underrated novelist.

Marjoe A combination of Mary (see below) and Joe. Also Marjo.

Marjorie A variation of Margaret (see above). Marjorie McCoy lives in Taft, Okla. When President John F. Kennedy appointed attorney Marjorie McKenzie Lawson to a judgeship in the District of Columbia, she became the first black woman so appointed.

Marla A form of Marlene (see below).

Marlee A blend of Mary (see below) and Lee in occasional use.

Marlene A blend of Mary (see below) and Magdalene. Also Marlaina, Mariane, Marlayne, Mariea, Marleen, Marlena, Marley, Marlyn, Marlynne, Marna. The name appears as Marline among 1800s free black women.

Marquetta The origins of this name are not clear. Marquetta Haynes is a school teacher and wife of basketball great Marques Haynes.

Marsena The origins of this unusual name are unclear.

Marsha This form of Marcia (see above) appears in the

1800s among black women. Marsha Warfield is an outrageous comedian.

Marta   A variation of Martha (see below).

Martha   *Biblical/Aramaic:* Lady. Also Martella, Martelle, Martina. In the New Testament, Martha, the sister of Mary, prepared dinner while Mary sat at the feet of Jesus to hear His message. Martha is documented among black women in the 18th century. Sociologist Martha Mae Jones is a clothing designer. As an entrepreneur, she operates the Downstairs Market, where her one-of-a-kind chic attire is sold in the famous Chelsea area of Manhattan.

Marthena   A variation of Martha (see above) appearing in the index of unusual names. Also Marthenia.

Marva   *Latin:* Wonderful. Also Marvela, Marvella, Marvelle. Marva Louis at one time was the wife of heavyweight champ Joe Louis.

Mary   *Hebrew:* Bitterness. "Call me not Naomi [the pleasant], call me Mara [the bitter] for the Almighty hath dealt very bitterly with me." Ruth 1:20. *Greek:* A form of Mirian, which means rebellious. In English, however, Mary is most closely associated with the Virgin Mother of Jesus Christ, which accounts for its overwhelming popularity. In the 18th century, Mary followed Sarah, Rachael, and Phillis as the fourth most often documented name among free black women. The overwhelming popularity of Mary required middle names to distinguish between the many girls with the name: Mary Ann, Mary Jo, Mary Lou, Mary Sue. The imposing intellect of Mary Frances Berry has served African-Americans well. As a historian, educator, lawyer, government official, and civil and human rights activist, Berry is an unflagging advocate for black America. Included in her stellar repertoire of accomplishments is the authorship of five important books. Mary McLeod Bethune rates among the most outstanding women in African-American history. Among her signal achievements is the founding of Bethune Daytona Educational and Industrial Institute, which is now known as Bethune-Cookman College. A friend of Eleanor Roosevelt, Bethune dedicated her entire life to uplifting African-Americans. Mary Eleanora McCoy is called the mother of clubs because of her involvement in numerous organizations devoted to black causes. She was influential in the life of her husband, inventor Elijah McCoy. Jazz pianist Mary Lou Williams was greatly influenced by Earl Hines. Mary J. Blige, according to Maurice Butler in *Black Beat*, became "quite large in a short amount of time." Apparently armed with a ton of confidence, Blige parlayed a tape made at a mall into one smash single after another.

Maryland The name of this state located on the northeast coast is found as a female name in Pine Bluff, Ark., in 1936.

Maryse A form of Mary (see above) or a feminine version of Maurice.

Marzetta This compound found among Puckett's names appears to have its origins in African-American invention.

Matilda *German:* Mighty in battle.

Matoka Collected by Puckett.

Mattie A short form of Martha (see above) and Matilda (see above) frequently used as a given name in the early part of this century.

Mattiwilda Coloratura soprano Mattiwilda Dobbs, following her graduation from Spelman College in 1946, found a career in opera impossible in the U.S. But she sang in all the major European opera houses. She was the first African-American to sing a principal role in La Scala in Milan.

Mattline Perhaps a phonetic spelling of Madeline (see above).

Maude Originally a short form of Matilda (see above), now an independent name. Also Maude Mae, Maudie, Maudie Mae.

Maureen *Irish:* Little Mary.

Maurisha Maurisha Joseph, star basketball player for McAuley High School in New York, was the valedictorian of her class.

Mauve *Latin:* Violet, lilac-colored.

Mavis *French:* The song thrush. Occasionally used by black parents. Mavis Staples is the soulful lead of the Staple Singers.

Maxine *Latin:* Greatest. Also Maxene. Distinguished and articulate, Maxine Waters has been a resounding advocate for her constituency. Elected to the California State Assembly in 1976, Waters is considered the most powerful woman in California political circles.

May *Greek:* Mother. *Latin:* Great one. May is the Anglicized version of Maia, the Roman goddess of springtime for whom the month of May is named. May France is a two-name combination appearing in *Black Names.* May Miller was one of the most celebrated playwrights of the Harlem Renaissance.

Maya A variation of Maia (see above) that has enjoyed regular use among black parents since the legendary poet, author, and college professor Maya Angelou emerged on the national scene. She has enthralled the nation with her poems, one of which she read at President Bill Clinton's inauguration.

Maybelle A popular compound. Big Maybelle was the first to record "You Ain't Nothing But a Hound Dog," but Elvis Presley's cover made a wider impact.

Maychell A variation of May (see above) listed in Puckett's unusual names of schoolgirls.

Maydelle Appears in the index of unusual names.

Maydia A variation of Maida (see above) found among Puckett's unusual names for females.

Mayline Documented in Pine Bluff, Ark., in 1936.

Maynell A contemporary use of May (see above) as a prefix. Maynell Thomas is a film producer.

Mayola   A combination of May (see above) and Ola (see below).

Mazella   Documented in Washington, D.C., 1880–64.

Medea   *Greek:* Ruling. In Greek myth, the enchantress Medea murdered her own children. Its negative connotation of death and destruction makes use of the name extremely rare.

Medora   *English:* Mother's gift.

Megan   A Welsh form of Margaret (see above) that now enjoys widespread popularity as a girl's first name throughout the English-speaking world.

Melanie   *Greek:* Black, of a dark complexion. In Greek mythology, Melania was an epithet for Demeter, the earth goddess. Melanie Hamilton, a character in *Gone With the Wind,* was the impetus for this name's popularity.

Melba   Some sources report Melba as a variation of Melva. Most, however, attribute its use to fondness for Nellie Melba, the Australian operatic soprano, who took her name from her hometown of Melbourne. The dessert Peach Melba was created in the singer's honor by a chef at the Savon Hotel in London in 1892. Melba Liston is a jazz trombonist. Melba Moore is a famous actress and singer who achieved stardom on Broadway. Melba Joyce Boyd is a poet and college professor.

Meleda   Also Meledia. Meleda appears in Puckett's index of unusual names.

Melia   Also Milia. Unusual names documented in the 1700s.

Melina   *Greek:* Honey.

Melinda   *Greek:* Honey. Melinda is said to have been invented to complement Belinda (see above). Inda, a fashionable name element among white families of the 18th century, has remained quite popular among black parents until the recent explosion of inventions. Documented in Washington, D.C., 1863–64.

Melissa *Greek:* Honey bee. Melissa Renee Maxwell, a writer and director, served as creative associate on the critically acclaimed *Boyz N the Hood.*

Melody *Greek:* Song, beautiful music.

Mel Rosa This unusual name is found in Puckett's collection.

Melvina *Irish:* Chief. Also Melvine. Melvina Miller, a steelworker, won $22 million in the Illinois lottery. She had faithfully played the same digits for ten years.

Melvinda A rare name appearing in *Black Names.*

Melzetta Appears in Puckett's index of unusual names.

Melzore Appears in Puckett's index of unusual names.

Memphis The name of this city in Tennessee is noted among schoolgirls.

Mena Documented in Montgomery, Ala., 1877–1937.

Mendora Another Puckett gem.

Menora Noted in the late 18th century.

Mentha Mae A combination appearing in Puckett's collection.

Mercedes *Spanish:* Merciful, compassionate. Quietly fashionable.

Meredith *Welsh:* Magnificent lady. Born and raised in the Crown Heights section of Brooklyn, track star Meredith Rainey is slated to achieve great success. Smart, talented, and determined, this 24-year-old looks forward to a bright future on and off the racing circuit.

Meta A diminutive for Margaret (see above). Meta Varick Fuller was an acclaimed sculptor.

Mettlenunoo Mettlenunoo Nanabeka is a junior high school student in Brooklyn.

Mia *Italian:* My. An English diminutive for Maria (see above).

Michaela *Hebrew:* Like unto the Lord; a feminine form of Michael showing a recent surge in use. Also Micaela,

Michaella, Michala, Michaelina, Michaeline, Mickala, Mykela.

Michelle *Hebrew:* Like unto the Lord; by far the most often used feminine form of Michael. Michelle has enjoyed enormous popularity as a high-fashion name since the 1950s. Michelle Segue is an art director in Bloomfield Hills, Mich. Michele Wallace is the author of *Black Macho and the Myth of the Superwoman.*

Mikki A popular pet name for Michelle (see above) that is sometimes used as an independent name. Mikki Garth-Taylor is fashion and beauty editor for *Essence.*

Milagron *Spanish:* Miraculous.

Mildred *English:* Gentle strength. Mildred Greene operates a travel business in Harlem.

Milly A popular short form of Mildred (see above).

Mima An unusual name of uncertain origins appearing in the 1800s.

Mimi A diminutive for Mildred (see above) rarely used as a given name.

Mineola An unusual compound appearing in Puckett's 1877–1937 list in Montgomery, Ala.

Minerva *Latin:* The thinking one. Minerva is the Roman goddess of wisdom.

Minnie A diminutive for Wilhemina (see below). Also Minny. The late Minnie Gentry played Gram Tee on "The Cosby Show."

Minta Called an 18th-century literary name, Minta is documented in that century among free black women.

Mirabelle *Latin:* Wonderful. Also Mirabel.

Miranda *Latin:* Admirable. Appearing in the 19th century.

Miriam *Hebrew:* The meaning of Miriam is widely disputed. But it is agreed that it is closely related to Mary (see above). Miriam Makeba is an illustrious South African singer.

Missouri Although never widespread, for a short period from the end of the 19th into the early 20th century, the state name Missouri was used as a girl's name, especially in the Southwest.

Missy A diminutive for Melissa (see above) appearing in Puckett's early list, Missy appears among contemporary schoolgirls.

Mitzi A German pet form of Maria (see above).

Modelia An apparent African-American invention appearing in Pine Bluff, Ark., in 1936, according to Puckett.

Modelle An unusual name appearing in 1877–1937 in Montgomery, Ala.

Modjeska Modjeska Simkins is a well-known educator and civil rights activist.

Molien Molien Watley lives in Highland Park, Mich.

Molly A diminutive for Mary (see above) appearing among free blacks in the 1700s. Also Mollie. Pharmacist Mollie Moon was a well-known civic worker and activist.

Mona *Irish:* Aristocratic. Also Monia. Occasionally used by black families.

Moneta This unisex name may be used for a girl. Moneta Sleet is a photographer.

Monica This name is said to have originated in Africa because of St. Monica, who was from that continent, but its meaning is unknown. It has been well-used by black parents. Monica Roberts is the merchandise manager for the Calvin Klein Collection.

Monique This French form of Monica (see above) has flourished since a burst of popularity in the late 1950s. Monique R. Payne of Whitney M. Young High School in Chicago is listed as one of the Top High School Seniors of 1993 by *Ebony*.

Montana *Spanish:* Mountain; Montana is a western state.

Monzora Noted by Puckett.

Morena *Spanish:* Brown, brown-haired.

Morgena *Welsh:* Bright sea dweller; a feminine version of Morgan. However, Morgan is now seen among females.

Mosetta Documented among black women in 1877–1937, in Montgomery, Ala.

Mozelle *Hebrew:* Savior; a female form of Moses. Also Moselle, Mozell. Found among contemporary black women. Mozelle Boyd is a public relations expert.

Mozetta Documented in the late 19th century, Mozetta is found among contemporary black women.

Muriel *Irish:* Shining sea.

Murilla A variation of Muriel (see above).

Myra *Latin:* Sweet-smelling oil; a feminine form of Myron. Steadily fashionable, Myra is a consistent choice.

Myrlie A variation of Myrtle (see below). In 1987, Myrlie Evers became the first black woman appointed commissioner to the Board of Public Works in Los Angeles. She is the widow of the slain civil rights leader Medgar Evers.

Myrtaline An African-American variation of Myrtle (see below). Also Myrteline.

Myrtis A form of Myrtle (see below) used since the late 19th century. Also Merdis, Mertis, Murdis.

Myrtle *English:* A dark green bush with pink or white blossoms.

Nada *Russian:* Hope, one of the three holy virtues: faith, hope and charity. Also Nadia. Virtue names, as they are sometimes called, were common in early America. While Faith and Hope have remained active, Charity seems to have fallen out of favor.

Nadine *French:* Hope. In French this form of Nada (see above) may also represent a pet name for Bernadette (see above). It appears among black women, 1877–1937. Nadine White is an artist of increasing repute.

Najah Brooklyn Tech's Najah Adams demonstrated her winning form by capturing the triple jump at the 1993 New York State Track and Field championship.

Nan *Hebrew:* Grace; a pet form of Hannah (see above) or Ann (see above). Nan Bearden is a choreographer with her own dance company.

Nana *Hebrew:* Grace; a short form of Hannah (see above).

Nancy *Hebrew:* Grace. Originally a pet name for Hannah (see above) or Ann (see above), Nancy is now well-established as an independent name. Noted on Puckett's "In the Beginning, 1619–1799" list, Nancy has remained in use by black parents. Nancy Wilson is one of the all-time great jazz singers.

Nanetta This French form of Nancy (see above) is noted in the 19th century. Also Nanette, Netty, Nettie. Nettie Glenn is a vocalist.

Nanine A French form of Nan (see above).

Nannie A short form of Nancy (see above). Nannie Helen Burroughs was a civil rights activist and accomplished orator.

Naomi *Biblical/Hebrew:* Sweet, pleasant. The sweet beauty of Naomi Sims led to a highly successful modeling career. She is now a successful entrepreneur and author.

Narcissa *Greek:* Daffodil; a version of Narcissus (see below). The use of this unusual name is documented in Washington, D.C., 1863–64.

Narcissus *Greek:* Daffodil. In Greek mythology, Narcissus was the name of a young man of great beauty who became so enchanted with his own reflection that he fell in love with himself. Today, narcissism refers to exaggerated self-love or conceit. Noted in the 17th century among free black women, the name, though rare, appears today among schoolgirls.

Nartashia Nartashia Lassiter lives in Baltimore.

Na'Sheeman Na'Sheeman Hillman is an outstanding member of the Trinity High School girls' basketball team in Garfield Heights, Ohio.

Natalie *Latin:* Nativity, birthday of Our Lord; often given to girls born on Christmas. Also Natala, Natalia, Nathalie. According to Puckett's 1877–1937 list, Natalie was frequently used in Southern cities. Natalie Daise is a Gullah tour operator and storyteller based in South Carolina. Singer Natalie Cole is the daughter of the legendary Nat "King" Cole.

Natasha *Russian:* Birthday of our Lord; a form of Natalie (see above).

Natha Lee An obvious African-American variation of Natalie (see above) appearing in Puckett's index of unusual names.

Nathalia Nathalia T. Jeffrey is a dentist in Jamaica, N.Y.

Nazarie Also Nazlee, Nazarine, Nazrinie. Nazarie represents a series of names using the Naz sound.

Neala *Irish:* Champion; a feminine form of Neal.

Nealtha A feminine form of Neal appearing among African-American women, 1877–1937.

Neda *English:* A sanctuary. Also Nedda.

Nedra Nedra Wheeler is a bassist in New York City.

Nefertia A variation of Nefertari, queen of Egypt. Also Neferatri. Neferatri Bordain was a recipient of the YWCA's Young Baptist Future Award.

Nefira Found in Puckett's index.

Negina *Hebrew:* Melody.

Nekita Nekita Beasley is a college track star.

Nelia A pet form of Cornelia (see above).

Nelka An unusual name noted in Puckett's index.

Nell Diminutive for Eleanor. Also Nelly, Nella, Nellia, Nelline. Nell and Nelly appear as independent names among free black women in the 1700s. Nellie enjoyed a brief moment of popularity. Olympian Nell Cecelia Jackson was an outstanding athlete, coach, and educator. Nellie Lutcher was a famous rhythm and blues singer of the 1940s and 1950s. Nurse-turned-novelist Nella Larsen was the first black woman to receive a Guggenheim Award.

Nelsena An unusual variation of Nell (see above) or Nelson found in Puckett's index.

Nelta Interior decorator and space planner Nelta Brunson says she is named for a woman who once employed her mother. This white lady stood up for her black employee in the face of discrimination.

Neola *Greek:* Young one.

Nercelia An apparent invention appearing in Puckett's index.

Nerine Nerine was a sea nymph in Greek mythology.

Nerissa A form of Nerita (see below). An unusual name appearing in Puckett's index.

Nerita *Greek:* A sea snail.

Nerolia *Italian:* Nerolia was a princess who is said to have discovered neroli oil by distilling flowers from the orange tree.

Nessa *Scandinavian:* A high rock projecting into the sea, a promontory.

Nessie A Welsh pet form of Agnes (see above).

Nesta A Welsh pet form of Agnes (see above). Also Neta, Netta.

Netta *Hebrew:* A plant or shrub. Also Neta.

Nettie Diminutive for names such as Annette (see above) and Nanette. Also Netty. Nettie enjoyed a brief stint of popularity as a first name for girls.

Neva *Spanish:* Snowy.

Nevada The name of this state with its snow-capped mountains is found in Puckett's 1877–1937 list. In rare but contemporary use as a girl's name by both black and white parents.

Newanna An early invention using the favored Wanna name element, it appears on Puckett's index of unusual names.

Neysa *Greek:* Pure.

Nezza Appears in Puckett's index.

Nia A suffix now infrequently used as an independent name.

Nicola A variation of Nicole (see below) appearing among black women, 1877–1937.

Nicole *Greek:* victory of the people; a feminine form of Nicholas. Also Nichelle, Nichola, Nichole, Nicholette, Nicolea, Nicolene, Nicoletta, Nicolette, Nicolina, Nikolia. Nichelle Nichols played Lt. Uhura in the original "Star Trek" show of the 1960s. Astronaut Mae Jemison says Nichols's role helped inspire her.

Nikki A nickname for Nicole (see above). Poet Nikki Giovanni, born Yolanda Cornelia Giovanni, came of age in the turbulent 1960s when her militant poetry helped to define the times. Hip-hop artist Nikki D brought the notoriously tough Apollo audience to their feet while she was still an unsigned unknown.

Nilia An unusual name appearing in Puckett's index.

Nina *Spanish:* Girl. Born Eunice Kathleen Waymon, Nina Simone is regarded as the high priestess of soul. For her renditions of "Four Women" and "Mississippi Goddam" during the civil rights movement, black music aficionado Donald Bogle called her a political diva.

Nodie An unusual name appearing among black females in Puckett's 1877–1937 list.

Noel *French:* Christmas; a unisex name. Also Noela, Noeleen, Noelene, Noeline, Noella, Noelle, Noelynn.

Nola *Irish:* White shoulders.

Noleta *Latin:* Unwilling. Also Nolita.

Nona *Latin:* Ninth. Singer Nona Gaye is Marvin Gaye's daughter.

Nonie Collected by Puckett and also found among contemporary women.

Nora *Greek:* Light; a short form of Eleanor (see above) or Honora (see above). Nora Antonia Gordon (1866–1901) is noted for her work at Spelman College in Atlanta, where she trained missionaries for Africa.

Norberta *German:* Brilliant northerner; a female form of Norbert.

Noreen An Irish diminutive for Nora (see above).

Norine A variation of Noreen (see above). Also Norena, Norene, Norina, Norrine.

Norma *Latin:* A rule, principle. Norma Holloway Johnson is a federal court judge in the District of Columbia. Norma Merrick Sklarek is an accomplished architect.

Norwida This unusual name appears in Puckett's index.

Norzell Norzell sounds like an African-American invention. It appears on Puckett's index.

Novella A variation of Nova appearing among black women in 1877–1937. Actress Novella Nelson was remarkable in the Public Theatre's version of *The Chalk Circle.*

Novia *Spanish:* Girlfriend. Also Nova. Appears in Puckett's index.

Nozelle Collected by Puckett.

Nyceta An unusual name appearing in Puckett's index.

Nydia *Latin:* Nest.

Nykesha Nykesha Sales is a valuable member of the Bloomfield High School girls' basketball team, Bloomfield, Conn.

Obedience Name found in Puckett's list, "In the Beginning, 1619–1799." One of the virtue names so popular among the Puritans, Obedience is now obsolete.

Obelia A variation of Odelia (see below) appearing in Puckett's collection.

Octavia *Latin:* Eight; a feminine version of Octavius. Noted as Octavie in Puckett's collection. Writer Octavia Albert (1859–1899) was the author of *The House of Bondage,* a series of conversations with former slaves.

Odalis The meaning of this name with its roots in Spanish is not known.

Odele *Greek:* Song. *German:* Rich. *The New American Dictionary of Baby Names* describes Odele as derived from Odell, which comes from the old English place name, Woad Hill. Also Odela, Odelet, Odelette, Odell, Odella, Odelle.

Odelia *Hebrew:* I will praise the Lord. Also Oda, Odeelia, Odele, Odelinda, Odella, Odilia. Appears among schoolgirls, 1877–1937.

Odell Form of Odele. Also Odella. The names appear on Puckett's 1877–1937 list.

Odessa *Greek:* Long voyage; the name of a port city in Russia.

Odesta This variation of Odessa (see above) is found among schoolgirls, 1877–1937.

Odette *French:* Wealthy. Also Odetta. Odetta Holmes Minter has been at the forefront of the folksong movement since the 1950s.

Ola The derivation of this name is disputed. It is said to come from the Norwegian Olga, to be the feminine form of Olaf, or to be a form of the German Olesia, which means man's defender. However, given the long use of the name among African-Americans, it is not farfetched to speculate that it is rooted in Olu, Ole, and Ola, all African prefixes. Six-year-old Ola Malana Hearndon of West Kingston, R.I., bears the name of her great grandmother, a name said to have been in her maternal family for several generations. The long-popular Ola Mae appears among contemporary women.

Olalee This form of Ola (see above) appears among schoolgirls, 1877–1937.

Olena *Russian:* Light; a form of Helen (see above). Also Olene. The names appear in Puckett's list of unusual names of schoolgirls.

Olenka Appears in Puckett's index of unusual names.

Olenza Indexed by Puckett.

Oletha Variation of Aletha (see above). Also Olethea,

Oleta. Oletha appears in Puckett's list of unusual names of schoolgirls.

Olga *Russian:* Holy, devout. Rarely used by black parents.

Olivetta Form of Olive (see below). Also Olivette. Olivetta Sanders lives in Wichita, Kansas.

Olivia *Latin:* The olive tree. Also Olive. Educator Olivia Davidson Washington assisted her husband, Booker T. Washington, in the founding of Tuskegee Institute.

Olympia *Greek:* From Mount Olympus. In Greek mythology, Olympus was the home of the gods. The name appears among contemporary schoolgirls.

Omelia A variation of Amelia (see above).

Omera An unusual name appearing in Puckett's index.

Ometa Collected by Puckett.

Omizell This has all the markings of an African-American creation. It appears on Puckett's 1877–1937 list.

Oneida *Native American:* Long-awaited.

Onella *Greek:* Light.

Oneta An unusual name appearing in Puckett's index.

Onetha This form of Oneta (see above) is found among contemporary schoolgirls.

Onia This name appears on Puckett's 1877–1937 list.

Onie Lee Found among Puckett's list of unusual names of schoolgirls.

Opal *Sanskrit:* Precious stone.

Ophelia *Greek:* Wisdom. Also Ofelia. Ophelia comes from a Greek word for serpent, which in ancient Greece represented wisdom. However the character Ophelia in Shakespeare's Hamlet loses her senses, and in biblical history the serpent is deceitful. Ophelia Settle Egypt was a prodigious scholar and dedicated social worker.

Oprah The origins of this name are not clear. One source calls it a variation of Ophelia (see above), another calls it a variation of Orpah (see below). Superstar Oprah Winfrey is a paragon of success.

Ora *Latin:* Pray for us. Orabel and Ora Lee are popular versions of the name. Appearing in the 19th century, Ora is found among contemporary schoolgirls.

Oralia *Latin:* Golden; a form of Aurelia (see above). Also Orlena, Orlene, Oralie.

Ordella *German:* Spear.

Orea *Greek:* From the mountain.

Orece Found in Puckett's 1877–1937 list.

Orela *Latin:* A divine announcement.

Orelia This form of Oralia (see above) appears in Augusta, Ga., in 1899, as well as among contemporary schoolgirls.

Oremia Found in Puckett's list of unusual names of schoolgirls.

Orena An unusual name appearing in Puckett's index.

Oreta Noted among schoolgirls in 1877. Found among contemporary schoolgirls as Oretta.

Oriana *Latin:* Dawn, golden sunrise.

Orleas Appearing among free black names, 1800–60, Orleas resonates with African-American creation.

Orlena This unusual name appears on Puckett's list of schoolgirls' names.

Orpah *Hebrew:* A fawn.

Orpha An unusual name appearing in the 1800s.

Orra A variation of Ora (see above) found among free black women, 1800–60.

Oshell A Puckett gem.

Osie Ola A Puckett pearl.

Otelia *German:* Prospers in battle. Otelia Cromwell, an outstanding educator, was the first black graduate of Smith College.

Otha Dell A two-name combination noted in Puckett's list of unusual names of schoolgirls.

Othelia A variation of Ophelia (see above).

Ottielee Appears in Puckett's index of unusual names.

Ovetta An unusual name appearing in southern cities, 1877–1937. Ovetta appears among contemporary schoolgirls.

Ozela Also Ozella. These inventions appear in Puckett's collection.

Ozia This apparent invention appears among free black women, 1800–60.

Ozora *Hebrew:* Strength of the Lord.

Paige *English/French:* Young attendant. Also Page, Pagett, Payge. In medieval times, page was the title given to young boys training for knighthood. Later it came to be a surname indicating an ancestor who was a page. Its use as a girl's name is recent.

Palmira *Greek:* Land of palm trees. Also Palma.

Palmyra This variation of Palmira (see above) appears among black women of the 19th century.

Paloma *Spanish:* A dove. Also Palometa, Palomita. Although Paloma did not gain wide recognition until the popularity of designer Paloma Picasso, the daughter of artist Pablo Picasso, it is noted among black women in Puckett's index.

Pam A nickname for Pamela (see below). Actress Pam Grier gained a certain amount of notoriety during the 1970s making "blaxploitation" films.

Pamela Created in 1590 by Sir Phillip Sidney as the name of a character in *Arcadia*. Also Pamelia.

Pandora *Greek:* The all-gifted one. In Greek mythology, Pandora disobeyed the Oracles and opened a box, allowing all human ills to escape.

Pansy *French:* A flower name; from pensee, which means a thought.

Pantha Variation of Panthea (see below). Also Panthie. Both versions appear in Puckett's index of unusual names.

Panthea *Greek:* Home of all the gods. Also Pantheia, Pantheya.

Paquita A Spanish diminutive for Frances (see above), which in Latin means from France; a feminine version of Paco.

Paralee Also Pari Lee, Parolee. Paralee appears in Puckett's collection.

Paris The name of the capital city of France is used as a given name for both boys and girls.

Parmalee Found in Puckett's index of unusual names.

Parnella *French:* Little rock; a feminine form of Parnell. Also Pernella.

Parnie Appears in Puckett's collection.

Parthenia *Greek:* Virginal.

Pascale *French:* Easter.

Pat A diminutive for Patricia (see below).

Patience A popular virtue name often used by the Puritans. Noted as one of the 19 most frequently used southern free black female names in the 1700s. Given the contemporary lack of patience, it is no wonder the name is out of use.

Patrice A version of Patricia (see below). Also Patreece,

Patreice, Patryce. The name has enjoyed enormous popularity among black parents. Patrice Green is a publicist.

Patricia *Latin:* A woman of noble birth, a patrician; a feminine form of Patrick. Patricia Roberts Harris has a distinguished career as lawyer and educator. Patricia Williams is currently among the most celebrated black women lawyers.

Patrina An unusual variation of Patricia (see above) appearing among black women, 1877–1937.

Patsy A pet name for Patricia (see above).

Patty A diminutive for Patricia (see above). Also Patti, Pattie. Patty is documented among free black women in the 1700s. Patti La Belle is a noted singer.

Paula *French:* Little; a feminine form of Paul that connotes small in stature, but big in love and steadfastness. Also Paule, Paulettea, Paulette, Paulie, Pauline, Paulita, Pollie, Polly. Novelist Paule Burke Marshall is the acclaimed author of *Brown Girl Brownstones.*

Pauli A feminine form of Paul. The talented Pauli Murray is a prime example of a genuine woman of letters, with noteworthy achievements in the fields of law, poetry, scholarship, writing, education, administration, civil rights activism, and Christian ministry.

Pauline This feminine version of Paul predates Paula (see above).

Peach The name of a fruit used as girl's name.

Pearl A jewel name. Also Pearla, Pearlie, Pearlina, Pearlinda, Pearline, Pearly Lee. Pearlimae appears among contemporary schoolgirls. Pearl Bailey is a singer and actress. Pearl Duncan is a writer.

Pearlie Lee A popular two-name combination often used in the early 20th century. Also Pearlie Mae.

Pecola Pecola Breedlove is the protagonist of Toni Morrison's compelling novel, *The Bluest Eye.*

Peggy Originally a diminutive for the Greek Margaret (see above), which means pearl, Peggy is well-established as an independent name. Also Peg. Peggy is documented in the 1700s. Peggy Boyd is a scientific consultant and grants expert.

Penelope   *Greek:* A weaver. In Greek myth, Penelope is the loyal wife of Odysseus, who wove each day and tore her work apart each night. She did so to confound the many suitors who believed that her wandering husband was dead. Penelope told her admirers that she could not marry until she finished the tapestry she was weaving.

Penny   A popular nickname for Penelope (see above), which has become an independent name. Also Pennie. First noted in the 1700s, Penny appears among contemporary school children.

Peony   *Latin:* A flower name.

Pepita   A Spanish nickname for Josephine (see above). Also Peppy.

Pernella   *Greek:* Rock.

Pernesa   Found in Puckett's index.

Perneta   With its origins apparently rooted in African-American sound preferences, Perneta appears in the index of unusual names.

Peta-Gay   Peta-Gay Marie Jackson graduated magna cum laude from Howard University in 1993.

Petrina   *Greek:* Like a rock; a female form of Peter.

Petunia   *French:* A flower name. It appears in Puckett's collection, but was never widely used.

Pheba   Possibly a variation of Phoebe (see below), this unusual name is documented among black women of the 1700s.

Philana   *Greek:* Loves humankind.

Philantha   *Greek:* Loves flowers.

Philberta   *English:* Brilliant one.

Phillippa   *Greek:* Lover of horses; a feminine form of Phillip. Also Philida, Phillina, Philina, Philippa. Pianist

Philippa Duke Schuyler was a child prodigy who by the age of 12 had won many awards for her piano recitals.

Phillis *Greek:* A green branch. This form of Phyllis (see below) was noted in the 17th century as one of the 19 most frequently used southern free black female names.

Philomela *Greek:* The nightingale, lover of the moon, lover of song. Also Philomen, Philomena. In Greek mythology, the maiden Philomela was changed into a nightingale.

Phoebe *Greek:* Bright one, radiant. Appears among free black names in the 1800s.

Phylicia An alternate spelling of Felicia (see above). The multitalented Phylicia Rashad, costar of the all-time hit "Cosby Show" TV series, joined the cast of Broadway's hit musical *Jelly's Last Jam* on June 15, 1993.

Phyllis *Greek:* A green branch. Poet Phillis Wheatley was born in Senegal, West Africa, and brought to the U.S. at the tender age of 8 as a captive. She is considered the first major African-American poet.

Pia *Latin:* Pious.

Pink The name of a color used as a girl's name. Also Pinky.

Pleasant An unusual first name appearing in the 1800s. Very rare indeed.

Polly A variation of Molly (see above), itself a diminutive for Mary (see above). Also Pollie, Pollyanna. Polly appears in the 1700s.

Pomona *Latin:* Fruitful. This name for the mythical Roman goddess of fruit appears among free black women in the 1800s.

Portia *Latin:* An offer. Also Posha. Portia was the heroine of Shakespeare's *Merchant of Venice.* The name appears among contemporary schoolgirls as Porsha.

Precious This name certainly announces what the parents feel about their daughter. It appears among contemporary Oklahoma City elementary school girls.

Prettie Lee An interesting two-name combination appearing in Puckett's index of unusual names.

Princess *English:* Of royal birth. Appearing in the 1700s, Princess has been consistently although infrequently used by black parents.

Princetta A variation of Princess (see above) more often employed by black parents.

Priscilla *Latin:* Ancient. Appearing in the 1700s, the name occurs among contemporary schoolgirls as Prisilla. Priscilla Baskerville is a prominent opera vocalist.

Prudence *Latin:* Exercises caution and wisdom; a virtue name.

Prunella *Latin:* Small plum. Appears in Puckett's index of unusual names.

Pyrena *Greek:* Fiery one.

Quandra Quandra Prettyman Stadler is a poet.

Queen Also Queenella, Queenesta, Queenetta, Queennie, Queenie May, Queen Esta, Queen Esther. Documented by Puckett, 1877–1937, Queen and its numerous variations have enjoyed good use by black parents. Queen Afua is a nutritionist who specializes in vegetarian diets. Queen Latifah is a famous hip-hop artist. The ageless Audrey Moore is best known as Queen Mother Moore.

Queenie   Queenie Dooley was a secretary at Wayne State University.

Querida   *Spanish:* Beloved, darling.

Quillia   Appears among Puckett's unusual names of schoolgirls.

Quinsetta   This unusual name appears in Puckett's index.

Quintelia   Listed in Puckett's index of unusual names.

Quintina   *Latin:* Fifth child; a feminine form of Quentin.

Quitha   Appears among Puckett's list of unusual names of schoolgirls.

Quiviene   Documented among free black names, 1800–60.

Rachel   *Biblical/Hebrew:* Ewe, female sheep; the wife of Jacob. Also Rachael, Racheal, Rachele, Rachelle, Raquela, Raquella, Rawquelle, Raychel, Raychelle, Rashell, Rashelle. A popular name among the Puritans, Rachel appears on Puckett's "In the Beginning, 1619–1799" list. Recently it has again become fashionable among black parents. One of our most distinguished Rachels is the widow of Jackie Robinson. Rachel Robinson is chairperson of the Jackie Robinson Foundation.

Radella   *English:* Elfin counselor.

Radious   Noted in *Parade,* Radious Guess is a multicultural education specialist in Lincoln, Neb.

Rae A short form of Rachel (see above) now used independently. Also Raylene. Anthropologist Rae Alexander Minter, a grandniece of the eminent painter Henry Ossawa Tanner, was named after her father, Ray.

Rahsheda A spelling variation of the Arabic Rashidah, which means wise, mature.

Raina *Latin:* Queen; a variation of Regina (see below). Also Rayna, Rayne, Reyna, Rine.

Rain Perhaps parents are thinking of a lovely spring shower when this word is chosen to name a baby girl. Actress Rain Pryor is the daughter of comedian Richard Pryor.

Raissa *French:* Thinker, believer.

Ramona *Spanish:* A mighty or wise guardian; a feminine form of Ramon or Raymond.

Rana *Scandinavian.* In Norse mythology, Rana was the goddess of the sea. In Sanskrit, it is a title for a queen.

Randi A feminine form of Randy. Randi Hofer is an international relations expert.

Ranita *Hebrew:* Joyous song.

Raquel A Spanish form of Rachel (see above).

Raven *English:* A large black bird.

Rayevelyn A combination appearing in Puckett's index of unusual names.

Raynoma Raynoma Gordy was Berry Gordy's first wife.

Reatha Also Retha, Rether. Reatha is documented on Puckett's 1877–1937 list.

Reba Short for Rebecca (see below), sometimes used as an independent name. Also Reyba, Rheba. Reba Binion lives in Detroit.

Rebecca *Biblical/Hebrew:* A firm bond, such as the marriage vow. Also Rebeca, Rebecka, Rebeka, Rebekah. In the Old Testament, Rebecca was a beautiful maiden who became the wife of Isaac.

Redell An apparent recent creation appearing among Puckett's unusual names of schoolgirls.

Redessa Noted among Puckett's unusual names of schoolgirls.

Redolia Redolia is apparently of African-American coinage; it appears in Puckett's index of unusual names, *Black Names in America.*

Redonia An indication of Re as a popular phoneme among African-Americans, it appears in the index of unusual names.

Regina *Latin:* Queen.

Reholda Appears in Puckett's index of unusual names.

Reietta Appears among free black names, 1800s.

Remal Also Remel. From Puckett's pearls.

Rena *Hebrew:* Melody. Also Reena, Reina, Rina.

Renata *Latin:* Born again.

Rene A diminutive for Irene (see above).

Renee *French:* Reborn; a form of Renata (see above). Also Renae, Rene, Renell, Renelle. During the second half of the 20th century, Renee has enjoyed enormous popularity among black parents. Renee Turner is a newswriter and producer for NBC television's Chicago bureau.

Renetta Appearing in Puckett's index of unusual names and found among contemporary schoolgirls. Renetta may be a variation of Renita (see below) or a spontaneous African-American creation.

Renita *Latin:* A rebel.

Reola Appears in Pine Bluff, Ark., 1936.

Reselle Appears among Puckett's unusual names of schoolgirls.

Reva The derivation of Reva is disputed. It is variously reported as Latin for regaining strength, as a variation of the French Riva, which means riverbank, or as a variation of Vera (see below). Also Rever.

Rhea *Greek:* Flowing. In Greek mythology, Rhea was the mother of the gods.

Rheolia Documented in Puckett's unusual names of schoolgirls.

Rheta *Greek:* An eloquent orator. Also Rhetta.

Rhoda *Greek:* A rose. Also Rhodia.

Rhona *Scandinavian:* Rough isle.

Rhonda *Welsh:* Fierce, noisy waters. Also Ronda, Rhonette. Rhonda Henderson works for IBM.

Ria An element of names such as Victoria (see below), now used as an independent name.

Richardine A feminine form of Richard. Also Richardeen, Richidine. Richardine is quite popular among black parents when the father's name is Richard.

Richette Appears in Puckett's index of unusual names.

Rilaestine An African-American invention. Also Rellestine. Rellestine Smith Wilkins lives in Muskegon, Mich.

Rita *Greek:* A pearl; a diminutive for Margarita now used as an independent name. Following in the footsteps of Gwendolyn Brooks, Rita Dove was named poet laureate of the U.S. She is professor of literature at the University of Virginia.

Riva *French:* Riverbank. Also a variation of the Hebrew name Rebecca (see above).

Robbie Diminutive for Roberta (see below) infrequently used as a given name. Also Robby. Robbie McCauley is a widely acclaimed performance artist in New York City.

Roberta *English:* Bright, shining fame; a feminine form of Robert. Also Robertha. Singer Roberta Flack's abilities have not diminished since her emergence in the late 1960s.

Robin *English:* Bright, shining fame; a feminine version of Robert. Also Robena, Robene, Robenia, Robina, Robinette. Actress Robin Givens, once married to boxer Mike Tyson, is making a brilliant comeback on the screen.

Rochelle *French:* From the little rock.

Rodelia An unusual blend appearing in the index of unusual names.

Rodella This unusual combination appears in Puckett's 1877–1937 list and is found among contemporary black women.

Rolanda *German:* From the famous land; a feminine version of Roland. Rolanda Watts is a highly skilled broadcaster.

Ronetta An unusual name appearing on Puckett's list.

Rosa *Latin:* A rose. Also Rosalia, Rosalie. Our beloved Rosa Parks, the legendary first lady of the civil rights movement, was a recipient of an Essence Award in 1993.

Rosalind *Spanish:* Beautiful rose. Also Rosalyn, Rosalinda, Roslyn. Actress Rosalind Cash appeared in the TV version of *Ceremonies in Dark Old Men,* a play by Lonne Elder III.

Rosamond *German:* Famous protector. *Latin:* Rose of the world.

Rose *Latin:* A flower name. Also Rosena, Rosina, Rosey, Rosetta, Roselyn, Rosita, Roslyn, Roslynn, Rozlyn, Rosezena, Rosenna. Rose has enjoyed enormous popularity among black parents. During the 1940s and 1950s, hair stylist Rose Morgan owned the largest beauty salon in the country. Women traveled to New York from all regions of the country to have their hair styled at the famous House of Beauty. Singer Rosetta Tharpe is widely heralded for singing gospel songs. She is credited with taking this precious music to Europe.

Roseanne A popular combination involving Rose (see above).

Roselle A variation of Rose (see above). Also Rozella.

Rosemary *Latin:* Dew of the sea. Also Rosemarie, Rosemari, Rosemay. Rosemari Mealy is the author of *Fidel & Malcolm: Memories of a Meeting.*

Rowena *Welsh:* Slender. Also Roweena, Roweina, Rowina. Rowena is a character in *Ivanhoe.*

Roxann *Persian:* Brilliant one. Also Roxanne.

Rozell A variation of Rose (see above) found among African-American women.

Rozetta A variation of Rose (see above) found among African-American women.

Ruby *French:* A precious gem. Also Rubie, Rubye. Actress Ruby Dee, wife of Ossie Davis, is an accomplished actress. Rubye Nely is a spokeswoman for Jackson State College.

Rubena Noted among Puckett's unusual names of schoolgirls.

Rudene Beautiful and talented Rudene T. Mercer of Jacksonville, Fla., is a Sunday school teacher and math tutor. She was designated a top high school senior by *Ebony* magazine.

Rufina *Latin:* Red-haired; a feminine form of Rufus.

Ruth *Biblical/Hebrew:* Beautiful, compassionate. Also Ruthie, Ruthy, Ruthalee, Ruthelle, Ruthene, Ruthia, Ruthia Mae, Ruthlyn. Many consider the story of Ruth in the Old Testament one of the most beautiful stories of faithfulness and obedience in the Bible. To her Hebrew mother-in-law, the widowed Moabite woman said, ". . . entreat me not to leave thee or to return from following after thee for where you go, so shall I go." Ruth 1:16. Appearing among black women in the 1700s, the name Ruth has been enormously popular until the recent craze for name elaboration. Business executive Ruth Bowen was the first black woman to establish a talent and booking agency in New York. Her work for black artists, including Dinah Washington, Sammy Davis Jr., Aretha Franklin, and Ray Charles, allowed her firm, the Queen Booking Corp., to top the million-dollar mark annually. Educator Ruth B. Love was the first black person named superintendent of the Chicago school system.

Sabaloo A Puckett pearl.

Sabina *Latin:* From the Sabine. When Rome was being settled, the ancient Sabine tribe lived in what is now central Italy. The Sabine women were kidnapped by Romulus to provide wives for the the men of Rome, a historical event often referred to in literature as the rape of the Sabines.

Sabra The origins of Sabra are disputed. Most sources report it as Hebrew, meaning to rest. However, in the 13th *Golden Legend,* Sabra is the daughter of Ptolemy, king of Egypt. In modern Israel, Sabra refers to a native-born Israeli. Black parents have occasionally used the name. It appears in Puckett's index of unusual names and among contemporary schoolgirls.

Sabrina *Latin:* From the boundary line.

Sadia Sadia Nell Graham is fashion and beauty coordinator for *Essence.*

Sadie *Hebrew:* Princess; a diminutive for Sarah (see below) sometimes used as an independent name. Sadie Mae Owens lives in Muskogee, Okla. Sadie Tanner Mossell Alexander of the prestigious Tanner and Alexander families was the first black woman to be awarded a law degree from the University of Pennsylvania.

Sage *Latin:* Wise.

Salenia A variation of Selina (see below). Salina,

Selena, Selene, and Saline also appear in *Black Names in America,* 1800s.

Salinda An unusual combination documented among black women in 1936.

Sally *Hebrew:* Princess; a diminutive for Sarah now well-established as an independent name. Also Sall. It is first documented among black women in 1619–1799. Sally McCoy is a collector of rare African-American artifacts.

Salome *Biblical/Hebrew:* Peace. Salome, the daughter of Herodias, performed the dance that seduced King Herod to behead John the Baptist. Salome took John's head to her mother.

Salona This variation of Salome (see above) appears in Puckett's index.

Samalla An unusual name of obscure origins. Also Sannella. Samalla appears in Puckett's collection.

Samantha *Biblical/Hebrew:* Asked of God.

Sametta Noted in the 19th century and among contemporary women.

Samuella An unusual feminine version of Samuel. Also Samella. Samuella appears among schoolgirls in 1877–1937. It is also noted among contemporary black women. Samella Sanders Lewis has amassed an impressive record. Her centerpiece, *Art: African American,* is a standard textbook in colleges and universities.

Sandra *Greek:* Helper of humankind. Originally a pet name for Alexandra, the high-fashion Sandra has enjoyed extraordinary popularity in black families.

Sandy *Greek:* Helper of humankind. Also Sandi. There is a rapidly growing trend toward using this pet name for Sandra as an independent name.

Saphronia An African-American adaptation of Sophronia (see below). Also Safronie. Saphronia appears in the 1920 census records among adult women and is documented by Puckett on his 1877–1937 schoolgirls' list. Saphronia enjoyed a brief stint of popularity, but was quickly lost in the early migrations to big eastern and northern cities.

Sapphire *Hebrew:* A beautiful and treasured jewel. Despite its compelling meaning, it is surprising to find the name in use, given the stigma attached to it. Sapphire of the "Amos and Andy" radio and TV show epitomized the stereotypical, loudmouth, hostile, negative black woman. For a period the name was employed as a term of abuse. Parents who use it today may not be aware of Sapphire's unsavory past and associate it with the precious jewel.

Sara This version of Sarah (see below) is first listed among college students, 1930s.

Sarah *Biblical/Hebrew:* Princess. Sarah was the wife of Abraham and the mother of Isaac in the Old Testament. Sarai, her name before it became Sarah, meant quarrelsome. Sarah is noted in *Black Names in America* as one of the 19 most often used southern free black female names. Sarah Vaughan was called "the divine" because of her melodic voice. She was one of the top jazz singers. Sarah Breedlove became Madame C. J. Walker, inventor of hair preparations for African-Americans. She is the first black woman millionaire in the nation.

Sarata Noted among schoolgirls, 1877–1837.

Sarella A compound of Sara (see above) and Ella (see above), noted in the late 19th century.

Sarena Noted in Puckett's index.

Saretta A sassy name documented by Puckett.

Saundra An elaboration of the spelling of Sandra (see above).

Savannah *Spanish:* Treeless. Savannah Churchill was a rhythm and blues singer.

Savilla Appears in 1877–1937 among schoolgirls.

Savory This rare use of the name of a sweet herb is found in *Black Names in America,* 1800s.

Scarlett *English:* Scarlet, a bright red cloth; originally a surname referring to someone who dealt in scarlet. Also Scarlet, Scarlette. The tragic character Scarlett O'Hara of Margaret Mitchell's *Gone With the Wind* and the name's association with the biblical scarlet woman, the mother of harlots (Revelations 17:3) may have curtailed its use.

Scylla Found in *Black Names in America,* 19th century.

Sealy Sealy appears in Puckett's collection of the 1800s. If it was ever more than a one-time choice, its current association with the mattress company lays it to rest.

Sebana The origins of this unusual name among school-girls, 1877–1937, appear to lie in African-American creativity.

Sebra Found in Washington, D.C., 1863–64.

Sedalia Sedalia resonates with the sounds of African-American creativity. It appears in Puckett's index. Sedalia Davis lives in San Diego.

Sedna *Eskimo:* The goddess of food. In Eskimo mythology, Sedna lives in the sea. When angered, she will blow up a storm.

Sedonia *Latin:* Woman from Sedon; the name of an ancient seaport in Phoenicia. In Hebrew, Sidon implies to ensnare.

Segusta This unusual name, documented among adult women, 1877–1937, is probably an African-American invention. Like some of the more unusual creations, Segusta may have occurred only once.

Sela *Hebrew:* A rock.

Selima A variation of Selina (see below). Also Selema.

Selina *Greek:* The goddess of the moon. Also Selena, Selene, Selinda, Seline, Selie. Selina appears among black women in the late 19th century.

Selma *German:* Divine helmet. Sculptor Selma Burke is best recalled as the designer of the FDR engraving on the dime.

Sema This name is documented among schoolgirls, 1877–1937.

Senalda *Spanish:* A signal.

Senethia Noted in the early 20th century.

Sennetta Noted in 1877–1937.

Sennie Appears among schoolgirls, 1877–1937.

Senora Senora Early is a magazine subscription fulfillment manager.

Seraphina *Hebrew:* Ardent. Also Sarafina. The seraphim are the highest-ranking angels, distinguished for their adoration of the Almighty.

Serena *Latin:* Tranquil, serene one.

Serilda *German:* Armored warrior maid.

Shaba Shaba Ranks is a performer.

Shahara Shahara Ahmad-Llewellyn lives in East Hampton, N.Y.

Shaina *Hebrew:* Beautiful.

Shakari Shakari Bonds is the daughter of baseball superstar Barry Bonds.

Shana Collected by Puckett, this lovely name is early evidence of an attraction to the Sha prefix.

Shanice Popular R&B singer Shanice is often featured in *Black Beat.*

Sha Niesha Sha Niesha Ty-Kiera Donaii Brown's mother says her infant daughter's first name means princess of the world in Arabic.

Shannon *Irish:* Ancient.

Shari A version of Sharleen (see below) or Sherry (see below). Shari Belafonte is a model and actress.

Sharima Sharima Wilder is on the girls' basketball team of Clinton High School in New York.

Sharleen *French:* Petite and womanly; a variation of Charlene (see above), which is itself a variation of Charlotte (see above). Also Sharlene.

Sharon *Hebrew:* Princess. Sharon Brown is a broadcast journalist.

Sharwyn Sharwyn Dyson is a teacher at the College of New Rochelle.

Sharyn Sharyn Hemphill is a junior high school teacher in Brooklyn.

Sheba *Hebrew:* From Sheba. The queen of Sheba, whose given name was Makeda, is famous for her alliance with and later marriage to King Solomon.

Sheena *Hebrew:* The Lord is gracious; a form of Jane (see above).

Shefroi Noted in Puckett's index of unusual names.

Sheila An Irish variation of the Latin Cecilia, which means blind. Also Sheelah, Sheilah, Seila, Shayla, Shela, Shelagh. Sheila has enjoyed enormous popularity among black parents. Sheila Stainback is a TV news commentator.

Shelldonia This unusual combination appears among schoolgirls, 1876–1937.

Shelleene Shelleene Ravette Johnson graduated in 1993.

Shemeka This spelling is by far the most popular version. Senior Shemeka Banger is class president at Central High School in Memphis.

Shenikwa Shenikwa Nowlin Cox has demostrated an indomitable spirit. Her promising career as a ballerina with the Dance Theater of Harlem was cut short by a crippling car accident. Wheelchair bound, she is married and a lawyer for Greyhound Lines.

Shelley *English:* Dweller in the meadow on the ledge.

Sherry An American variant of Sharon (see above), Sarah (see above), Shirley (see below), or Cherie. Also Sherri, Sherrilyn, Sherrie, Sheree. Sherry Bronfman is a mother and patron of the arts.

Sheryl *German:* Man; a variation of Cheryl (see above), which is a variation of Charlotte (see above). Also Sherill, Sherryl, Sheryll. A solid contributor when it comes to blacks in publishing, Sheryl Hilliard Tucker is vice-president of editorial operations and executive editor of *Black Enterprise.*

Shirley *English:* From the bright meadow. Shirley has been enormously popular among black parents as it epitomizes fashion and pretty sound. Shirley Anita Chisholm personifies the unstinting advocate for the civil and human rights of black people. She is a consummate politician of high principle and integrity, whose life is highlighted by achievement. Pundits consider overcoming the obstacles of race and class to be elected to the House of Representatives in 1968 as her crowning achievement. African-American women all around the country were inspired to stand up and achieve in the face of adversity.

Shula From Puckett's index of unusual names.

Sibyl *Greek:* Prophetic. Also Sybil.

Sigrid *Scandinavian:* Beautiful counselor.

Silva *Latin:* A maid for the woodlands.

Simia An unusual name appearing among black women in 1877–1937.

Simone *Hebrew:* One who listens carefully; the French feminine form of Simon. Also Simona, Simonetta, Simonette, Simonia, Simonne.

Sina A rare name found in the 1800s that one source says originates in the Irish Sine. Also Sineta.

Sirelia Found in Puckett's index of unusual names.

Sirena *Greek:* She who ensnares. In ancient Greek and Roman myth, sirens were sea creatures who were half-bird and half-woman. Their melodious song so enchanted sailors that the sailors starved to death.

Sisly In the late 19th and early 20th centuries, Sis and Sister were popular nicknames for elder daughters in black families. Sisly is noted in the 1800s as an independent name.

Sissieretta A most unusual combination of Sissie and

Retta. Sissieretta Jones (1869–1933) was a famous opera singer. Of great talent, she was born Matilda Sissieretta Joyner in Portsmouth, Va.

Sissy A diminutive for the Latin Cecilia (see above), which means blind.

Sojourner The powerful legacy and legend of Sojourner Truth are beloved. A devout Christian, she changed her name from Isabella and began abolitionist and feminist activities that secured her place in history. Her legacy is triumph despite the odds.

Solonia A gem of a name collected in *Black Names in America.*

Sonnie A once popular pet name for boys, sometimes used as an independent name for girls.

Sonya *Russian:* Wisdom; a variation of the Greek Sophia (see below). Also Sonia, Sonja.

Sophenia An unusual variation of Sophia (see below) appearing in Puckett's index.

Sophia *Greek:* Wisdom. Also Sophie.

Sophialea A variation of Sophia (see above) found in Puckett's index.

Sophronia *Greek:* Prudent, practical, cautious. Also Sofronia. In steady use at the turn of the century.

Sree Appears among black women, 1877–1937.

Stacey *Greek:* Resurrection; a surname derived from Eustance and a pet name for Anastasia. Also Staci, Stacia, Stacie, Stasee, Stasey, Stasia. Formerly a boy's name, it now is more often used for girls.

Star *English:* A brilliant heavenly body. Also Starette, Staretta, Starla, Starleena, Starlena, Starlene, Starletta, Starlette, Starlyn, Starlynn.

Stella *Latin:* Star.

Stephanie *Greek:* Crowned one; a feminine form of Stephen. Also Stefani. Stephanie Stokes Oliver is editor of *Essence.*

Steveanna Variation of Steve. Also Stevetta. Steveanna appears among names of schoolgirls in 1877–1937. Stevetta Nelson is a union representative in Detroit.

Sudella A probable creation in Puckett's index.

Sudie Appearing in Puckett's index and noted among contemporary women.

Sue A diminutive for Susan (see below) frequently used as an independent name since the 17th century. Sue Thurman's faith in God and loyal support of her husband, Howard Thurman, informed her unfailing efforts of spiritual uplift.

Suella A combination of Sue (see above) and Ella (see above) noted in Puckett's index.

Sula Collected by Puckett, Sula has roots in Africa. It is also the title of a Toni Morrison novel.

Sunny A diminutive for Sunshine (see below), this cheerful name is sometimes used independently.

Sunray A name referring to the brightness of the sun and perhaps displaying the character of the parents' affection for their little girl, it is found in Puckett's index of unusual names.

Sunshine Found in Puckett's index, Sunshine is infrequently employed as a given name.

Surderia Noted in 1877–1937.

Surice Noted in Puckett's index, Surice appears among contemporary schoolgirls as Sureese and Sureace.

Surilla Found in Puckett's index of unusual names.

Susan *Hebrew:* Graceful lily. Also Shoshana, Shoshanna, Shoshanna, Susanna, Susannah, Susie, Suzanne, Suzzette. In use consistently since the 17th century. Physician Susan McKinney Steward was a women's rights activist and hospital founder. The grace-filled Susan Taylor, editor-in-chief of *Essence,* personifies her name's meaning. Nurse, activist, and author Susie King Taylor is one of our unsung heroes whose remarkable life bears more scrutiny. Long-time Motown executive and movie producer Suzanne de Passe worked closely with Berry Gordy and played a key role in packaging the Jackson Five. Suzette Charles was a Miss America.

Suvena Suvena certainly has sounds that have been favored by many African-Americans. It appears in Puckett's index.

Suzene A variation of Susan (see above) noted in 1877–1937.

Suzon Suzon Christine Kirksey graduated in 1993.

Sybil *Greek:* Prophetic. Derived from Sibyl (see above), this is now the more common spelling. Sybil Smith Stephens, the first black woman swimmer to earn NCAA Division I All-American status, was inducted into the hall of fame of the Athletic Department at Boston University.

Sylvania Derived from Sylvia (see below).

Sylvannah A variation of Sybil (see above) appearing among black women in the 1800s.

Sylvia *Latin:* Wood; a derivative of Silva, which means wood. Also Silvey, Silvia. Rhea Silvia is the mythical goddess of nature said to be the mother of Romulus and Remus. Silvia was the original spelling, but Sylvia has predominated throughout the 20th century. Sylvia A. Boone was the first black woman given tenure at Yale. Sylvia Wood owns and operates Harlem's famed Sylvia's, a soul food restaurant that has become a favored stop for tourists from around the world.

Symora A lyrical gem collected in *Black Names in America.*

Synesta An unusual name rooted in the African-American lexicon.

Synestine With the sounds of black coinage, Synestine appears in 1877–1937 among schoolgirls.

Synestube Found in Puckett's index of unusual names.

Syphronia A variation of Saphronia (see above)

Syretha Found in 1877–1937 among schoolgirls.

Tabatha *Aramaic:* A child of grace, a child of the Lord; a version of Tabitha (see below). Tabatha is noted among black women in the 1800s.

Tabby A nickname for Tabitha (see below) infrequently used as an independent name. Also Tabbee, Tabbey, Tabbi, Tabbie.

Tabina *Arabic:* Muhammad's follower. This Arabic name that greatly resembles Tabitha is noted among New York City schoolgirls.

Tabitha *Aramaic:* A child of grace. Noted among contemporary women.

Tacita *Latin:* Silent.

Taff A variation of Taffy (see below) appearing among Puckett's schoolgirls' names.

Taffy *Welsh:* Beloved.

Taj As a member of the hot ghetto soul group Sisters With Voices, Tamara Johnson is known as Taj.

Tajama Athlete Tajama Abraham is an outstanding basketball player at Kecoughtan High School, Hampton, Va.

Talitha *Aramaic:* Damsel, a maiden of gentle or noble birth.

Tallulah *Native American:* Among the Choctaw people of Georgia, Tallulah was a place name used to identify the beautiful Tallulah Falls in Georgia. Also Talley,

Tallie, Tally. Tallulah Bankhead, a famous American actress, is closely associated with the name. It appears among Brooklyn high school girls.

Tamara *Hebrew:* Palm tree. Also Tamra, Tamarah, Tamarra, Tamary, Tamera, Tamma, Tammara. In special favor, noted among New York City high school girls.

Tammy A popular nickname, now a frequent independent name. Also Tammi, Tammee, Tammey, Tammie. Tamm E Hunt is a supper club singer in the New York area.

Tamyene A form of Tammy (see above) noted among free black women of the 1800s.

Tandra Tandra Dawson is a criminal attorney in New York.

Taniesha Athlete Taniesha Grizzle won the New York State championship for 800 meters in the competition among high school girls.

Tanya *Russian:* An abbreviated form of the Russian Tatiana (see below), said to come from Tatius, the name of a king of the Sabines, but the meaning of Tanya is not known. Also Tana, Tahnya, Taneea, Tania. It is quite popular among contemporary parents. Arizona State University's high jumper Tanya Hughes finished in first place at the 1992 NCAA games in Austin, Texas.

Tara *Irish:* Tower. The ancient Irish kings lived in Tara's Halls, where the bards sang of their heroic deeds. Enjoying a current spate of popularity, Tara is noted among school students.

Tareazer Documented in the 1800s.

Tarvia Tarvia Lucas is the daughter of NBA coach John Lucas.

Tasha *Russian:* Christmas; a pet name for Natasha (see above). Also Tasia, Tasya.

Tate A surname infrequently used as a given name.

Tatiana The meaning of this Russian variation of the

Italian Tizianna is not known. It is occasionally used in America by both black and white parents.

Tatum   *English:* She who brings cheer to others.

Tawana   Also Twana, Twanna. The unhappy Tawana Brawley episode may have cut into the popularity of this name. Brawley is a student at Howard University. Twana Mazyck is a community college student. Twanna Terry is a high school track and field champion.

Taylor   *English:* An occupational name for a tailor. Formerly exclusively a boy's name, the use of Taylor as a girl's name is growing.

Teacake   This affectionate nickname appears in Puckett's schoolgirls' list as a given name.

Tecora   An unusual name appearing among schoolgirls, 1877–1937.

Tedessa   Tedessa Naves is a certified nursing assistant.

Telissa   Lyrical Telissa is documented in 1877–1937.

Telma   Telma Hopkins is an actress.

Temperance   *English:* One who uses self-control and restraint. This virtue name appears in Puckett's collection and among contemporary women.

Templa   *Latin:* A sanctuary.

Tene   Tene Williams is an emerging vocalist.

Tennessee   Use of this state name as a given name was noted in 1899 among black women.

Teresa   *Greek:* Harvester; a popular spelling variation of Theresa (see below). The name is well-used by black parents.

Teretha   Teretha represents a different sound elaboration of Teresa (see above). It appears today among high school students.

Tess   First a pet name for Teresa (see above), Tess is noted among contemporary high school students as an independent name.

Tessa   This diminutive for Teresa (see above) is noted

among contemporary high school students as an independent name.

Tessie The sassy Tessie, found among schoolgirls in 1877–1937, represents an early use of a short form of Teresa (see above) as an independent name.

Texanna A most unusual name elaboration found among schoolgirls, 1877–1937.

Thais The origins of this name are not clear. It may have roots in Spanish. Also Tyees, Tyes. Thais Davis was the 1993 recipient of the Korean Merchants Association of Greater New York Scholarship, awarded to promote racial harmony.

Thalia *Greek:* In bloom. In Greek mythology, Thalia is the muse of comedy.

Thea An element used rarely as a given name.

Theady An expansion of Thea (see above) noted in Puckett's 1877–1937 unusual names of schoolgirls. The variation Theda is found among North Carolina high school students.

Theatrice An elaboration of Thea (see above).

Thelma Coined in 1877 by Marie Corelli for her novel *Thelma,* it comes from the Greek Thelema, which refers to will. Thelma McQueen is best known as actress Butterfly McQueen. Educator Thelma Etoria Avant Dinwiddie, an award-winning teacher at Detroit's showcase Renaissance High, is known on the Detroit supper club circuit as singer Kris Lynn.

Theodora *Greek:* Given by God. Also Theodosia. Noted by Puckett among schoolgirls, Theodora is found among contemporary high school students.

Theodosia Theodosia J. Tucker is the daughter of Reverend E. Theophilus Caviness, pastor of the Greater Abyssinian Baptist Church of Cleveland.

Theola *Greek:* Heavenly scent.

Theophilla *Greek:* God-loving.

Theresa *Greek:* One who brings in the harvest. Due to

the popularity of St. Teresa of Avila, and St. Thérèse of Lisieux, Theresa has been widely used by Catholic families. Its popularity has spread to include black and white families, especially spelled Teresa.

Thessia Noted in 1877–1937 among schoolgirls.

Thomasena *Biblical/Hebrew:* Twin; a popular feminine form of Thomas. Noted by Puckett and among contemporary high school students.

Thomasine A feminine form of Thomas not frequently used.

Thulani Thulani Davis is a writer.

Tia *Spanish:* Aunt. Also Tiana, Tiara.

Tiffany *Greek:* God appears. Also Tiffaney, Tiffani. Tiffany was originally associated with the Epiphany, which occurs on January 6 as Christians rejoice in the manifestation of Christ to the Gentiles.

Tina Pet form of names such as Christina and Ernestina. Also Tena. They appear as given names in 1877–1937. The beautiful Tina Turner is one of the world's most fabulous entertainers.

Tinah This spelling variation of Tina is found in 1619–1799 among free black names.

Tiny This affectionate reference to size is infrequently employed as a given name.

Tiombe A student at Arsenal Technical High School in Indianapolis, Tiombe Burton is called a top high school senior by *Ebony.*

Tisha Probably a variation of Letitia (see above) or Tricia (see below). Also Tish, Tisher. Tisha is noted in 1899. Tisha Anne Johnson of Dallas is fondly called Tish by those close to her.

Toby *Hebrew:* The Lord is good. Also Tobi. More often used by black parents as a boy's name.

Toma An unusual name documented in 1899.

Tommie A boy's nickname for Thomas sometimes used for girls.

Tonja A variation of Tonya (see below). Tonja Buford of Illinois University won the 100-meter hurdles at the 1993 Alabama University relays.

Tony A diminutive for Antoinette (see above) and Antonia whose frequency as a given name has recently increased. Also Toni. Nobel and Pulitzer Prize–winner Toni Morrison is preeminent among African-American women novelists and one of the most significant novelists of the twentieth century. Her centerpiece work is the best-seller *Song of Solomon.* Photographer Toni Parks is the daughter of the famed Gordon Parks.

Tonya A popular alternative spelling of Tanya (see above). Jamaican-born actress Tonya Lee Williams is the intelligent and beautiful Olivia Barber Hastings on "The Young and the Restless," a top rated soap opera. Writer Tonya Bolden is the editor of *Rites of Passage: Stories About Growing Up by Black Writers From Around the World.*

Tracy Originally a diminutive for Theresa (see above), Tracy is well-established as an independent name. Also Tracey, Traci. Tracey Reese is a hot fashion designer.

Treasie This name appears among free black women, 1619–1799, but its origins are not known. It may be a form of Tracy. Also Treacy, Trecy.

Trese A rare name found in Puckett's collection.

Tricia *Latin:* Aristocratic; a pet form of the popular Patricia (see above).

Trina *Greek:* Pure; a popular short form for Katrina.

Trudie A diminutive for Gertrude (see above) as a given name. Also Trudi, Trudy. Never in widespread use.

Trudier This name appears to be strictly an African-American variation of Trudie (see above). Trudier Harris is a famous folklorist.

Truzella An unusual elaboration of Trudie (see above) documented in 1877–1937. This name is perfect evidence of our consistent desire to distinguish the names of our children.

Tulie This unusual name documented in 1899 sounds remarkably like Thule (or Thuli) Dumakude, a South African singer in New York.

Tyra Tyra Banks is a supermodel. Tyra Natasha Turner graduated in 1993. Tyra Farrell is an actress with star potential.

Udele *English:* Wealthy. Also Udella, Edelle, Yudella, Yudelle.

Ulrica *German:* Power of the wolf; a feminine form of Ulric.

Ulebelle A combined name noted in Pine Bluff, Ark. in 1936.

Uloise An unusual variation of Eloise (see above).

Ulyssandra A college student with this name explains that it is a combination of her parents' names, Ulyssis and Sandra (see above).

Ulyssese This feminine form of Ulysses is noted among South Carolina schoolgirls.

Ulystine Found in Puckett's index of unusual names.

Una *Latin:* One. Una Mulzac is the founder and owner of Liberation Book Store in Harlem. Her collection of black-themed books serves the needs of antiquarians.

Undine *Latin:* Of the sea. Undine Smith was a gifted composer, arranger, and teacher who taught music for 45 years at Virginia State College. Among her students are included such notable artists as Billy Taylor and Leon Thompson.

Unis An apparent invention appearing among free black names in the 1800s. Also Uniska. It appears today as Unice.

Unita In 1976, Unita Blackwell was elected mayor of Mayersville, the first black mayor in Mississippi.

Ura An element of Urania (see below). Also Urada, Uralee. Ura appears as an independent name in Puckett's index.

Urania *Greek:* Heavenly. Noted among free black names, 1800–60.

Ursal Also Ursaline. Noted among Puckett's unusual names.

Urshaa Found in Puckett's index of unusual names.

Ursula *Latin:* Young female bear. Ursula appears among free black names in the 1800s and among schoolchildren today.

Utah The use of the name of this western state as a girl's name is noted in Puckett's index.

Uterina Found in Puckett's collection.

Utrice Utrice Leid was a leading member of the founding team for the New York–based *City Sun,* a weekly newspaper. She served as editor-in-chief of the paper for its first eight years.

Uzee Tecomia An unusual two-name combination noted in the Puckett collection.

Val *Scandinavian:* Famous battle heroine; said to be rooted in Valda, a feminine form of Valdemar, the hero of the battle, Val is also a diminutive for Valerie (see below). A number of names found on Puckett's list attest to the popularity of this name element.

Valaida Valaida Snow (1900–56) was a musician, singer, and dancer of some note.

Valedia The rhythmic sound of Valedia brands it as a recent African-American invention. Noted in 1877–1937.

Valeira This lyrical name is noted in Puckett's index.

Valencia *Latin/Spanish:* Vigorous. Also Valentia. Valencia Elana Harris is a preschooler.

Valenda Valenda is another indication of a fancy for the element Val.

Valentina *Latin:* To be strong; a feminine form of Valentine. It appears among Brooklyn high school students.

Valentine *Latin:* Healthy. Appears among black women in the 1800s.

Valera This form of Valeria is listed in Puckett's index.

Valeria *Latin:* One who is vigorous. The use of Valeria is rare at best. However, Valeria is noted among contemporary women.

Valerie *French:* Strong; a form of Valeria (see above). Also Valaree, Valarey, Valaree, Valerye. Valerie has enjoyed popularity among black parents. Valerie Wilson

Wesley is executive editor of *Essence*. Valerie Simpson is the female half of the composing and marital team of Ashford and Simpson.

Valinda A blend of Val (see above) and Linda (see above). Also Verlinda. Valinda is found on Puckett's list.

Valisha Appearing in Puckett's index, Valisha represents an early indication of the current infatuation with the phoneme *sha*.

Valonia *Latin:* From the valley.

Valora *Latin:* Valorous.

Valzora A rarefied use of sounds noted in the late 1800s.

Vana This short form of Ivana (see above), the Russian feminine form of John, or of Vanessa (see below) has gained high visibility as a given name through the celebrity of Vanna White.

Vanessa By contrast to names rooted in antiquity and the medieval period, Vanessa is a recent literary invention coined by Jonathan Swift to name a character in *Gulliver's Travels.*

Vanetta While it does not appear in most name books, one source says it is a recent invention arising out of Vanessa (see above). The very similar Venetta, however, is noted by Puckett in *Black Names in America.*

Vanity The use of this word as a name is noted among contemporary elementary school girls.

Vanora *Irish:* White wave.

Vashti *Biblical/Persian:* Thread of life, beautiful. This name appears in the Old Testament Book of Esther.

Veatrice An unusual variation of Beatrice (see above) in Puckett's index.

Vedette *French:* Movie star. Also Vedetta.

Velma The origins of this name are disputed. It apparently came into use in the late 19th century.

Velvet This word, which describes the smooth, soft, silky texture of a type of cloth, is now used as a girl's name.

Vendetta *Italian:* A guardian. Also Vendette.

Venella Collected by Puckett.

Venera Found in Puckett's index.

Veneta This name probably arose from Venetia, which in Latin refers to a woman from Venice. Also Venita, Vinita, Venetia. Venetia Nelson lives in Oakland, Calif.

Venetta Documented in 1877–1937.

Venie Appears in the 1800s.

Venus *Latin:* Love and beauty. Noted among free black women of the 1700s, the name for this mythical goddess of love and beauty is rarely used by contemporary parents. No wonder Venus is not widely used, given its personification of feminine perfection and the growing tendency to distort its implications of love to mean sexual prowess.

Vera *Slavic:* Faith. Well-used by black parents, Vera is noted among contemporary New York City high school students.

Verda An unusual name perhaps arising out of the French Verdi, which means springlike.

Verdell Also Verdelle. Verdell appears in Puckett's index.

Verena *Latin:* Truth.

Verlalia Noted by Puckett.

Verlee A rhythmic use of Ver as a prefix. Also Verlenia.

Verlee Lee A popular type of rhythm often seen among black names, especially in the first half of the 20th century. Appears among schoolgirls in 1877–1937.

Verlie A location in France. Also Virlie. Verlie appears in Puckett's index, but perhaps the meaning is coincidental.

Verlina Black Panther Party member Verlina Brewer was a survivor of the shootout in Chicago in which Fred Hampton and Mark Clark were brutally murdered by law enforcement officials.

Verline Noted in *Free Black Names in America.*

Vermell   One of the many names beginning with Ver that are found in Puckett's index.

Vermona   Vermona Fisher says her name is a derivative of her grandmother's Vernonia.

Verna   *Latin:* Spring. Also Vernia. Vernia Mae Margaree is a college student.

Verneka   *Black Names in America* notes this blend of American and African sounds.

Vernel   Collected by Puckett.

Vernell   An example of a penchant for Ver. Also Vernella, Vernelle. Appears among New York City schoolgirls as Vernal.

Vernessa   Noted by Puckett, it appears among contemporary schoolgirls.

Vernetta   Also Verneta. Documented in the late 19th century, Vernetta appears among contemporary women. Verneta Gaskins, class of 1993 at Benjamin Banneker High School in Washington, D.C., is a member of the National Honor Society.

Vernice   Noted by Puckett and in contemporary use.

Vernola   Noted by Puckett. Vernola Foreman lives in Kansas City.

Verona   Noted in 1877–1937.

Veronica   *Latin:* True image. According to legend, a young woman named Veronica wiped the face of Christ on His way to the crucifixion. The cloth, preserved in Rome, is said to be imprinted with the true image of the Lord. This high-fashion name is first noted among free blacks in Washington, D.C., in 1863–64. The 20th-century popularity of the Archie comics and the character Veronica may have done much to inhibit widespread use. But it is occasionally used by black parents.

Verta   The origins of this unusual name are probably rooted in the Smart family of Fairfax, S.C. Verta Mae Smart Grosvenor is a writer and culinary anthropologist.

Vertille   Documented in Puckett's index of unusual names.

Vesta *Latin:* Goddess of the house. Vesta was the myth-ical Roman goddess of the household. In Roman my-thology, the six vestal virgins who tended her altar were buried alive if they lost their virginity. Vesta Mae Finch lives in Muskogee, Okla.

Viana Documented in 1899.

Vicky A popular nickname for Victoria (see below) now in widespread use as a given name. Also Vicki, Vickee, Vikki. Vicki Ward lives in Staten Island, N.Y.

Victoria *Latin:* Victorious. Victoria Binion is a civic ad-ministrator.

Vicy An unusual name noted in the late 19th and early 20th centuries.

Videlle Noted among schoolgirls, 1877–1937.

Vidonia *Latin:* A vine.

Villete *French:* Dweller at the country estate.

Vina Noted in the 1800s.

Vincenta *Latin:* One who conquers; a feminine form of Vincent.

Vinnette A French nickname for Winifred.

Vinney An apparent diminutive for Vinnette (see above). Also Vinne, Viney, Vinie, Vinnie. Vinney appears among free black women in the 1700s. Its use in contemporary America appears to be confined to black families. Vinie Burrows is an outstanding actress, director, and radio producer.

Viola *Latin:* Violet.

Violet *Latin:* Purple.

Violetta Also Violette. Found in Washington, D.C., 1863–64. Violette Benjamin is a college student.

Virgie A nickname for Virginia (see below) that has been used regularly but infrequently as an independent name. Also Vergie, Virgie Mae, Virgie Lee.

Virginia *Latin:* Virgin. Virginia Dare, born in 1587, was the first white child born in what is now the U.S. First documented in 1877, the name Virginia has enjoyed widespread use among black parents. Virginia Lacy Jones is a well-known librarian and educator. Virginia Randolph was an influential educator.

Virtula An unusual name found among schoolgirls, 1877–1937.

Vivian *Latin:* Lively; once a male name now exclusively used for girls. Also Viviana, Viviane, Vivianna, Vianne, Vivien, Vivienne, Vivyan, Vivyana, Vyvyan, Vyvyana.

Vonetta Vonetta McGee is a singer and actress.

Vynetta Also Vinette. Vynetta is found in Puckett's index. Vinette K. Pryce is a writer for the New York *Amsterdam News.*

Wacila Noted in the 18th century and found among contemporary women.

Wahlena Also Walenia, Wylena. Wahlena was found by Puckett.

Waltena A female version of Walter, noted in the 19th century.

Wanda *German:* The wanderer. Also Wanda Lee, Wanda Mae, Wonda, Wondy.

Wanza Documented in 1877–1937.

Wardena Collected among early 20th-century names.

Warenna A feminine version of Warren appearing in Puckett's index of unusual names.

Warrenette A feminine version of Warren that occurs among contemporary schoolgirls.

Wendy A diminutive for Wanda (see above).

Wenzola Appears among black women during the early 20th century.

Westina Appears in the index of unusual names.

Wheirda Mae A rarefied name appearing in Puckett's index.

Wheirmelda Collected by Puckett.

Whitney *English:* White island. Given the overwhelming popularity of singer Whitney Houston, this traditionally male name will likely be regularly used for girls.

Whoopi Born Caryn Johnson in New York in 1950, actress and comedian Whoopi Goldberg has captured the imagination of America.

Wilberetta A feminine version of Wilbur. Also Wilbetta.

Wilda *English:* Forest dweller. Also Welda.

Wildetta Found in Puckett's index of unusual names.

Wiletta A feminine variation of Will. Also Willetta. Willetta Powell lives in Taft, Okla.

Wilhemina *German:* Determined protector; a feminine form of William. Also Wilhemine, Wilhelmenia.

Willa *German:* The desired.

Willadean Found in Puckett's index of unusual names. Willa Dean is a popular two-name combination.

Willafred Noted in 1877–1937.

Willene Noted in the late 19th century.

Willianna Appears in Puckett's index.

Willie Principally a boy's name, Willie is sometimes used for girls. Also Willye. Willye White is the only American woman ever to appear in five straight Olympics.

Willie Mae An enormously popular two-name combination for much of the first half of the 20th century. Also Willa Mae. Willie Mae Ford is a pioneering evangelist.

Wilma A popular diminutive for Wilhemina (see above). World-class sprinter Wilma Randolph first appeared in the Olympics at age 16. Four years later, she was the star of the 1960 Olympics.

Willola A blend of Will and the ever-popular Ola (see above), found in 1877–1937.

Willow Mae Noted among contemporary adult women, this two-name combination has been used by black parents.

Wilzetta An interesting use of Wil found in the index of unusual names.

Winifred *German:* A friend of peace.

Winna Documented among free black names in the 1700s. Found among high school students in Brooklyn, 1993.

Winney A popular diminutive for Winifred (see above). Also Winnie. Winney is noted among free black names in the 1700s. Winnie Mandela is the indomitable freedom fighter of South Africa.

Winona *Native American/Sioux:* Firstborn daughter. Also Wynona.

Wonderful This word that connotes the marvelous is occasionally used as a girl's name.

Wubnesh Wubnesh Hylton is a Hunter College student.

Wylena Also Wylene. Wylena is found in Puckett's index of unusual names.

Wylona Found in Puckett's index of unusual names.

Wyolene Noted in Montgomery, Ala., 1877–1937.

Wyomia Wyomia Tyus was the first person to win back-to-back titles in the Olympic 100 meters, in 1964 and 1968. She is a motivational speaker from Los Angeles.

Xanthe *Greek:* Yellow-haired. Also Xanthia. Xanthia Place is a street name in Tulsa.

Xavia Noted in Puckett's index and appearing among contemporary schoolgirls in New York.

Xenia *Greek:* Hospitable. Also Xeenia, Xena, Zeena, Zena, Zenia, Zina, Zyna.

Xermona Born in Muskogee, Okla., Xermona Clayton was the first black woman to host a television show in the South—"The Xermona Clayton Show," televised in Atlanta.

Xylecia Xylecia Genesis Ison attends Spelman College.

Xyline *Greek:* Dweller in the woods. Also Xylia, Xylina, Xylona.

Yalina *Russian:* Light; a form of Helen (see above). Also Yelena.

Yanick Yanick Rice Lamb is president of the New York Association of Black Journalists.

Yasmin *Arabic:* Jasmine. Also Yasmine.

Yolanda *Greek:* Violet flower. Yolanda is quite in vogue these days.

Yonah Yonah A. Cox attends Howard University.

Yvette A diminutive for Yvonne (see below). Yvette Noel-Schure is a writer for *Black Beat*.

Yvonne *French:* Archer. Also Yevonne. Yvonne Watson Brathwaite Burke was elected to the U.S. Congress from the 17th Congressional District in Los Angeles in 1972.

Zandra A variation of Sandra (see above).

Zandra-Iolani Zandra-Iolani Maria Coles is an honor student at the School of New Resources, College of New Rochelle.

Zara *Hebrew:* Brightness, dawn. *Arabic:* Princess.

Zebra The use of this name of the beautifully striped animal appears among high school students in Brooklyn.

Zeda An unusual name appearing among free black names in the 1800s.

Zelda *German:* Gray maid of the battle; a diminutive for Griselda.

Zelena Found among schoolgirls in 1877–1937.

Zella Unusual name found among schoolgirls, 1877–1937.

Zellena Found among schoolgirls, 1877–1937.

Zelma *German:* Under divine protection. Zelma Watson George is a noted sociologist, educator, and musicologist.

Zenith The use of the word as a name.

Zenobia *Greek:* Given life by Zeus.

Zeola Unusual name among schoolgirls, 1877–1937.

Zerlinda *Hebrew:* Beautiful dawn.

Zerline Unusual name among schoolgirls, 1877–1937.

Zettie   Also Zettee, Zettie Lee. Zettie appears among schoolgirls, 1877–1937.

Zia   *Latin:* Grain.

Zilphy   Found in Puckett's index of unusual names.

Zina   *Greek:* Hospitable. Also Zena, Zeena, Zeenia, Zeenya, Zenia, Zina, Xenia. Tennis star Zina Garrison-Jackson is a world-class player.

Zoa   *Greek:* Life. Also Zoe.

Zodie   Zodie Johnson was a well-known educator in Detroit.

Zola   *Italian:* A clump of earth.

Zona   *Greek:* A girdle. Appears in 1937 in Augusta, Ga.

Zora   *Slavic:* Dawn. Appears among Brooklyn high school girls. Anthropologist, folklorist, and novelist Zora Neale Hurston was a major player during the Harlem Renaissance. She is the award-winning author of the classic *Their Eyes Were Watching God,* a must-read book about a woman's struggle for identity and fulfillment.

Zura   Also Zuri. Zura was noted in 1937.

Zylpha   An Old Testament name whose meaning is unknown. Also Zilpha. Zilpha Elaw was a notable 19th-century Christian leader. Zylpha Mapp-Robinson, humanitarian and former school psychologist, received her doctorate in 1993 at age 83.

African

Names for Girls

So how shall we name you, little one?
Are you your father's father, or his brother,
*   or yet another?*
Whose spirit is it that is in you, little warrior?

   —UGANDA, A MOTHER TO HER FIRST BORN

Aba *Akan/Fante:* Born on Thursday.

Abam *Akan:* Next child after twins. Although this name is good for a boy or a girl, its very specific meaning curtails its use.

Abayaa *Akan:* Born on Yawda (Thursday).

Abayomi *Yoruba:* She brings joy.

Abebi *Yoruba:* We asked for her and she came.

Abeje *Yoruba:* We asked to have her.

Abeke *Yoruba:* We wanted her to love her.

Abena *Ashanti:* Tuesday's child.

Abenaa *Akan:* Born on Benada (Tuesday).

Abeni *Yoruba:* Behold she is ours.

Abeo *Yoruba:* Her birth brings happiness.

Abidemi *Shekiri:* She was born in want of parents. The name implies a child who has lost her parents and will be raised by grandparents, or perhaps by a father.

Abimbola *Yoruba:* Born to be rich. Also Abimola.

Abiola *Yoruba:* Born in honor. More often used for boys. Abiola Sinclair is media and culture critic for the New York *Amsterdam News.*

Abir *Arabic:* Fragrant.

Ablah *Arabic:* Perfectly formed.

Abwooli *Uganda:* Cat.

Adanma *Yoruba:* A beautiful daughter.

Adanna *Yoruba:* Father's daughter.

Adanne *Yoruba:* Mother's daughter.

Adaoha *Yoruba:* Daughter of the people.

Adeola *Yoruba:* Born with a crown.

Adebomi *Yoruba:* The crown covers my nakedness.

Adeleke *Yoruba:* The crown brings happiness.

Aderinola *Yoruba:* Crowned she walked toward wealth.

Adiba *Arabic:* She is cultured, refined.

Adesina *Yoruba:* The coming of this girlchild opens the way for more children. This name is often given when the parents have waited a long time for a firstborn.

Adia *Swahili:* A gift from God has come.

Adiva *Arabic:* Gentle, agreeable.

Adoa *Akan:* Born on Dwowda (Monday).

Adoma *Akan:* Born on Minminda (Saturday).

Adun *Shekiri:* I struggle alone.

Adwoa *Akan:* Born on Monday.

Aduke *Yoruba:* Much loved.

Adunni *Yoruba:* Sweet to love.

Adwoa *Fante:* Born on Monday.

Afafa *Ewe:* First child of second husband.

Afiya *Swahili:* Healthy.

Afra *Arabic:* White.

Afryea *Ewe:* Born during good times.

Afua *Ewe:* Born on Friday.

Aida *Arabic:* Reward.

Ain *Arabic:* Precious.

Aina *Yoruba:* She came by a complicated delivery.

Aisha *Swahili:* Life. In the newly created names section are many spinoff names derived from the sounds in Aisha. In that sense it can be called a favorite. Aisha Sales is a writer and teacher in New York.

Aishah *Arabic:* Prosperous. The wife of the prophet Muhammad.

Akanika *Yoruba:* Born during the festival.

Akanke *Yoruba:* To know her is to pet her.

Akatwijuka *Uganda:* God remembered the parents. Although the name is difficult, the expression of gratitude is very special.

Akenke *Yoruba:* To want her is to love her.

Akiiki *Uganda:* Ambassador.

Akilah *Arabic:* Bright, logical, one who reasons well.

Akili *Ibo:* Born wise.

Akos *Akan:* Born on Kwesida (Sunday).

Akosua *Akan/Ewe:* Born on Sunday. During the 1970s, at the peak of the name change movement, Akosua was a frequent choice.

Akua *Ibo:* Sweet messenger. Akua Weekes is a freelance writer in New York City.

Alake *Yoruba:* She will be petted if she lives. A name for a sickly child.

Alero *Shekiri:* The earth is fertile. This Shekiri name is reserved for a first daughter.

Alike *Yoruba:* She is beautiful.

Alile *Yao:* She weeps.

Alima *Arabic:* Cultured.

Aliyah *Arabic:* Exalted.

Aluna *Mwera:* Come here.

Alzena *Arabic:* Woman.

Ama *Akan/Ewe:* Born on Saturday.

Amadi *Ibo:* Rejoicing.

Amadoma *Akan:* Born on Minminda (Saturday).

Amani *Arabic:* Aspirations.

Amina *Swahili:* Trustworthy, faithful. Amina Baraka is a poet and editor, and the wife of Amiri.

Aminah *Arabic:* Honest, faithful.

Aminata A version of Amina (see above). Aminata Moseka is the name given to singer Abbey Lincoln by President Sekou Toure of Guinea.

Amonke *Yoruba:* To know her is to pet her.

Araba *Akan:* Born on Benada (Tuesday).

Asabi *Yoruba:* One of high birth.

Asha *Swahili:* Life.

Ashanti This name of a West African ethnic group is often used by black parents as a girl's name.

Asesimba *Swahili:* Born noble.

Asma *Arabic:* Precious.

Atta *Akan:* Twin. Atta is one of many names in

Ghana and throughout the continent that can be used for a girl or boy.

Atwooki *Uganda:* She is beautiful.

Awali *Ibo:* Joy.

Awelewa *Yoruba:* Dainty, refined.

Ayanna *Swahili:* She is a beautiful flower. Ayanna Ajenke is a minister who resides in Brooklyn.

Ayo *Yoruba:* Joy. Ayo Hogan is a counselor and cultural activist.

Ayobami *Yoruba:* I am blessed with joy.

Ayobunni *Yoruba:* Joy has come.

Ayodele *Yoruba:* Joy comes at last. This name may be given by a family that has waited a long time for a child. Spelman College graduate Ayodele Nailah Roach is a member of the class of 1993.

Ayofemi *Yoruba:* Joy.

Ayoola *Ibo:* There is joy in wealth.

Aziza *Swahili:* Precious.

Azuka *Yoruba:* We all need support.

Baaba *Akan:* Born on Yawda (Thursday).

Baba *Fante:* Born on Thursday.

Babirye *Uganda:* Elder twin sister.

Baderinwa *Yoruba:* Worthy of respect.

Bahati *Swahili:* She brings luck.

Bakesiima *Uganda:* The parents have luck.

Bayo *Yoruba:* Joy is found.

Beduwa *Akan:* The tenth-born child. The chances

of this name being used for its meaning are slim. For beauty of sound, however, it might be attractive.

Beedzi *Akan:* This child eats well. Also Beedzidi.

Bejide *Yoruba:* Girl born during a rainstorm.

Bimkubwa *Swahili:* A great lady.

Birungi *Uganda:* Nice.

Boahimmaa *Ewe:* An ex-patriate. This name is usually given to an adult who has chosen to live in a different community.

Bolade *Yoruba:* Honor arrives.

Bolanile *Yoruba:* She is the wealth of this home.

Bunmi *Yoruba:* My gift.

Bupe *Nyakyusa:* Hospitality.

Buseje *Yao:* Ask me.

Chaonaine *Ngoni:* She has seen me.

Chausiku *Swahili:* Born at night.

Chemwapuwa *Shona:* That which you are given.

Chiku *Swahili:* Charterer.

Chimodu *Ibo:* God the protector. Chimodu is used for girls and boys.

Chimwala *Yao:* A stone.

Chinue *Ibo:* God's own blessing.

Chioma *Ibo:* The good God.

Chiosa *Ibo:* God of all.

Chipo *Shona:* A gift.

Chotsani *Yao:* Take away.

Cohila *Ovimbundu:* The young are quiet about the things that hurt them.

D

Dada *Yoruba:* She has curly hair.

Dalila *Swahili:* Gentle.

Dalili *Swahili:* Sign, omen.

Dayo *Yoruba:* Joy arrives.

Dikeledi *Tswana:* Tears.

Do *Ewe:* First child following twins.

Dofi *Ewe:* Second child following twins.

Doto *Zaramo:* Second born of twins.

Douye *Ibo:* We got what we sought.

Duku *Akan:* 11th born.

Dziko *Nguni:* The world.

E

Ebi *Ibo:* Good thought.

Ebun *Yoruba:* A gift.

Efia *Fante:* Born on Friday.

Efie (E fee) *Akan:* Born on Fida (Friday).

Efua *Akan:* Born on Fida (Friday). During the 1970s, a peak period of name changing among African-American women, Efua was popular not for its meaning but for its lovely sound.

Ekuwa *Akan:* Born on Wukuda (Wednesday).

Enomwoyi *Benin:* One who has grace and charm.

Enyonyam *Ewe:* It is good for me.

Eshe *Swahili:* Life.

Esi *Fante:* Born on Sunday. *Ewe:* Born on Kwesida (Sunday).

Etan *Shekiri:* God's love never ceases.

Etemi *Shekiri:* I was not put to shame (a modest way of saying I am proud).

Ezinwene *Ibo:* A good sister.

Fabayo *Yoruba:* A lucky birth is joy.

Fadilah *Arabic:* Virtue.

Fadwa *Arabic:* Self-sacrificing.

Faizah *Arabic:* Victorious.

Fari *Wolof:* The queen.

Faridah *Arabic:* Unique.

Farihah *Arabic:* Joyful.

Fashola *Yoruba:* God's blessing.

Fatima *Arabic:* Daughter of the prophet.

Fatinah *Arabic:* Captivating.

Fatuma *Swahili:* Daughter of the prophet.

Fayola *Yoruba:* Good fortune walks with honor.

Femi *Yoruba:* Love me.

Fola *Yoruba:* Honor.

Folade *Yoruba:* Honor arrives.

Folami *Yoruba:* Respect and honor me.

Folashade *Yoruba:* Honor gets a crown.

Folayan *Yoruba:* Walk in dignity.

Foluke *Yoruba:* Placed in God's care.

Fuju *Swahili:* Born after parents' separation.

Fukayna *Arabic:* Scholarly, studious.

Ghadah *Arabic:* Beautiful.

Ghayda *Arabic:* Young and delicate.

Ghika *Ibo:* God is the greatest.

Goumba *Wolof:* Blind. The type of blindness Goumba implies is that of one who does not see anything but the will of God. She is blind to the surroundings of the world.

Habibah *Arabic:* Beloved.

Hadiya *Swahili:* A gift from God. This name is frequently noted among contemporary women.

Hadiyah *Arabic:* Guide to righteousness.

Hadiyyah *Arabic:* Gift

Halima *Swahili:* Gentle.

Hana *Arabic:* Happiness.

Hanifah *Arabic:* True believer.

Haniyyah *Arabic:* Pleased, happy.

Haqikah *Arabic:* Truthful.

Hasanati *Swahili:* Good.

Hasina *Swahili:* Good.

Hasna *Arabic:* Beautiful.

Hawa *Swahili:* Longing.

Hayfa *Arabic:* Slender, beautiful body.

Ibadiran *Yoruba:* The one with the velvet behind who walks with grace.

Ifama *Ibo:* All is well.

Ife *Yoruba:* Love.

Ifeakawa *Ibo:* There is nothing better than a child.

Ifeanyichuckwu *Ibo:*

Nothing is impossible with God.

Ifeoma *Ibo:* A good thing.

Ifetayo *Yoruba:* Love brings happiness.

Ige *Yoruba:* Delivered feetfirst.

Ikuseghan *Benin:* Peace surpasses war.

Imani *Swahili:* Faith. This is a word closely related to Iman, the Arabic word for faith. Imani Douglass is an actress and director.

Isoke *Benin:* A good gift from God.

Iverem *Tiv:* Blessing and favor have arrived. Esther Iverem is a journalist for *New York Newsday.*

Izegbe *Benin:* Long-expected child.

Jaha *Swahili:* Dignity.

Jala *Arabic:* Lucid.

Jamila *Swahili:* Beautiful.

Jamilah *Arabic:* Beautiful. Jamilah Shaka is a student in Silver Spring, Md.

Japera *Shona:* We are finished. This name might be given to a girl where family feels it beneficial not to have more children. The name is an affirmation of their desire.

Jaribu *Swahili:* One who tries. As a member of Serious Business with her husband Ngomo, Jaribu Hill has sung political messages for more than a decade. As a law school student, she was one of three recipients of the inaugural Thurgood Marshall Fellowship awarded by the New York City Bar Association.

Jemine *Shekiri:* The Lord let me have mine. Also Jemi.

Jendayi *Shona:* Give thanks.

Jokha *Swahili:* The robe of royalty.

Jolomi *Shekiri:* The Lord has settled me.

Jubemi *Shekiri:* The Lord has answered my prayers.

Jumanah *Arabic:* Silver pearl.

Jumapili *Mwera:* Born on Sunday.

Jumoke *Yoruba:* Everyone loves this child.

Kakra *Fante:* Youngest twin.

Kalila *Arabic:* Sweetheart, beloved.

Kamaria *Swahili:* Beauty of the moon.

Kamilah *Arabic:* The perfect one.

Kanika *Mwera:* Black cloth.

Kantayeni *Yao:* Go and throw her away. If this name is to be interpreted literally, then the only reason one might choose it would be for its lovely, rhythmic cadence. The Yao people of Malawi may interpret just the opposite of its literal meaning.

Katou *Uganda:* Small.

Kefilwe *Tswana:* I receive.

Kehinde *Yoruba:* Younger twin.

Kesi *Swahili:* Born when father was in trouble.

Khadija *Swahili:* Born prematurely. Khadija and its African-American variations are popular among many contemporary African-American women. Young and lovely Khadija Mohamed got her picture in *New York Newsday.* Her 95.6 GPA put her centerstage as valedictorian of her class at St. Peter's High School in Staten Island, N.Y.

Khadijah *Arabic.* Name of prophet Muhammad's wife.

Khalidah *Arabic:* Immortal.

Khalilah *Arabic.* If this name is a feminine version of Khaleel, as it appears to be, it means sincere friend. Khalilah Ali-Camacho describes herself as a sincere friend of her former husband Muhammad Ali.

Kibibi *Swahili:* Little lady.

Kifimbo *Swahili:* A very thin baby.

Kigongo *Luganda:* Born before twins.

Kiiza *Luganda:* A child who follows twins.

Kisakye *Uganda:* God's grace.

Kissa *Luganda:* Born after twins.

Kizuwanda *Zaramo:* The last born.

Kobungye *Uganda:* Freedom comes.

Kokumo *Yoruba:* This one will not die. Parents who have lost children before use this name to affirm the life of the newborn. Kokumo becomes an affirmation of life.

Kolugyendo *Uganda:* Born while parents were on a trip.

Kukua *Fante:* Born on Wednesday.

Laini *Swahili:* Sweet and gentle, soft. Laini "Muki" Brown is an aspiring record company executive.

Lama *Arabic:* Darkness of lips.

Lamis *Arabic:* Soft to the touch.

Lamya *Arabic:* Dark-lipped.

Lateefah *Arabic:* A pleasant, gentle woman.

Latifah *Arabic:* Gentle, kind. Queen Latifah is a not always gentle rap artist.

Layla *Swahili:* She was born at night.

Leldo *Pulssar:* Unique child.

Lerato *Tswana:* She brings love.

Limber *Tiv:* Joyful.

Lina *Arabic:* Tender.

Liziuzayani *Yao:* Tell someone.

Lolli *Wolof:* Fall. Among the Wolof people of Senegal, Gambia, and surrounding West African countries, this is a very special name. Fall is deemed the best time of the year, because the crops are at the end of their cycle. The farming time is over, and it is party time.

Lulu *Swahili:* A pearl.

Lumusi *Ewe:* Born facedown.

M

Maanan *Akan:* Fourth-born child.

Madihah *Arabic:* Praise-worthy.

Mafaune *Bachopi:* Soil.

Maizah *Arabic:* Discerning.

Majidah *Arabic:* Glorious.

Makeda *Ethiopian:* The beautiful Makeda was the legendary queen of Ethiopia best known as the queen of Sheba. Exceedingly rich, she journeyed to Jerusalem to hold court with King Solomon. Makeda Benjamin is an aspiring dancer and writer in New York City.

Malak *Arabic:* Angel.

Maliaka *Swahili:* Queen, of high attributes. Also Malaika. Maliaka Headley is a preschooler. Malaika Adero is an editor for Amistad Press. This name is very popular among black parents who prefer African names.

Mama *Fante:* Born on Saturday.

Manar *Arabic:* Guiding light.

Mande *Uganda:* First day.

Mandisa *Xhosa:* Sweet.

Mansa *Akan:* Third-born child.

Maram *Arabic:* Aspiration.

Marjani *Swahili:* Named for the beautiful coral.

Masani *Luganda:* Has gap between teeth.

Masika *Swahili:* Born during the season of the rains.

Mawusi *Ewe:* In the hands of God.

Maysa *Arabic:* To walk

with a proud, swinging gait.

Mbafor *Ibo:* Born on a market day.

Mbeke *Ibo:* Born on the first day of the week.

Mesi *Yao:* Water.

Mkegani *Zaramo:* Child of disrespectful wife.

Mkiwa *Swahili:* Orphaned child.

Modupe *Yoruba:* I am grateful.

Mogbeyi *Shekiri:* This one is my joy.

Monifa *Yoruba:* I have luck. Monifa has been widely used by African-Americans. Monifa White is a program coordinator and producer at WLIB in New York City.

Montsho *Tswana:* Black.

Mosi *Swahili:* The first-born.

Mpho *Tswana:* Gift.

Msiba *Swahili:* Born during mourning.

Mudiwa *Shona:* Beloved.

Mukamutara *Rwanda:* Mutara's daughter, or a girl born during King Mutara's reign.

Mukarramma *Arabic:* Honored.

Mulekwa *Uganda:* Child who has no father.

Mumbejja *Uganda:* Princess.

Muna *Arabic:* Wish.

Muteteli *Rwanda:* Dainty.

Muzaana *Uganda:* The wife of a princess, or a lady serving a king's palace.

Mwaka *Swahili:* Born during the start of the farming season.

Mwamuila *Zafamo:* Born during the war.

Mwanaidi *Swahili:* Born during the Idd festival.

Mwanawa *Zaramo:* First-born child.

Mwanjaa *Zaramo:* Born during a famine.

Mwasaa *Swahili:* Born on time.

Naadu *Ga:* One from Sempeh region. This is a clan name associated with a region of Ghana. Naadu Blankson is a journalist.

Nabirye *Luganda:* Mother of twins.

Nabukwasi *Luganda:* Bad housekeeper. Nabukwasi is an example of a name earned by one's actions.

Nabulungi *Luganda:* Beautiful one.

Nabwire *Uganda:* Born during the night.

Nada *Arabic:* Full of generosity; dew.

Naeemah *Arabic:* Benevolent. Naeemah Binion attends Michigan State University.

Nafisah *Arabic:* Precious thing.

Nafula *Abaluhya:* Born during rainy season.

Nafuna *Luganda:* Born feetfirst.

Nailah *Arabic:* She who will succeed, one who acquires.

Naimah *Arabic:* Lives a quiet, enjoyable life.

Najibah *Arabic:* Of noble birth.

Najla *Arabic:* Wide eyes.

Nakampi *Uganda:* Short.

Nalongo *Luganda:* Mother of twins. This is another example of a name acquired as an adult.

Namalwa *Uganda:* Born during the party or celebration.

Namono *Luganda:* Younger twin.

Nanyamka *Ewe:* God's gift.

Nasiche *Uganda:* Born

during the time of the locust.

Nathifa *Arabic:* Clean, pure.

Nayo *Yoruba:* We have joy.

Ndiadiane *Sereer:* Amazing.

Ndidi *Ibo:* Child born with the gift of patience.

Neema *Swahili:* Born during prosperity.

Ngozi *Ibo:* A blessing has come.

Ngulinga *Ngoni:* Weeping.

Niara *Swahili:* Of high purpose. Niara Sudarkasa is the first woman appointed president of Lincoln University. Historically black and all male for much of its history, Lincoln is now coeducational.

Njemile *Yao:* Upstanding.

Nkechi *Ibo:* This is for God.

Nkosazana *Xhosa:* Princess.

Nkroma *Akan:* The ninth-born child.

Nneka *Ibo:* Her mother is outstanding.

Nnenia *Ibo:* Her grandmothers look alike.

Nobanzi *Xhosa:* Width.

Nomalanga *Zulu:* A sunny disposition.

Nombeko *Xhosa:* Respect.

Nomble *Xhosa:* Beautiful.

Nomuula *Xhosa:* Rain.

Nonyameko *Xhosa:* Patience.

Nonzamo *Xhosa:* One who in her life will go through many trials. The life of Nonzamo Winifred "Winnie" Mandela personifies the meaning of her name. Winnie Mandela is loved and respected worldwide for her unfailing opposition to the draconian oppression of an apartheid state.

Nourbese *Benin:* A wonderful child.

Nsonwa *Akan:* The seventh-born child.

Ntosake *Zulu:* She who comes with her own things, or she who walks with lions. Also Ntozake. Born Paulette Williams, Ntozake Shange is one of our most brilliant poets. Her *for colored girls who have considered suicide / when the rainbow is enuf* brought her fame.

Nuru *Swahili:* Born in daylight.

Nwakaego *Ibo:* She is more important than money.

Nwakego *Ibo:* A child is greater than money.

Nwazuoaa *Ibo:* Maybe all granted.

Nyameke *Akan:* Gift from God.

Nzingha *Matamba.* Also Zinga. The meaning of this great 17th-century African warrior queen's name is obscured by her brilliance as an administrator and organizer. But perhaps her most important legacy is her unstinting commitment to peace.

Obialumani *Ibo:* I know a peaceful mind.

Oboego *Ibo:* The child that came with money.

Ogorehuekwu *Ibo:* Gift of God.

Olabisi *Yoruba:* Joy is increased.

Olabunni *Yoruba:* We are rewarded with honor.

Olaniyi *Yoruba:* Glory in wealth.

Olufemi *Yoruba:* God loves me.

Olufunke *Yoruba:* A gift from God to love.

Olufunmilayo *Yoruba:* God gives joy.

Oluremi *Yoruba:* God consoles me.

Omagbemi *Shekiri:* This child saved me. Also Ogbemi.

Omaone *Shekiri:* I have a child. A parent celebrates the birth of a child with this affirmation of her presence.

Omolara *Benin:* Born during the night.

Omorenomwara *Benin:* This child will not suffer.

Omorose *Benin:* My beautiful child.

Omosede *Benin:* A child counts more than a king.

Omosupe *Benin:* A child is the most precious thing.

Oni *Benin:* Desired. *Yoruba:* Born in a sacred place.

Onyeka *Ibo:* Who is the greatest.

Orisetimeyin *Shekiri:* The Lord is behind me, or the Lord is supporting me. Also Oritseweyinmi. Popular abbreviations include Oti, Weyinmi, Timeyin.

Osayiomwabe *Benin:* God will help us.

Oseye *Benin:* The happy one.

Ozigbodi *Ewe:* Patience.

Panya *Swahili:* Tiny like a mouse.

Panyin *Fante:* Elder of twins.

Pasua *Swahili:* Born by Caesarean.

Pili *Swahili:* The second-born child.

Preye *Ibo:* God's gift or blessing.

Radhiya *Swahili:* Agreeable.

Ramla *Swahili:* Predicts the future.

Rashida *Swahili:* Righteous.

Raziya *Swahili:* Easy to get along with.

Rehema *Swahili:* Of great compassion.

Rufaro *Shona:* Happiness.

Rukiya *Swahili:* She rises on high.

Sada *Swahili:* Help has come.

Sade The meaning of this Nigerian name is unknown. Sade, the beautiful and brilliant singer from London, is the daughter of a Nigerian father and a British mother.

Safa *Arabic:* Clarity, purity.

Safiya *Swahili:* Clearminded, pure. Also Safiyah. This name has enjoyed a great deal of

popularity among African-American
women who have changed their names, as well as among parents naming their children.

Safiyyah *Arabic:* Serene, pure, best friend. Safiyyah Marks lives in New York City.

Sagirah *Arabic:* Little one.

Salama *Swahili:* Peace.

Salma *Swahili:* Safe.

Sangeya *Shona:* Hate men.

Sanura *Swahili:* Kitten. A name for a baby who looks like a kitten.

Sauda *Swahili:* Of a dark complexion.

Sazidde *Uganda:* Fourth day.

Sekelaga *Nyakyusa:* Rejoice.

Selma *Arabic:* Secure.

Serwa *Ewe:* Royal woman.

Shani *Swahili:* Marvelous.

Sharifa *Swahili:* Distinguished.

Shiminege *Tiv:* Let us see the future in this child.

Shoorai *Shona:* Broom.

Shukura *Swahili:* Be grateful

Sibongile *Ndebele:* Thanks.

Siboniso *Zulu:* Sign.

Sigele *Ngoni:* Left.

Sigolwide *Nyakyusa:* My ways are straight.

Sisi *Fante:* Born on a Sunday.

Ssanyu *Uganda:* Happiness.

Subria *Swahili:* Patience rewarded.

Suhailah *Arabic:* Gentle.

Sukutai *Shona:* Squeeze.

Suubi *Uganda:* Hope.

Syandene *Nyakyusa:* Punctual.

Tabia *Swahili:* Talented.

Tahirah *Arabic:* Pure. *Taiwo:* Firstborn of twins.

Takiyah *Arabic:* Righteous.

Tale (tah lea) *Tswana:* Green.

Tawia *Akan:* Next child after the twins.

Tebesigwa *Uganda:* People are to be trusted.

Teleza *Ngoni:* Slippery.

Thema *Akan:* Queen.

Themba *Zulu:* One to be trusted.

Thandiwe *Xhosa:* Loving.

Titilayo *Yoruba:* Happiness is eternal.

Toju *Shekiri:* The Lord's is uppermost.

Tosan *Shekiri:* God knows the best.

Tsoyo *Shekiri:* I'll see this one as my joy.

Tulimbwelu *Nyakyusa:* We are in the light of God.

Tulinagwe *Nyakyusa:* God is with us.

Tumwebaze *Uganda:* Let us thank God for this child.

Tumpe *Nyakyusa:* Let us thank God for this child.

Uchechuckwu *Ibo:* God's sense.

Udoka *Ibo:* Peace is better.

Uliyemi *Shekiri:* Home suits me. Also Yemi.

Urbi *Benin:* Princess.

Uwimana *Rwanda:* Daughter of God.

Waseme *Swahili:* Let them talk.

Wesesa *Musoga:* Careless.

Wudha *Uganda:* Younger twin sister.

Yaa *Ewe:* Born on Thursday. Unisex.

Yadikone *Wolof:* You were here before. This name may be given to an especially bright child to imply that she has the wisdom of an older person.

Yahimba *Tiv:* There is no place like home.

Yaminah *Arabic:* Right and proper.

Ye *Ewe:* Elder of twins.

Yejide *Yoruba:* She has her mother's face.

Yetunde *Yoruba:* Mother comes back.

Zahra *Swahili:* Flower

Zakiya *Swahili:* Intelligent.

Zalika *Swahili:* Wellborn.

Zawadi *Swahili:* A gift has come.

Zesiro *Luganda:* The firstborn twin.

Zuwena *Swahili:* Good.

Newly Created

Names for Girls

He believed that a man's life proceeds from his name, in the way that a river proceeds from its source.

—N. Scott Momaday
The Names: A Memoir by N. Scott Momaday, 1976

Among her peers, the infant girl of the 1990s who is called the rhythmic Mattie Mae, Esther Fay, or plain old Jane, may in fact sport the most uncommon name!

A

Aaisha
Aarianne
Aarica
Aarika
Aartee
Aarti
Aatifa
Abanessa
Abani
Abasha
Adara
Adawna
Adayshia
Adeidra
Adelicia
Adenike
Adjanaye
Adjua
Adysseus
Aeliveau
Afara
Afiah

Ahagrace
Aheesha
Ahleesha
Ahmana
Ahmeena
Aiken
Aisia
Aissata
Aiyana
Aiyanna
Aja
Akeiba
Akeita
Akela
Akelia
Akemi
Akerria
Akeshia
Aketa
Akeya
Akeyla
Akia

Akila
Akilah
Akira
Akiya
Alahna
Alaice
Alani
Alanika
Alanya
Alberea
Aleachia
Aleah
Aleda
Aleena
Aleisha
Alelea
Aleshia
Aletrice
Alethea
Alfair
Alfena
Alfenita

Alfrenita	Amarita	Annaka
Alfretta	Ambrea	Annalee
Alichia	Ambreia	Annella
Aline	Ami	Annquinette
A'Lishan	Amiebelle	Anshanta
Alleva	Amiell	Anthria
Almeera	Amiika	Antoneshia
Almena	Amika	Antrina
Almesha	Aminah	Anysha
Almetta	Aminata	Anza
Alnese	Amira	Anzetta
Alnita	Amisha	Aprili
Alodia	Amishia	Aquaisha
Alonda	Amrita	Aqueela
Alondra	Amyelita	Ara
Alosoua	Amyna	AraBell
Aloya	Anada	Arbedella
Alphenia	Ananasa	Arcola
Alqueen	Andrameda	Aria
Altasha	Andriena	Arielle
Altheia	Aneatra	Arindella
Althia	Aneca	Arlise
Altrionette	Aneeka	Arnetia
Al Vareeta	Aneesa	Arnitta
Alyce	Anegie	Aronika
Alysha	Anelia	Atara
Alzena	Anese	Artavaya
Alzine	Anitia	Artavia
Amaquah	Anique	Artesha
Amara	Ankara	Arthie

Arthuree
Artisia
Arverna
Arvita
Arzela
Arzella
Aseelah
Ashanea
Ashanee
Ashani
Ashanique

Asharee
Ashlee
Asia
Asukile
Asya
Athel
Atiya
Audythe
Auh
Aundra
Auria

Averall
Avonella
Ayala
Ayisha
Azalee
Azalie
Aziza
Azlonia
Azure-De

Badia
Baiesha
Baine
Ba Kendra
Balita
Banesa
Banesha
Banisha
Batrina
Beatris
Becka
Belindra

Belinette
Bendalynn
Beneature
Beneisha
Beneshea
Beneta
Beniesha
Benishia
Benitta
Bennicia
Bennilyn
Berenis

Beritshia
Bernessa
Bernetha
Bernietta
Bernilya
Bernita
Berrastina
Bertice
Bertita
Beverlyn
Bibiana
Birrilla

Birthale
Blayne
Bless
Blomer
Blondee
Boishea
Bonique
Bradice
Brandee
Brandi
Branyell
Breanna
Bree
Breena
Brencia
Breona

Bresha
Breshay
Breshia
Bretta
Breya
Breyana
Breyanb
Bria
Briahna
Bricole
Brieanna
Brilyn
Brina
Brinia
Brinna
Briona

Brione
Brionna
Brionne
Brisa
Brisha
Brishetta
Brissa
Brita
Britia
Brushira
Brynesha
Brynishia
Burbette
Byrna

Cadymae
Calberto
Calisa
Calisha
Calissa
Calista
Calitia

Calletta
Callista
Callrissa
Callula
Calretha
Calvina
Calvinetta

Camalla
Camelita
Camella
Camenisha
Cameri
Cameria
Cameshia

Camika	Carisse	Carshara
Camria	Carita	Carshena
Camryn	Carlaena	Carsina
Camyll	Carlandra	Carysa
Camylle	Carleta	Casaundra
Candalyn	Carletha	Casedra
Candelle	Carletta	Cashundra
Candice	Carliqua	Casinda
Candiss	Carlisha	Cassenia
Candita	Carlisia	Cassina
Caneika	Carlissia	Cateel
Caneisha	Carlista	Cateka
Canesha	Carlonda	Cateria
Canice	Carltissa	Catia
Canietha	Carmisha	Catiana
Canisha	Carnella	Catie
Cannelle	Carnesha	Catina
Cannie	Carnesia	Catisha
Cantara	Carnetta	Catissa
Cantrella	Carnette	Catreece
Caprina	Carnika	Catrelle
Capritta	Carnisha	Catrice
Carenna	Carnthia	Catricia
Caressa	Carressa	Catteeka
Caretha	Carrilla	Cautauqua
Caretrice	Carrisa	Cavasi
Carimisha	Carrissa	Cawanda
Carisa	Carrita	Cayta
Carisia	Carronda	Ceaira
Carissa	Carsha	Ceanda

Ceddrina	Chakaria	Chanika
Cedreka	Chakeia	Chanique
Cedrina	Chalayna	Chanisa
Ceey	Chaleeta	Chanita
Ceiaira	Chalena	Channie
Ceirria	Chalissa	Chanovia
Celisha	Chalonda	Chanquita
Celisia	Chalsma	Chantae
Celissa	Chamaikha	Chantai
Celisse	Chamara	Chantara
Celissia	Chamaria	Chantasis
Celustia	Chambray	Chantay
Cemetrius	Chameka	Chantaye
Cenda	Chamelia	Chanteese
Cendra	Chamia	Chantell
Ceolia	Chamika	Chantelsha
Ceporah	Chamila	Chanthina
Cerease	Chamique	Chantoya
Ceretha	Chandesia	Chantra
Cerilla	Chandre	Chantrell
Cerissa	Chandrea	Chantrice
Cerita	Chandrelle	Chantrill
Cerrina	Chandrenia	Chanyell
Cessli	Chanecqu	Chaquana
Chabre	Chanekka	Chaquanta
Chabreka	Chanesse	Charasika
Chabrielle	Chanetta	Chardesia
Chadae	Chaneyll	Chareka
Chaela	Chanice	Charena
Chakara	Chaniece	Charesa

Charetta
Charice
Chariese
Charika
Charina
Charisa
Charisha
Charisse
Charista
Charkeshia
Charlana
Charlanda
Charlanna
Charlanne
Charleana
Charleate
Charlena
Charlesena
Charlessa
Charlessena
Charlice
Cha Rae
Charel
Charmeka
Charmisa
Charnele
Charnesha
Charniqua
Charnita
Charon

Charonda
Charonia
Charsha
Charvanda
Charvenisia
Charvetta
Charyl
Chastidy
Chatisa
Chau
Chaundra
Chaunell
Chaunetta
Chauneva
Chavon
Cheezelle
Chekeria
Chekesha
Chekita
Cheneka
Chenequa
Chenesha
Chenetta
Chenette
Chenice
Chenika
Chenita
Chennistique
Chenterra
Cheranda

Chereena
Chereka
Cherella
Cheresa
Cherice
Cherida
Cherika
Cherina
Cherise
Cherkita
Cherlisa
Cherna
Cheron
Cherone
Cherran
Cheryle
Chesley
Chetaria
Chevarlyn
Chevon
Chevaun
Chevonna
Chicquetta
Chika
Chikara
Chimere
Cherina
Chiquita
Chiquon
Chirisa

Choe
Chona
Chrishana
Chrisssy
Christal
Christel
Christella
Christelle
Christen
Chrlyne
Chumequa
Cienate
Cirmesha
Claetha
Claretha

Clarrusha
Claudie
Clayella
Clevea
Clynta
Codelia
Consistoy
Cormeka
Cormelizi
Corrianne
Cortisha
Cotha
Cranesha
Creasie
Cree

Creola
Crissanda
Cruzita
Cubie
Curtaziad
Curtisha
Curtissa
Curtrisa
Cyna
Cynedra
Cynethia
Cynetria
Cyniece
Cynteria

Dackeyia
Daesha
Daeshavon
Dahlia
Dahne
Dainice

Daisha
Daishia
Dakia
Dakiesha
Dakima
Dakisha

Daleashanti
Daleisha
Daletha
Dalila
Dalinia
Dalishua

Dalishya	Daria	Deatonia
Dalma	Darika	Deatrix
Dalresha	Darisha	Deaudre
Dalvessa	Darita	De Aun
Dalvis	Darnesha	Deeandra
Dalynna	Da Tisha	Deena
Damali	Datra	Deenie
Damalyn	Datrice	Deensha
Dameeka	Daufreda	Deesha
Damenica	Davah	Deitra
Damesha	Da Vetta	Deja Devorah
Danaya	Daviedra	Dejana
D'Andra	Davita	Dejanee
Daneeka	Davona	Dekendra
Daneesha	Davonda	Dekenya
Daneka	Dawanna	Dekoven
Danelia	Dawnette	Delaine
Danelle	Dawnia	Delana
Danesha	Daydrill	Delaree
Danessa	Dayna	Delcine
Danetra	DD'Anna	Deleena
Dani	Deanda	Delena
Dania	De Andra	Delesha
Danice	De Andre	Delfloria
Daniece	Deandrea	Delinda
Danisha	Deandria	Delisa
Danishea	DeAngela	Delise
Danyell	Deanna	Delisha
Daquetta	Deare De Fay	Delissa
Daree	Deasha	Dellaphine

Deloise
Delonda
Delondyn
Delphia
Delvaughn
Delyn
Delynden
Delyse
Demaria
Demeisha
Demisha
Dena
Denda
Deneisha
Denell
Denesha
Denika
Denique
Denita
Denitia
Deondidre
Dequandra
Dera Estee
Derilyn
Derinda
Derrianne

Deshanda
DeShawana
DeShay
Desreta
Dessie
Destiny
Detra
Devanei
DeVella
De Vera
DeVette
Devonna
Devora
Devya
Dezere
Dianda
Diandra
Diandre
Dianora
Diasha
Diazina
Dineka
Dinora
Diondra
Dionette
Dionisia

Dirra
Djane
Dollaree
Domika
Donella
Donesha
Donette
Donisha
Donnia
Dorinda
Doroughtia
Dovina
Doylene
Drena
Drina
Drosella
D'shae
Durr
Dwania
Dyeasha
Dylana
Dyshaneta
Dyshia
Dywonda

E

Eadie
Ealie
Earlatta
Earleas
Earlecia
Earlena
Earlicia
Earlique
Earlisha
Earmine
Earnasha
Earnisha
Earthalyn
Ebonique
Ebonisha
Edlisha
Ednita
Egreather
Eiesha
Ekeira
Ekeya

Elayesha
Elcares
Eleesha
Elese
Elesha
Elethia
Elethie
Elett
Elgina
Elisandra
Elisheba
Elizer
Ellenia
Elneatria
Elnesa
Elnetra
Elonra
Elsey
Elwanda
Emeka
Emera

Emeshia
Emiko
Emmaliese
Emmastine
Emna
Endera
Endura
Eniola
Enise
Enishia
Ennis
Enza
Era
Ermene
Ernesha
Ernisha
Esaterica
Eslyn
Essline
Essola
Estrella

Etha
Etorya
Eulaisha
Eulaie
Eulalia
Eunique
Euralea

Euralene
Euree
Evanesa
Evangelyan
Evanthia
Evelisa
Everleen

Evonda
Evoni
Evonia
Eyamba

F

Fabiana
Fabiola
Fabreena
Fadora
Faiola
Falaka
Falakika
Falami
Faleisha
Faleshia
Fanelissa
Fanesia
Fantasha
Farrusa

Fasha
Fateisha
Fatesha
Fatiya
Faydra
Faykita
Fayrell
Faytandria
Fedena
Feleasha
Felesha
Feonia
Fera
Ferrari

Ferresha
Ferrilyn
Fiorella
Fiorisela
Flanice
Fleisha
Florende
Florisa
Fonie
Fraysina
Freisha
Funmilayo
Fylesha

G

Gaisha
Gakeshia
Galayna
Gamelba
Garene
Garmeika
Garmeisha
Garnetta
Gehell
Gemace
Generra
Genesa
Genesia

Genia
Genice
Geniqua
Genita
Georgettea
Gequetta
Gerica
Gerika
Gerisa
Gerlia
Getoria
Ginessa
Ginette

Ginika
Ginneisha
Gisela
Glennisha
Glentoria
Glikerya
Glorisha
Glynitra
Glynova
Goldzene
Gwenisha
Gwennetta

H

Habiba

Hafeza

Hakima

Ha Lea

Haliegh

Hamishia

Harikila

Harrianna

Harrjanna

Harva

Hasha

Hashia

Haydelisa

Hazea

Hazelee

Hazelene

Hazeline

Hedaya

Helayna

Hezkialena

Herlean

Herleen

Herlina

Herlinda

Hermenia

Hersha

Hessie

Himali

Himani

Hisazo

Hoshelle

Hoshoma

Howneshia

Hulda

Hydirah

Hyturia

I

Icey
Idlyene
Iduna
Ieasha
Ieashah

Ieashia
Ieashiah
Ieesha
Ieeshia
Igela

Ikesha
Ilecia
Ilee
Incentlee
Indira

J

Jaanai
Jacara
Jacenda
Jackia
Jackquel
Jacquetta
Jacodi

Jaconda
JaCoya
Jacqui
JaDeana
Jadera
Jadine
Jadrianne

Jadrien
Jaedra
Jaela
Jaeleen
Jaenae
Jaenett
Jafra

Jahaidia	Jamaam	Ja-Min
Jahaira	Jamaka	Jamira
Jahalia	Jamara	Jamnesha
Jaharra	Jamari	Jammisha
Jahkiisha	Jamarra	Jamora
Jahmonique	Jameela	Janada
Jahnesseh	Jameelah	Janae
Jahvonda	Jameice	Janaesi
Jahzinga	Jameisha	Janderra
Jaika	Ja Meka	Jandra
Jakala	Jameka	Janece
Jakeela	Jamela	Janecia
Jakeisha	Jamelia	Ja'Neece
Jakeisia	Ja'Mell	Janeen
Ja Kenda	Jamelya	Janeesa
Ja Kesha	Jameria	Janeia
Jaketta	Jamesa	Janeika
Jakisha	Jamese	Janeisha
Jakira	Jamesetta	Janeka
Jakiya	Jamesha	Janella
Jakorra	Jameshia	Janelle
Jalaina	Jameta	Ja Neva
Jalaine	Jamethia	Janicka
Jalayna	Jametta	Janieasha
Jaleisa	Jamiera	Janiece
Jalena	Jamika	Janika
Ja Lessa	Jamilah	Janique
Jalessa	Jamilla	Janisa
Jalinda	Jamilota	Janisha
Jalisa	Jamilya	Janissa

Jannella	Jayna	Jennora
Jannelle	Jaynell	Jenyne
Jannisha	Jeana	Jequita
Janith	Jeanice	Jericka
Janora	Jeanis	Jerika
Janur	Jehna	Jerina
Jaquandra	Jehnese	Jermecia
Jaquane	Jekina	Jermell
Jaquanna	Jekira	Jermesha
Jacquete	Jelena	Jermice
Jacquetta	Jelissa	Jermika
Jaquette	Jeloni	Jermila
Jaquinda	Jemelia	Jernice
Jaramaji	Jemesha	Jeronise
Jarina	Jemika	Jerothea
Jarika	Jena	Jetisha
Jarita	Jeneka	Jevon
Jarushia	Jenell	Jikeeta
Jashona	Jenene	Jikeka
Jaskia	Jenesia	Jilisa
Jasmer	Jenessa	Jimel
Jatarra	Jenice	Jimisha
Jateira	Jenicka	Jimysha
Ja Teka	Jenika	Jinean
Jatori	Jenique	Jinessa
Jatoria	Jenisha	Jo Anee
Jaunkita	Jenissa	Joarvonia
Javana	Jenneta	Jobyna
Javeeka	Jennika	Jocelle
Javonda	Jennisa	Jo Dell

Jofran
Johnell
Johnesha
Johnique
Johnisha
Johnnisha
Jokay
Jolene
Joletha
Jomeka

Joneil
Joneisha
Jonelle
Jonika
Jonique
Jonisha
Jonmekya
Jontae
Jonzeeta
Josehanny

Jovan
Jualeah
Juauna
Julander
Julene
Julissa
Juquetta
Jylla
Jynesin
Jyvonda

Kaala
Kaara
Kaari
Kaarina
Kachia
Kachonda
Kacia
Kacindra
Kadeidra
Kadeja
Kaesha

Kahlae
Kailea
Kaishawn
Kaitha
Kaitia
Kaitisha
Kalana
Kalani
Kalea
Kalean
Kaleisha

Kalena
Kalesha
Kalesta
Kalika
Kalima
Kalina
Kalinda
Kalisha
Kalissa
Kalista
Kalondra

Ka Lynn	Karmonique	Keischa
Kamala	Karnesha	Kelesha
Kamara	Karriem	Kelisha
Kamari	Karry Ann	Kemisha
Kameela	Kashawn	Kencle
Kameelah	Kashay	Kendretta
Kamesha	Kashonna	Kenisha
Kamila	Ka Tara	Kenteria
Kamilia	Ka Teira	Kentreia
Kamilah	Katessa	Kera
Kamira	Katheia	Keria
Kamilal	Katish	Kerima
Kamisha	Katrice	Kesha
Kamishia	Katrisa	Kestia
Kandra	Kavita	Keteva
Kandalsiha	Kavitha	Ketura
Kaneisha	Kavonna	Keyanna
Kanesha	Kayi	Keyasha
Kanika	Kayota	Keyka
Kandra	Kaysha	Keyonna
Kamilal	Kaytoya	Khalian
Kamini	Kaywan	Kiah
Kaprisha	Keannya	Kialyn
Kariesha	Keeanna	Kiana
Karina	Keesha	Kianna
Karisha	Keewanda	Kiendra
Karlisha	Kefira	Kienyata
Karlitha	Keiandrea	Kierna
Karlyn	Keionda	Kijianna
Karmela	Keis	Kimani

Kimesha
Kimetha
Kimika
Kimmell
Kimwanna
Kina
Kindra
Kini
Kira
Kisa
Kisha
Kishan
Kishandra
Kishauna
Komeka

Kondria
Konhasha
Konishia
Kovey
Kresenda
Kreshia
Kreshonda
Krisa
Krisanda
Krisandra
Krista
Krushetta
Krysha
Krysia
Krystle

Kuchita
Kwaneisha
Kwanetta
Kyatona
Kyeisha
Kyesha
Kym
Kyma
Kyndra
Kyneesha
Kyshanwnda
Kyshona
Kyshonda
Kyteva

L

Laara
Labonnie
Labredna
Labresha
Labrisha
Labritney
Lacara

Lachana
Lachanda
Lachandice
Lachandra
La Channa
Lachanta
Lachante

Lachear
La Chelle
Lachelle
Lacherika
Lacheryl
Lachina
Lachonda

Laconduas

Lacoria

Lacrecia

La Creasia

Lacrissa

Lacrista

Lacyndora

Ladaisa

La Daisha

Ladaisha

Ladaishia

Ladara

Ladaseha

Ladassa

Ladavia

Ladawn

La Deana

La Deeta

Ladeeta

La Deidra

Ladesha

Ladi

Ladina

Ladiva

Ladon

Ladona

La Donna

Ladonna

Ladonne

Ladonya

La Doris

Ladrica

Laeeersha

Laesha

Lafondra

La Guardia

Lajessica

Lajohna

Lajoia

Lajuana

Lajuanna

La Juanta

Lajuliette

La June

La Junia

Lakaiya

La Kasha

Lakasha

Lakazia

Lakea

Lakecia

Lakedia

Lakedra

Lakeela

Lakeena

Lakeesh

La Keisha

La'keisha

Lakeisha

Lakendria

Lakentra

La Kenya

Lakenya

La Kesa

Lakesbia

Lakesha

Lakesia

Lakessa

Laketha

Laketia

Laketrice

Laketta

Lakeysha

Laki

La Kia

La'kia

Lakia

Lakida

La Kiesha

Lakiesha

Lakila

La Kirah

La Kisha

Lakisha

Lakishia

La Kita

Lakita

Lakitra

Lakitta

Lakiya

Lakonya	Lanetra	Laqunia
Lakranda	Lanieka	Laquonda
La Kresha	Lanielle	Laquondra
Lakresha	Laniesha	Laqushia
Lakreshia	Lannette	La Rae
Lakrisha	Lanora	Larayne
Lakshana	La Paula	Lareesa
Lalania	Lapaula	Lareesea
Lalondra	La'petra	Lareisha
Lamanica	Laqualia	Larena
Lamara	La Quan	Larenda
Lamarra	Laquana	Laresa
Lameeka	Laquanda	La Resha
La Meka	Laquarius	Laresha
Lamesha	Laqueal	Laretha
Lametria	Laqueena	Larinda
Lamika	Laquela	Larissa
Lamisha	La Quesha	Larita
Lamona	Laquesha	La Ronce
Lamonda	Laquetta	Laronda
Lamonica	La Quianas	La Rosianna
Lanata	Laquilla	Lartrice
Landria	La Quisha	La'sandra
Landyce	La'quisha	Laseanna
Lanecia	Laquisha	Lashana
Laneetra	Laquinda	La Shanda
Laneisha	Laquinia	Lashanda
Lanesa	Laquinta	Lashanna
Lanesha	La Quita	Lashannon
Lanetha	Laquita	Lashannova

Lashanta
La Shante
Lashante
Lashaquonta
Lashaun
Lashaunda
Lashaunia
Lashaunna
Lashaunta
Lashawn
La Shawnda
Lashawnda
La'shay
Lashea
Lasheba
Lasheele
La Sheena
Lasheka
Lashelia
Lashell
Lashelle
Lashenia
Lasherri
Lashika
Lashirelle
Lashon
La'shona
Lashona
La Shonda
Lashonda

Lashonde
Lashondia
Lashondra
Lashonne
Lashunda
Lashundra
Lasonda
Lasonia
Lasonya
La Staisha
Lastarr
Lata
Lataisha
Latandra
Latania
La Tannae
Latanya
Latarisha
Latarra
La Tarsha
Latarsha
La Tasha
Latasha
Latashia
Latavis
Lataysha
La Tazia
Lateasha
Lateisha
Latedra

Lateefa
Latenna
La Tesa
Latesha
Latessa
Latice
Latifa
LaTina
La Tisha
Latisha
Latishia
Latissa
Latissha
Lativia
Latoia
Latonia
La Tonica
Latora
Latosha
La Trecia
Latrecia
La Treece
Latreece
La'treesh
Latrell
La Trenda
La Trese
La Trice
Latricia
Latrina

Latrisa	Lenelle	Linderdene
Latrisha	Lenesha	Lineasha
Lauralywn	Lenika	Linique
Laurisa	Lenisa	Lioneshka
Laurita	Lenise	Litisha
Lavanna	Leomia	Lodie
LaVaska	Leondra	Loniesha
LaVelle	Leonella	Lonisha
Lavelta	Leonette	Loranesha
La Vesta	Leora	Lorea
La Von	Leshanda	Loressa
Lavonia	Leshandra	Loretha
La Wanda	Leshara	Lorissa
Lawanda	Le Tasha	Loroshia
Lawanza	Lether	Loryce
Le Andra	Le Treasha	Louester
Le Ann	Letrice	Louvennia
Le Anna	Levedra	Luchia
Leareather	Leyvonne	Lucreasha
Ledeath	Lezora	Lukia
Lededra	Lhtoria	Lukisha
Lekeisha	Lian	Luladaye
Lekesha	Licenture	Lu Liesha
Le Keshia	Licha	Luqueasha
Lekeyia	Lickarisa	Luttie
Lekisha	Lidona	Luveda
Leleti	Lieana	Lydria
Leloa	Ligia	Lynair
Lenedra	Likeshia	Lynesha
Leneice	Likita	Lynikia

Lynnesia
Lyria

Lyrissa
Lysondra

Maalika
Macaela
Machaela
Machamma
Machisa
Madella
Madelon
Madina
Madrena
Maeene
Mai
Maisha
Majassa
Majayla
Makaela
Makaila
Makara
Makaya
Makayla

Makeesha
Makeeva
Malayna
Maleeka
Maleka
Malena
Malene
Malenna
Malessa
Maleta
Maliasha
Malisa
Malkresha
Malori
Malree
Maltoria
Malusha
Malynda
Mamiesha

Maneesha
Manefa
Maneka
Manessa
Manika
Manisa
Manisha
Manolia
Maquesha
Maquita
Marcarsha
Marchessa
Marchetta
Marchita
Mardy
Marellene
Marelyn
Mariamu
Maricka

Maricsa	Markia	Martonette
Mariesa	Markiessha	Marvie
Mariesha	Markisha	Marzae
Mariessa	Markishia	Mashanda
Marija	Markita	Mashanna
Mariska	Markitha	Mashara
Maritha	Markiya	Mashayla
Maritsa	Marlainna	Mashedia
Mariza	Marlanna	Matefia
Marizela	Marlayna	Matisha
Marja	Marleasa	Matiya
Markasa	Marlisa	Matosha
Markeeda	Marlisha	Matoya
Markeesha	Marlissa	Matrisha
Markeeta	Marna	Maudene
Markeia	Marnique	Maudest
Markeidra	Marquashia	Maudell
Markeila	Marqueda	Meddie
Markeisha	Marquedia	Medria
Markeita	Marqueita	Meela
Markeka	Marquenda	Meisha
Markela	Marquise	Mekell
Markeria	Marquita	Mekelle
Markesha	Marquiva	Mekenna
Markeshia	Marshae	Melesha
Marketa	Marshana	Melishea
Marketha	Marshayla	Melishia
Marketta	Marshika	Melisia
Markeva	Marteka	Melitha
Marki	Martesha	Merble

Merikay
Merlenda
Merlyr
Messina
Metaweise
Mevelyn
Mia Ayana
Micaiesha
Micalyne
Michandra
Micolette
Micsrisha
Mieka
Miesha
Mikeita
Mikella
Mikia

Mikita
Mikyria
Mikysha
Milanka
Malique
Milika
Miltoneisha
Milvette
Minica
Mintie
Minna
Miquesha
Miri
Misu
Mitra
M'Kaila
Modesbine

Moisie
Monesha
Moneshea
Moneshia
Monetta
Monicka
Monie
Monika
Monikia
Monikka
Monisha
Montina
Monzetta
Myreda
Myrena
Myshanae
Mystik

N

Naadira
Nabila
Nacala
Nacarra

Nacona
Na Coral
Nacosta
Nacrina

Nadisha
Nadiya
Nadria
Naeisha

Nahtasha	Nakeysha	Nashanna
Nahvon	Nakia	Nashanda
Naidi	Nakiesha	Nashauna
Naikeya	Nakima	Nashay
Naila	Nakisha	Nasheena
Naimi	Nakitha	Nasheeta
Naina	Nakita	Natacky
Naisha	Nakitta	Natasa
Naitore	Nalani	Na Tasha
Najtassa	Nalanie	Natasha
Nakala	Nalesia	Natarsha
Nakayla	Naleta	Natarshia
Nakea	Nalicia	Natena
Nakeanya	Nalisa	Natesha
Nakedra	Namika	Nathifa
Nakeema	Nadria	Natika
Nakeesha	Nantonia	Natira
Nakeeta	Naquania	Natisha
Nakeia	Naquasha	Natishia
Nakeidra	Naquesha	Natoka
Nakeisha	Naquima	Natonja
Nakeita	Naquita	Natosha
Nakeithra	Nara	Natya
Nakeitra	Narisa	Nava
Nakeitta	Narkita	Navesha
Nakenyia	Naromie	Navika
Nakeria	Narsha	Naya
Nakesha	Nartisha	Nazamova
Nakeshea	Narvelene	Nazarene
Naketa	Nashadra	Nazia

Nazlie
Ndidi
Neca
Neche
Nechesa
Necia
Neda
Nedenia
Neekia
Neesha
Neeti
Neha
Neheh
Neidra
Neikeishia
Neisha
Nejuan
Nekarah
Nekeda
Nekeena
Nekeisha
Nekelia
Nekema
Nekesha
Nekia
Nelisha
Nequa
Nequita
Nerissa
Nesa

Nesha
Neshonda
Netanya
Nevi
Neyla
Neyle
Neysa
Niaisha
Niani
Nicadia
Nicalia
Nickeia
Nickenya
Nickesha
Nickeya
Nickosi
Nidell
Nidia
Nikeesha
Nikeeta
Nikell
Niketa
Nikeya
Nikida
Nikisha
Nikiya
Nikota
Nimone
Ninona
Nirosha

Niroshi
Nirusha
Nisa
Nisha
Nishali
Nisheka
Nishell
Nishkala
Nitika
Niurka
Nneka
Nomi
Nomiki
Nomsa
Nona
Noni
Nordia
Norita
Norshawna
Novlette
Nurlean
Nyema
Nyesha
Nyeemah
Nykeadra
Nykele
Nykeva
Nykia
Nykita
Nyla

O

Oatoya
Oberlina
Occassana
Octeria
O'dasha
Odean
Odelia
Okeshia
Okevia
Okasna
O'Keshia
Olabisi
Olamara
Olenka
Olesya
Olicia
Olunda
Omara
Omesha
Omnique
Omnisha

Ondrea
Oneasha
Oneretta
Onicia
Onietha
Onika
Onisha
Onita
Ontencia
Onyeka
Onzanikka
Oqudra
Oqueria
Ora
Ora Lee
Ora Mae
Oreana
Oree
Orelia
Orenda
Oressa

Oreteria
Orisa
Oritisha
Orkia
Orla
Orlinda
Ornesha
Ornicka
Orquidea
Orretta
Ortaria
Ortavea
Ortavia
Orteekqua
Osceetta
Oscette
Oshay
Osheka
Osra
Oteen
Otisha

Ouida   Owillinda
Oveita   Ozella

Padocia   Patrishia   Peshonna
Padra   Patrizia   Petesha
Padrina   Pauletha   Phelesha
Pagona   Paulisa   Phozia
Pakoya   Pavitra   Phyllisteen
Palesa   Pear   Phyllsteen
Panise   Pearlita   Piezella
Pankita   Pedelia   Pollene
Paria   Pektra   Ponchitta
Parisa   Pema   Ponzie
Parissa   Penci   Porita
Pasha   Peora   Preeti
Patarisha   Perdita   Preeya
Patisha   Periscia   Prenise
Patona   Perisha   Previtte
Patreka   Perita   Prim
Patresa   Pernice   Princella
Patrese   Pernisha
Patrina   Pertisha

Qauntilla
Qeysha
Qiana
Qiarra
Quachell
Quainette
Qualisha
Qualonda
Quamika
Quana
Quanda
Quanece
Quaneisha
Quanesha
Quanika
Quanique
Quanisha
Quanta
Quantae

Quantara
Quantay
Quantel
Quantenique
Quanteria
Quantiara
Quantisha
Quan'ya
Quashanda
Quashia
Quaunteka
Quavetta
Quayla
Quazina
Queenika
Quenchell
Quenesa
Quenetta
Quenikka

Quenisha
Quentrese
Querida
Queshia
Queshonda
Quiana
Qui'Ann
Quichell
Quimae
Quimay
Quinae
Quindara
Quinika
Quinetta
Quinshana
Quinta
Qulack
Quonda
Quonyette

R

Rachelle
Racquell
Racretia
Radeca
Radekah
Radiah
Raea
Raeairra
Raeana
Rae Chelle
Raeisha
Raeleesha
Raeneisha
Raesha
Raeshelle
Raessa
Raffy
Rahsheita
Rai
Raia
Raishada

Raishonn
Raissa
Rajena
Rakeisha
Rakenya
Rakesha
Rakisha
Ralinda
Ralisha
Ralonda
Ramaya
Ramika
Ramina
Ramonique
Ramonita
Ranasha
Ranata
Randaya
Raneesha
Raneka
Ranell

Ranelle
Ranesha
Raneshia
Ranesna
Rani
Ranice
Raniece
Ranika
Ranisha
Ranita
Raniya
Ranola
Raqueria
Ra Shae
Rashae
Rashana
Rashanda
Rashanta
Rasharia
Rashaunda
Rashaundra

Ra Shawn
Rashawn
Rashawna
Rasheema
Rasheda
Rasheeda
Rasheeta
Ra Sheia
Rasheka
Rathenna
Ravena
Ravonda
Ra Yanda
Rayanna
Rayelle
Rayena
Raymae
Raymesha
Rayneisha
Raynese
Raynetha
Rayshan
Reana
Reatha
Reaundra
Redosha
Regale
Reichelle
Reisha
Rekisha

Rekiya
Rema
Remattie
Remeika
Remeka
Remmy
Remonda
Remona
Renarda
Renaysha
Renda
Renea
Reneisha
Reneka
Renell
Renelle
Renesha
Renetia
Renitza
Requita
Reshae
Reshana
Reshaunda
Resheka
Reshonda
Ressa
Retasha
Revonda
Rezarta
Rheatte

Rhodus
Rhondeisha
Rhonesha
Rhudine
Rhumette
Ricardel
Richanti
Richeena
Richette
Richonda
Rickeesia
Rickell
Rickesha
Rickya
Rihannan
Rikeisha
Rikita
Rikkara
Rilla
Rilma
Rinesha
Risa
Risha
Rishona
Robenia
Robercina
Robersena

Roedeana   Ronesha   Rounette
Roelanzye   Ronessa   Rovonna
Rohama   Ronika   Rowanda
Rohan   Roninese   Royqesha
Roheeda   Roniqua   Ruenda
Rokeria   Ronjuanee   Rula
Romeka   Ronkena   Rukina
Romysha   Ronneisha   Runaka
Ronail   Ronnella   Ruqqiya
Ronata   Ronsha   Ruthelaine
Rondai   Roquanda   Ruthene
Roneeka   Roshanla   Rycca
Roneria   Roshanna   Rynesha
Roneisha   Rotha   Rysheema

Saaqshai   Sabryee   Sahisha
Saarecka   Sacora   Saincellya
Sabaya   Sada   Sajedah
Sabela   Sadarah   Sakara
Sabika'Sabira Sadra   Sakeena
Sabreena   Safeya   Sakendra
Sabriya   Saheli   Sakeria

Sakevia	Sanaa	Sayyida
Sakima	Sana-Shae	Saznette
Sakinah	Sandya	Scherie
Sakira	Sanelra	Schlonda
Sakithiya	Sanessa	Schneida
Salandra	Sanika	Schneiqueka
Salatha	Sanise	Schnella
Salathia	Sanisha	Schnetta
Saleeha	Saquanda	Schquita
Saleema	Saranique	Seandra
Saleena	Saraya	Searcey
Saleha	Sareesha	Sedera
Salinda	Sareeta	Sedika
Salisha	Sareka	Sedionna
Salishya	Sarena	Sedona
Salita	Saresa	Sedora
Saloni	Sareta	Se Gusta
Salynn	Saretta	Sehrisa
Samaiya	Sarilla	Seletha
Samarj	Sarissa	Selueni
Samarra	Saroyra	Seneka
Samaya	Satarra	Sequana
Sameera	Satedra	Sequinta
Sameria	Saterra	Sequita
Sametra	Sausha	Serissa
Sammeka	Savedra	Seritta
Samonia	Saveena	Shaadi
Samoria	Savena	Shaakira
Samuetra	Savii	Shaalee
Samya	Sayaka	Shabba

Shacondra	Shakena	Shalonda
Shadara	Shakendra	Shalondra
Shadaria	Shakeria	Shalonna
Shadaryl	Shaketa	Shalquindra
Shadawm	Shaketha	Shaluana
Shaday	Shakeema	Shamanika
Shaela	Shakeeya	Shamanique
Shafaye	Shakeya	Shamarla
Shafonda	Shakeyra	Shamarra
Shailenda	Shakia	Shambra
Shaina	Shakiera	Shambray
Shajuana	Shakietta	Shambre
Shaka	Shakina	Shambreka
Shakara	Shakira	Shambria
Shakeda	Shalae	Shameeka
Shakedra	Shalamar	Shameika
Shakeela	Sha Lana	Shameke
Shakema	Shalana	Shametra
Shakeema	Shalanda	Shamiesha
Shakeena	Shalaya	Shamique
Shakeerah	Shalayne	Shamiska
Shakeeta	Shaleah	Shamonique
Shakeeyah	Shalene	Shamonya
Shakeia	Shalesa	Shamora
Shakeidra	Shalesta	Shanada
Shakeila	Shaleta	Shanara
Shakeisha	Shaletha	Shanawl
Shakeita	Shalise	Shancela
Shakeitha	Shalisha	Shanda
Shakela	Shalisia	Shandalyn

Shandelle	Shanti	Sharmyra
Shandelyn	Shantisha	Sharna
Shanderla	Shantizia	Sharnae
Shaneeka	Shantyl	Sharnay
Shaneese	Shaokira	Sharndell
Shanekra	Shaquan	Sharnease
Shanel	Shaquana	Sharnell
Shanell	Shaquetta	Sharnetta
Shanena	Shaquria	Sharona
Shanequa	Sharalee	Sharonda
Shanesha	Sharalyn	Sharonne
Shanessa	Sharanda	Sharoya
Shanetha	Sharasa	Sharquita
Shanetta	Sharde	Shartoya
Shanette	Sharece	Sharvelle
Shaneya	Shareen	Shasha
Shaneza	Sharell	Shatara
Shani	Sharena	Sha Tasha
Shanicka	Sharene	Shateka
Shanicqua	Sharesa	Shatika
Shaniea	Sharess	Shatrice
Shanikqua	Sharhonda	Shaula
Shanique	Shariffa	Shauna
Shantal	Sharinda	Shaunquetta
Shantanika	Sharisha	Shaunta
Shante	Shariss	Shavanta
Shan'tel	Sharland	Shavaroughn
Shantel	Sharmika	Shavonna
Shantelle	Sharmista	Shavonte
Shantesa	Sharmonique	Shaw Ann

Sha Waya	Shemuel	Shonnette
Shawnda	Shenece	Shonta
Shawneequa	Shenequa	Shontae
Shawnikia	Shenik	Shontaz
Shawnsa	Sheniqua	Shonte
Shawnte	Shenique	Shontedra
Shawntelle	Shepera	Shontika
Shayda	Sherae	Shorinette
Shayla	Sheranda	Shoronette
Shaylea	She Ray	Shrenda
Shayli	Sherdonna	Shyeda
Shayvonne	Shereka	Shymeca
Sheeja	Sherelle	Shyra
Shekeisha	Sherian	Siriboa
Shekena	Sherita	Slanice
Sheketa	Sheron	Sonceria
Shekevia	Sherrice	Stana
Shelanda	Shina	Starasia
Shelayna	Shinelle	Stasha
Sheleatha	Shinequa	Sulibel
Shelecia	Shineta	Sulimar
Shelina	Shiwishi	Surnell
Shelita	Shondalette	Surquonna
Shelvon	Shondalyn	Swanzetta
Shemeque	Shondel	Swayzine
Shemeika	Shondria	Sylver
Shemikia	Shongo	Symra
Shemina	Shonnett	

T

Tabrinna	Tahmea	Takiya
Tabrisha	Tahnisha	Takreasha
Tacara	Tai	Talandra
Tachika	Taiese	Talaria
Tacorra	Taiesha	Talasea
Tacorvia	Taijara	Taleesha
Tacquira	Taikenya	Ta Lena
Tadra	Taileisha	Talesa
Taeashia	Taina	Talisha
Taedra	Taisha	Tamaique
Taemika	Taiwanna	Tameca
Taeneka	Takeana	Tamedra
Taesha	Takeela	Tameeka
Taevia	Takeisha	Tameika
Tafaria	Takema	Tameira
Taffia	Takendra	Tameisha
Tafisa	Takeria	Tameka
Tahasha	Takeya	Tamellia
Taheera	Takira	Tamesha
Taheisha	Takisha	Tamieka
Taheria	Takishea	Tamika

Tamiko	Ta Ronia	Teyonka
Tamilya	Tarsha	Thandeka
Tamisha	Tarsheka	Thelathia
Tamm E	Tarvana	Theolanda
Tamora	Tasanna	Thimuelle
Tanae	Ta Sha	Tiawanna
Tanaeya	Tasha	Tichanda
Tanaisha	Tashanda	Tichina
Tanaua	Tasharah	Tiesha
Tanecia	Tashondra	Tika
Ta Neisha	Taundra	Tikoa
Taneka	Tavonda	Tilmona
Tanequa	Tawnya	Timandra
Tanesha	Teadra	Tim' Esha
Tangala	TeAna	Tineaka
Tangela	Tefera	Tisha
Tangi	Tekeyia	Tishanna
Tangie	Teletha	Tiyomby
Taniqua	Telsa	Toi
Tanisha	Temeka	Tomecia
Tanita	Temequa	Tomeka
Tanneisia	Tenaye	Tonesha
Tannesia	Teneshia	Tonice
Tanshay	Tenieka	Tonija
Taquanna	Tenisha	Tonique
Taqueesha	Teraza	Tonisha
Tarai	Terralee	Tonneda
Taranette	Terretha	Tonnisha
Tareka	Terrish	Tonzia
Tarnise	Tesha	Tovette

Tquana
Tramonia
Trantina
Trasha
Trashiba
Trenia
Trenice
Trensa

Trese
Trevaia
Tria
Trinidell
Tsia
Tulani
Tuliza
Twanda

Tychell
Tyesha
Tyiesha
Tyisha
Tykera
Tykidra
Tywonna

Ubanisha
Ukaya
Ulana

Uldean
Umeka
Umeko

Unica
Uthona
Uyen

V

Vadidehi
Vaileigh
Vakeesha
Vakisha
Valdaze
Valeeka
Valena
Valera
Valeshia
Validra
Valnise
Valona
Vamoece
Vamonda
Vancenia
Vanica
Vaniesha
Vaniessa
Vannice
Va-Rhonda
Varsha

Vasanta
Vashanda
Vashawn
Vashonda
Vastine
Veda
Vedessa
Veeda
Vela
Velmanette
Velva
Veneca
Veneeda
Veneka
Venesha
Venita
Verdelle
Verena
Verenis
Vergie
Verica

Verita
Verline
Verlondrea
Verly
Vermenka
Vermishia
Vernadine
Verndine
Verneka
Vernell
Vernesha
Vernessa
Vernether
Veronich
Verrissa
Verron
Vershonda
Vertasha
Vertavia

Veryl	Vinisha	Vondra
Veta	Vira	Vondrea
Vickona	Virdelle	Vonesha
Vida	Virlisha	Vonica
Vietta	Vishakha	Vonshae
Vinique	Vonderline	

W

Wadioni	Wealetta	Wykelia
Wadonna	Welda	Wykysha
Wakena	Wendi-Autumn	Wyneshia
Wakesha	Weslene	Wytashanika
Waheshia	Whitne	Wyvonna
Walisha	Willia Metta	Wyzena
Wanesa	Wilsoneka	Wyzenna
Wanisha	Wilynda	
Waynisha	Wondy	

X

Xandria	Xiomara
Xavia	Xyomara

Y

Ya Keshia	YaMaya	Yaritza
Yacheka	Yameeka	Yarleis
Yadira	Yamiche	Yarlene
Yadreece	Yamikani	Yarnetta
Yahira	Yamila	Yashakii
Yakeba	Yamilya	Yashi
Yakeshea	Yanae	Yashica
Ya Keshia	Yanick	Yashoda
Yakima	Yaniqua	Yasomattie
Yakimah	Yaritsa	Yatae

Yaunee
Yauntia
Yavette
Yavonda
Yeasha
Yelissa
Yesenia
Yevola

Yevone
Yevonessa
Yolette
Yomara
Yontae
Yorishia
Yorlanda
Yoshiko

Youlanda
Youshaima
Youvonnie
Yulda
Yulinda
Yulonda
Yvelise
Yvoone

Zackeisha
Zaddie
Zadelsa
Zadie
Zadonne
Zaferne
Zheera
Zhiyah
Zara
Zahara
Zaheera
Zahra
Zakaria

Zakaya
Zakeeshia
Zakia
Zakiya
Zalika
Zalean
Zandra
Zandrea
Zanella
Zaneta
Zanishia
Zannah
Zannette

Zanovia
Zanquandria
Zaquina
Zaranika
Zareda
Zarenna
Zarina
Zarnika
Zarventra
Zarvondra
Zasha
Zatee
Zatina

Zatoria

Zaymara

Zaznette

Zdena

Zeandra

Zearlisha

Zechari

Zekial

Zela

Zeldreana

Zellie

Zenedra

Zerricka

Zestina

Zettisha

Zia

Zihesa

Zinah

Ziva

Zkiah

Zollerita

Zondra

Zonya

Zorine

Zuleika

Zulekha

Zuleyka

Zulmira

Zunilda

Zuri

Zurisha

Zykeisha

Zykia

AND BABY MAKES THREE...
COMPREHENSIVE GUIDES BY
TRACIE HOTCHNER

CHILDBIRTH
&
MARRIAGE

The Transition to Parenthood
75201-8/$10.95 US/$12.95 CAN

PREGNANCY
&
CHILDBIRTH

Revised Edition
75946-2/$11.00 US/$13.00 CAN

THE
PREGNANCY
DIARY

76543-8/$10.00 US/$12.00 CAN